THE BEGINNINGS OF THE TEACHING
OF MODERN SUBJECTS IN ENGLAND

THE BEGINNINGS OF THE
TEACHING OF MODERN
SUBJECTS IN ENGLAND

BY

FOSTER WATSON, M.A.

Republished S. R. Publishers Ltd., 1971
First published Sir Isaac Pitman & Sons Ltd., London, 1909

Republished 1971 by S. R. Publishers Limited,
East Ardsley, Wakefield,
Yorkshire, England,

by kind permission of the copyright holder.

ISBN 0 85409 704 X

Reprinted by Scolar Press Ltd.,
Menston, Yorkshire, U.K.

Bibliographic note

The many students of the history of education who have experienced difficulty in obtaining a copy of this volume will appreciate the reasons for its reprint. Originally published in 1909, it still remains the basic source work and has yet to be superseded.

For the first time within the pages of a single volume the historical facts concerning the beginnings of the teaching of modern subjects in England were made known, and made known in connection with the history of the social forces which brought them into the educational curriculum. The book was not written with the object of bringing the educational practices of past periods into comparison with the highest theoretical educational standards of the early twentieth century, and with all the assumed vantage-ground of patronage, to praise the past when it came near to those heights, or to condole with it for any marked deficiencies, judged by the then current theory or practice.

On the contrary, and herein lies the value of a facsimile reprint of this particular work over six decades after its original publication, any history of educational subjects should encourage and deepen within us the habit of looking with a keener interest for indications of the sound adaptation of educational provision to the felt social, economic, political and religious needs of a community in a past period, from the point of view of the contemporary aims and scope of knowledge of that period. If, further, such a study stimulates the exercise of thought on the multitudinous problems which have arisen in every period, and leads us to identify ourselves in real interest with the aims and methods of the solutions attempted to those problems, then our judgement is strengthened for forming decisions as to the educational difficulties of the present age.

The Beginnings of the Teaching
of Modern Subjects in England

The Beginnings of the Teaching of Modern Subjects in England

BY

FOSTER WATSON, M.A.

PROFESSOR OF EDUCATION IN THE UNIVERSITY COLLEGE
OF WALES, ABERYSTWYTH ; AUTHOR OF " THE ENGLISH
GRAMMAR SCHOOLS TO 1660," AND TRANSLATOR
OF THE *Linguae Latinae Exercitatio* OF JUAN
LUIS VIVES, UNDER THE TITLE OF
" TUDOR SCHOOL-BOY LIFE "

LONDON : SIR ISAAC PITMAN & SONS, LTD.
No. 1 AMEN CORNER, E.C.   1909

PRINTED BY SIR ISAAC PITMAN
& SONS, LTD., LONDON, BATH
AND NEW YORK .   . 1909

THIS WORK IS DEDICATED TO

THE RIGHT HONOURABLE LORD RENDEL,

PRESIDENT OF

THE UNIVERSITY COLLEGE OF WALES, ABERYSTWYTH,

AS A TOKEN OF HIGH APPRECIATION,

SHARED BY ALL THE MEMBERS OF THE STAFF,

OF HIS ACTIVE GOODWILL TO, AND INTEREST IN,

THE COLLEGE.

PREFACE

Owing to the rapid development of a system of
County and Municipal Secondary Schools in England
and Wales, at the present time, a special interest
is centred on the place and function of the " modern"
subjects in the Secondary Schools. The sole aim
of this book is to present the essential facts and
circumstances relating to the introduction of these
subjects into English education. The book is not
written with the object of bringing the educational
practice of past periods into comparison with the
highest theoretical educational standards of to-day,
and with all the assumed vantage-ground of patronage, to praise the past when it came near to our
heights, or to condole with it for any marked
deficiencies, judged by our present theory or practice.
It is not even suggested that the gain from the study
will be of direct assistance " in the right paths."
If a history of any educational subject encourages
and deepens within us the habit of looking with a
keener interest for indications of the sound adaptation of educational provision to the felt social,
economic, political and religious needs of a community in a past period, *from the point of view of the
contemporary aims and scope of knowledge of that*

period, then that study justifies itself. If, further, such a study stimulates the exercise of thought on the multitudinous problems which have arisen in every period, and leads us to identify ourselves in real interest with the aims and methods of the solutions attempted to those problems, then our judgment is strengthened for forming decisions as to the educational difficulties of the present age. It will be generally admitted that it is high time that the historical facts with regard to the beginnings of the teaching of modern subjects in England were known, and known in connexion with the history of the social forces which brought them into the educational curriculum. This is precisely what is now attempted for the first time, as far as the writer knows, within a single volume.

Wherever possible, reference is made to fixed dates or places, of the earliest inclusions, in England, of any modern subject, as, for instance, in the Statutes or Orders prescribing school curricula. So, too, bibliographical details as to the earliest text-books are emphasised, in so far as they afford important indications of aims and methods. The bibliographical subject-lists are intended to convey a general impression of the chief directions and scope of contemporary knowledge in the subjects in which the information is not readily accessible.

I have to acknowledge the courtesy of editors in assenting to my use of articles which have already appeared in print, as follows : in the *Journal of Education* (June, 1899), " The First Text-book in Civics in England " (*Excursus* to Chapter II) ; in the *Educational Times* (August, 1895), " A Museum of Cromwell's Time " (*Excursus* to Chapter V) ; and in the *Gentleman's Magazine* (September, 1899), " Some Private Teachers of Arithmetic " (*Excursus* to Chapter VIII).

F. W.

Queen's Square House,
Aberystwyth.

CONTENTS

xi

CONTENTS

CHAPTER I

THE TEACHING OF ENGLISH

CHAPTER II

THE TEACHING OF HISTORY

CONTENTS

CHAPTER III

TEACHING OF GEOGRAPHY IN ENGLAND UP TO 1660

CHAPTER IV

THE TEACHING OF DRAWING

CONTENTS

CONTENTS

CHAPTER VII

THE TEACHING OF MATHEMATICS

CHAPTER VIII

THE TEACHING OF ARITHMETIC

CONTENTS

CHAPTER IX

THE TEACHING OF GEOMETRY

CHAPTER X

THE TEACHING OF ASTRONOMY

CONTENTS

CHAPTER XI

THE TEACHING OF MODERN LANGUAGES

I. French

CHAPTER XII

THE TEACHING OF MODERN LANGUAGES

II. Italian

CHAPTER XIII

THE TEACHING OF MODERN LANGUAGES

III. Spanish

CHAPTER XIV

THE TEACHING OF MODERN LANGUAGES

IV. The Teaching of German and Dutch

CONTENTS

CHAPTER XV

THE TEACHING OF MODERN LANGUAGES

Polyglottism

CHAPTER XVI

CONCLUSION

The Triumph of English

" To speak our own Mother-English Tongue purely, properly, elegantly, is (for aught I know) as commendable as to speak French, Spanish, Latin, or any other exotic and foreign language."

Note : " I speak not this to undervalue those more learned languages, whence all Civility, Learning, yea, Religion and Salvation, too, comes streaming down to us, *but to provoke in us a love of our own language and learning therein contained.* Many go farther and fare worse."—From the Preface to the *Phraseologia Puerilis* (1638) of John Clarke, Head Master of Lincoln Grammar School from 1624 onwards, certainly up to 1654 and perhaps later.

Introduction

GENERAL MOVEMENTS LEADING TO THE INCLUSION OF MODERN SUBJECTS IN ENGLISH EDUCATION

IT is usually assumed that institutions connected with royalty, the nobility and the gentry, are conservative, and that democratic institutions are progressive. Such a view requires modification, if it is to be applied to educational history. The English Grammar Schools were essentially democratic ; Mr. A. F. Leach has shown with overwhelming evidence that these schools were "free," i.e. required no fee from those for whom the school was founded. Nevertheless, the Grammar Schools, though more progressive than is ordinarily supposed, were relatively reactionary and conservative compared with the educational arrangements for the children of the nobility. The reason is not far to seek. The Grammar Schools were controlled largely by authority,[1] which, after the manner of authority, sought to economise energy by drifting into tradition. The education of the higher classes was free as the winds. Subjects of direct usefulness or of social prestige could be chosen and could be pursued,

---

[1] e.g. by the statutes of founders, the authority of the diocesan in licensing of schoolmasters, in visitations and examinations ; by the prescription of text-books by the King and Privy Council.

often under favourable conditions. Experiments could be tried. *Rapport* could be established between methods tried in this country and in foreign countries. A subject of study could receive its educational place in so far as it tended to raise the index of the personal efficiency of the noble. There was thus the amplest scope for the introduction of new subjects in the education of the nobles, whilst in the Grammar Schools authority and tradition offered passive resistance to the conscious introduction of any subjects unrelated to the two outstanding interests of religion and the languages of religion (Latin, Greek and Hebrew). We have to recognise that in the sixteenth and seventeenth centuries, modern subjects, e.g. mathematics, natural sciences, and the vernacular languages, foreign and English, advanced with mighty strides, yet to these subjects the doors of the Grammar Schools, for the most part, remained closed.[1] Substantially, the Grammar Schools stood by the developments of the two subjects of the mediaeval Trivium, viz., grammar and rhetoric, letting the formal study of the third subject of the Trivium, viz. logic, drop out of the school course. They were thus, as indeed Edward Leigh in 1663 describes Eton, Winchester and Westminster, " trivial " schools. In Puritan England, the Bible, the " holy "

---

[1] Such a case as that of Blackburn Grammar School is exceptional. There the Statutes (1597) suggest that " the principles of arithmetic, geometry and cosmography, with some introduction into the sphere *are profitable* " (*Vict. Hist. Lancashire*, vol. ii, p. 591).

languages which elucidated it, Latin, Greek and Hebrew, and the general sense of antiquity common to them all which bound up these languages with religious associations were closely connected with and helped by the studies of grammar and rhetoric. Hence, to the Grammar School point of view, the subjects of the Quadrivium, viz., arithmetic, geometry, astronomy and music, were, to a large extent, irrelevant to the aims of a thorough education. At most they were " extras," and often this was marked by the payments of fees for them, if taught at all, whilst classical instruction was " free."

An illustration of the permeation of the religious aim of the Grammar School can be seen by the attitude towards natural science. John Milton, in 1644, could include in his suggested curriculum Pliny's *Historia Naturalis* and Seneca's *Questiones Naturales*. But it is clear that Hezekiah Woodward, a schoolmaster who taught in a Grammar School and also established a private school of his own, and probably was " progressive " as a Puritan, was an advocate of the study of the " creatures," i.e. natural phenomena as disclosed in the Biblical account of the Creation. The natural science of the Grammar Schools, therefore, followed the lines of John Swan's *Speculum Mundi* and Joshua Sylvester's *Divine Workes and Weekes* (i.e. a translation of Du Bartas's *Première Semaine*). It had taken generations to build up the classico-religious tradition, and accordingly every attempt to obtain a lodgment of a new subject into the strongholds was resisted as an alien, such as Sébastien Castellion, or Servetus, was repelled in Calvin's citadel of thought at Geneva. " Progress " meant the conversion of classical writings like those of Pliny and Seneca as far as subject-matter went, into observations with regard to natural phenomena, interpreted into moral and religious maxims founded on scriptural analogies.

But the Quadrivium, arithmetic, geometry, astronomy, and music had attractions for the noble, since they were the arts which particularly had relation to the activities of the practical world, whilst the Trivium of grammar, rhetoric, and logic, though a basis of intellectual training, could not confine the noble's energies. It was, of course, from the Quadrivium as basis that the differentiation and variety of modern subjects sprang, and accordingly the nobles not only received the advantage of having intellectual interests naturally drawn to these subjects, but in many cases, particularly in the seventeenth century, they contributed in no mean measure to their progress and development. Some leading names in the advancement of gentlemen's education call for mention, since they will help to bring out the historical suggestions for the inclusion of various subjects in the educational curriculum.

In 1531, Sir Thomas Elyot wrote the *Gouvernour*, the first Renascence book in English on education. It is of outstanding importance in its treatment of physical education, in its pioneering suggestions for the teaching of drawing, cosmography and history, in addition to its progressive views on the teaching of Latin and Greek. In 1555 followed the less conspicuous anonymous *Institution of a Gentleman*, which, like Elyot's *Gouvernour*, advocates the study of history. The ground given is that history is "very necessary to be read of all those which bear office and authority in the Commonwealth." In 1560 Laurence Humfrey, one of the English refugees from the Marian persecution, published at Basle the Latin text of his book on the Nobles (*Optimates*). Humfrey emphasises history and civil knowledge, that is, the knowledge of law, antiquity and the *statutes of our realm*. To these subjects he adds arithmetic, geometry, geography. Above all, nobles must study religion. In 1561, Sir Thomas Hoby produced his translation of Count Baldassare Castiglione's *Cortegiano* (originally published 1528). This was the greatest of the Italian courtiers' books, and advocated training in state-discourses, manners, physical exercises, languages, ancient and modern, music, and, permeating all, gracefulness, dignity and ease of bearing. Castiglione is also remarkable for his treatment of the training of the gentlewoman. "She should be learned and sure in the most necessary languages, a good musician, able to draw and paint, be a good housewife, able to devise sports and pastimes, and a good dancer." In 1607 John Cleland wrote his *Institution of a Young Nobleman*, an eminently practical treatise. It praises the culture of the mother-tongue. It suggests the ingenious method of teaching handwriting by tracing letters on Venetian glass laid over a model copy. For Latin, Cleland advises the study of the colloquies of Vives and Corderius. Correct French speaking is to be learned. History, logic, mathematics are to be taught. Geometry begins from map-drawing and architectural designing. Astronomy and geography are to be studied. Law is to be read in Justinian, but the noble must also know the Common Law, and he must read the statutes of his country. In 1622 came Henry Peacham's *Compleat Gentleman*, undoubtedly the most representative contemporary account of educational practice in the first quarter of the seventeenth century, particularly in the subjects of history, cosmography, geometry, poetry, music, drawing and painting in oil, heraldry, exercises of the body, in travel, war, fishing. Nor must the name of Milton be omitted, for his tractate *Of Education* in 1644 describes a gentleman's comprehensive course in ancient authors, and also in modern subjects such as mathematics, natural history, modern languages, physical exercises, medicine and anatomy and (what is so strikingly realistic when we think of the contemporary Great Civil War) Military matters and the observation of the Naval possibilities of our country, on holidays ; and the serious study of Constitutional Law and the Statutes.

One remarkable development of opinion in education extant in MSS., entitled *Exercitatio of Schooling*,[1] must here be described. This consists of the Notes of John Dury, dated 1646. Dury had written a " Motion tending to the Public Good, an expression very frequent in the first half of the seventeenth century, and associated in Dury's mind

---

[1] Brit. Mus., *Sloane MSS*. 649 (p. 52).

particularly with educational schemes. In the MSS. papers of 1646 are linked together the *Exercitatio of Schooling* and the *Education of Nobles and Gentlemen*. The progressive aspect of Dury is marked in the usual recognition of the writers on the education of noblemen, of the intensive side of education, but Dury is significant also in continuing the extensive side of admitting " the vulgar " to the benefits of the education laid down for the nobles, each class to have the fullest and most liberal education for its special needs. Thus to take the question of the school curricula, Dury suggests all schools should be public, but of two sorts. The first kind should be *common to all*, and in these everyone should come into a knowledge of " things," and learn in the *mother tongue* " the right (*a*) notions, (*b*) names of things, (*c*) expressions. In the school teaching of languages, some should learn (*a*) Hebrew, (*b*) Greek, (*c*) Latin ; others should learn the languages of training for commerce ; (*d*) French, (*e*) Spanish, (*f*) Italian. Of the various arts and sciences : (1) " the vulgar " should be equipped with those necessary for trades and servile work ; (2) the learned, for increase of science and the training up of others ; (3) the nobles should be fitted for " public charges in peace and war." Dury's proposals are permeated with the Puritanic sense of responsibility of the fulfilment of all the duties of every occupation in the Commonwealth and the adequate training for it, both in liberal studies and in technical instruction.

To return to the books on the education of

nobles. . The *Gentleman's Calling* and Clement Ellis's *Gentile Sinner or England's Brave Gentleman* represent the Puritan-Gentleman ideal, and the recoil from the gentleman-gallant of the age, and include training in the liberal " arts and sciences." In 1678, J. Gailhard wrote his *Compleat Gentleman*. This is particularly valuable in its details of the arrangements for the Grand Tour of the gentleman, showing how he was to learn foreign languages and music abroad, as well as be trained in the exercises of dancing, running, wrestling, fencing, and above all to " ride the Great Horse." Other subjects to be acquired at towns *en route* are mathematics, geography, and a new subject even for the noble, " chemistry," together with the gentleman's time-honoured subject of physic at Padua or Montpellier, and of civil law at Orleans or Angers. Gailhard would even like his gentleman to acquire not only Latin and Greek, but also Hebrew, Chaldaic, Syriac, and Arabic. About 1728, Daniel Defoe wrote the *Compleat English Gentleman*.[1] Defoe is willing to dispense with Latin and Greek, but the gentleman was to learn natural and experimental philosophy, mathematics, astronomy, history, geography, and (again a new study) *navigation*. Defoe insists that for all these studies Latin is not necessary. " Not one sea-faring man in twenty understands Latin," and yet a man without it may be an " artist " in navigation. Defoe marks a new era. " You may," he

---

[1] In 1890 this book was edited for the first time by Dr. Karl Bülbring.

declares, "be a gentleman of learning, and yet reading in English may do all for you that you want."

The subjects which we have thus found mentioned in the books on the education of nobles include substantially all which we call "modern." Nobles were chiefly taught by private tutors at home and by travel with "governors" abroad. There had prevailed in mediaeval times a system of bringing up of the young nobles in the households of great princes and lords, but as a system such household education, together with the old training of knights through service as pages and as squires, had lied out with the Middle Ages: the end of the practice is roughly marked in England by the Wars of the Roses. The new nobility of the Tudors represented the energy, good fortunes, and sterling qualities of a new class of the successful men of the world of diplomacy, courtiers' service, and of commerce and enterprise of seamanship under the Tudors. It became orthodox to proclaim that nobility was determined not by blood but by personal merit. The famous question raised in the *Don Quixote*[1] of Cervantes as to the precedence of letters over arms was often discussed, and usually settled as by Cicero : *cedant arma togae*. Another searching problem of the sixteenth century was whether court-life or country-life were preferable. Many decided practically in favour of the country, and the type of the English scholarly country gentleman has been of great significance in the advancement of

---

[1] Part i, chap. xxxviii.

learning, especially in the natural sciences, outdoor exercises, and the belles-lettres.

Historically, the growth of the class of nobles and gentry in the Tudor times was very rapid, and the barriers between grades of society were incomparably easier to break down than they had been in the Middle Ages. The constant infusion of new blood into the nobility from individuals who won their patent of nobility by the energy of their characters caused a greater readiness of comprehensive outlook with regard to the education of their children towards branches of learning and accomplishments far away from the limitations of the " mere " poor scholar of the Grammar Schools and Universities. Hence we find the nobles studied such subjects as mathematics, the natural and experimental sciences, modern languages, and, of course, the personal accomplishments of physical exercises. Thus these studies seemed largely to carry a class distinction, except that the professional training of the physicians often led them also to some of these scientific studies.

Or, again, the general aim of the training of the noble or gentleman had many points of contact with the professional training of the lawyer. Probably the distaste often shown by the noble for the Universities was due to the ecclesiastical traditions of the old mediaeval Universities. The new Tudor nobility, especially after the Reformation, were essentially civil and non-ecclesiastic in tendencies, and approximated in some respects to the lawyer-type. So far was this the case that in the fifteenth century onwards, whether the noble or gentleman went to the University or not, he often was trained in the Inns of Court. We are fortunate in possessing a description of the Inns of Court, with their educational aims, methods, and practice, in the *de Laudibus Legum Angliae*, written in Latin c. 1463 by Sir John Fortescue, and translated into English in 1616 by John Selden. The facts given by Selden in the following account of course represent the latter date. After passing through the lesser Inns of Chancery, students are admitted, Selden tells us, into " the Inns of Court, properly so-called. Of these there are four in number. In that which is the least frequented, there are about 200 students. . . . The students are sons to persons of quality ; those of an inferior rank not being able to bear the expenses of maintaining and educating their children in this way. As to the merchants, they seldom care to lessen their stock in trade by being at such large yearly expenses. So that there is scarce to be found throughout the Kingdom an eminent lawyer who is not a gentleman by birth and fortune ; consequently they have a greater regard for their character and honour than those who are bred in another way.

" There is both in the Inns of Court and in the Inns of Chancery a sort of Academy or Gymnasium, fit for persons of their station ; where they learn singing and all kinds of music, dancing and such other accomplishments and diversions (which are called revels) as are suitable to their quality, and such as are usually practised at Court. At other

times, out of Court, the greater part apply themselves to the study of the law. Upon festival days,
and after the offices of the Church are over, they
employ themselves in the study of sacred and
profane history. Here everything which is good
and virtuous is to be learned. All vice is discouraged
and banished. So that knights, barons and the
greatest nobility of the kingdom often place their
children in those Inns of Court, not so much to
make the laws their study, much less to live by the
profession (having large patrimonies of their own),
but to form their manners, and to preserve them
from the contagion of vice."

But at times both the Universities and the Inns
of Court were felt to be inadequate to the needs of
the education of the increasing number of the nobles
and gentry, and project after project of Academies
was put forward to meet the want. The suggestions
as to curricula in these proposed new institutions
are entitled to be described as highly progressive.
The first important proposed organisation was that
of Sir Humphrey Gilbert, called *Queen Elizabeth's
Academy* c. 1570. It was intended for " the Queen's
Wards and others the youth of nobility and gentlemen." The suggested provision of teaching was as
follows : For Latin, Greek, one schoolmaster and
four ushers ; a teacher of Hebrew ; also one for
logic and rhetoric ; one teacher for moral philosophy,
and one in natural philosophy, and a reader in physic.
The last-named two were required to conduct
experiments and were afforded a " physic-garden "
for the purpose. The rest of the staff included a

reader of civil law and one for divinity ; a lawyer for grounds of the Common Law, who shall cut down and teach exquisitely the office of a Justice of the Peace and Sheriff ; one teacher of French (with an usher) ; one of Italian (with an usher) ; one of Spanish ; one of the High Dutch, i.e. German ; one master of defence ; of dancing and vaulting ; of music (with an usher) ; one herald of arms, and, of course, a teacher of riding the Great Horse. Students will thus "study matters of action most for present practice both of peace and war." These subjects were to be taught in English, and text-books in English were to be encouraged.

In 1620, a scheme devised by Edmund Boulton for an Academy was actually referred to a Committee of the House of Lords, on the proposal of the Lord Admiral Buckingham. Provision was to be made that the King's Wards might have a fit breeding and an education given them in England, *instead of going abroad where alone they could get the instruction needed*, but " where it proved costly to their souls many times, as much as their bodies." The subjects of study were to be mathematics and all kinds of noble exercises. In 1635, Sir Francis Kynaston offered his house in Covent Garden as an Academy, under the name of *Musaeum Minervae*. The Academy was incorporated, and had a common seal allotted, and a grant of arms. Professors were nominated for philosophy, physic, music, astronomy, geometry, and languages. Other professors were to be appointed for horsemanship, dancing, painting, engraving, etc., and the various professors were expected to lecture each on a number of subjects allied to that of his chair.

In 1648 Sir Balthazar Gerbier projected an Academy at Bethnal Green. There were to be taught a large number of subjects, but Gerbier was an adventurer, and the enterprise must not be regarded too seriously.[1] In the year 1700, Lewis Maidwell petitioned the House of Commons for a Committee to report on his scheme of an Academy in Languages, Arts and Physical Exercises. The scheme[2] failed. In 1705 Maidwell changed his scheme of an *Academy* to a " School of Navigation and Languages."[3] He says : " Had Charles II founded a school like this, in place of his Mathematical School[4] (Christ's Hospital) he had then outrivalled his neighbour's pretensions." Maidwell refers to the ordinances of Louis XIV, which he says " so magnificently testify to his care for instructing and supporting youths throughout the kingdom in the art of Navigation."

The schemes of the Academies show the new subjects on the verge of entering into the actual curricula of educational institutions. They are therefore more vital to the subject of this book than the imaginative schemes of ideal States, in which education receives a treatment. Yet we can hardly

---

[1] *See* p. 505 *infra.*

[2] *See Collectanea*, vol. i, ed. Fletcher. Oxford Historical Society (1885), pp. 269 *et seqq.*

[3] *Ibid.*, p. 294.

[4] As to the Mathematical School in Christ's Hospital *see* p. 312 *infra.*

pass by without recalling such books (dealing incidentally with education) as Sir Thomas More's *Utopia* c. 1518; Thomas Campanella's *Civitas Solis* c. 1620; *Nova Solyma*, 1648; and above all, in its era-making suggestions of training in experimental science, Francis Bacon's *New Atlantis*, 1627. These books were educationally of high importance in familiarising the intellectual world with the necessity of open-mindedness with regard to new lines of culture and scientific inquiry, and of the filtration from such new fields of study of new subjects and methods of instruction for the young.[1]

The thirst of enterprise and novelty in ideal states found its counterpart in real life in the rise and development of the great merchant class, and the transition from the Nobles to men of Commerce is not so abrupt as might at first appear. The great livery companies imitated the state and display of the great nobles so that a City Company's Hall was almost "the replica of the house of the noble" who lodged his little army of retainers and held sac and soc within his city during the Middle Ages."[2] Corporately, a City Company

---

[1] The idea of experiment in education was thus recognised. The following passage shows the application of the plans of an Academy to the specialised education of the Deaf and Dumb: "I began," says John Bulwer, "in idea to conceive the model of a new Academie, which might be erected in favour of those who are . . . deaf and dumb," in the Preface to *Philocophus* (1648). But Bulwer relates that talking of the plan to some "rational men," "it did rather amuse them than satisfy their understandings."

[2] George Unwin: *Gilds and Companies of London*, p. 176.

controlled its particular trade, and the conditions of training the young in it, by apprenticeship. Individual merchants often won honour and dignity in the Elizabethan era, and later, in no degree inferior to that of barons themselves.

There was an astounding variety of kinds of preparation, in the individuals who achieved distinction as merchants. On the whole, the most successful merchants' early training was not ordinarily through the Grammar School and University. Robert Ashley (1565–1641), who was at Southampton Grammar School, under Adrian à Saravia, who taught his pupils French [1]—a most unusual Grammar School subject, we are told—" exchanged the 'arts' for ' marts,' " and this seems typical of the usual separation of the two. The " marts " boy, i.e. the boy desiring a commercial career, was outside of a congenial atmosphere in the Grammar School. We may judge so, at any rate, from the case of Sir Dudley North, son of Lord North. Born in 1641, Dudley North was sent as a boy to Bury St. Edmund's Grammar School to learn Latin. But he " had too much spirit (for his book), which had rather to be employed in regular action." His brother, Roger North, says that Dudley " had a strange bent to traffic, and while he was at school drove a subtle trade amongst the boys by buying and selling. In short, it was considered that he had learning enough for a merchant, but not phlegm enough for a sedentary occupation." He was next sent to a writing

---

[1] *See* p. 396 *infra*.

and arithmetic school for some time, and then bound apprentice by his father to a "Turkey Merchant." The apprenticeship of the sons of noblemen and gentlemen to merchants was a recognised method of training. Francis Osborn[1] explains that if a gentleman becomes a merchant, he has advantage in his travelling abroad by having "the law of nations and articles of a reciprocal amity to protect him." Dudley North was sent to Archangel, and then to Smyrna. In those voyages, "he had an eye for everything worth observing, and kept a regular journal of all that he saw." He became wealthy. He acquired skill in the practice of the Turkish law, and is said to have tried over 500 cases without employing interpreters. He compiled a Turkish Dictionary, and it was said "No Frank ever spoke the vulgar idiom (of Turkish) so correct and perfect as he did." He became a London merchant, M.P., Commissioner of Customs, and a Lord of the Treasury.

But more frequently than Turkish, Arabic was learned in various degrees by English merchants in the East. The scholarly study of that language must have been quickened and strengthened by the residence at Smyrna and Aleppo of members of the Levant Company. Thus, Edward Pococke had served as chaplain to that Company, 1630–1636. At Aleppo he had learned to speak Arabic fluently and studied "Hebrew, Samaritan, Syriac and

---

[1] *Advice to a Son* (1656), p. 59. Osborn suggests as an alternative to becoming a merchant that a youth should join the retinue of an ambassador.

Ethiopic." On his return to England in 1636, Pococke was appointed by Archbishop Laud as Professor of Arabic at Oxford, a post he held till his death in 1691. The study of Oriental languages, it will be seen, must have been strongly stimulated by the training in Commerce, in the East, of the young apprentice and employé. This interest in Arabic even reached Westminster School, in the time of Dr. Busby, who is said himself to have taught Arabic to the boys.[1]

The case of Sir Thomas Gresham may be cited as typical of a boy who was sent first to the University (Gonville College, Cambridge) and afterwards apprenticed to his uncle, Sir John Gresham, who was a trader to the Levant, and one of the founders of the Russia Company. Sir John Gresham, after the manner of Elizabethan merchants, founded a Free Grammar School at Holt, in Norfolk, in 1546. Sir Thomas Gresham, in later life, recognised that he owed his wide commercial knowledge to the apprenticeship he served with his uncle. As one of the merchant-princes of Queen Elizabeth's time, Gresham showed the educational wide-mindedness of the merchant-class in his foundation of Gresham College. He endowed professorships in divinity, astronomy, music, geometry, law, medicine and rhetoric. He urged in his directions to professors that they should remember that the hearers of the lectures would be " merchants and other citizens," and therefore he says the lectures are not to be

---

[1] *See also* p. 522 *infra.*

" read after the manner of the Universities, but let the reader cull out such heads of his subject as may best serve the good liking and capacity of the said auditory." The Astronomy Professor was to read " the principles of the sphere and the theoriques of the planets, and to explain the use of common instruments for the capacity of mariners," and he was to apply " these things " to use by reading geography, and the art of navigation. The geometry professor was to lecture for one term on arithmetic ; the next on theoretical geometry ; and the third on practical geometry. In music " the lecture was to be read, the theoretic part for one half-hour or thereabouts, and the practical part by help of voices or instruments for the rest of the hour." It will thus be seen that Sir Thomas Gresham brought into useful study modern subjects not then taught in Grammar Schools, and but little in the Universities, that he encouraged practical methods to be used, and that he required the subjects to be taught in English, and not in Latin.

One further example is worth citing to illustrate the relation of Commerce to Education. Sir William Petty, the son of a clothier, was born in 1623, at Rumsey, in Hampshire. When a boy, Aubrey says " his greatest delight was to look on the artificers, e.g. smiths, watchmakers, carpenters, joiners, and at 12 years old, he could have worked any of these trades." [1] He went to school, and by

---

[1] Aubrey's *Brief Lives* (ed. Clark), vol. ii, p. 140. Aubrey says of himself : " As a boy my greatest delight was to be continually with the artificers that come to Easton (Wilts),

12 years of age learned a competent smattering of Latin, and was entered into the Greek. He was bound apprentice to a sea-captain, and at 15 years of age " he went into Normandy, to Caen, in a vessel that went hence with a little stock, and began to merchandise, and had so good success that he maintained himself, and also educated himself. Here he learned the French tongue, and perfected himself in the Latin, and had Greek enough to serve his turn. Here, at Caen, he studied the arts. At Paris, he studied Anatomy." Petty made the " Down Survey " in Ireland, was an original member of the Royal Society, and was one of the earliest of our theoretical economists. He was at one time Professor of Anatomy at Oxford, at another Professor of Music at Gresham College. His active, varied experience led him to a keen interest in education. His views were expounded in a most suggestive, unconventional, and progressive tractate entitled *W. P.'s Advice concerning the education of Youth.* [1]

The active influence of enterprising careers was even more directly felt in the schools by the presence of men like Sir Henry Savile, and Sir Henry Wotton, who had both been diplomats, and both of whom were provosts of Eton College. So, too, William Malim, who was headmaster of Eton, 1561–1571,

---

(e.g. joiners, carpenters, coopers, masons) and understand their trades." *Ibid.*, vol. i, p. 35. So also for the fascination of the arts of practical life on the boyhood of Sir Isaac Newton *see* Brewster's *Life of Newton*, ed. Lynn (1878), p. 5.
[1] *See* p. 225 *et seqq. infra.*

had travelled, and, as he says himself, "seen Antioch, Constantinople, Jerusalem, and other Eastern cities." Or, again, there was the great schoolmaster, Thomas Farnaby (1575 ? – 1647), who was educated in a Jesuit College in Spain. He had sailed in Drake's and Hawkins's last voyage, and on his return was an "abcedarian" at Martock, in Somersetshire, and afterwards opened the most successful private school of the age in Goldsmith's Alley. Men of such an active temperament as that of Farnaby (who is said, further, to have been a soldier in the Netherlands) were no doubt exceptional, but the general atmosphere of adventure and enterprise at least cannot be said to have been entirely absent from the school, when one of Drake's companions was a schoolmaster.

The Nobles and the Merchants, then, were among the progressive forces bringing about the origins of the modern subjects in education. So, too, the smaller tradesmen and craftsmen have their place in educational history, though it is not so conspicuous, and in other directions. The smaller tradesman's son went, for the most part, to the local Grammar Schools,[1] but after he had been there he usually learned his trade, and if the tradesman were allowed by his guild, he took several other apprentices, to whom he was bound to teach his trade in all the details of its practice. It is evident that this training in a trade, at any rate, might be of considerable significance for education. Mr. Froude

---

[1] *See* the present writer's *English Grammar Schools,* p. 531.

went so far as to say, "*the old English education was the apprentice system.*" Anyway, we cannot fail to recognise that the process of acquiring a trade or craft by the teaching of the apprentice by the master is the origin of technical and of manual instruction in England. Obadiah Walker in his *Of Education* (2nd ed., 1673) refers to the method of this teaching. " In manual arts the master first showeth his apprentice what he is to do ; next works it himself in his presence, and gives him rules, and then sets him to work." Walker insists that this also is the right method of " breeding a gentleman or scholar."

In earlier times, the position of an apprentice seems to have had dignity, but apprenticeship eventually lost its old estimation ; not, however, without protest being made. In 1629, Edmund Boulton, the projector of an Academy for nobles, wrote the *Cities Advocate*, repelling by appeal to history and law the suggestion that " apprenticeship " extinguished " the claim to gentry." But the economic conditions of society in the seventeenth century had produced a large mass of children who were a source of inconvenience and even danger if not brought into some sort of discipline. Froude says : " In every parish in England, the larger householders, the squire and the parson, the farmers, smiths, joiners, shoemakers, were obliged by law to divide amongst themselves according to their means, the children of the poor, who would otherwise grow up unprovided for, and clothe, feed, lodge and teach them in return for their services, till they were old enough to take care of themselves." Thus, at

Wanstead, in Essex, entries in the parish register show that female parish children were passed over to the lace school there, as apprentices to the trade of tambour-worker till twenty-one years of age at £4 premium.[1]

The association of poor, destitute children with apprenticeship naturally brought down the *status* of apprenticeship. It will be remembered that Edward VI (in 1553) gave his palace of Bridewell to the City of London, and that it became a hospital, a workhouse, and a house of correction combined. One of the provisions of the Orders was to receive manufacturers who should take apprentices for seven years, when the latter were to receive their freedom and a donation of £10 to set them up in trade. Bridewell, however, served to degrade the standing of apprentices by associating them with the vagrants who were to be " corrected " and the poor " to be set on work," and unfortunately this combination of functions became a model for further similar institutions throughout the country. Trade schools, however, were sometimes isolated from the house of correction, and the poor, young and old, " set on work," the material being supplied by municipal authorities. Thus as early as 1516, the Mayor of Lincoln brought a clothier to that city to teach the improved methods of the art. In 1591 a knitting-school was established (later on held in the cloisters, under the Grammar School), and John Cheeseman, the knitter, undertook to " set on work " in his science " all such as

---

[1] *Vict. County Hist., Essex,* vol. ii, p. 486.

were willing to come to him or were sent to him by the aldermen, and to hide nothing from them that belongeth to the knowledge of the said science." In 1596 we find from the Leicester Town Records,[1] the wife of Thomas Clark, shoemaker, was allowed a loan of £20 for a year for stock in teaching children kersey knitting. Thus there were both men and women teachers in these municipal Trade Schools, and both boy and girl[2] pupils. The origins of individual manual and technical education are therefore to be sought in the institution of apprenticeship in trades and crafts, and of class instruction in the town Trade and Craft Schools. Sir William Borlase's Free School was founded at Great Marlow in 1628, and provided for the teaching of twenty-four poor boys and twenty-four poor girls. It was prescribed by Borlase's will that the girls learn to knit, spin and make bone-lace. In 1672 the Aylesbury overseers paid Mary Sutton five shillings to teach the workhouse children to make lace.[3] The teaching of manual work has therefore formed part of the education of the poor, locally, in England.

The establishment of Christ's Hospital in 1552 marks the beginning of an important era in schools for the poor. At first the children at Christ's Hospital were sent to Bridewell, four or five at a time, to learn a trade, though they resided in the Hospital.

---

[1] Edited E. Bateson, vol. iii, p. xlviii.

[2] In 1642 Mr. Humphrey Walcot founded a school to teach sixteen poor girls of Lydbury North to spin flax and wool in an outhouse, a widow being engaged to teach them. —*Vict. Hist. Shropshire*, vol. i, p. 429.

[3] *Vict. County Hist. Bucks*, vol. ii, p. xlviii.

The Hospital admitted infants, namely, the found-lings, as well as older children. A headmaster and " petty " or ABC assistants were appointed. It was not till 1673 that an order of the Court enacted that no children be taken into the school under seven years of age. Girls were admitted as well as boys. It was the original intention that children of the Hospital, after their elementary education, " if not given to learning," should be apprenticed, and Christ's Hospital may be regarded as a preparatory school for apprentices. Sea-faring and colonising opened up careers of apprenticeship for a long succession of generations of the boys. In 1640, so keen were boys for adventurous careers, that an order[1] was passed that " the consent of parents must be obtained before children be sent to New England." The great Trading Companies and especially the East India Company, took over boys " to be employed in their affairs beyond the seas." After the foundation of the Mathematical School of Christ's Hospital in 1673, the teaching of Mathe-matics and Navigation, in which subjects Christ's Hospital was the pioneer school, prepared directly for apprenticeship to sea-captains serving in the Indian Navy.

After the model of Christ's Hospital in its later developments, Blue-coat Schools were established in many parts of the country, providing for the entire charge of the living of pupils, together with their elementary education and the payment of premiums

---

[1] *See* E. H. Pearce : *Annals of Christ's Hospital,* pp. 282-3.

for their apprenticeship. At Westminster, the boys and girls formed a Grey-coat School.[1] The boys of this school also went in large numbers as apprentices in the Navy service. This fact led to the proposal in 1700 to teach the brighter boys Arithmetic and Navigation. In the minutes there is recorded a request from a " proposer of Salt Works in Pennsylvania for two or three children from this house, apprentice." It is only by accounts of this kind that we see how directly the educational system tended to follow the needs of the extension of our empire by land and sea. So, too, occasionally even Grammar Schools were influenced in the same direction.

The Statutes of Woodbridge (Suffolk) Grammar School, 1662, require the ten free boys, " sons of the meaner sort of the inhabitants," to learn Latin and Greek

> that thereby they may be made fit for the University (if it be desired) ; but in case any of them be unapt to learn those languages, and not likely to be fitted for the University, or if their parents, or those that have the government of them, desire that they be taught only Arithmetic, and to write, to be fitted for trades or to go to sea ; that then the schoolmaster shall teach them accordingly and fit them for such employments as shall be so desired.

In 1707 an Act of Parliament required the appointment at Plymouth *Workhouse* of a schoolmaster

> to teach the poor children to read, write, and cast accounts, and " to teach such as have a capacity and inclination to learn, the art of navigation, and such part of the mathematics as tend thereunto."

---

[1] Miss Day has written an interesting account of the school under the title *An Old Westminster Endowment*.

A *Yellow*[1] School was established at Cirencester in 1722, where twenty boys were to be taught reading, writing, and the art of weaving worsted stockings, and twenty girls to read and spin. The institution of the "Charity" Schools on a large scale belongs to the eighteenth century, but it seems clear that the girls were required in those schools ordinarily to receive manual training in the subjects of sewing, knitting or some local handicraft.

With regard to the highly skilled needlework and embroidery, these rather belonged to the domestic than to the school education of the upper classes. In the *Life of Nicholas Ferrar* by Dr. Jebb, the Religious Community of Little Gidding is described as having a school-house, where the young girls always had at hand the young women of the House, who had acquired long and skilled experience in manual work. Dr. Jebb says: "They were curious at their needles, and they made their scissors to serve the altar or the poor. They were fine surgeons,[2] and they kept by them all manner of salves, oils and balsams: a room they had on purpose to lock up these and cordial waters of

---

[1] Colston's Foundation at Bristol (1634) is still known as the *Red* Maid's School. For distribution to girls leaving school, £10 or £20 were to be given to girls for dowries.

[2] *See* Prof. J. E. B. Mayor's *Nicholas Ferrar*, p. 231 n. for instances of ladies' skill in surgery. *See* also Joseph Payne's Lectures on the History of Education, p. 34, as to the practical proficiency of ladies in *mediaeval* times, in the same subject. Surgery, apparently, was a lady's subject, physic a gentleman's, and in mediaeval and later times these were often part of the education of the young of the higher classes.

their own distilling. . . . None of them were nice
of dressing with their own hands poor people's
wounds, were they never so offensive ; but as for
prescribing physic, their uncle understood it well
himself, yet he never practised it, and he forbade
them to tamper or meddle with it." The manual
work of the Collett sisters in the household of
Nicholas Ferrar included bookbinding and gilding.
The books of harmonies of the Scriptures which these
ladies produced were of beautiful workmanship in the
embroidery which covered them. But the educational subject of manual work in embroidery,
samplers, and plain needlework was an old one.
The modern aspect is the inclusion of the teaching of
needlework of some kind in almost all the schools,
secondary and elementary, established for girls in the
seventeenth century.[1]

In 1643 Mrs. Perwick kept a Girls' School in
Hackney, from which the biographer[2] of Mrs.
Perwick's daughter, Susanna, states that there had
been eight hundred girls educated in that school,
and that Susanna in her accomplishments surpassed
them all. From this account we see that music,
instrumental and vocal, was the chief subject, and
then dancing, both pursued to high proficiency.
Next, " whatever curious works of the needle or
otherwise can be named, which females are wont to

---

[1] The history has been comprehensively dealt with in
Samplers and Tapestry Embroideries by Marcus B. Huish.
See also the interesting chapter on the subject in Miss Eliz.
Godfrey's *Home Life under the Stuarts,* pp. 247–258.

[2] Mr. John Batcheler.

be conversant in, whether by silver, silks, straws, glass, wax, gums, or any other of the like kind, to say nothing of the pen for 'being an accountant' as well as the arts of good housewifery and cooking " —all these subjects had been practically studied by Susanna Perwick, and presumably by the rest of the eight hundred old pupils of Mrs. Perwick's school.

None of the above curriculum can be described as modern, except perhaps the accountancy. The requirement of " accounts " was made from girls as well as boys in the Elementary Schools which sprang up in the seventeenth century. But this probably only meant elementary arithmetic.[1] With regard to book-keeping, it may be mentioned that the first treatise in English was by James Peele, Clerk to the Governors of Christ's Hospital. It was entitled—

> *The pathewaye to perfectnes in the accomptes of debitour and creditour, in manner of a dialogue very pleasant and profitable for merchauntes and all other that minde to frequent the same, once again set forth and very much enlarged by James Peele, citizen and salter of London, Clercke of Christes Hospitall, practiser and teacher of the same.* London, 1569, fol.

The *Pathway* is in dialogue form in English between the Merchant and the Schoolmaster. The schoolmaster says : " My close school hideth itself to the profit of my scholars, but the same being close, is not generally known to all men, whereby my number and gain is the less." As far as we can judge, Peele's school for book-keeping is the first in this modern subject, and as Peele was the Clerk

---

[1] *See* p. 303 *infra.*

INTRODUCTION

to Christ's Hospital, an association in the pioneering of the teaching of this subject is established with that institution.

After Peele there followed writers of text-books on book-keeping such as Oldcastle,[1] Millis. The subject was one pursued outside of the school course and usually after leaving the ordinary school. Sometimes girls studied book-keeping. In 1678 a tractate was issued entitled *Advice to the Women and Maidens of London,* strongly urging girls " instead of their *usual* pastime and education in Needlework, Lace, and Point-making " to apply themselves more generally to the " practice of the method of keeping books of account, whereby either single or married, they may know their estates, carry on their trades, and avoid the danger of a helpless and forlorn condition, incident to widows." It is a clever and capable tract, and is a really modern document in its advocacy of a commercial education for girls.

Mrs. Bathsua Makin, who taught a school at Putney and afterwards at Tottenham High Cross, in 1673 wrote her *Essay to Revive the Ancient Education of Gentlewomen.* Mrs. Makin points out what is " generally done " in the private secondary schools for girls. " In most schools the teaching of the Needle and Housewifery are quite enough. I do acknowledge," she says, " that women should be accomplished in those things that concern them

---

[1] *See* de Morgan : *Arithmetical Books,* p. 28. *See also Excursus on Private Teachers of Arithmetic,* pp. 321–331 *infra.*

Line 5, for *Millis* read *Mellis.*

as women. My meaning is, what should be done with the *overplus time*, etc. ? " Her demands for the curriculum of girls are thus detailed : " To buy wool and flax, to dye scarlet and purple, requires skill in Natural Philosophy. To consider a field, the quantity and quality, requires knowledge in Geometry. To plant a vineyard requires understanding in Husbandry. She (the woman) could not merchandise without Arithmetic. She could not govern a family well without knowledge in Politics and Economics. She could not look well to the ways of her household except she understood Physic and Chirurgery (Surgery.) " Mrs. Makin adds by no means apologetically : " This seems to be the description of an honest, well-bred, ingenious, industrious Dutch-woman. I desire our women (whose condition calls them to business) should have no other breeding but what will enable them to do those things performed by this woman." When the close connexion of English with Dutch history in the time of Queen Elizabeth, and the growing sympathies of England with the Dutch refugees here in England are considered, we see the direct sources of Mrs. Makin's appeal to the model of the Dutch " Learned Maid."

But not only with the Netherlands, but with all the Protestants of Germany, France, Switzerland, Italy, Spain, Protestant England entered into close ties in the days of their meeting in Strassburg, Frankfort and Geneva, when the English Protestant leaders had to escape from England. Similarly, in the days of persecution, the Huguenot and other Protestant refugees found so warm a welcome in England as to raise the accusation (not, indeed, unfounded,) that greater liberty of conscience was allowed them than to our own dissentients from the doctrines and practice of the Established Church. The consequences in the introduction of new trades and crafts and to the commerce of this country from the presence of the religious refugees were conspicuous.[1] The important place they held in the development of the teaching of modern languages will appear in the chapters of this book dealing with those subjects.

In connexion with experimental science, the era-making influence in bringing into general notice the results of the advance in science of the seventeenth century was the Royal Society. The Royal Society was by far the keenest intellectual force in the second half of the seventeenth century, in its direct influence as a Society, as well as through the close connexion of individual members with the University life of Oxford and Cambridge, with Gresham College, and the College of Physicians. The new knowledge, and particularly the new methods, spread, at any rate, in the Universities, though some parents refused to allow their sons to be taught experimental subjects and even higher mathematics, " lest," as they said, " they should be smutted with the black art." The association with the Royal Society of essentially religious men such as Bishops Seth Ward and John Wilkins, together

---

[1] For a full account *see* Prof. W. Cunningham's *Alien Immigrants to England*, especially Chapters iv, v, vi.

with laymen of the religious stamp of Robert Boyle
and John Evelyn, the sympathy and co-operation
in large numbers of the aristocracy, beginning with
Charles II, and the outstanding ability of the members (to mention only one, Sir Isaac Newton) gave
the Society a unique position in both the pursuit and
in the dissemination of knowledge. Primarily, perhaps, the forces which concentrated in the Royal
Society are to be traced to that spirit of enterprise
and discovery which produced our great Trading
Companies but with their energies transferred to
the intellectual plane. Largely, England owes the
development of the seventeenth century experimental study of science to the successors of the
mighty merchants and men of commerce who had
made possible the wealth and leisure for nobles,
gentlemen, and scholars, e.g. the group who fore-
gathered at Great Tew, near Oxford, under Lord
Falkland,[1] and afterwards with others, established
the Royal Society, determined to pursue and track
out the " secrets " of Nature as fearlessly as their
predecessors had probed the geographical " secrets "
in the pursuit of adventurous commerce. The
schools for the young took a long time before they
appropriated the new subjects developed by the
Royal Society, into their curricula. In our survey,
limited by the end of the seventeenth century, we
can only attempt to trace the recognition rather
than any general adoption of the new experimental

---

[1] Clarendon's *History of the Great Rebellion*, Book VII,
§ 220.

subjects, except such as had reference to such a practical art as Navigation.

The close connexion of the progress of differentiation of subjects and the widening of the curriculum of educational institutions—with the course of national history becomes more unmistakable, the closer we study the subject. We have noted some of the chief forces making for progress, in the modern subjects in the sixteenth and seventeenth centuries. Instances could be multiplied indefinitely of direct influences on the academic curricula and methods exercised by political, social, and religious historical changes and events. The Reformation directly produced authoritative textbooks such as the Catechism, the Primer, and by attraction, so to say, an authoritative Latin Grammar. The realisation of English heroism in the old French wars gave rise to an authoritative book on Civics in Latin, though the stimulation of English patriotism through a foreign language was short-lived, even when done authoritatively.

The Fires of Smithfield made Protestant sermons of eloquent preachers of unusual preciousness, and shorthand came into the schools from the necessity of trying to get the boys to present *verbatim* reports for preservation, and for handing down sound doctrine. The Protestant refugees from abroad brought their arts, their culture, and their languages with them, and many actually set up as schoolmasters. The Great Civil War brought constitutional questions to the fore, and quickened legal studies, and even had a stimulative effect on astrology. The same war, from another standpoint, brought Hobbes's reflexion that it had been the obsession of the minds of the boys trained in the Grammar Schools, by classical studies which had made English people seek to emulate the civil conflicts which they found recorded as occurring in Greece and in Rome, and thus from the political point of view Hobbes advocated an English rather than a classical education. Francis Osborn[1] was discouraged from advocating heartily the inclusion of history as a subject of study when he " considered with what contradiction reports arrived at us, during our late Civil War." I have mentioned above the direct recognition of Louis XIV's ordinances for the provision of Navigation—used as an argument in application to equal English needs for similar provision. The needs in our large Merchant-service of sea-captains for apprentices, and the adaptation of the schools by the provision of the teaching of Navigation and the training of boys for service in the New England Colonies, all these instances are typical of the close and direct relations which may be traced between national life and new suggestions in education and their inter-relations. The inclusion of new subjects in the school curricula was of course part of the adaptation of the school to its environment. The more deeply we study the inter-relations the more we realise that the " school " in the sixteenth and seventeenth centuries (taking the term to include all educational institutions,

---

[1] *Advice to a Son* (1656), p. 6.

public and private, preparing for the active duties of life) was not only related to the course of the national life, as it always must be, explicitly or implicitly, but that in these centuries, important active elements in the community eagerly sought and intelligently followed up into practical effort, the educative suggestions and implications received from the most progressive national and social forces of the age.

It will be necessary, in our survey, to trace the history of the contents, and the development of the teaching, of each of the main modern subjects coming into the educational domain in the period, one by one, viz. English, History, Geography, Drawing, Physic and Natural History, Experimental Natural Philosophy, Mathematics, with the divisions, Arithmetic, Geometry, Astronomy; the Modern Languages, French, Italian, Spanish, German and Dutch, Polyglottism; and finally to take stock of the outstanding triumph of the English language in school and general education at the end of the seventeenth century.

The Beginnings of the Teaching of
Modern Subjects in England

CHAPTER I

THE TEACHING OF ENGLISH

THE idea of erudition in the Renascence time dominated all the educational institutions including the schools. The restraining plea of *festina lente* finds a place in school statutes. The haste to be rich is a modern analogue to the Renascence haste to become learned. Success in education resolved itself into the production of precocity. The early stages were neglected because they bore so little immediate fruit. Hence Mulcaster's valiant protest that the early stages were, in sober fact, the most important, educationally. Logically Mulcaster was obliged to stipulate for instruction in the vernacular, since the vernacular is vital for sound early instruction. But where the very language of instruction and of erudition was Latin, the goal to be reached as quickly as possible was Latin-speaking and Latin-reading. All the earlier stages of vernacular speaking must be reduced to a minimum as a waste of time. To speak nothing but Latin up to seven years of age, like Montaigne, was a consummation devoutly to be wished.

The interesting fact must be realised that the " return to the ancients " of the Renascence, " the

1

revival of Learning," led to the recognition of the value of the vernacular languages, partly because the study of philology could not be limited by its starting point of Latin, and also because the energy of thought which was awakened by the Renascence, was as penetrating intellectually as the voyages and discoveries in the same period were enterprising physically. At the same time political causes led to the consciousness of a national spirit in the chief countries of Europe, and this led to the expression of aspirations, experiences and ideals on a national basis, and in the vernacular.

Still, the consciousness of the value of a national language, as embodied in literary products, does not lead necessarily to a recognition of the disciplinary value of training in the vernacular language in the schools. It will be necessary to trace some indications of the growing recognition of the value of English both as an instrument of speech and as an educational influence, though the subject found scant recognition in the school curriculum for a long time. Yet the value of a vernacular was discovered early, at any rate by one writer.

In 1523, in his *de Tradendis Disciplinis*, Juan Luis Vives[1] says :

Let the teacher know with exactitude the vernacular language of the boys, so that he may teach the learned

---

[1] Vives (1492–1540) was educated at Valencia and at Paris. He came to England in 1523, and was attached to the Court of Henry VIII. He also was appointed to lecture at Oxford, where he became Fellow of Corpus Christi College. His reputation as a writer on education linked his name with Erasmus and Budaeus.

languages more satisfactorily and easily. For unless he speaks in the language of his country and makes use of words suitable to his subject-matter he will mislead his boys, and this error will accompany them persistently when they are grown-up. For boys do not understand even sufficiently well their mother-tongue, unless everything, bit by bit, is explained to them in the most careful manner. Let the teacher, further, keep in his memory the ancient forms of his mother tongue, and not only the knowledge of recent words, but also of the old words and those which now have passed out of common use, for unless this happens where any language shall receive its manifold changes, books written a hundred years previously would not be understood by posterity.

Nothing approaching this utterance (itself in Latin) in its appreciation of the vernacular from a pedagogic point of view appears in the English language for nearly sixty years. The first book in the English language on Moral Philosophy (and cognate subjects relating to the education and equipment of the *Governor* of a state) was Elyot's the *Boke called the Gouvernour* in 1531. But it was only in 1582 that Mulcaster published his *Elementarie* which boldly urged the teaching of English as a language worthy of study by English men and English children.

The inadequacy of the knowledge of the vernacular language possessed by schoolmasters even, is shown in the following passage from John Palsgrave's Dedication to King Henry VIII of his translation of *Acolastus*, 1540.

Some other furthermore there be, which though they have by their great study, at your grace's universities, so much profited in the Latin tongue, that to show an evident trial of their learning, they can write an **Epistle** right Latin like, and thereto speak Latin, as the time shall minister occasion, very well, yea and have also by their diligence attained to a comely vein in making verses ; yet for all this, partly because of the rude language used in their native countries, where they were born & first learned (as it happened) their grammar rules & partly because that coming straight from thence, unto some of your grace's universities, they have not had occasions to be conversant in such places of your realm, as the purest English is spoken, they be not able to express their conceit in their vulgar tongue, nor be sufficient, perfectly to open the diversities of phrases between our tongue and the Latin (which in my poor judgment is the very chief thing that the schoolmaster should travail in). In so much that for want of this sufficient perfection in our own tongue, I have known divers of them which have still continued their study in some of your grace's universities, that after a substantial increase of good learning, by their great and industrious study obtained, yet when they have been called to do any service in your grace's commonwealth, either to preach in open audience, or to have other administration, requiring their assiduous conversanting with your subjects, they have then been forced to read over our English authors, by that means to provide a remedy unto their evident imperfection in that behalf.

Within the years 1531–1582, even the writing in English on subjects of scholarship was not altogether approved. Not infrequently an author showed the recognition of the transitional stage by writing in Latin and translating his book into English, as, for instance, Laurence Humfrey in his *Optimates* published at Basle in 1560, translated into English and published in London in 1563.[1]

---

[1] The further title (of the Latin edition) is : *Optimates, sive de Nobilitate, ejusque antiqua origine, naturâ, disciplinâ, lib. 3. Basle. 1560. 8°.* The English title is : *The Nobles, or of Nobilitye. The Original Nature, dutyes, right and Christian Institucion thereof three Bookes. London. 1563. 12°.*

But earlier than this, in 1545, Roger Ascham had written the *Toxophilus* in English. He feels, however, that it would have brought him more credit had he written in Latin, but he is writing for archers, who may some of them know English better than Latin. Still, Ascham's explanation of his choice of English for the language in which to write his book is substantially an apology for not writing in Latin :

If any man would blame me, either for taking such a matter in hand, or else for writing it in the English tongue, this answer I may make him, that when the best of the realm think it honest for them to use, I, one of the meanest sort, ought not to suppose it vile for me to write ; and though to have written it in another tongue, had been both more profitable for my study, and also more honest [honourable] for my name, yet I can think my labor well bestowed, if with a little hinderance of my profit and name, may come any furtherance to the pleasure or commodity of the gentlemen and yeomen of England, for whose sake I took this matter in hand. And as for the Latin or Greek tongue, everything is so excellently done in them, that none can do better : in the English tongue, contrary, everything in a manner so meanly both for the matter and handling, that no man can do worse. For therein the least learned, for the most part, have been always most ready to write. And they which had least hope in Latin, have been most bold in English : when surely every man that is most ready to talk is not most able to write. He that will write well in any tongue, must follow this counsel of Aristotle, to speak as the common people do, to think as wise men do : and so should every man understand him, and the judgment of wise men allow him. Many English writers have not done so, but using strange words, as Latin, French, and Italian, do make all things dark and hard.

Thomas Wilson in his *Art of Rhetoric* in 1553 wrote the first important text-book treating of

Line 36, for *Thomas Wilson* read *Thomas Wilton*.

composition in the English language.[1] Wilson states the difficulty with which the writer of English at the time had to contend. Since the Renascence, England had come into contact with foreign countries (France, Spain and Italy particularly), and the English traveller, usually well-instructed and influential, had made it the fashion to imitate foreign expressions, in an age when the English language itself had not become fixed in standard by the possession of a long-established, continuous national literature. Wilson lays down the maxim that the English writer should write genuine English :

Among all other lessons this should first be learned, that we never affect any strange ink-horn terms, but to speak as is commonly received, neither seeking to be over fine, nor yet living overcareless, using our speech as most men do, and ordering our wits as the fewest have done. Some seek so far for outlandish English that they forget altogether their mother's language. And I dare swear this, if some of their mothers were alive they were not able to tell what they say ; and yet these fine English clerks will say they speak in their mother tongue, if a man should charge them for counterfeiting the King's English. Some far-journeyed gentlemen at their return home, like as they love to go in foreign apparel, so they will powder their talk with over-sea language. He that cometh lately out of France will talk French English, and never blush at the matter. Another chops in with English italianated and applieth the Italian phrase to our English speaking. . . . The lawyer will store his stomach with the prating of pedlars. . . . The unlearned or foolish phantastical, that smells but of learning (such fellows

---

[1] Leonard Cox (Headmaster of the Reading Grammar School) wrote *The Art or Crafte of Rhetoryke*, 1524, but it was only an elementary and technical manual.

as have seen learned men in their days), will so Latin their tongues that the simple can not but wonder at their talk, and think surely they speak by some revelation. I know them that think rhetoric to stand wholly upon dark words ; and he that can catch an inkhorn term by the tail him they count to be a fine Englishman and a good rhetorician.

In 1557, Sir John Cheke [1] says : " I am of this opinion that our own tongue should be written clear and pure unmixt and unmangled with borrowing of other tongues, wherein if we take not heed betime, ever borrowing and never paying she shall be fair to keep her house as bankrupt."

And again George Chapman, [2] the translator into English of Homer : " For my varietie of new words I have none Inckepot I am sure you know, but such as I give pasport with such authoritie, so significant and not ill sounding, that if my countrey language were an usurer, or a man of this age speaking it, hee would thank mee for enriching him."

But the love of odd, bizarre, foreign, pretentious, extravagant terms reached its climax in John Lyly's *Euphues* published in 1579 at the time

---

[1] In a letter to Sir Thomas Hoby, the translator of Castigliano's *Courtier*. Still earlier (*c.* 1540) Sir Thomas Smith in an oration to University students on his appointment as Professor of Civil Law in the University of Cambridge, said that English " where its use was marked by precision and purity, might compare even with the Latin, for beauty and force of expression." —Mullinger, *University of Cambridge*, vol. ii, p. 132. Yet, it may be noted, Smith was delivering his address in the Latin language.

[2] In the instalment of Homer's *Iliad* called *Achilles' Shield*, 1598, under the title : " To the Understander." *See* Gregory Smith's *Eliz. Crit. Essays*, vol. ii, p. 305.

when the greatest of the Elizabethan poets, Spenser, and the greatest English writer, Shakespere, were in the preparatory stage towards the richest and completest power of expression in English.

Ascham's *Scholemaster*, published in 1570, is significant in the development of the use of English. In contrast to his *Toxophilus* of 1545, when he apologised for writing a book of Archery in the English language, he writes a treatise on learning and education, in English—the *Scholemaster*—without a shadow of an apology. Ascham felt now even a book on scholarship might be written in the vernacular, without misgiving. The time was ripe for the further step of not only justifying the use of English, but of glorying in it. Richard Mulcaster came forward, and said the fitting word. His *Elementarie* in 1582 contains the most able, the deepest, and most patriotic words which had yet been said on the English language. He says :

> Our natural tongue being as beneficial to us for our needful delivery as any other is to the people which use it ; and having as pretty and as fair observations in it as any other hath, and being as ready to yield to any rules of art as any other is, why should I not take some pains to find out the right writing of ours, as other countrymen have done to find out the like in theirs ?

He returns, again and again, to this delightful theme. Mulcaster discovered the great merits of English as a language. How could he justify his pleasure to a learned world that, by tradition and use, only thought of Latin as a literary language ? He must show, in the first place, its antiquity.

EFFECT OF TRADE ON LANGUAGE

Our language cannot be called young :

Unless the German himself [itself] be young, which claimeth a prerogative for the age of his [its] speech of an infinite prescription ; unless the Latin and Greek be young, whose words we enfranchise to our own use, though not always immediately from themselves, but most-what through the Italian, French, and Spanish ; unless other tongues, which be neither Greek nor Latin, nor any of the forenamed, from whom we have somewhat, *as they have from ours*, will, for company's sake, be content to be young, that ours may not be old. But I am well assured that every one of these will strive for antiquity, and rather grant it to us than forego it themselves.

In bold, noble language, instinct with the patriotism of the Elizabethan age, Mulcaster speaks of the English nation as being of " good credit," even in the language of its detractors and enemies. He then shows that the matter of our speech is as significant and lófty as that of any other nation. He discusses, with admiration, the effect that chivalry must have had in increasing and refining vocabulary. The inspiriting effect of war, "its true and untrue reports, its projects, devices, and multitude of discourses," are vigorously shown, and, finally, Mulcaster draws attention to the influence of trade in expanding ideas, and in provoking apt expression :

If the spreading sea and the spacious land could use any speech, they would both show you where, and in how many strange places, they have seen our people, and also given you to wit that they deal in as much and as greater variety of matters as any other people do, whether at home or abroad.   Which is the reason why our tongue doth serve to so many uses, because it is conversant with so many matters, in so sundry kinds of dealings. Now all this variety of matter and diversity of trade make both matter for our speech and means to enlarge it.

9

Mulcaster's *Elementarie* is the earliest text-book on the teaching of English. It is emphatically a teacher's book of method for the teaching of the vernacular. The consciousness of the author of the glorious possibilities of the English language, a few years before Spenser and Shakespere wrote,[1] makes the book unique. It is remarkable that it has never been reprinted.

Mulcaster addresses a long peroration to his readers at the end of his *Elementarie*. In it he returns once more to the advocacy of the English language as a subject for teaching and as worthy of cultivation. He is a head master of a classical school, he is an able Latin writer, and yet his call to the study of English is stronger than any writing for, probably, over two hundred years.

One passage more, perhaps the best known, from the peroration to the *Elementarie*. It is on the value of the English *v.* Latin as a literary language :

Our own language bears the joyful title of our liberty and freedom, the Latin remembers us of our thraldom and bondage. I love Rome, but London better ; I favour Italy, but England more. I honour the Latin, but I worship the English. . . . I honour foreign tongues, but wish my own to be partaker of their honour. Knowing them, I wish my own tongue to resemble their grace. I confess their furniture, and wish it were ours. Why not [write] all in English, a tongue of itself both deep in conceit and frank in delivery ? . . . I do not think that any language,

---

[1] The *Elementarie* was printed in 1582, Shakespere's first play was written about 1590, and Spenser's *Faerie Queene*, 1590–96.

be it whatsoever, is better able to utter all arguments either with more pith or greater plainness than our English tongue . . . not any whit behind either the subtle Greek for crouching close, or the stately Latin for spreading fair. [1]

Looked at from the point of view of the writers in the English language, the later Elizabethans were not all unconscious of their great literary men. Richard Carew c. 1595–6 proudly asserts : [2] " Whatsoever grace any other language carrieth in verse or prose, in tropes, or metaphors, in echoes or agnominations, they may all be lively and exactly represented in ours. Will you have Plato's verse ? Read Sir Thomas Smith. The Ionic ? Sir Thomas More. Cicero's ? Ascham. Varro ? Chaucer. Demosthenes ? Sir John Cheke (who in his treatise to the Rebels hath comprised all the figures of rhetoric). Will you read Virgil ? Take the Earl of Surrey. Catullus ? Shakespere and Marlowe's fragment. Ovid ? Daniel. Lucan ? Spenser. Martial ? Sir John Davies and others. Will you have all in all for prose and verse ? Take the miracle of our age, Sir Philip Sidney. Carew

---

[1] Sir Humphrey Gilbert in his proposed *Queene Elizabeth's Achademy* (*c.* 1572) suggested that the public " readers " (*i.e.*, lecturers) every six years should be required to set forth some new book in print according to their several professions, and every three years make some translation of a good foreign book " into the English tongue."

[2] In a MSS. Epistle on the Excellency of the English Tongue (Brit. Mus. MSS.) reprinted in Mr. Gregory Smith's *Elizabethan Critical Essays*, ii, p. 293. Modern critical judgment would not confirm all Carew's illustrations of the best writers of English of his period.

has elsewhere [1] excellent remarks to offer on the teaching of Latin, but he offers no method of teaching his native language.

Peacham, [2] similarly, in 1622, delights in the reading of English literature. He considers that no gentleman's education is complete without a knowledge of our great authors. Indeed, a scholar is often inferior in his knowledge of English literature to a well-trained gentleman ; in other words, the study of English is, in Peacham's view, important, but at the same time is recognised as non-academic. " I have known," he says, " even excellent scholars so defective this way, that when they had been beating their brains, twenty or four and twenty years about Greek etymologies or the Hebrew roots and Rabbins, could neither write true English in true orthography ; . . . otherwise, for their judgment in the arts and other tongues very sufficient."

The directions which Peacham gives for the study of English literature and composition are clear and instructive. " To help yourself herein (i.e. to speak and write good English), make choice of those authors in prose who speak the best and purest English." For this purpose, he goes on to say : [3]

"I would commend unto you (though from more antiquity) the *Life of Richard III*, written by

---

[1] *The True and Ready way to learn the Latin Tongue*, Published by Samuel Hartlib, 1654.

[2] In *The Compleat Gentleman Fashioning him absolute in the most necessary and commendable Qualities concerning Minde or Bodie that may be required in a Noble Gentleman.*

[3] *Compleat Gentleman*, p. 53.

Sir Thomas More ; the *Arcadia* of the noble Sir Philip Sidney, whom Du Bartas makes one of the four columns of our language ; the *Essays and Other Pieces* of the excellent master of eloquence, my lord of St. Albans, who possesseth not only eloquence but all good learning as hereditary by both father and mother. You have then Mr. Hooker's *Polity* ; *Henry IV*, well written by Sir John Hayward ; that first part of *Our English Kings* by M. Samuel Daniel. There are many others I know, but these will taste you best, as proceeding from no vulgar judgments ; the last Earl of Northampton, in his ordinary style, was not to be mended. Procure, then, if you may, the speeches made in Parliament, frequent learned sermons, in term time resort to the Star Chamber, and be present at the pleadings in other public courts, whereby you shall better your speech, enrich your understanding, and get more experience in one month than in other four by keeping your melancholy study and by solitary meditation.''

When Peacham deals with Poetry, he especially desires the study of Latin classical poets, and then later writers of Latin verse. But he also advocates the English poets as a subject of study.[1] This is what he says of Chaucer : ''Of English poets of our own nation, esteem Sir Geoffrey Chaucer the father ; although the style for the antiquity may distaste you, yet as under a bitter and rough rind, there lieth a delicate kernell of conceit and sweet invention.

---

[1] *Compleat Gentleman*, p. 94.

What examples, similitudes, times, places, and above all, persons, with their speeches and attributes, do as in his *Canterbury Tales* (like those threads of gold, the rich arras), beautify his work quite thorough!"

Other English writers whom Peacham chooses out for a gentleman's reading are Gower, Lydgate. Then followed Harding, and after him Skelton,[1] Earl of Surrey, Sir Thomas Wyat, Sternhold, John Heywood, Sir Thomas More, Phaer, Golding. Of the writers in the golden age of Queen Elizabeth Peacham's choice falls as follows : " To omit Her Majesty, who had a singular gift herein, above others, were Edward Earl of Oxford, the Lord Buckhurst, Henry Lord Paget, our Phœnix, the noble Sir Philip Sidney, Mr. Edward Dyer, Mr. Edmund Spenser, Mr. Samuel Davies, with sundry others whom (together with those admirable wits yet living and so well known), not out of envy but to avoid tediousness, I overpass. This much of poetry."

On the other hand, Samuel Daniel in his *Musophilus: or Defence of all Learning* in 1602–3 says :

"How many thousands never heard the name of Sidney, or of Spenser, or their books ? "

Mentioning Daniel, I cannot forbear to quote his prophetic lines :

When as our accents equal to the best,
Is able greater wonders to bring forth :
When all that ever hotter spirits exprest,
Comes bettered by the patience of the North.

---

[1] A "poet laureate for what desert I could never hear," says Peacham.

And who, in time, knows whither we may vent
The treasure of our tongue, to what strange shores
This gain of our best glory shall be sent,
T' inrich unknowing Nations with our stores ?
What worlds in th' yet unformed Occident
May come refin'd with th' accents that are ours ?
Or, who can tell for what great work in hand
The greatness of our style is now ordain'd ?
What powers it shall bring in, what spirits command,
What thoughts let out, what humours keep
        restrain'd,
What mischief it may powerfully withstand,
And what fair ends may thereby be attain'd.

It may appear to be straying from the subject of writers on the Teaching of English to include this last quotation from Samuel Daniel, but to the student of the history of English education the direct call to the consideration and study of English writers, especially in the earlier stages, is a point of great importance ; first, directly in itself, and, secondly, indirectly, in the competitive position of the vernacular, with respect to Latin and Greek as subjects of educational discipline. The direct reference to the " unformed Occident," and the importance of the preservation of the integrity of the English language, and honour for it, because of its indefinitely great prospective influence in the New World, makes the passage one which should be better known than it is in both England and America.

Passing by the writers of books on the teaching of the reading [1] and spelling of English, one writer

---

[1] *See* the author's *English Grammar Schools to* 1660, chap. x. John Cleland in his *Institution of a Young*

who clearly realised the problem involved in the teaching of the vernacular was John Brinsley, in the *Ludus literarius* (1612). His treatment needs full quotation, as it marks an epoch in the development of the teaching of English :

The Necessity for the further teaching of English.

But to tell you what I think, seems unto me, to be a very main want in all our Grammar schools generally, or in the most of them ; whereof I have heard some great learned men to complain ; That there is no care had in respect, to train up scholars so, as they may be able to express their minds purely and readily in our own tongue, and to increase in the practice of it, as well as in the Latin or Greek ; whereas our chief endeavour should be for it, and that for these reasons : 1. Because that language which all sorts and conditions of men amongst us are to have most use of, both in speech and writing, is our own native tongue. 2. The purity and elegancy of our own language is to be esteemed a chief part of the honour of our Nation : which we all ought to advance as much as in us lieth. As when Greece and Rome and other nations have most flourished, their languages also have been most pure : and from those times of Greece and Rome, we fetch our chiefest patterns, for the learning of their tongues. 3. Because of those which are for a time trained up in schools, there are very few which proceed in learning, in comparison of them that follow other callings.

Complaint of want of care in our schools for growth in our own tongue, as in the Latin.

Our chief endeavour should be for our own tongue. Reasons.

Nobleman (1607) requires for the private pupil the systematic teaching of English before learning Latin. The boy is to be trained " to read with a sweet accent, not pronouncing verse as prose, or prose as verse, but with a pleasant harmony, reading at the beginning with leisure, pausing at the full periods, and taking his breath at the broken points, lifting or basing his voice as the subject requireth and the admiration or question offereth."

As to the deficiency, Spoudeus [1] is even more emphatic. He says :

For schools which have any regard for our English tongue. This complaint is not without just cause : for I do not know any school, wherein there is regard had hereof to any purpose ; notwithstanding the general necessity and use of it, and also the great commendation which it brings to them who have attained it : but I think every minute an hour until I hear this of you how my trouble and shame may be avoided, and how I may obtain this faculty to direct my children, how they may go thus forward, not only in reading English perfectly, but also in the propriety, purity, and copy [= Latin, *copia*] of our English tongue, so as they may utter their minds commendably of any matter which may concern them, according to their age and place.

Philoponus then supplies a description of his method of English teaching and right reading of all other things learned in Latin, the daily use of Lily's rules construed into English, the continual practice of English grammatical translations of all the school authors and the learning by heart of Latin and English. But, further, Philoponus urges the practice of writing English "heedily" in true Orthography—writing epistles or familiar letters to their friends in English, as well as in Latin. Then he goes on to suggest " the reporting of a fable in English, or the like matter, trying who can make the best report." He does not say whether he would have this composition oral or written, or both. Further, he advocates the taking of notes of sermons, and delivering them again. For the rest, see to the

---

[1] p. 22, Brinsley's *Ludus Literarius* takes the form of a colloquy, in which Spoudeus generally states the common practice of teachers and Philoponus suggests the methods of educational reform.

translations into English first, in propriety, then in purity.

On the earliest stages in teaching English, Hezekiah Woodward, in 1641, says :

" Certain it is the child understands more of his own tongue in one month from his nurse (after he can speak articulately) than he gains from a school in any three in any language ; which clearly showeth of what force Nature is. . . . I confess my thoughts are not ripened here, though it is no disparagement to go even so low ; for the mother-tongue is the foundation of *all*." Woodward refers his readers to Mr. Carew,[1] a man of long experience gained by travel, and to Mr. Hodges'[2] large " tractate." Woodward prophesies that the elementary teacher will some day receive " a good encouragement " in his salary, " to come down so low." He adds : " This will be thought upon when times mend, and the day clears up ; then our judgment and foresight will clear up too." In the meantime, good scholars are not forthcoming as elementary teachers. Hence good teachers cannot be got for the mother-tongue, and such teaching will be left to the meanest and worst teachers.[3] " There," says he, " I have it

---

[1] *See* p. 11 *supra*.

[2] *See English Grammar Schools*, pp. 184–5.

[3] *Cf.* Mulcaster's incisive passage in the *Positions*, p. 130 : " Some will say, perhaps, to train up children, what needs so much cunning, or in so petty a matter what needs so much labour ? . . . The matter is not so mean, which is the readiest mean to so great a good, but if it were mean, the *meanest matter requireth not the meanest master* to have it well done ; and the first ground-work should be laid by the best workman." *See* also Mulcaster's *Positions*, p. 233.

given in the Mistress her hands, *for there is no remedy.*" [1]

Woodward, later on,[2] urges that the practice of the mother-tongue is the true guide to "concords" in teaching Latin. The child will not say: "Him did read," but " He did read." What the child says at home gives him the right direction, for use (i.e. practice) has established it in his mind. " *Me* pray you, mother ? " No, *I* do pray you." " *I* is in a fault ? " " No. *I am.*" Woodward had read his Mulcaster, but the conviction of the importance of some English teaching as a basis to all high instruction, is his own.

For the Petty School, [3] Charles Hoole in 1660 suggested a method of teaching English, and teaching English literature. It might be expected that, *a fortiori*, he would advocate English in higher instruction. But the glamour of a purely classical education even in 1660 was predominant, and any direct English teaching was relegated to the Elementary School except such as might be included in Rhetoric.

It is still necessary to consider in some detail the books of the period which might have served as school text-books had the subject been considered worthy of a place in the curriculum. For there were books which were paving the way to a body of knowledge on the English language and literature. These were making the vernacular a subject of inquiry and

---

[1] *A Light to Grammar*, 1641, cap v.
[2] *Ibid.*, cap. vii.
[3] *See English Grammar Schools*, chap. viii.

investigation, and were thus placing it in line with other academic studies. Some teachers, principally private teachers and tutors, were actually bringing English into the teaching arena for one class in the nation, chiefly the gentry, who happened to have tutors who were interested in the research, or in some rare instances, who considered a knowledge of our own language and literature a necessary part of true patriotism, and a nobleman's privilege. Again when the French influence came into the Court of Charles II, curiously enough, there was an impetus by way of reaction, not so much calculated to strengthen Latin, as to discover the value of a training in English. By that time, too, as we shall see, text-books for almost every branch of learning were available in English.

I will now describe the books on the English language, in their chronological order.

First, must be named here the great philological work of research done by Mr. A. J. Ellis for the Philological Society, in making known early books on the English language.

> *On Early English Pronunciation, With especial reference to Shakespeare and Chaucer : containing an investigation of the Correspondence of Writing with Speech in England from the Anglo-Saxon Period to the present day, preceded by a systematic notation of all spoken sounds by means of the ordinary Printing Types. By Alexander J. Ellis, F.R.S.* For the Philological Society. Part I, 1869 ; Part II, 1869 ; Part III, 1871 ; Part IV, 1875 ; Part V. 1889.

The authorities named by Mr. Ellis between 1500 and 1660 in this subject are the following : **1530,**

John Palsgrave ; 1545 and 1550, Louis Meigret ; 1547 and 1567, W. Salisbury ; 1555, Sir John Cheke ; 1568, Sir Thomas Smith ; 1569, John Hart ; 1570, Peter Levins ; 1573, John Baret ; 1611, Randle Cotgrave ; 1611, John Florio ; Mr. Ellis also treats of Bullokar, Gill, Butler, Ben Jonson, Willis,[1] Wallis.[2]

To turn now, in more detail, to the early books on the teaching of English :

1580. WILLIAM BULLOKAR.

> *Bullokars Booke at large, for the Amendment of Orthographie for English speech ; wherein a most perfect supplie is made, for the wantes and double sounde of letters in the olde Orthographie, with Examples for the same, with the easie conference and use of both Orthographies, to save expences in Bookes for a time, untill this amendment grow to a generall use, for the easie, speedie and perfect reading and writing of English, (the speech not changed, as some untruly and maliciously, or at least ignorantlie blowe abroade) by the which amendment the same Authour hath also framed a ruled Grammar, to be imprinted heereafter, for the same speech, to no small commoditie of the English Nation, not only to come to easie, speedie and perfect use of our owne language, but also to their easie, speedie and readie entrance into the secretes of other Languages, and easie and speedie pathway to all Straungers, to use our Language, heeretofore very hard unto them, to no small profite & credite to this our Nation, and stay thereunto in the weightiest causes. There is also imprinted with this Orthographie a short Pamphlet*

---

[1] Thomas Willis : *Vestibulum Linguæ Latinæ.* 1651. For an account of this book *see Educ. Review* (1895), p. 330.

[2] John Wallis, the mathematician : *Joannis Wallisii Grammatica Linguæ Anglicanæ Cui præfigitur De Loquela ; sive de sonorum omnium loquelarium formatione : Tractatus Grammatico-Physicus.* 1675. First ed. 1653 ; 2nd, 1664.

*for all learners, and a Primer agreeing to the same,
and as learners shall go forward therein, other necessarie
Bookes shall speedily be provided with the same Orthographie. Hereunto are also ioyned written Copies with
the same Orthographie.*

Give God the praise, that teacheth alwaies.

When truth trieth, errour flieth.

*Seene and allowed according to order. Imprinted
at London by Henrie Denham. 1580. (4to. 59 pp.)*

The preface to this long-titled book is headed
" Bullokar to his Countrie." In this preface, Bullokar
states that when he wrote his book he had not seen
works on the same subject by Sir Thomas Smith
and Master Chester,[1] otherwise he would have offered
them his services in orthography.

One interesting feature of this book is that Bullokar gives his experience with regard to the teaching
of his own children, and is thus a pioneer not only
in language-study but also in child-study, as a basis
for pedagogical method.

The voyce should give names to letters.

But yet I have founde by handling of mine owne children
(whome I have used to mine owne liking in teaching
them true Ortography written, for lacke of the printed) that
reading and writing may be had perfectly, in the time that
my helpes before used could be perfectly conceyved and
halfe followed, by reason that in true Ortography, both
the eye, the voyce, and the eare consent most perfectly,
without any let, doubt or maze. Which want of concord

---

[1] The book to which Bullokar refers appears to be :
*A Methode or comfortable beginning for all unlearned,
whereby they may be taught to read English, in a very short
time, with pleasure : So profitable as straunge, put in light
by J[ohn] H[art] Chester Heralt. Henrie Denham. London.
1570. 4to.*

in the eye, voice, and eare, I did perceyve almost thirtie yeares past, by the very voyce of children, who guided by the eye with the letter, and giving voyce according to the name thereof, as they were taught to name letters, yeelded to the eare of the hearer a cleane contrary to the word looked for.

The following passage shows Bullokar as an inquirer into the language.

Of xxxvii parts scant six perfect [*i.e.,* in our English Alphabet]

Hereby grewe quarels in the teacher, and lothsome-nesse in the learner, and great payne to both : and the conclusion was, that both teacher and learner must go by rote, or no rule could be followed, when of xxxvii parties, xxxi kept no square, nor true joint. For xii parts greatly needefull, lacked altogether, or were furnished with the other xxiii partes, by peecing and contrary hewing of which xxiii (if they be well viewed) they are so mangled, that there are but sixe partes in perfect use : whereof (as occasion hath offered) I have complayned to divers of the art of learning, whereunto some have yeelded, some not conceyved of it, some loth to graunt it, and some old customaries could not abide to heare of any spedie way to knowledge, were it never so good. 1594.

> *Grammatica Anglicana, praecipue quatenus a Latina differt, ad unicam P. Rami Methodum concinnata . . . authore P. G.* [*P. Greenwood ?*] *Vocabula Chauceriana quædam selectiora . . . ipsæ hodie Poetarum deliciæ, una cum eorum significatis . . . eodem authore J. Legatt ; Cantabrigiæ* 1594. 8vo. (pp. 36.) Also 1598.

This is an English Grammar written in Latin. It contains short chapters on letters, syllables, parts of speech. As an illustration in treating of the verb is quoted :

> "Not Philip's son, who all the world subdued,
> Achilles ne, in Hector's blood imbu'd :
> Not all the worthies stout which ever lived,
> With this our Peer, were worthy be compared."

At the end of the tiny book is a little dictionary of English words occurring in the text, with the Latin equivalent. Two passages are given for grammatical " analysis " or what we call parsing. The model for the process gives the parsing done in Latin throughout. [1] Finally there is a Vocabulary of Chaucerian words.

1596.   Coote's *English Schoolmaster*.[2]

The great merit of Coote is that he attempts to explain the manner of learning for the pupil and of teaching for the teacher in the English language. The book is essentially for the elementary pupil.

1619.   Alexander Gill. 2nd ed. 1621.   For an account of the two Alexander Gills *see* Masson's *Milton*, vol. i, chap. 3.

> *Logonomia Anglica. Quâ gentis sermo faciliùs addiscitur Conscripta ab Alexandro Gil, Paulinæ Scholæ magistro primario.   Secundò edita, paulò correctior sed ad usum communem accommodatior.* Sm. 4to.

Alexander Gill's *Logonomia Anglica. Nach der Ausgabe von* 1621 *diplomatisch herausgegeben von Otto L. Jiriczek.* In *Quellen und Forschungen zur Sprach-und Culturgeschichte der Germanischen Völker. Strassburg. Trubner,* 1903.

Gill suggests a phonetic system of English spelling. He would propose to use Anglo-Saxon signs for the

---

[1] Reflecting the Grammar School method. We know from John Brinsley's *Ludus Litirarius* (p. 80) that the parsing lessons in the Grammar School were supposed to be conducted by questions and answers in Latin.

[2] *The Englishe Schole-Maister, Teaching all his Scholars, of what age soever, the most easie, short and perfect order of distinct Reading, and true Writing our English tongue, that hath ever been known or published by any.*

two sounds of *th* and other symbols. Whilst dealing with grammatical and rhetorical figures Gill quotes from Spenser, Sidney, Wither, Daniel, and other English poets. He even prefers Spenser to Homer.

What France had done for Sidney in the quotation of passages from *Arcadian Rhetoric* (1588) Gill did for Spenser in *Logonomia Anglica*.

Gill's method of teaching is by illustrative passages from many English writers, but especially he quotes rhetorical passages from Spenser's *Faerie Queene*, *Shepherd's Kalendar*, and the *Ruines of Time*.

He also quotes from : " Noster " Lucanus, Sam. Daniel, " Noster " Juvenal, Geo. Withers, Stanyhurst Aeneis, Sir P. Sidney, and takes his definitions from Mancinellus, Despauterius, etc. The examples taken from Spenser's *Faerie Queene* are very numerous. One definition ($\pi\epsilon\rho\acute{\iota}\phi\rho\alpha\sigma\iota\varsigma$) is taken from Farnaby.

Harrington's translation of Epigrams (Martial) is quoted. So is the *Arcadia* of Sir Philip Sidney. Spenser appears in Gill as *noster Homerus*. The quotation of passages occur chiefly in illustration of the figures of rhetoric and grammar. There are nearly seventy quotations from Spenser alone.

It is thus clear that Gill leads his readers to look for illustrative passages from the great English writers. This is done in the interests of rhetoric, and it is in connexion with the subject of rhetoric that we recognise the nearest approach to the study of English literature as a subject of teaching and culture in the seventeenth century.

25

1624.

> *A Perfect Survey of the English Tongue, taken according to the Use and Analogie of the Latine. And serveth for the more plaine exposition of the Grammaticall Rules and Precepts, collected by Lillie, and for the more certaine Translation of the English tongue into Latine. Together with sundry good demonstrations by way of Sentences in either tongue. Written and collected by Io : Hewes, Master of Arts. Principiis cognitis, multo facilus extrema intelligitur. Cic. pro Cluentio. London. Printed by Edw. Allde, for William Garret. 1624. 4to. Also 1632.*

With 16 pages at the end of " The Author his Counsel and Exh⁻rtation to his beloved Pupils, and those of all Ages."   John Hewes claims that he has made for those that are English as *a posteriori* the English tongue the first groundwork to the Latin.   He therefore makes a special point of dealing with the English " signs" which do not find expression in the Latin.

Hewes prides himself on his divers examples whereby the pupil may learn to express again the particles or signs from the Latin into English. " Copious and fit examples are necessary to show the use of the rules we collect, wherein I seem not much to differ from the opinion of Manilius."

> Per varios usus artem experientia fecit,
> Exemplo monstrante viam.

After his signature Hewes adds :

Non tam praeclarum est scire Latine quam turpe nescire.

Hewes gives one page, a very full one, to a brief note of the moods, so of the tenses, both starting from English ;   then a one-page table of the more general rules of the syntax of the cases as they may be conceived in the English tongue ; then a table of exceptions to the syntax of the cases.

Hewes' book is a precursor of *The Treatise of English Particles* of William Walker (1623–1682), though he is not mentioned by the latter writer. His book is written to help the realisation of English Grammar and construction as an aid to learning Lily's Grammar. Lily's Grammar is itself epitomised to the smallest dimensions, and the main feature of Hewes' book is the copiousness of examples and the fewness of rules. The examples, moreover, are usually illustrative of the rules, as well as interesting quotations in themselves. As for example, treating of motion to a place requiring the accusative, Hewes gives :

Ne temere Abidum naviges. Sail not rashly to Abydos.
Non licet cuivis adire Corinthum. It is not lawful for all
    men to go to Corinth.

It is clear that such a method requires competent teachers, and it is for such that Hewes evidently is writing.

1633.   Charles Butler.

> *The English Grammar, Or the Institution of Letters, Syllables and woords in the English tung, whereunto is annexed an Index of woords Like and unlike.* By Charles Butler. Magd. Master of Arts.
> Arist. Polit. lib. 8. cap. 3. Grammatica addiscenda pueris, utpote ad vitam utilis. Oxford. Printed by William Turner for the Author, 1634.

(Of particular interest from the etymology of the Index. It is a genuine Accidence of the English Language.)

Butler in his Preface, holds :

The excellency of a language doth consist chiefly in :
1. Antiquity. 2. Copious Elegancy. 3. Generality. For
the first, Hebrew ; for the second, the Greek ; for the
third, the Latin ; for all, the English is worthily honoured.

He further quotes from Sir John Price : *Remains,*
chap. 3 :

(Whether more tartly or truly I know not) taxing our
Orthography to prefer his own saith that four good secretaries, writing a sentence in English from his mouth, differed
all, one from another, in many letters : whereas so many
Welsh, writing the same in their tongue, varied not in any
letter.

He goes on to point out that the—

Uncertainty of our writing is due to the imperfection
of our Alphabet.

Butler, like Gill, utilises the Anglo-Saxon signs
for the different sounds of *th*, and makes use of other
symbols for phonetic distinctions. The index of
words like and unlike is very valuable as showing
the pronunciation of Butler's time. He takes care
to distinguish words nearly alike, thus he says :
Wound (past participle of to wind) *tortus;* a *wound,*
vulnus.

1640. Simon Daines.

> *Orthoepia Anglicana : or the first principall part of*
> *the English Grammer Teaching the Art of right speaking*
> *and pronouncing English, With certaine exact rules*
> *of Orthography, and rules of spelling or combining of*
> *Syllables, and directions for keeping of stops or points*
> *between sentence and sentence. A work in it selfe abso-*
> *lute, and never knowne to be accomplished by any before ;*
> *No lesse profitable then necessary for all sorts, as well*
> *Natives as Foreigners, that desire to attaine the perfection*

of our English Tongue. Methodically composed by the industry and observation of Simon Daines, Schoolemaster of Hintlesham in Suffs. Perficit omnia tempus. London. Printed by Robert Young and Richard Badger for the Company of Stationers. 1640. 4to. (96 pp.)

Daines endeavours to bring English spelling to such method as may be possible. After which the curious paragraph :

Onely here for the further practice of little ones, that their parents may need to buy them no other book for the reading English,[1] we have here annexed some hard words confusedly compound, though in an alphabetical order, and after them the first chapter of S. Matthew, *to inure them a little to those Hebrew Names.*

Then follow rules as to " points " (punctuation) and directions for the writing of epistles. [2]

1640.

The English Grammar Made by Ben Jonson. For the benefit of all strangers, out of his observation of the English Language now spoken and in use. Consuetudo, certissima loquendi Magistra, utendumque, plane sermone, ut nummo, cui publica forma est. Quinct. Printed MDCXL. (Sm. Fol. pp. 84.)

The first four chapters are of grammar and the parts, of letters and their powers, of the vowels and of the consonants. These are given with the

---

[1] This is by no means an isolated reference to the unwillingness of parents to expend money on school books. Edmund Coote says (1596) : " Thou canst not move all their parents to be willing to bestow so much money in a book at first. Tell them from me, they need buy no more " [than the *English Scholemaister*].

[2] For letter-writing as a school exercise *see English Grammar Schools*, chap. xxv.

English Grammar on one side of the opened book and a Latin commentary—*Grammatica Anglicana*—on the other.

The following is the Preface to this well-known book :

> The profit of grammar is great to strangers, who are to live in communion and commerce with us ; and it is honourable to ourselves. For by it we communicate all our labours, studies, profits, without an interpreter. We free our language from the opinion of rudeness and barbarism, wherewith it is mistaken to be diseased. We show the copy of it and matchableness with other tongues ; we ripen the wits of our own children, and youth sooner by it, and advance their knowledge.
>
> Confusion of language, a curse.
>
> Experience breedeth Art : Lack of experience, Chance. Experience, Observation, Sense, Induction, are the four triers of Arts. It is ridiculous to teach any thing for undoubted truth, that sense and experience can confute. Zeno disputing of *quies*, was confuted by Diogenes, rising up and walking.
>
> In Grammar, not so much the Invention as the Disposition is to be commended. Yet we must remember that the most excellent creatures are not ever born perfect ; to leave bears and whelps, and other failings of nature.

The interest of Jonson's Grammar arises not so much from its worth in execution as in the new direction of grammar-teaching. Passing over the fact that he considered *English* Grammar worthy of study, a fitting deduction from the praise of the English language by Cheke, Ascham, Mulcaster, Daniel, Gascoigne and others, Jonson points out a method which it is not too much to say, is practised by the most modern of grammar-writers. The particular merit of Jonson, then, is the quoting of the older writers to illustrate the development and usage of English. Accordingly, in the syntax, there are frequent quotations from Chaucer, Gower, Lydgate, John Foxe, Sir Thomas More, Ascham, Cheke, Jewel. There are also now and again historical notes on the development of English grammatical usage.

The syntax contains about a hundred and thirty illustrative quotations, and of these about thirty are from Gower. Chaucer is cited twenty-five times, Lydgate and Sir Thomas More each about fourteen, the other chief authorities being Norton, Jewel, Fox, Sir John Cheke and the English Bible.[1]

There is one book which requires special notice in that it was explicitly intended for school use, viz :

1655.   J. Wharton.

> *A New English Grammar ; Containing All Rules and Directions necessary to be known for the judicious Reading, Right speaking and Writing of Letters, Syllables and Words in the English Tongue. Very usefull for Scholars before their entrance into the Rudiments of the Latine Tongue. With Directions for the use of this Book in Schools. Likewise for Strangers that desire to learn our Language, it will be the most certain Guide, that ever yet was extant. Composed by J. Wharton, Mr of Arts. London : Printed by W. Dugard, for Anthony Williamson, at the Queens Arms in S. Pauls Churchyard.* 1655.   8vo.   (pp. 109.)

Wharton's book deals with the following subjects : Letters and their force ; syllables and how to divide them ; of e final and its uses ; unsounded letters ;

---

[1] *See* G. C. Macaulay : *The Works of John Gower*, vol. ii, p. viii.

words sounded otherwise than written ; of rules for reading and writing some words : of the parts of speech ; of derivation of words ; of the composition of words ; of points in reading and writing. Wharton gives an important list of certain words like in sound but unlike in signification and manner of writing. These being brought together into one short sentence, the differences between them are more easily and certainly discussed and consequently their true manner of writing determined. There are twenty pages of these. Some of the expressions are curious, e.g. *blache* and *bleach.*

A Collie and a Fuller cannot dwell together, for the one doth *blache* or make black, the other doth *bleach* or whiten."

Wharton intends his book to be profitable for youth immediately before learning the rudiments of the Latin tongue both because of the importance of knowing their own tongue and also as preparative to learning Latin.

To strangers that desire to learn our language it will be a special help ; which they shall find not to be barbarous, confused, and irregular (as the common saying is), but familiar, orderly and easy, *equal to the Greek, and beyond the Latin for Composition, yea, happy above them both* in this ; not that it cannot be reduced to any ; but that indeed it *needeth little or no Grammar at all.*

Wharton makes the noteworthy declaration that *little* grammar [1] is a recommendation.

---

[1] In 1576, George Gascoigne had pleaded in the *Steele Glas :*

> " Grudge not at our English tong
> Bycause it stands by Monosyllables
> And cannot be declined as others are."

For whereas in the Latin tongue there are three score variations of the terminations of nouns, and six hundred of verbs, and in the Greek that number almost doubled ; in the English there is little variation at all ; and therefore needeth not any declensions of nouns, any conjugations of verbs, any rules of concord, or construction wherein the difficulties of any language doth consist, and which in the Latin and Greek cost much labour and toil. Now if any here object, what need of Grammar for that language which all speak of custom especially for ours which is so easy : to this I answer even the same that made the noblest of the Romans, when their tongue was come to the highest pitch, to write something of the Grammar thereof, that by Rules and Precepts it may be made yet more elegant, certain and permanent. And for this cause Charles the Great caused to be set forth a Grammar for the Teutonic tongue from which our English at first proceeded.

In like manner many worthie men, even of our nation, have in their several ages composed books of this nature, from all which I acknowledge more or less I have received light and direction. What herein is performed more than formerly I leave to the judgment of others, not doubting but that on further consideration and practice therein it may be reduced to a more perfect order than yet is done.

Mr. Mulcaster.
Mr. Coot.
Dr. Gill.
B. Jonson.
Mr. Butler.

I have not been able to see the following :

The English Schoolmaster compleated ; containing several Tables of common English words, from one to eight syllables ; both whole and divided, according to the Rules of true spelling ; with Prayers and Graces both before and after Meat ; Rules for Children's Behaviour with several other Necessaries suitable to the capacities of children and youth : also easie Rules for true and exact spelling, reading, and writing English, according to the present Pronunciation thereof ; with an Appendix containing the Principles of Arithmetick ; with an Account of Coins, Weights, Measures, Time, etc., Copies of Letters, Titles of Honour suitable for Men of all degrees and Qualities, Bills of Parcels, Bills of Exchange, Bills of Debt, Receipts and several other Rules and Observations fit for a youth's Accomplishment. By John Hawkins, Schoolmaster in Southwark. 8vo. (Advert. in Hoole's *Children's Talk,* 1697.)

1655. Joshua Poole.

The English Accidence. Or a short and easy way for the more speedy attaining to the Latin Tongue : so framed that young children may be exercised therein as soon as they can but indifferently read English, and thereby enabled to turn any Sentence into pure and elegant Latine. By Joshua Poole. Published by Authority ; and commended as generally necessary to be made use of in all Schooles of this Commonwealth. London. Printed by F Leach, for Richard Lowndes and are to be sol at the White-Lyon in St. Paul's Churchyard. 1655. 4to.

Poole gives the following account of his aim : " My drift and scope therefore is to have a child, so well versed in his Mother's tongue, before he meddle with Latin, that when he comes to the construing of a Latin author, he shall from the signification of his words in construing, be in some good measure able to tell distinctly what part of speech every word is, though he be not able to parse, vary, or give any other account of one word in his lesson, and when he is put to translation, or making of Latin, he shall know from his English both what part of speech every word is, and what Syntaxis, or ordering it should have in Latin, though in the mean time he never heard of one Latin word : And this I conceive may be in an indifferent manner affected by the Rules of this book, and the Praxis of them, according to these following directions."

In 1670, this same book appeared under the title *The Youth's Guide*. It is still described as " Published by Authority and commended as generally necessary to be made use of in all schools of this Kingdom."

Poole also wrote :

> *The English Parnassus : or, a Helpe to English Poesie. Containing a short Institution of that Art : A Collection of all Rhyming Monosyllables, The choicest Epithets and Phrases : With some General Forms upon all Occasions, Subjects, and Theams, Alphabetically digested. By Jos(h)ua Poole, M.A., Clare Hall, Camb.* 1657. 8vo.

(The Brit. Mus. copy has MS. notes by Dr. Isaac Watts.)

The proem is addressed "To the hopeful young Gentleman, his scholars in that private school at Hadley, near Barnet, kept in the house of Mr. Francis Atkinson, who, out of a design truly generous and public, endeavouring to prevent the inconveniences of irregulated youth, set up a School or Academy, for the education of a select number of Gentlemen's sons of good quality."

Poole dedicates his book to Mr. Atkinson. He says : " But for this book of mine, you are not ignorant of the difficulty of the attempt, what a strange multitude of Authors I have been forced, as it were, to anatomise, and that I may say without any great loss of modesty, that there never came yet abroad so methodical an Institution of English Poesie. For you who look on education through other prospective glasses than those of *necessity* or *advantage* know, that it requires a person of *generous* inclinations, that as an expressed Architect, lays the solid foundations of human life, and undertakes a business that hath the greatest influence on Policy, Morality and Religion."

Poole's *English Parnassus* is the outcome of the application of rhetorical methods to the English language. I have drawn attention to the place of rhetoric in the development of the study of English,[1] and Poole's work is a case in point. The *English Parnassus* was intended to be supplementary to a Rhetoric—supplying the material for practice in composition whilst the Rhetoric supplied the theoretical use of the phrases, etc., thus given.

This long work in 597 pages 8vo is divided into three parts. The first treats of all rhymes imaginable in English (i.e. it is a Dictionary of Rhymes), as the base and foundation of Poesy, according to their terminations. The second furnishes the diligent lover of the Muses with excellent choice and variety of apposite Epithets, somewhat in imitation of Textor's *Epitheta* for the Latin language. The third is an ample treasury of phrases and elegant expressions gathered out of the best esteemed English authors " that have writ in the several kinds of Poesy, not unlike that of *Thesaurus Poeticus*,[2] in Latin. . . . The design is absolutely new, there having not anything of this kind appeared upon the English stage before."

---

[1] *See* chapter xxvii on Teaching of Rhetoric in *English Grammar Schools*.

[2] Such as that of John Buchler (1633).

The English Language arriving daily to greater perfection and purity, Poesy must needs accordingly extend to all subjects and occasions incident to human life, and since it admits of the same division into species, as the Greek and Latin, we must, being obliged to them for their Terms, submit to their Method.

The different kinds of poetry are stated by Poole to be :

1. The Heroic or Epic.

2. The Lyric : Madrigals, Sonnets, Hymns, Ballets, Odes, (amorous, rural, military, jovial), Epithalamiums (nuptials), Epinicions (victories), Genethliacks (nativities), Congratulatories, etc. The greatest writers of this kind, Horace, Catullus.

3. Elegies, Threnodies and such like long-breathed poems in luctiferous subjects. Ovid in *de Tristibus* is the grand exemplar.

4. Dramatic poesy.
   " Tragedies, Comedies, Interludes, Masks, Entertainments, Dialogues, Satires, Frolics, Georgics, Pastorals, Piscotories, Nauticals, (these three called Eclogues), Memoralls, etc.

5. The Epigram.
   " Of vast extent, includes : Epitaphs, Characters, Emblems, Devices, Mottos, Hieroglyphics, Definitions, Rebuses, Problems. It is full of mirth and salt, sententious, directive as to Morality, Proverbial, Mythological, Enigmatical, in a word, hath all " human actions " and accidents to work upon, closing up all with a certain smartness of conceit. The numerous brood of it, are ingenious fallacies *in*, and *extra dictionem*, Encomiasticks, Vituperatories, Scoffs, Sarcasms, Jeers, Jests, Quibbles, Clinches, Quips, Bulls, Anagrams, Chronograms, Acrosticks, Criticisms, in a word, whatever is of succinct and concise Poetry, on what subject soever, handsomely couched and worded.

6. Poetical treatises concerning Learning, Science, or some particular sort of Philosophy, such as Lucretius, epistolary writings, such as those of Ovid (imitated by Mr. Drayton) and historical (imitated by the same Drayton and Daniel, and translated and supplied by Mr. Thomas May, both in Latin and English.)

Poole has studied Sir Philip Sidney's *Defence of Poesy*, Daniel's *Apology for Rhyme*, and Puttenham's *Art of English Poesy*. He offers the results of his studies to youth, as may be seen by the title of the second edition of his book. That the *English Parnassus* was regarded as a school-book is proved by the fact that Hoole prescribes the book for Form IV of a Grammar School.

The significance of this school-book in the history of the development of the vernacular and its literature is extremely marked. As the book is little known, it is desirable to give the list of English authors, from whom Poole so copiously quotes, to do for English what *Textor* in his *Epitheta* and Buchler in his *Thesaurus Poeticus* had done for the Latin language.

Poole gives :

The Books principally made use of in the compiling of this work.

Dubartas' *works*. Ben Jonson. Browne's *Pastorals*. Randolph's *Poems*. Drayton. May's *Lucan*. Quarles' divine Poems. Quarles' *divine Fancies*. Sandys' Ovid's *Metamorphoses*. Sandys' *Paraphrase on the Canticles*. Herbert's *Poems*. Tottham's *Poems*. Withers' *Poems*. Orlando *Furiose*. Heywood's *Dialogues and Dramas*. Chapman's *Homer*. Overbury's *Characters*. Balzac's *Epistles*. Cowley's *Blossoms*. Horace translated. Ovid's works translated. Johnsonus. Spenser's *Faery Queen*. Gomersal's *Levite's Revenge*. Sir Philip Sidney's *Arcadia*. Shakespeare. Heywood *of Angels*. Carew's *Poems*. Daniel

OUSTED ENGLISH AUTHORS

May's *Edward* III. Quarles' *Emblems.* Quarles' *Argalus et Parthenia.* Sandys' *of Christ's Passion.* Habington's *Castara.* Sir John Beaumont's Poem. *The Valiant Bruce.* Burton's *Melancholy.* Chapman's *Hero and Leander.* Blunt's *Characters.* Massinger's *Secretary.* Lovelace's *Pastorals.* Virgil translated. *Cooper's Hill. Elegies on Mr. King.* Chaucer. Aviso. Holiday's *Persius.* Comedies and Tragedies, many. Quarles' *Solomon's Recantation.* Quarles' *Eclogues.* Howel's *Instruction for foreign travel.* Howel's *Vocal Forest* and England's *Tears.* Fuller's *Holy State.* Donne's *Poems.* Malvezzi. Davenant's *Poems.* Waller's *Poems.* Milton's *Poems.* Sandys' *Paraphrase on Job, on Psalms. Ecclesiastes,* etc.

This list is almost as remarkable as it is long. Over 160 pages are studded with adjectival epithets gathered from these authors on all sorts of subjects. Then follow over 340 pages of an English Anthology again, on, all kinds of subjects. Poole very early states the author of the particular passages he quotes, so intent is he on its value, as an illustration of the subject described. But the student of those days, accustomed to use his " Textor " and his " Buchler " and other multitudinous phrase-books, would find with pleasant surprise how susceptible was the English language of Poole's time of similar treatment. The material for English composition in prose and in verse was laboriously collected, and Poole produced an English *Copia Verborum et Rerum,* which in its *copiousness,* almost eclipses Erasmus's Latin apparatus. He was conscious that to supply merely the material was not enough ; and he intended to put forth an *English Rhetoric* to show how this material should be used. This, unfortunately, he did not produce.

1665. Owen Price.

> *The Vocal Organ : or a new art of teaching Ortho-graphy, by observing the instruments of pronunciation, and the difference between words of like sound, whereby any outlandish or mere Englishman, woman, or child, may speedily attain to the exact spelling, reading, writing, or pronouncing of any word in the English Tongue, without the advantage of its fountains, the Greek and Latin.* Oxford, 1665.
>
> *English Orthography*, 1668 and 1670.

In 1657 Owen Price was Headmaster of Magdalen College School, Oxford, and in 1658 apparently the Independents thought to displace Busby at Westminster and substitute Price. Price suggests in a letter to Scobell[1]: "Let any scholars in Oxford be appointed to make trial of my boys here ; or I will wait upon the Governors to the School at Westminster and they shall hear me teach." He claims during the eight years he has been school-master he can produce "more godly men and preach-ers (some of whom have passed the approvers) than some (that make greater noise than I do) have with their twenty years' labour."

George Snell in his *Right Teaching of Useful Knowledge* (1649) regards it as the function of teaching, "to prepare children in a sweet and pleasant way, that they may be able in a gentle manner to converse with all sorts of persons." Snell therefore holds the teaching of English in high esteem. He directs how to teach the primer and English grammar, and proposes an authorised English

---

[1] *See* Bloxam : *Registers of Magdalen College, Oxford,* i, p. 181.

lexicon to do for English what Nicole[1] had recently done for the French language. Every word included in such a lexicon "ought to be of a fair and ear-pleasing sound." Etymologies should be furnished. Only words in use should be admitted. When a word is taken from another language, a characteristical letter should be inserted to note the Anglicism by which it is admitted into our " national corporation," e.g. for labor, write labour ; for peris, perish. Further Snell suggests there should be an edict to ratify and settle the English language, that all words henceforth to be used have only their metal from the lexicon, and their stamp from a similarly authorised grammar. Further he would have an English *Florilegium*. In it, Snell proposes should be placed all the best English forms and phrases of speech, and all the witty and pleasant expressions which are plentifully extant in the words of our great " predicants " and famous comedians, and " in those innumerable tractates that have been more purely and more ingeniously penned in late times than in any time heretofore in memory."

With regard to the teaching of English we have no knowledge that it was cultivated seriously in any public Grammar School[2] by 1660, in spite of Hoole's recommendation that Poole's *English Parnassus*

---

[1] Nicole (1625–1695) was to become one of the leading names of the Port-Royalist group, who especially insisted on the place of the mother-tongue in the French schools.

[2] Charles Hoole, mentioned above, was master of a *private* Grammar School.

should find a place there. Yet if one school can be singled out as likely to have had more attention paid to English, that school would probably be St. Paul's School, for there, Richard Mulcaster was Head Master from 1596 to 1608, and he was followed by the two Gills, father and son, 1608–40; and John Langley 1640–57 who seems to have had wide interests in history, archaeology and rhetoric. Still, the fact stands out that it was the private schools such as those of Wharton and Poole and Hoole, in which the innovation of the serious study of the vernacular was earliest developed.

Poole and Wharton, in different ways, deserve to be placed by the side of Mulcaster as pioneers in the teaching of English.

In his address to the courteous reader, Wharton (in 1655) argues—

Our mother-tongue . . . is as capable of any scholar-like expressions, as any whatsoever. Besides the purity and elegancy of our own language is to be esteemed a chief part of the honour of our Nation, which we all ought to our utmost power to advance. Lastly, because for *one* that is trained up in the Grammar Schools to any perfection, fit for the University, or any learned Profession, a hundred are taken away before ; of whom the most, very shortly after, wholly in a manner, forget their Latin ; so that if they be not bettered in the knowledge of their Native Language, their labour and cost is to little or no purpose.

Here is an appeal for a sound knowledge of English "which we all ought to our utmost power to advance," and the recognition of the importance of the ninety-nine who do not reach " any perfection " in Latin at the Grammar School. Such boys soon forgot their Latin, and certainly Wharton commands the sympathy of our generation when he urges, that at least these youths might have had a good grounding in their native language. If we wish to realise the progress made in the proposals for the teaching of English we cannot do better than compare the view of Wharton in 1655 with that of the Founder of Bruton School in 1519. In the Foundation Deed of that school it is prescribed :

> And the sd maister shall *not teche his scolers song nor other petite lernynge as the Cross Rewe, Redyng of the mateyns, or of the psalter or such other small things, neither redyng of Englissh butt such as shall concern lernynge of gramer :* ffor the ffounders of the said scole intend wt. our lordes mercy oonly to have the grammer of latyn tongue so suffi- ciently taught that the scolers of the same profityng and provyng shall in tymes to come for ever be after their capacities perfight Latyn-men.

The development of a knowledge of English in the English schools was, however, greater than would appear from any search for its direct encouragement. Indirectly, the study of Rhetoric brought about a keen and ready appreciation of expression in speech of appropriate and striking imagery. It was indeed Latin and Greek rhetoric that was aimed at, but by attraction and analogy, equally appropriate and striking forms of expression were sought in the English renderings of Latin and Greek idioms. Since Latin and Greek oratory was the highest development of Grammar School work, there was always a *tendency amongst the best schoolmasters and the best pupils* to make the English language used in dealing with composition exercises parallel in pitch and effort with the classics. Otherwise, it would be difficult to understand how the boys from the Elizabethan and Stuart Grammar Schools became such eloquent English writers, preachers, politicians, and publicists.[1]

There is one statement of method of using " histories " in connexion with an Academy for noblemen's sons which has special interest in its emphasis on the use of English in oratorical exercises. The following is Sir Humphrey Gilbert's requirement of duties (in the projected Queen Elizabeth's Academy for the education of Her Majesty's Wards) from the teacher of logic and rhetoric. He is " to see his scholars dispute and exercise."

The exercises and orations to be in English.

When the Orator shall practise his scholars in the exercise thereof, he shall chiefly do it in Orations made in English, both politic and military, taking occasions out of Discourses of histories, approving or reproving the matter, not only by reason, but also with the examples and stratagems both antique and modern. For of what commodity such use of art will be in our tongue may partly be seen by the scholastical rawness of some newly commen from the universities : besides, in what language soever learning is attained, the appliance to use is principally in the vulgar speech, as in preaching, in parliament, in council, in commission and other offices of Common Weal. I omit to show what ornament will thereby grow to our tongue, and how able it will appear for strength and plenty, when, by such exercises, learning shall have brought unto it the choice of words, the building of sentences, the garnishment of figures, and other beauties of Oratory,—whereupon I have heard that the famous knight Sir John Cheke devised to have declamations, and such other exercises, sometimes in the universities performed in English.

---

[1] On the subject of the influence of the teaching of Rhetoric on English *see English Grammar Schools*, p. 451–3.

CHAPTER II

THE TEACHING OF HISTORY AND AN *EXCURSUS* ON THE FIRST TEXT-BOOK IN CIVICS IN ENGLAND

IN the Pre-Reformation Schools, the subject of history received little attention, unless indeed we accept the reading of Legends of the Saints as representative of a historical course. The effect of the Renascence was not directly productive of an educational interest in history, except to stimulate a desire to understand the circumstances of the events and incidents alluded to in the reading of the classics. In this sense, Erasmus's *Adages* and *Apophthegms* may be said to have promoted effectively the anecdotal and incidental side of historical interest. The provision made at every stage of instruction in post-Reformation times, for what may be termed the allusive references to history was ample, and the results of investigations of scholars in all departments of classical, historical research filtered into the dictionaries, phrase-books, excerpts, and commonplace books, so that scholars, both older and younger, lived in an atmosphere of quotations and allusions. In modern pedagogical terminology, they "turned to use" all the history they found. Fragmentary historical knowledge thus helped the variety and " copiousness " of illustration, which every scholar wished to have freely at command, for the purpose of his " themes " and " orations."

There were, however, the serious limitations from the point of view of historical study, that such interest was largely confined to ancient times, and again, there was no continuity in the study of history. It was not studied as an end in itself, but as a means to elegance of expression and fullness of illustration and example. The ancient historians were not studied for their subject-matter, but for their style.

To speak of English history, the old Latin chroniclers, Gildas, Bede, the Anglo-Saxon Chronicle, William of Malmesbury, Giraldus Cambrensis, Hoveden, Matthew Paris, Higden, are of course much more accessible now than they were, say, in the Elizabethan Age. When historians began to write in English the audience of readers was chiefly found amongst the members of noble families. Accordingly, Robert Fabyan's *Chronicle or Concordance of Histories* first published by Pynson in 1516 marks an era in historical study. Lord Berners' translation of the Chronicles of Froissart was also printed by Pynson, in 1523–5. In the preface to his translation of Froissart, Lord Berners states his conception of the value of historical study. The whole preface is eloquently written, though too long to quote in full. But the gist is the following passage : " The most profitable thing in this world for the institution of the human life is history. Once

46

the continual reading thereof maketh young men equal in prudence to old men ; and to old fathers stricken in age it ministereth experience of things. More, it yieldeth private persons worthy of dignity, rule and governance : it compelleth the emperors, high rulers and governours to do noble deeds, to the end that they may obtain immortal glory : it exciteth, moveth and stirreth the strong, hardy warriors for the great laud that they have, after they be dead, promptly to go in hand with great and hard perils in defence of their country, and it prohibiteth reprovable persons to do mischievous deeds, for fear of infamy and shame. So thus, through the monuments of writing, which is the testimony unto virtue many men have been moved, some to build cities, some to devise and establish laws right profitable, necessary and behoveful for the human life, some other to find new arts, crafts and sciences, very requisite to the use of mankind. . . . It is the keeper of such things as have been virtuously done, and the witness of evil deeds, and by the benefit of history, all noble, high and virtuous acts be immortal." Clearly this splendid plea for the reading of history is addressed to the nobles and gentlemen of England. History, in Lord Berners' view, is the subject which will draw them on, " stirred up," in Milton's words, " with high hopes of living to be brave men, and worthy patriots, dear to God and famous to all ages."

In 1534, nearly half a century before Mulcaster wrote, Polydore Vergil, an Italian had published,

at Basle, his *Historia Anglica*.[1] But Polydore
Vergil was an Italian, and though his attitude of
" disinterested spectator " of the field of English
history from Henry VI to Henry VIII constitutes
a claim to high consideration on the modern historian, this very reason handicapped him in the
age immediately succeeding the publication of
his work. Hall's Chronicle (founded on Polydore
Vergil), which applauds Henry VIII, was more in
accordance with the spirit of the times and Hollinshead's Chronicles, first published in 1557, mark an
era in historical work, both on account of diligence
in compilation, and also as the source of historical
information for English people who were not
Latinists. But all these writers, though significant
of the coming importance of history as a field for
scholarship, were of no direct influence on school-
work. Indirectly, as offering the material for
dramatists of historical plays, no doubt they
brought subjects for contemplation before the minds
of the rising generation, not only in the case of
those boys who belonged to the companies of actors,
but in their class-mates, who were spectators of
their friends' performances, and in the general
spirit of the times, which found its reflection
in boys' minds, from the conversation of their

---

[1] Of which Sir Henry Ellis says : " It was the first of
our histories in which the writer ventured to compare
the facts and weigh the statements of his predecessors ;
and it was the first in which summaries of personal character
are introduced in the terse and energetic form adopted in
the Roman classics."

elders who were playgoers, entering into the vivid realisation from stage-performances of the history of their kings, and the noble ancestors of their Virgin-Queen.

John Stow helped to popularise the reading of English history by his *Summary of English Chronicles* in 1561.   His *Survey of London* (1598) showed enthusiasm in thoroughness of description, and power to inspire historical, local interest.

The following translation is indicative of the growing interest in historical study at a stage beyond the school :

Thomas Blundeville.

> *The true order and Methode of wrytung and reading Hystories, according to the Precepts of Francisco Patritio and Accontio Tridentino, no less plainly than briefly set forth in our vulgar speach, to the great profite and commoditye of all those that delight in Hystories.*   London. 1570.   8o.

The latter part of Queen Elizabeth's reign saw a remarkable development of historical study.

Of the first importance in the development of historical study of English sources was the publication in 1586 of the learned William Camden's *Remains concerning Britain and a survey of the British Isles, containing their Languages, Names, Surnames, Allusions, Anagramms, Armories, Moneys, Impresses, Apparel, Artillerie, Wise Speeches, Proverbs, Poesies, Epitaphs, written by William Camden, Esquire, Clarenceux, King of Arms.*

This was an inquiry into all questions connected with the Roman occupation of Britain. It was written in Latin, and originally was a small octavo volume of 556 pages. The later editions, in English, reach to four volumes folio. In 1603, Camden published at Frankfort his *Anglica*, *Normannica*, *Hibernica*, *Cambrica*, which brings together the chief chronicles of the history of England, Normandy, Ireland and Wales. His *Britannia* was translated by Philemon Holland in 1610, and is described as a " chorographical description of the most flourishing kingdoms, England, Scotland, and Ireland." Camden was Headmaster of Westminster School (1593–9) and the writer of the famous standard Greek Grammar. Camden travelled throughout Britain to collect materials as far as possible, on the spot, for each place he described. He thus followed the example of John Leland (*c.* 1500–1552), who was appointed by King Henry VIII King's Antiquary and Commissioner, to examine into the libraries of colleges and religious houses for the collection of historical material.

Besides Camden, there were in the early years of King James I's reign, men like Speed, Stow, Cotton, the two Spelmans, Usher, Dugdale, Raleigh, and Selden. These formed a strong historical circle,[1]

---

[1] An attempt was made to establish a College or Society of Antiquaries in 1589. This failed. Again, in James I's reign a further attempt was made. This again failed. James I took a " mislike " to such an institution, and would not grant a charter of incorporation fearing a religious or political significance in such a society.

but their combined influence was not sufficient to give history such a *status* as to find a foothold in the schools. The most that could be done was to establish the subject academically in the Universities of Oxford and Cambridge. William Camden himself, in 1622, endowed a Readership in the University of Oxford.

There was also a lectureship in History established at Cambridge in 1628, by Lord Brooke. The qualifications required of the lecturer were that he must be an M.A. of five years' standing, an unmarried layman, and to have shown in published works ability in Greek and Latin, cosmography and chronology. The lectureship was open to foreigners, and preference was to be given to candidates who had travelled beyond seas and who knew foreign languages.[1] The qualifications thus laid down show remarkable insight. Mr. Mullinger points out the inferiority of English historical literature at the time to that of France.[2] The first Cambridge History Lecturer was a foreigner, Is. Dorislaw, of Leyden.

The first Camden Reader in History at Oxford was Degory Wheare, who wrote out his lectures as—

De ratione et methodo Legendi historias. Lond. 1623.

July 12, 1623, is the date of the Dissertation. The dedication appropriately is to William Camden. The London edition was enlarged and published at Oxford, 1625, and still further enlarged in 1637. It

---

[1] Mullinger, *University of Cambridge*, ii, 421.
[2] *Ibid.*, p. 423.

was translated into English in 1694, and enlarged by Edmund Bohun. The third edition of the translation contains Mr. Dodwell's Invitation to Gentlemen to acquaint themselves with Ancient History. Its title had become :

> *The Method and Order of Reading both Civil and Ecclesiastical Histories, in which the most Excellent Historians are reduced into the Order in which they are successively to be Read ; and the Judgments of Learned Men, concerning each of them subjoined.*

This deserves to be noted as a method of study of history. It is not perhaps a method of teaching, though indirectly suggestions could be deduced. The " Invitation," as expressed, is significant. History even in 1698 is seen to be still pre-eminently a gentleman's study. The book was used as a textbook at Cambridge up to the beginning of the eighteenth century.[1]

A similar book is that of—

> Prideaux (Matthias). *An Easy and Compendious Introduction for the Reading of all sorts of Histories.* Oxon. 1648, 1655, 1664.

An Article of Laud's Statutes (Oxford University, 1636) reads : " Of the lectures in history, Mondays and Fridays, between one and two in the afternoon the lecturer in history to lecture in Lucius Florus or any other historians of ancient date and repute." The auditors were to be : "All bachelors of arts

---

[1] *Dictionary of National Biography* (under Wheare).

who were bound to attend from Easter next, following the day of their first presentation till they were promoted to the master's degree; and, in like manner, the civil law students until they were presented as bachelors of law."

Speaking generally, history if studied at all by University students, was post-graduate. Emphatic reasons were, however, given for the reading of histories. The writers of the time speak of History as the *Speculum Mundi*. They point out that " examples are more taking than precepts binding." Law gives the precepts : history supplies the examples. They quote Seneca :

> " Longum iter per praecepta, breve et efficax per exempla."

They quote Cicero to the effect that we can by history be seated free from danger and yet acquaint ourselves with the perturbations of all the kingdoms of the world.

From the point of view of the age, we can perhaps judge of the place of history by Heylyn's summarising of the " benefits of history ": [1]

1. It is the rule of direction, by whose square we ought to rectify our obliquities, and in this sense the Orator calleth it *Magistra vitae*.

2. It stirreth men to virtue and deterreth them from vice.

3. It hath been not only the inventor but also the conserver of all arts, such especially whose end consisteth in action.

---

[1] In the *Cosmographie containing the Chorography and Historie of the whole world.* By Peter Heylyn. 1625, etc.

4. It informeth a man's mind in all particular observations, making him serviceable to his prince and country.

5. It is the best schoolmaster of war, the teacher of stratagems, and giveth more directions than a whole Senate.

6. It is the Politician's best assistant and chief tutor.

7. It is most available to the study of Divinity.

8. It is (lastly and least of all), the study which affordeth a man the greatest aid in discoursing; it delighteth the ear, and contenteth the mind.

There can be no doubt that the great Civil War amongst its many results quickened the study of history. Thus it was in 1648, that Heylyn (who had announced in 1627 that he would not further write on the subjects of his small book called the *Microcosmos*) set himself to the great work of compiling a vastly extended *Cosmography* published in 1652, which contained over 1,100 folio pages. The spirit in which he wrote may be judged by his statement in the address to the reader : " Without any by-design to abuse the reader, though the history and geography of the world be my principal business, yet I have apprehended every modest occasion of recording the heroic acts of my native soil, and filing on the registers of perpetual fame, the gallantry and brave achievements of the people of England exemplified in their many victories and signal services in Italy, France, Spain, Scotland, Belgium, in Palestine, Cyprus, Africa, and America,

and indeed, where not ? " Heylyn, however, realises that his great book cannot find a public amongst
the people at large. " For the people in the Body
collective have not abilities to read and much
less to judge. . . . I look on the Nobility, Clergy,
Gentry, as their representatives in this kind ;
to whose favourable and ingenuous acceptance I
submit the same. Which if I can attain unto, it is
all I aim at."

Heylyn's description of the divisions of History
throws light on the seventeenth century views
regarding it.[1] History is seen to include natural
history, astronomy, geography, politics, law, apophthegms, as well as branches still recognised. William
London's Catalogue of Books (1658) includes under
the heading " History " such subjects as Rhetoric,
Books of Manners, English Dictionaries, Foreign
travel, and, of course, what we call Natural History.

Heylyn realises that the sources of " history "
are : (1) Commentaries ; (2) Annals ; (3) Diaries or
Journals ; (4) Chronologies. History is, as it were,
" a quintessence extracted out of these four
elements."

---

[1] Heylyn's scheme recalls Lord Bacon's divisions of
History in the *de Augmentis Scientiarum* (1623), Book ii.
Bacon associates history with poesy and philosophy—
as parts of human learning. Heylyn's scheme shows
the position of history in the minds of his contemporaries and represents probably somewhat closely historical
teaching (when it was given). Bacon's treatment of
history, of course, is more searching and philosophical in
its theory. Bacon states the " defects " of " literary "
history, in the *Advancement of Learning*, Book ii (1605).

The different kinds of history are as follows :

Histories are *either* of the {Great World,
Lesser World, *or* of man,
that Μικρₒκοσμος

The former is {

Universal. Of the world and all things in it. This is Cosmography, and is best handled by Pliny in his Natural History.

Particular. Of Heaven and its affections. This is Astronomy, and is beholding to Aratus and Ptolemy.

Of the Earth and her parts : this is Geography, and is set forth by Strabo, Mela, etc.

The latter tell {

The inward works of man, as his opinions touching religion or philosophy, whose history is compiled by Diogenes Laertius.

The outward works, which are {

Actions. {

Manners, Customs and Laws, these belong to Policy and Statesmen.

Of the Tongue {

Of some length, and such are Orations and Speeches.

Succinct.

Of one man and are called Apophthegms.

Of many, and are called Proverbs—digested best by Erasmus.

Of the Hand, which branch themselves into two parts, being :

Either of one man alone. Such histories are called Lives and are best done by Plutarch.

Or, of many whose History is {

Universal, belonging to the whole in general with relation to the particular, or such of them as are of note.

Particular {

Ecclesiastical, which describeth the acts of the Church, her beginning, increase, decrease, restoring and continuance.

Civil, which relate the occurrences of commonwealths, their beginnings, etc.

Heylyn then gives a list of the best writers of the three last-named kinds of history.

The best writers of :

General History. These are Moses, Berosus, Trogus Pompeius, Diodorus Siculus, Eusebius, Bede, Zouaras, Abbas Uspergensis, Philip Bergomensis, Carion, Paulus Jovius, Thuanus, Sleidan, Sebastian Munster. Lastly, Sir Walter Raleigh's *History of the World.*

On this last-named work Heylyn says : " When it meeteth with a judicious and understanding reader, it will speak for itself. For my part I only say what Martial spake of Sallust, it is *primus in historia.*"

The best writers of—

Ecclesiastical History ;

I. The Jews : The Word of God in the Old Testament. Philo Judaeus, Flavius Josephus, Egesippus.

II. The Christians. The New Testament. Eusebius, Socrates, Sozomen, Theodoret, and Evagrius for the first 600 years after Christ. Mr. Fox in his *Acts and Monuments* till the year 1558 ; Sleidan in his *Ecclesiastical Commentaries,* from the year 1517, in which Luther began to batter down the walls of Popery till 1560 ; *Historia Magdeburgensis .* Platina *de vitis Ponteficum ;* Philip Mornay ; Du Plessis, *History of the Papacy.*

III. The Heathens : St. Austin, Civitas Dei ; Clemens Alexandrinus ; Arnobius *adversus gentes ;* Laetantius Firmianus *de falsa religione ;* Orosius *against the Pagans ;* Giraldus *de Diis omnium gentium ;* John Gaulis *de religione veterum.*

Heylyn then gives the best writers on Civil History. He extends his survey to the Assyrians, Chaldeans, Medes, Persians, and Parthians, to the

8—(2407)

historians of Greece, Rome and Italy, Germany, France, Spain, Turks and Saracens, Muscovites and Tartars, and Asia, Africa and America. [1] Lastly of the British Isles. The historians named are : Gildas, Polydore Vergil ; [2] Geoffrey of Monmouth : [3] voluminous Hollingshead and Stowe ; [4] Speed ; [5] Martin ; " pieces of history " by Lord Bacon, Sir Thomas More, Sir John Hayward, Matthew Paris ; Daniel. For Scotland, Heaton Boetius and Buchanan. For Wales, Humfrey Lloyd and David Powell. For Ireland, Giraldus Cambrensis. For them all, Andrew du Chesne, of Touraine, in France, " who wrote one body of story for all parts of the British Isles up to 1612, such as never any native durst undertake or had hope to achieve. But for all and above them all, judicious Mr. Camden in his *Britannia* hath given great light to histories already extant, and to such as future ages shall produce."

There is one text-book much shorter than Heylyn's [6] written for the purpose of instruction

---

[1] The list for Africa and America joined together is : " Leo Afer ; Francisco Alvarez ; Aloyssius Cadamistus ; Acasta ; the navigations of Columbus, Vespatius, Patritius and others as Oviedus, Cortez, Gusman, Nonius, Gomara, Benzo, Lyrius, etc."

[2] " Sufficiently good if not overladen with malicious or accidentary untruths."

[3] " A writer merely fabulous."

[4] " Full of confusion and commixture of unworthy relations."

[5] " Delighteth the ear, and not a little informing the mind."

[6] For an account of Heylyn's *Cosmographie*, as a geographical book, *see* p. 125 *et seqq.*

in history for the young noble and gentleman
entitled :

> *A Survey of History, or a Nursery for the Gentry
> contrived and comprized in an Intermixt discourse
> upon Historicall and Politicall relations ; a work
> inviting the approbation of the judicious.* Lond.
> 1638.

The writer, Richard Brathwait, following French
writers, asks : " Would you be enabled for company ?
No better medium than knowledge in history."
He has still deeper reasons to offer for its study.
" History is that which hath reduced tradition
into profitable knowledge. It tempers the mind
and forms it to a perfect shape and symmetry. We
may by history reconcile the future and present
tense, see Asie in England, travel the Holy Land,
and go to the Holy War with Mr. Fuller, see the
Grand Seignory in the *Seraglio*, compass the world
with (Sir Francis) Drake. Would you see the
wars and actions of the Roman Empires ? You
may see them tread the stage again with less cost
or hazard than at first. You may, by the study
of history, live in all ages, see Adam in Eden, sail
with Noah in the Ark, sit and consult with Julius
Cæsar, converse with Seneca, confer with all the
wise philosophers, go to school at Athens, and with
a free access hear all disputes and much more
from this study of history."

Edward Leigh, in his *Religion and Learning*
(1663), says to the same purpose : " I think it best
with Plato, when weary with other studies, to sport
myself with reading of good histories." A passage

from a letter of Oliver Cromwell deals with the educational value of reading history. Cromwell, in giving advice to his son, said : " Recreate yourself with Sir Walter Raleigh's History ; it's a body of History and will add more to your understanding than fragments of story."

Raleigh's *History of the World* was published in 1614. It was not a history in the scientific sense of the term. It may perhaps be described as a medley of miscellaneous material with legal, theological, mythological, military and political digressions, though pursuing its way through the course of the ages. Thus it begins with the Mosaic account of Creation, and contains fifteen sections on the position, together with a map, of Paradise. It describes the trees in the Garden of Eden, and raises the question whether the Tree of Knowledge was a kind of fig. After dealing with Jewish history, Raleigh writes of Greece and Rome. The book contains an immense amount of reflective digression and miscellaneous information. Cromwell's advice was probably sound, for Raleigh was interesting, and took great delight in tracing the rise and fall of empires. The largeness of scale and extent of time over which his history ran were contrasts to the ordinary historians of his day. Raleigh's style, too, —as for instance (at the end of the work) the address to Death—could rise to a high pitch.

In 1652, Alexander Ross, Head Master of the Southampton Grammar School, attempted a continuation to Raleigh's *History of the World*. In the Preface to the *Continuation* he quotes Quintilian to show that history is necessary for school-masters, *so that pupils may have matter for their orations and exercises.* In 1650 Alexander Ross had engaged on the congenial task of abridging Raleigh, and issued his book under the title of *The Marrow of History.* There is, however, no evidence that either of those two books of Alexander Ross were used in the school, though the employment of passages from historical writers for Latin composition was a common practice.

Another schoolmaster historian was Richard Knolles, who published a general history of the Ottoman Turks, in 1603, was for ten years Head Master of Sir Roger Manwood's Grammar School at Sandwich. Knolles was at work on the history during the period of his Headmastership.

Mr. John Langley, Head Master of St. Paul's School in the Commonwealth, who died in 1657, "was a learned man . . . a historian, cosmographer . . . and a great Antiquary in the most memorable things of this nation. Into whatsoever parts of the land he travelled, he was able to refresh, and to instruct his fellow travellers. . . ." [1] We may conjecture that such a schoolmaster would be willing to impart his historical knowledge in the schoolroom as well as to fellow travellers on a journey.

---

[1] Dr. Reynolds' Funeral Sermon for Dr. Langley. Other schoolmaster historians were John Twyne, Head Master of King's School, Canterbury, and John Hyrd, Head Master of Lincoln Grammar School (1580), writer in Latin verse of *Historia Anglicana.*

The young " gentleman " at the University, as we learn from Earle,[1] " shows his gentlemanliness as a contrast to scholarliness by reading on ' foul days ' some short History or a piece of Euphormio (i.e. the *Argenis* of John Barclay). His main loitering is at the Library where he studies Arms and Books of Honour, and turns a gentleman-critic in Pedigrees. Of all things he endures not to be mistaken for a scholar."

The author of *Heroick Education* in 1657 advised the learning of history by the young noble and gentlemen, whilst the memory is fresh and " easy to take impressions." By history he looks to " open the understanding to reason." The tutor is to discourse on all events, not only simply reading them over like Romances. The pupil must have his " common sense " exercised in observing the causes and reasons of things. He that teaches history should draw out the most material passages from historians and make a pithy epitome or " Body of History very succinct." This will open the way to an universal knowledge of history, and be a great help to memory. But especially he should receive a deep impression of modern histories " which concern us more nearly."

It should be added that the author (who simply describes himself as " J. B.") considers that the public schools have grave disadvantages for the youth. The boy " wallows eight or ten years in that dust, only to learn the Latin tongue, and a

---

[1] *Microcosmography*, 1628.

*few shreds of history, worth nothing, because they are
but pieces disjointed, which have no dependence."*

The general trend of views with regard to history
as an educational subject may be said to be that it
was important for the noble or gentleman, but not
for the mass of the people. The Grammar School,
it may be repeated, was not intended originally
for the rich but for the poor, and the rich man's
studies differed from the Grammar School curriculum. They belonged to the courtly type. In the
books on noblemen's education there was always a
recognition of the principle of *noblesse oblige*, and
it was held not only desirable, but also necessary,
that the noble should both know and take a pride
in the great deeds of his ancestors, and this implied
a knowledge, at any rate, to some extent, of the
history of the country. The education of the noble
and gentleman was essentially private education
by tutors and teachers, chosen usually for their
specialistic knowledge. The attempt made to found
the *Musaeum Minervae* by Sir Francis Kynaston[1]
in 1635 shows that even the Universities did not
provide the subjects which were thought necessary
for a gentleman's education. Boys from an early
age were to be taught throughout their course of
studies, which were planned for seven years. "The
Regent is to remember," say the Constitutions of
the *Musaeum Minervae*, "as he shall see opportunity
from time to time, both publicly and privately,

---

[1] He points out that the masters of public schools are
ordinarily young, and " serve their apprenticeship at their
scholars' cost, as new physicians do in hospitals."

to excite the Noblemen and Gentry to virtuous and heroic minds by the example of the most renowned, (but especially to set before their eyes the images of the) Worthies of our own nation, and of their own Ancestors in their several families ; so that having taken impression in the *Musaeum* from the best ideas, the whole kingdom of inferior people, in those several counties where they shall be distributed to live, and shine, may find example, help, reason and happiness in and being under them." [1]

Biography was always a particularly attractive subject in a course for gentlemen. Vives, who was very scrupulous as to the reading for girls, permitted them this reading. A considerable literature had grown up of individual biographies, and also of collections of biographies. The Great Civil War, for instance, produced the collections of great popularity of David Lloyd and John Walker. But the greatest work of the kind was Thomas Fuller's general collection of the lives of the *Worthies of England* in 1662.

In the *Musaeum Minervae* the specified subjects which could be counted as historical are : Heraldry, Blazon of Coats and Arms, Practical Knowledge of Deeds and Evidences, Principles and Processes of Common Law, Knowledge of Antiquities, Coins, Medals, Husbandry. And these courses the Regent (i.e. the Principal) " shall see performed."

---

[1] So, too, the proposed *Academy* of Sir Balthazar Gerbier included history as a subject (1649).

The study of history was then advocated in the period up to 1660 for the nobles and gentlemen, both on educational grounds and also as a class distinction. Further, it was considered that history required a sound judgment as to affairs, based upon a profound study of the Aristotelian trilogy of moral sciences, viz. Ethics, Politics, and Economics. Such a conception necessarily involved the postponement of historical studies to a more mature age than the school, and even a riper age than the University courses.

Of educational writers of the period, Mulcaster and Brinsley, it should be noted, do not treat of history or teaching. Naturally it was the publicists such as Sir Thomas Elyot and Sir Thomas Smith who especially laid stress upon the practical value of historical study.

The opinion of Elyot in the *Boke called the Gouvernour* (1531) with regard to history is that if it be studied seriously and diligently no subject has equal " commodity " and pleasure for a noble man. More exactly stated, Elyot's testimony is to the value of the reading of the writings of the Roman and Greek historians. He names Demetrius Phalareus, Livy, Xenophon, particularly *Paedia Cyri*, Quintus Curtius. Then are commended Julius Caesar and Sallust for their " compendious " writing. Elyot finds the *Conciones*, i.e. the addresses of generals to their troops, particularly attractive. The collection of *Orationes et Conciones*, thus taken out from classical historical writers must have been widely read at any rate in the seventeenth

Line 14, for *history or teaching* read *the teaching of history*.

century, when they were included in the *Elzevir* publications. Tacitus is to be read as combining " majesty " and compendious eloquence. Though style is important, it is in Elyot's view chiefly for their subject-matter that historical writers are to be read. For in history we see occasions of wars, counsels and preparations, the conduct of battle. Then again we see the prosperity or decay of commonwealths, good and evil qualities in rulers, the " commodities " of virtue and " discommodities " of vice.

The interest of Elyot may thus be described as bringing history into the province of rhetoric, and as providing material for ethical disquisitions. The outcome of such views, which were common to the Renascence writers, determined the direction of historical interest. It became, as Professor Woodward says,[1] " fragmentary, artificial, a *cento* of examples, of commonplaces, of biographical idealisations."

In his inaugural lecture in the University of Cambridge as Professor of Civil Law, c. 1541, Sir Thomas Smith said he had endeavoured to guard against the barrenness of current dialectical studies, by a wide range of reading " embracing not only logic, rhetoric, and philosophy, but also ancient and modern history, and did time permit he could point to more than six hundred passages from the Pandects, which demanded all these subjects for their complete elucidation." [2]

---

[1] In his *Erasmus, Concerning Education*, p. 131.
[2] Mullinger, *University of Cambridge*, ii, p. 130.

The Institution of a Gentleman, **1555,** urges the reading of histories and avoiding of idleness. The ground is : " to encourage noble hearts to read their doings by which they may be moved to do worthy deeds and avoid the contrary." In 1560, Laurence Humfrey recommends the young nobleman to the study of Greek historians, Plutarch, Appian, Thucydides ; amongst the Hebrews, Josephus, the Books of Genesis, Exodus, Judges and the Kings ; amongst the Latins, Caesar, Livy. Humfrey, however, is especially worthy of mention in recommending the histories written by his contemporaries, though these are not names which carry great attraction to the ordinary student now—Sleidan, Jovius, Bembus.

Peacham laid stress on the study of history. As Humfrey had emphasised the study of contemporaneous foreign history, Peacham (1622) made an appeal for a knowledge of the history of our own country. [1] " While I wander in foreign history, let me warn you, *ne sis peregrinus domi,* that you be not a stranger in the history of your own country, which is a common fault imputed to our English travellers in foreign countries ; who curious in the observation and search of the most memorable things and monuments of other places can say (as a great peer of France told me) nothing of their own country of England, being no whit inferior to any other in the world, for matter of antiquity and rarities

---

[1] *Compleat Gentleman,* p. 50–1.

of every kind worthy of remark and admiration. Herein I must worthily and onely prefer unto you the glory of our nation, Mr. Camden, as well for his judgment and diligence as the purity and sweet fluence of his Latin style ; and with him the rising star of good letters and antiquity, Mr. John Selden of the Inner Temple."

Whilst Peacham thus recommends the study of English historians, he points out that Giraldus, Geoffrey Higden, Ranulph of Chester, Walsingham did " cum saeculo caecutire," and as for Polydore Vergil, " so that his own history might pass for current, he burned and embezzled the best and most ancient records and monuments of our abbeys, priories, and cathedral churches."

Coote, in his *English Schoolmaster*, 1556, made a " brief Chronology " for practising " hard " words and for understanding the Bible and other histories. " By this Chronology, too, a Grammar-scholar may learn to know when his authors both Greek and Latin lived and when the principal histories in them were done." It is the barest list of events and dates, some naïvely conjectural, e.g. the Law of Moses given 858 years after the Flood, followed by Phaethon, burnt, the next date being 40 years after the " Law given "—Joshua brought the people into the Land of Canaan. Nevertheless, Coote's *English Scholemaster* was designed for pupils at the earliest stages of learning, and is therefore important in tracing the development of history teaching.

Line 16, for 1556 read 1596.

Milton regards history [1] as a province of Political Philosophy. The student is " to know the beginning, end and reasons of Political Societies ; that they may not in a dangerous fit of the Commonwealth, be such poor, shaken, uncertain reeds, of such a tottering conscience, as many of our great counsellers have lately shewn themselves, but steadfast pillars of the state. After this they are to dive into the grounds of law and legal justice ; delivered first and with best warrant by Moses ; and as far as human prudence can be trusted in those extolled remains of Grecian law-givers, Licurgus, Solon, Zaleucus, Charondas, and thence to the Roman Edicts and Tables with their Justinian ; and so down to the Saxon and Common Laws of England and the Statutes. [2] Sundays also and every evening may be now understandingly spent in the highest

---

[1] Tractate, 1644.

[2] Laurence Humfrey in 1560, in *The Nobles,* required that nobles be instructed in—

" Justinian's Institutions, the Pandects and the whole course of the civil law. And both all antiquity and the law and statutes of our own realm, wherein so skilful ought he to be, as he dare profess it. For, the Nobles' palaces ought to be the whole country's Oracles. Plato had I almost overpassed, with whose laws and commonwealth, he ought, most familiarly acquaint him." Sir Nicholas Bacon, in his *Articles* (1561) *for the bringing up of the Queen's Wards,* suggested that " at and after the age of sixteen, they were to attend lectures upon temporal and civil law as well as *de disciplina militari*. Sir Humphrey Gilbert in his projected Queen Elizabeth's Academy provides for a " lawyer for grounds of common law, who shall set down and teach exquisitely the office of a justice of the peace and sheriff. . . . 100 *li*."

matters [1] of Theology and Church history ancient and modern."

Milton and other educational writers laid no stress on the direct school teaching of history, yet it is easy to understand their view. For all these writers, the value of history is clearly seen on its ethical side ; Milton especially values its political import. In no case had history an independent position as a science, nor was there any room for its treatment as such. In no case was there any ground afforded for the inclusion of history as a separate academic study, in any way suggestive of fitness for school purposes. Yet the *de Officiis* of Cicero as a typical ethical treatise was a part of the course in some schools, and it is likely that such a book was a peg on which historical examples were hung. It was in this indirect way that history was taught.

With regard to Milton's views quoted above there is much to be found reflected in the practice of the times. In the first place, the Ten Commandments

---

[1] One other book may be mentioned as specially attractive to Puritan tastes, viz., the translation of *La Semaine : or the Birth of the World* by the Huguenot Guillaume de Saluste, Seigneur du Bartas, translated into English, 1579–84, by Joshua Sylvester, under the title *Du Bartas, his Divine Weeks and Works*. This gives in rhyme the Creation and the Fall, goes through an account of the Laws of Moses, through Jewish history, up to the time of Christ. It is " decorated and enriched with every ornament of classic literature and scientific knowledge, not without collateral aid from the gothic ages and legendary tales." It cannot be said to be a school text-book, but it is precisely the sort of history in which the first half of the seventeenth century delighted, and has an interest in its similarity at points with Milton's " *Paradise Lost*."

were often learned with the A B C, and Scripture history in some form was an important School subject. The Greek law-givers were familiar names, and stories of them are to be found in books of selections. The Roman edicts and Tables were fully discoursed upon in Godwin's *Romanae Historiae Anthologia* (1614).

Milton had suggested the reading of Justinian, and an exceptional instance is to be found in which he was prescribed for school-teaching. The Statutes of East Retford Grammar School (1552) explicitly name Justinian as an author to be read in the school.

With regard to Theology and Church history, there was systematic instruction in " lectures " and sermons and text-books such as the following :

> *The Abridgment of Christian Divinitie So exactly and methodically compiled that it leads, as it were, by the hand To the Reading of the Scriptures, ordering of commonplaces, Understanding of Controversies, clearing of some cases of conscience* by John Wollebius Doctor of Divinity and ordinary Professor in the University of Basel. This book was translated by Alexander Ross (himself a remarkable schoolmaster of Southampton Grammar School) 1650.

As to Church history, it is interesting to note that Thomas Fuller wrote the *Church History of Britain from the Birth of Jesus Christ until the year* 1628. Written in an attractive and conciliatory style, it was a book calculated to draw readers of every kind, without the *animus* of the partisan historians preceding him. But a book much more important from the popular point of view, and one which must have been familiar to most Puritan households was John Foxe's History of the *Acts and Monuments of the Church*, or as it is better known, the *Book of Martyrs*, which throws the searchlight on the sufferings of the Protestant Martyrs in 1555–8, in the fires of Smithfield. Only second to the letterpress, in graphic portraiture, but much more fascinating to the children-members of the family, were the terribly realistic illustrations of the burning anguish of the martyrs of the Protestant faith, which to succeeding generations made the Persecution live again into fierce and unforgettable enmity against the Catholics. Church history of this kind came to the child as naturally as church-going, and independently of the school was probably to a boy of the Stuart period far more vivid than any instruction imparted in either the day school or the Sunday school of modern times.

These aspects of history were known in the domestic teaching of the time. They were familiar to the women and girls of the better Puritan families as well as to the men and boys.

Nehemiah Wallington[1] has given a picture of his mother, who may be taken as a type of a Puritan woman. "She was very ripe and perfect in all stories of the Bible, likewise in all the stories of the Martyrs, and would readily turn to them ; she was also perfect and well seen in the English Chronicles and in the descents of the Kings of England."

---

[1] Wallington (1598–1658) wrote a *Diary* chiefly of events of the reign of Charles I. It was first printed in 1869.

It was maintained in the sixteenth and seventeenth centuries that history is not a subject of knowledge or contemplation, but of action or practice, and close reflection and reasoning on actions. It was urged that " History is nothing but Moral Philosophy clothed in examples," and " Felix qui potuit rerum cognoscere causas." How could schoolboys be equal to such a difficult study ? Bartholomew Keckerman,[1] the logician, is the doughtiest exponent of this view. His argument is " that histories contain nothing but examples of precepts ; Precepts are generally delivered in a method, whilst examples are without any method." Keckerman boldly proceeds : " For as it were absurd for a man to desire to know and observe the examples of grammar, logic, or rhetoric, before he had learned the rules of those sciences, so it must needs be more absurd for one to desire to read seriously and professedly, and to observe histories, which are nothing but examples of Ethics and Politics, before he has learned the rules and method of Ethics and Politics." To teach youth history was to Keckerman the height of absurdity.

It required a strong man to meet the great logician, especially when he maintained the orthodox position. But Gerard Vossius was the greatest grammarian of his age, and a man of acute insight and unflinching courage. His answer was that languages can be well learned without knowing the grammar rules, hence it may be permissible that history may be studied

---

[1] In *de Natura Historiae*, part i, cap. i, p. 10.

73

before Ethics and Politics. Vossius further argues that Keckerman had not distinguished between reading histories, when written, and the very different task of writing them. To be a competent writer of history implies a sound training in Civil Philosophy, but as Quintilian says, the reading of history and orations is the way to train youth to become orators. Accordingly youth should be taught history. In spite of Vossius's view, however, there was no systematic teaching of history in the schools. The nearest approach was the use for composition of themes, of annals, emblems and apophthegms and adages, and, of course, the reading of classical historical writers, and the consultation of classic dictionaries of antiquities. Erasmus's *Adages* contained casual historical allusions of the very type which appealed to the schoolmasters. The *Apophthegms* of Erasmus are described as " the prompt, quick, witty and sententious sayings of certain Emperors, Kings, Captains, Philosophers and Orators as well Greek as Romans." Emblems were frequently connected with fables, mythology, heraldry and history. Pupils were required to collect material for themes from the histories of Plutarch, Valerius Maximus, Herodotus, Florus, Livy, Justinus Pliny, Pareus (*Medulla historiae*) and Aelian, and from the annals [1] of modern historians. The history

---

[1] These sources were recommended, for instance, in the *Apophthegmata* by Lycosthenes. In the material for themes, which he supplies, he quotes from annalists of modern (as well as ancient) countries, e.g. England, Austria, Flanders, Germany, Switzerland. So, too, with

learned in the Grammar School was a mosaic of gems without due realisation of the unity and continuity of history.

REPRESENTATIVE LIST OF HISTORY BOOKS TO 1652

The following list of books shows history on the way to the school. It follows the method of abridgements and epitomes. As in other subjects, when the books became smaller in size, they were regarded as more suitable to the capacities of children. Such seems to have been the idea of Coote, in introducing historical dates into his *English Schoolmaster*. This tendency towards epitome is therefore worthy of note.

Languet (Thomas) :

> *An Epitome of Cronicles conteining the whole discourse of the histories as well of this realme of England as all other countries . . . gathered out all most probable authors, etc. . . .* By T. Cooper. B.L. T. Berthelet, London, 1549, 4to.

Winstanley (William) :

> *England's Worthies, in the select lives of the most eminent persons from Constantine the Great to the death of Oliver Protector.* 8vo. 1660.

---

the *Symbola Heroica* of Reusner, historical illustrations for theme-writing were taken from *modern* as well as ancient history. So, again, in the *de Copia* of Erasmus, " copiousness " in an oration is to be cultivated by obtaining " examples " from divers nations, e.g. African, Hebrew, Spanish, French, English. This practice of using modern and contemporary historical examples may be said to be the earliest type of school use of historical study.

MODERN SUBJECTS IN ENGLISH SCHOOLS

Milton (John) :
> *History of Britain.* " From the first traditional beginning continued to the Norman Conquest, collected out of the antientest and best Authours thereof." 1670.

Lloyd (Ludowick) :
> *The Consent of Time.* 1590.
> *Diall of Daies.* 1590.

More (John) :
> *A Table (Chronological) from the beginning of the World to this day.* (Edited by N. Bownd.) J. Legatt, Printer to the Universities of Cambridge, 1593, 8vo.

Fulbecke (Wm) :
> *An historical collection of the continuall Factions Tumults, and Massacres of the Romans and Italians during the space of one hundred and twentie yeares next before the peaceable Empire of Augustus Caesar. Selected and derived out of best writers and reporters of these accidents . . . beginning where the historie of T. Livius doth end, and ending where C. Tacitus doth begin.* W. Ponsonby : London, 1601. 4to.

Davies (John) :
> *Microcosmos. The Discovery of the little World with the government thereof.* Oxford, 1603.

> " The poem describes the whole state of man, his condition, qualities and surroundings in a discursive manner which allows a short history of England to come in at p. 131."

Fulbecke (Wm) :
> *An Abridgment, or rather a bridge of Roman histories to passe the nearest way from Titus Livius to Cornelius Tacitus : under which for the spaces of six score yeares the fame and fortune of the Romans ebbs and flows* T. E. for R. More : London, 1680. 4to.

Philippson (Joannes) :
> *The Key of Historie. Or, a most methodicall Abridgement of the foure chief Monarchies, etc.* (Translated from the Latin.) Written by . . . John Sleidan. M. Flesher, for W. Sheeres, London, 1627. Also 1631, 1635.

Taylor (John) (the Water Poet) :
Memorial of all the English Monarchs, being in number 151, *from Brute to King Charles in Historical verse.* 1630. 8vo.

Isaacson (Henry) :
Saturni Ephemerides sive Tabula Historico-chronologica. 1633. Folio.

Aelianus (Claudius) : (translated by A. Fleming)—
A Register of Hystories, conteining Martiall exploites of worthy warriors, politique practises of Civil Magistrates, wise sentences of famous Philosophers, and other matters manifolde and memorable. Written in Greeke by Æ, a Romane ; and. delivered in Englishe . . . by A. Fleming. B.L. Imprinted . . . for F. Woodcocke, London, 1576. 4to.

Baker (Sir R.) :
A chronicle of the Kings of England, from the time of the Roman Government till the Reign of King Charles, containing all the passages of Church and State. 1643. Folio.

Hall (Robert), pseudonym for Heylyn (Peter) :
'Ηρωυλογια *Anglorum,* or *A help to English History.* 1641.

Heylyn (Peter) :
Cosmographie in four Books, containing the Chorography and History of the whole World and all the principall Kingdoms, Provinces, Seas and Isles thereof. Folio. 1652.

Cooper (Thomas) :
The Epitome of Chronicles, containing the whole Discourse of Histories as well of this Realme of England as all other countries from the beginning of the World to the Incarnation of Christ. By T. Languet, and thence to 1549 *by Thomas Cooper.* Lond, 1549, 1560. And augmented to the seventh year of Qn. Elizabeth's reign, 1565. 4to.

Grafton (Richard) :
An Abridgement of the Chronicles of England, gathered by Richard Grafton, Citizen of London. 1562. 8vo. Another edition, 1565, under title of :
A Manuall of the Chronicles of England.

Lily (George), Prebendary of Canterbury :

> *Anglorum Regum Chronicus Epitome.* Venice, 1548.
> Franc., 1565. 8vo. Basle, 1577.
> (Watts says, " This Author was the first who
> published an exact map of Britain.")

Stow (John) :

> *Summarie of English Chronicles,* 1565, 1570, 1575,
> 1579, 1590. 8vo. Continued to 1607 by Edmund
> Howes. 1610, 1611. 8vo.

Heylyn Peter :

> *Examen Historicum, a discovery and examination
> of the mistakes, falsities, and defects in some modern
> Histories.* 8vo.

Ross (Alexander) :

> *The Epitome of Sir W. Raleigh's History of the World.*
> *Observations on Sir W. Raleigh's History of the World.*

Raleigh (Sir Walter) :

> *The History of the World.* 1614.

Ross (Alexander) :

> *The Marrow of History,* 1650.
> *The Continuation of Sir Walter Raleigh's History
> of the World.* 1652.

Knolles (Richard) :

> *The General History of the Turks.* 1603.

Fuller (Thomas) :

> *The History of the Holy Warre.* 1643.

Drayton (Michael) :

> *Poly olbion.* 1622.

Beard (Thomas) :

> *The Theatre of God's Judgments ; wherein is repre-
> sented the admirable Justice of God against all notorious
> sinners, great and small, especially against the most
> eminent persons in the world ; collected out of Sacred,
> Ecclesiasticall, and Pagan Historians. Incomparably
> fit for all scholars, Ministers and studious Christians.*
> Folio. 1597.

EXCURSUS ON THE FIRST TEXT-BOOK ON CIVICS
IN ENGLAND

1580. CHRISTOPHER OCLAND.
Anglorum Praelia.

This is, I believe, the first book published in
England intended for school use with a view of
definitely giving to the youthful mind due and
proper material out of which patriotism might not
unreasonably be expected to develop.

The writer in question is Christopher Ocland,
and his book—written throughout, it should be
added, in Latin—has on its title-page (dated 1580) :
" *Anglorum Praelia : Ab anno Domini* 1327 *anno
nimirum primo inclytissimi Principis Eduardi eius
nominis tertii, usque ad annum Domini* 1558. *Car-
mine summatim perstricta. Christophoro Oclando
Buckingamiensi Anglo Authore.*" [In an edition
of 1582, on the title-page, Ocland is announced as
" primo Scholae Southwarkiensis prope Londinum,
dein Cheltennamensis, quae sunt a serenissima sua
Majestate fundatae, Moderatore."]

[To the 1582 edition is also added : " Item : *De
pacatissimo Angliae statu* [1] *imperante Elizabetha
compendiosa Narratio.*" And then the proud words :
" *Haec duo Poemata, tam ob argumenti gravitatem
quam Carminis facilitatem, Nobilissimi Regiae
Majestatis Consiliarii in omnibus huius regni Scholis
praelegenda pueris praecripserunt.*"]

In 1582 appeared a quarto edition and also an
octavo edition ; in 1589 a further edition of the

---

[1] This is described elsewhere as Εἰρηναρχία.

Elizabetheis. There is also a translation of the *Elizabetheis* into English, done by John Sharrock in 1585.

The title indicates the contents of the book. It is an account in Latin verse of the wars of England carried on between 1327 (the accession of Edward III) and 1558 (the death of Mary). There is a Latin poem by Richard Mulcaster, and also one by the well-known poet Thomas Watson, prefixed to the *Elizabetheis.* Readers of the *Positions* (1581) will remember the ecstasy of praise in which Mulcaster indulges over Queen Elizabeth. In these verses prefixed to Ocland's book, Mulcaster envies Ocland the subject of his verses after the strain :

"Nam quid nobilius sol nostra Principe cernit ? "

In the 1582 octavo edition of the *Anglorum Praelia*, on the page opposite to the dedication to Queen Elizabeth, and occupying the whole page, are the royal arms of Queen Elizabeth. The title-page had already announced " *Cum privilegio Regiae Maiestatis.*"

But the point which requires full recognition about Christopher Ocland is the fact that the Lords of the Privy Council ordered his *Praelia Anglorum* to be used in the grammar schools. I venture to transcribe the minute : [1]

"A letter to the Commissyoners for Causes Ecclesiasticall in London. That whereas there hathe bene of late a booke

---

[1] *Acts of the Privy Council of England.* Edited by J. R. Dasent. New series. Vol. xiii, A.D. 1581–82, pages 389–90.

written in Latyn verse by one Christofer Ockland, entituled *Anglorum Praelia,* which, as he enformeth, hathe bene by him at his great charges aboute half a yere sithence imprinted and published, and now againe lately imprinted with the addytion of a shorte treatise or appendix concerning the peaceable government of the Quenes Majestie ; Forasmuche as his travell therein with the qualitie of the verse hathe receyved good comendacion, and that the subjecte or matter of the said booke is such as is worthie to be read of all men and especially in the common schooles, where divers heathen poetes are ordinarily read and taught from the which the youthe of the Realme receyve rather infectyon in manners and educatyon than advauncement in vertue, in place of which poetes their Lordships thincke fitte this booke were read and taught in the grammer schooles, their Lordships therefore have thought good, as well for the commoditye of the said Ockland and for the incoraging of him and others that are learned to bestow their travell to so good purposes, as also for the benefitte of the youthe and the removing of such lascivyous poetes as are commonly read and taught in the said grammer schooles, requiring them uppon the receipt hereof to write their letters unto all the Bushoppes through the Realme requiring them to give commaundement that in all the grammar and free schooles within their severall Dyoces the said bookes *De Anglorum Praeliis* and peaceable government of her Majestie maye be, in place of some of the heathen poetes nowe read among them as Ovide *De Arte Amandi, De Tristibus,* or such lyke, may be receyved and publickly read and taught by schoolemasters unto their schollers in some one of their formes in the schooles fitte for that matter."

This remarkable minute is dated xxi Aprilis, at Grenewiche, 1582.

Perhaps the most interesting point that arises from the passage is the direct interference of the Privy Council in the recommendation of a text-book in history. The *mot d'ordre* is given to all schools (we should say all secondary schools) to use a certain book in place of works commonly read and on the whole less advantageous. It is important also to notice that the Privy Council, in its supervision of schools, works its will through the dioceses of the bishops. This is natural enough when it is remembered that the bishops had the licensing of schoolmasters in their hands, and also that in their visitations they also inquired into the way in which schools were being carried on throughout their dioceses.[1]

The reading of " heathen poetes," and the reconciliation of such a practice with a Christian teacher was a stumbling block with many of the pious in all generations of the Christian era. There were those, of course, who held that the broad highway of the classics was the only way to intellectual salvation. Ascham, for instance, often heard[2] Sir John Cheke say : " I would have a good student pass rejoicing through all authors, both Greek and Latin ; but he that will dwell in these few books only, first in God's Holy Bible and then join with it Tully in Latin, Plato, Aristotle, Xenophon, Isocrates, and Demosthenes in Greek, must needs prove an excellent man." Here, however, Sir John Cheke is speaking of " students," and his list is very choice. Dr. Laurence Humfrey, in his treatise *Of Nobility* (1563), on the other hand, pointed out the danger of indiscriminate classical teaching of the young, had protested against Ovid, and indeed only included

---

[1] *See English Grammar Schools*, pp. 19–23.
[2] Strype's *Life of Cheke*, Oxford edition, 1821, p. 153.

Terence because, as he says, " I saw Cicero so much esteem him."

In the *Anglorum Praelia* is given the copy of the Letters directed by the minute quoted above to be sent to all the bishops throughout England and Wales. It will be seen that it was drawn up sixteen days after the meeting of the Privy Council. It reads :

After our heartie commendations, etc. Whereas wee of hir Majesties high Commission Ecclesiastical have received letters from the Lordes of hir Highnesse moste honourable privie Counsell, That we should directe order to all the Byshops of the Realme, to cause to bee receyved and publiquely read and taught in all Grammar and Free Scholes within their severall Dioceses a Booke in Latine verse of late imprinted, entituled *Anglorum Praelia*, sette forth by one Christopher Ocklande, as by the true Copie of their Honours Letters, which wee sende you here inclosed, it may appeare unto you. *These* are therefore to require you, according to their Honours pleasures signified to us in that behalfe, forthwith upon receipt hereof to take present order within your Dioces for the due accomplishment of their sayde Letters accordingly. And so wee bidde you hearty farewell. From London the seaventh of May, 1582. Your Loving Friendes.

I have not as yet found any account of how the *Anglorum Praelia* was esteemed in the schools. But it is possible to form a judgment by remembering that the subject was the martial glory of England, and that these included the feats of Edward III and Henry V at a period three hundred years nearer to them than we are. " The matter of this book," the Commissioners themselves said, " is heroical and of good instruction." In fact, it would seem that Ocland's book was somewhat similar in its line of interest to books on the growth of our colonial empire of to-day. It was, however, written in Latin—much shorter and much more restrained in detail, though perhaps not always in its enthusiasm. The following is the account of Edward III and the Black Prince at Cressy :

> "Fulminat ense pater Princeps Edwardus, et eius
> Filius impubes ; illoque Britannica virtus
> Quanta sit eluxit bello, quo millia caesa
> Triginta aut plus eo, campique cruore madebant ; "

and so on.

Henry V at Agincourt is thus described :

> Ipse manu magno conatu rex rotat ensem,
> Nobilior faciebat idem pars, turbaque tota.
> Omne nemus resonat pulsatae cassidis ictu
> Armorum crebris tinnitibus insonat unda,
> Vicinique suis colles cum vallibus aegros
> Accipiunt gemitus morientum, sanguis inundat,

etc., from which it will be gathered that there is, for modern taste, rather too much enthusiastic gloating over bloodshed.

The " Elizabetha " is a panegyric of Ocland's queen in 1580, and a recital of the peaceable state of England. There is also an account of the members of Her Majesty's council. The following extract, from John Sharrock's translation, will give some idea of the matter and style of the verses. They deal with the towardness of Queen Elizabeth in her childhood :

> " But when her mother tongue she knew,
> Expressing signs of wondrous wit, and judgement to ensue :
> She at her prudent sayings made astonished men to stand,
> And books, desirous to be taught, would always have in
> hand.

She scarce the letters with her eyes intentive did behold,
Their several names, but thrice before by her instructors
    told :
But perfect them at fingers' end as two months taught,
Their figures diverse made, deciphering well, by judgements
    rare.
Yea, in few days (a marvel great it is to speak no doubt)
The princely imp by industry such sap had sucked
    out,
That, without counsel to assist, she anything could read."

With regard to Christopher Ocland himself, the facts to be gathered are few. While master at St. Olave's School in 1571, it appears that he received twenty marks a year, for which he was to teach ten or twelve boys at first and to help the usher to teach the " petytes." Ocland was also to be allowed to take six or eight scholars. This comes from the minutes of the vestry of the parish of St. Olave.[1] In the minutes of the same vestry, January 27, 1571, there is another schoolmaster, one John Payne.

There is a letter (quoted by Sir Henry Ellis in his *Collection of Letters*), written by Ocland to Sir Julius Cæsar, chiefly as to his poverty ; but the most pathetic letter is one to the great Lord Burghley, begging for relief in his distress. It is a vivid letter. It might be used as an apt illustration to Melanchthon's *Miseries of Schoolmasters*. After reading it one hardly needs more details of Ocland's life. No history of education can be complete which

---

[1] Quoted in Sir Henry Ellis' *Letters of Eminent Literary Men*, pp. 65–6.

does not include the sidelight afforded by such a letter. It takes us right into the midst of Ocland's life :

Help, my very good Lord, my singular good Lord, help I pray and most humbly desire your honour for God's sake, your poor and infortunate Christopher, that her Majesty may give me a prebend or benefice that will first fall. I never had anything at her Grace's hands for all my books heretofore made of her Highness. I trust my Lord Chancellor will give his good word with you and the other Lords of the Council. Or at the least speak to D. Aubrey, the Master of the Requests, and he will move my cause the sooner at your speech. At the writing of this, my lord, tidings come to me that one Hurdes, a serjeant of London, who cast me in the Counter, afore the feast of the Nativity of Christ last past, hath a *Capias utlagatum* out for me. I ought [owed] him but five pounds and he hath condemned me in forty pounds. The learned in the law say it to be ridiculous that I was bound in thirty pounds for payment of five pounds, and the condemnation upon the outlawry is risen to forty pounds. *Quid faciam ? Quo me vertam ? Mors est mihi lucro.*

He goes on to explain he has no relations to fall back on. His wife is paralysed—has been these three years—and grows worse every day on account of the misfortunes of her sons. Prison for Ocland would mean death to his wife and to their one daughter. He begs Lord Burghley, therefore, to get the writ of outlawry stayed. He then continues :

I teach school at Greenwich, where my labour will not find me bread and drink. I dare not teach in London where it would be better. For my debt is grown to twenty-three pounds in ten years, for so long ago it is since I gave over teaching school and began to get out *Anglorum Praelia* and my other books. I have compiled also at this time a book, the title is *De vitis aliquot illustrissimorum virorum in Anglia,* wherein I do not forget your honourable Lordship to have due place. I have opened myself to your Lordship, for truly it is said, *" Crescuntque tegendo vulnera."* Thus, having been too much tedious, I crave pardon, and pray God to send your Honour long life to the service of her Majesty in Council, the benefit of the realm, and the comfort of us all true English. Greenwich, this xiii. of October, 1590.—Your Lordship's most bounden for ever, most poor, and most wretched.

CHRISTOPHER OCLAND.

To the right Honourable and his singular good Lord, the Lord Burghley, Lord Treasurer of England.

There does not seem to be any indication as to whether Lord Burghley responded to the pathetic appeal, but Mr. Thompson Cooper, the writer of the notice on Ocland in the *Dictionary of National Biography,* gives us a reference to a petition to Prince Charles, preferred January 14, 1617, by Ocland's daughter (mentioned above), which met with response. Jane Ocland, the daughter, received a royal gift of twenty-two shillings. One's thoughts at once recur to Edmund Spenser's lines, printed, be it remembered, a few years after Ocland's letter was written :

" Full little knowest thou that hast not tried
What hell it is in suing long to bide * * *
To have thy prince's grace, yet want her peeres."

Ocland had made a bid for his prince's grace by his " Elizabetha," and for " her peeres," by his letter to Lord Burghley. But, apparently, he obtained neither. " Where I hanked after plenty,

I have run upon scarcity," said Ocland. It is little compensation, perhaps, that now he should turn out to be the first English writer of a book on civics. But the title does not seem to be undue to him. It is in the fitness of things that the first patriotic historical text-book should be written by an Elizabethan.

CHAPTER III

THE TEACHING OF GEOGRAPHY IN
ENGLAND UP TO 1660

In the long span of time of the Middle Ages, Mr.
Beazley [1] has shown that geographical progress,
though slow, was very marked, and has presented
a narration of what is, in the gross, a remarkable
achievement in geographical explanation and description. The story of the travel of pilgrims,
crusaders, diplomats, missionaries, merchants, presents as a whole a triumph of investigation, when
we bear in mind the resources at their disposal,
and brings us to the point of view that the
Tudor voyages came in a direct line of continuity
and were " prepared for " by the mediaevalists.
Mediaeval geographers produced effects slowly, for
the registering of results to be made universally
known was impossible in the days of MS. writing
and before the development of cartography. Hence
there was always the tendency to fall back upon
the biblical, the classical, the legendary. The
biblical views, and the authorised interpretation of
them placed limits to inquiry and investigation.
The classical knowledge was diffused through the
encyclopaedic collections of Martianus Capella and

---

[1] *The Dawn of Modern Geography*, vol. i, 300 A.D. to
900 A.D. ; vol. ii, 900 A.D. to 1260 A.D. ; vol. iii, 1260–1420.

Isidore of Seville, and geography only slowly emancipated itself to an individuality of its own. Ranulf Higden (who died 1364) marks a period since he jotted down the results of geographical study in England in the early chapters of his *Polychronicon*. Travel was represented by the book issued under the name of Sir John Mandeville in the fourteenth century. Maps were from time to time drawn up, as, for instance, in the Hereford *Mappa Mundi*, but these efforts were spasmodic and local. Hence the difficulty of general progress in a study, which requires organisation of effort, in registering the results of all inquiries and investigations. Geography was represented in early printing, Strabo appearing in a Latin translation as early as 1462. In 1480 Caxton produced *The myrrour and descrypcyon of the World*. Naturally, the earlier printed works, which by courtesy may be termed geographical, are of classical origin, and include works founded on those of Ptolemy and Proclus, which are rather astronomical or geometrical in nature. The differentiation between cosmography and geography was not always clear.

Hallam, in his *Literature of Europe*, attributes the growth in Renascence times of an interest in geographical knowledge, and the accompanying cartography, to the translations of Ptolemy's books on cosmography and to the discoveries on the coast of Africa made by the Portuguese, in addition to the more general causes of the progress of commerce and the evolution of knowledge as a whole. It may be added that the great impetus given to travelling, in visiting Italy, and other countries to which the learned went in pursuit of knowledge, necessarily made geography a practical interest.

Whatever the shortcomings of the educational writers on history and geography may be in the sixteenth and seventeenth centuries, these writers were unanimous in insisting on the close connexion, or as we say correlation, of history and geography.

Erasmus, [1] writing in 1511, sees the value of geography in reading histories and for the poets. It is a subject which gives us a knowledge [2] of the names ancient and modern, of mountains, rivers, cities ; and also of names of trees, plants, animals, dress, appliances, precious stones in which, adds Erasmus, " the average writer of to-day shows a strange ignorance." But the real use, in Erasmus's mind, of this knowledge for the teacher, is to have plenty of resource in the way of exposition and also for the purpose of supplying copiousness of phrase for composition of themes and " orations."

In 1523, J. L. Vives, perhaps the greatest of all educational writers of the Age of the Renascence, says [3] : " Let the pupil consult Strabo, the describer of the world, and contemplate the pictures of Ptolemy, if he can get them in an emendated form. He should add also the recent discoveries in the East and West from the Navigation of our people."

---

[1] Woodward, *Erasmus Concerning Education*, p. 145.

[2] *Ibid.*, p. 167.

[3] In the *de Tradendis Disciplinis*, book iv.

And, again, Peter Martyr, the Milanese, has fixed in the monument of letters an account of the navigations newly made in his time. But afterwards much more extended discoveries have been made and these latter will seem fabulous to posterity, though of the soberest fact. . . . Raphael Volaterranus has brought together a great deal about past achievements both in Anthropology and in Geography which have advanced his history greatly."

Sir Thomas Elyot, in the *Governour* in 1531, suggests that to " prepare the child to understanding histories " it is necessary that he study cosmography. For history is tedious, or at any rate less pleasant, when the names and position of countries and towns mentioned are not known. The old " tables " (i.e. pictures or maps) of Ptolemy are to be shown, " wherein all the world is painted, having first some introduction into the sphere, whereof now of late be made very good treatises and more plain and easy to learn than was wont to be."

With plans and maps and a good instructor the lessons in cosmography should be pleasant and easy. " For what pleasure it is," continues Elyot, " in one hour to behold those realms, cities, seas, rivers and mountains that uneth (scarcely) in an old man's life can not be journeyed and pursued ! What incredible delight is taken in beholding the diversities of people, beasts, fowls (birds), fishes, trees, fruits and herbs : to know the sundry manners and conditions of people and the variety of their natures, and that in a warm study or parlour, without peril of the sea, a danger of long and painful journeys.

Line 10, for *Governour* read *Gouvernour.*

I cannot tell what more pleasure should happen to a gentle wit than to behold in his own house every thing that within all the world is contained."

Such is the enthusiasm of the man of experience and thought less than forty years after the " discovery " of America by Columbus. The authors whom Elyot suggests are Strabo, Solinus, Mela and Dionysius.[1] With these " substantially perceived, it is time to induce a child to the reading of histories."

Cosmography, therefore, in Elyot's view, is the fore-train of history, and it is, he explicitly declares, *to all noble men*, not only pleasant but profitable also, and " wonderful necessary."

Engraving on copper is supposed to have been invented about the year 1460, and to have been applied to the production of maps for the first time [2] in the geography of Ptolemy, which was published at Rome in 1478. In 1550, Ramusio published a large collection of travels, which includes the account of Africa by Leo Africanus. Heylyn lays great store by Acosta's *History of the Indies*, published in 1590. The collections of voyages by Hakluyt were published 1598–1600 ; Purchas's *Pilgrims* 1613–1625.

Hallam gives the *Theatrum Orbis Terrarum* of Ortelius,[3] in 1570, as the first general atlas of modern

---

[1] The first three are the authors recommended by Erasmus.

[2] Hallam, *Literature of Europe* (1855), vol. i, p. 192.

[3] Hallam mentions that Ortelius gives a list of about 150 geographical works.

Europe, and as the " basis of all collections of maps since formed." The atlas of Mercator in the edition of 1598 marks still further progress.[1] The *Theatrum Orbis Terrarum sive Novus Atlas* of Blaew was published in 1648. Speed's Maps[2] were first published in 1611 under the title of *The Theatre of the Empire of Great Britain*, and in 1627, as : *A prospect of the most famous parts of the world drawn forth in Maps and descriptions of Asia, Africa, Europe and America*, etc. Hallam says that Speed's Maps[3] are by no means inferior to those of Blaew.

It was not till the end of the seventeenth century that de Lisle flourished, and Hallam considers de Lisle as the real founder of geographical science.

Geography had to claim a separate existence from astronomy, geometry, and history, with which it was not only related but also often confused.

---

[1] Hallam, *Literature of Europe* (1855), vol. ii, p. 354.

[2] Speed also published in 1611 his *History of Great Britain*, a distinctive work in history, in continuation of the *Theatre of the Empire*.

[3] Showing the difficulties of map illustration (at the end of the *Holy War*, 1639), Thomas Fuller says :

" Of thirty maps and descriptions of the Holy Land which I have perused, I have never met with two in all considerables alike ; some sink valleys where others raise mountains ; yea and rivers where others begin them ; and sometimes with a wanton dash of their pen create a stream in land, a creak in sea, more than nature ever owned. In these differences we have followed the Scripture as an impartial umpire. The latitudes and longitudes (wherein there be also unreconcilable discords) I have omitted, being advised that it will not quit cost in a map of so small extent." The map was engraved by the well-known engraver, W. Marshall.

Geographical facts were not investigated, but accepted on travellers' rumours. A book [1] like Coryat's *Crudities* (1611) gathered up stories, fables, and fiction as readily as facts, and whilst it stirred the imagination of its readers and was delightfully quaint, did little to stimulate precision of ideas, such as the separate studies of geometry and astronomy, from which geography sprang, began to demand.

Elyot had acutely pitched upon the solid value of cosmography on account of the " material figures and instruments " which can be brought to bear on its study. He is thus a forerunner of Eilhard Lubinus, who stated explicitly the educational value of illustration [2] as an aid to studies in general. In the case of geography it led to a development of the science itself.

Joseph Glanvill, [3] in 1668, compares the advance made by his time in geography with the knowledge possessed by antiquity. He notes that the ancients did not know that the earth was encompassed by the sea and could be circumnavigated. They were ignorant as to the Americas, north and south, and even of the remote parts of " their own Asia." They knew nothing accurately of Japan, the Javas, "the Phillippicks " and Borneo. The mighty empires of Mexico and Peru were not disclosed to them. But in his time, Glanvil says : " The frozen North, the Torrid Line

---

[1] Fynes Morison's *Itinerary*, published 1617, and Wm. Lithgow's *Total Discourse of the Rare Adventures and painfull Peregrinations*, 1632, should also be named.

[2] *See* pp. 143–4 *infra*.

[3] *Plus Ultra*, p. 49.

and the formerly unknown South are visited. The Earth hath been rounded by Magellan, Drake and Candish (Cavendish). The great motion of the sea is vulgar ; the diversities of winds stated ; the treasure of hidden virtues in the loadstone found and used. The spicy islands of the east, remote south and north are frequented, the people known, and their riches transmitted to us. Our navigation is far greater, our commerce more general, our charts more exact, our globes more accurate, our travels more remote, our reports more intelligent and sincere."

"Consequently," he proceeds, "our geography is far more perfect than it was in the elder times of Polybius, and Possidonius, yea · than in those of Ptolemy, Strabo and Pomponius Mela who lived amongst the Cæsars. . . . You will think so if you compare the Geographical performances of Gemma Frisius, Mercator, Ortelius, Stevinus, Bertius and Blaeu, with the best remains of the most celebrated Geographers of the more ancient ages."

William Wotton,[1] writing in 1694, referring to the progress made in modern knowledge over the knowledge of the Greeks and Romans, expands Elyot's idea of the value of " material figures and instruments." He connects together geography, astronomy and navigation as affected by the discovery of the property of the magnetic needle. He then points out that the improvements in navigation,

---

[1] *Reflections on Ancient and Modern Learning*, p. 249 *et seqq.*

which have made sea-coasts known, have been fastened upon the imagination and memory by the art of engraving on copper-plates. " For want of this," he continues, " the ancient descriptions even of those countries which they knew were rude and imperfect. Their maps were neither exact nor beautiful. . . . Velserus has printed some ancient maps, commonly called the Peutingerian Tables, that were made for the direction of the Roman Quartermasters, and if a man will compare them with Sanson's or Blaew's he will see the difference, which (adds Wotton) in future ages will certainly be vastly greater, if those countries which are now barbarous or undiscovered should ever come into the hands of a civilised or learned people."

The romantic history of maritime discovery and enterprise in the time of the Tudors and the Stuarts is detailed in the collections of Hakluyt and Purchas, and many another writer. This movement was parallel to the collections of historical annals and chronicles, and went through the routine of abridgements and epitomes on the way to popular dissemination of geographical knowledge. The drama in its references to wondrous lands and wondrous stories [1] of their inhabitants, brought vividly to the imagination the interest ever widening, but at first too full to grasp—of the Renascence Discovery of the World and of Man—the sense of the greatness of the knowledge ascertainable and recorded of Mother Earth. But perhaps the most noticeable

---

[1] e.g. Shakespere's *Tempest* with its Ariel and Caliban.

result of the extension of geographical knowledge and the " material figures and instruments " for its realisation, was to induce a new and intimate knowledge, a transfiguration by attraction, of the countries already known. For example, in England, we recognise in the Elizabethan age a deeper patriotism founded on a greater knowledge of our own country, by comparing it with the tales of travellers and discourses abroad. Thus, descriptions of England abound in Warner's *Albion* (1586), in Drayton's *Polyolbion* (1622), and the praise of Devon[1] in Carpenter's book on Geography, whilst there was a dissemination in all sorts of accounts of our country from the long descriptive passages of Camden's *Britannia* to lists of market towns and fairs, in an appendix to a primer.

As a directly educational discipline, however, geography developed late.[2] As with history, geography, or perhaps it should be said the wonderfully interesting compound called cosmography (which included references to natural philosophy, natural history, astronomy, astrology, hydrography, topography, chorography, navigation, geometry, history, taking man and his dwelling place, as its complex theme)—this was ordinarily a specifically

---

[1] *See* p. 120 *infra*.

[2] The first English University Readership in Geography was not established till 1887 in the University of Oxford. Nor has geography even yet its settled place in either the Elementary or Secondary School. Great strides have been made in recent years chiefly by the Royal Geographical Society in the encouragement of geographical teaching in Universities, colleges and schools.

gentleman's study. Various aspects of this many-sided subject, so to say, leaked out into separate treatises, and these, when small enough, and abridged enough, became " suitable " (by their brevity) for the " child's capacity." These, naturally, in their barest elements were lists of names of places and facts, and the human interest of the highly interesting subject in its first form completely vanished.

It was the humanistic aspect of geography which especially attracted the sixteenth and seventeenth centuries. In 1560, Laurence Humfrey in *The Nobles* says : " Great delight and profit bringeth Geography." He carries forward the traditions of Vives and Elyot.

Lord Herbert of Cherbury, writing in the early part of the seventeenth century, advocated the learning of geography : " It will be requisite to study geography with exactness, so much as may teach a man the situation of all countries in the whole world, together with which it will be fit to learn something concerning the governments, manners, religions, either ancient or new, as also the interests of states, and relations in amity, or strength in which they stand to their neighbours ; it will be necessary also, at the same time, to learn the use of the celestial globe, the studies of the both globes being complicated and joined together."

Peacham (1622) expects his *Compleat Gentleman* to study cosmography, " a science at once both feeding the eye and mind with such incredible variety, and profitable pleasure, that even the greatest kings and philosophers have bestowed the best part of their time in the contemplation hereof at home," and in travels abroad to increase their knowledge of geography.

In 1654 John Webster, in his *Examination of Academies*, says that in the Universities, geography, hydrography, chorography and topography are usually taught, and he names Nathaniel Carpenter's Geography as the text-book. He complains that cosmography is not taught properly. For cosmography is a perfect description of the " heavenly and elemental part of the world, nor are the theorems of Hydrography taught. These are of the utmost value for navigation and ought not to be neglected." The *Vindiciæ Academiarum* (1654) of Seth Ward answers Webster by saying that Sir Henry Savile required, in the terms of the foundation of the chair of Astronomy at Oxford, the Professor to lecture on these very subjects, " and no one has proved that he does not do so."

In 1657 the thoughtful educational writer who signs himself J. B. in his *Heroick Education* requires that the pupil " should be taught cosmography as exactly as possible, insomuch that he should carry, as 'twere, a little map of all the world in his imagination, after which it will not be very difficult to teach him the art of fortification with all the inventions, engines and instruments of war."

The correlation of history and geography is emphasised by Willam London in 1658. " Geography," he says, " stirs up and provokes many profitable searchers in the bowels of history. . . . From my own experience, I assure thee (i.e. the reader of his book) a world of pleasure and of great advantage, especially if thou tracest thy history with a map lying before thee, it takes a double impression in thy mind ; first of the history thou readest, and then of the remembrance of all circumstances about both, not without a deep impression of the situation of all places."

The passages quoted so far especially relate to the education of the noble and the young gentleman. The actual teaching of geography is mainly connected with the academies and private tuition. The following passage illustrates the private tuition in geography in the period up to 1660. John Crowther, the tutor, writes to Ralph Verney, his pupil : " I have not yet initiated you into Geography. If you cannot have leisure to come over hither, I will attend you for a week or so at Claydon till I have showed you the principal grounds."[1] Crowther also writes with regard to the " sale of a study at the second-hand. I have bought two books scarce and fit for your use, Grymston's *Estates and Principalities of the World*, 20s., and the *History of Venice*, 10s., which I will let you have or reserve them myself at your pleasure."[2]

The first notice of geography teaching in England appears to be that of Richard Hakluyt. For before he wrote, in 1589 his first edition, and in 1598 the enlarged edition, of *Principall Navigations, Voiages, and Discoveries of the English Nation*, it is stated,

---

[1] *Verney Memoirs*, iii, p. 119.
[2] *Ibid.*, iii, p. 120.

after taking his degree, M.A. Oxford (Christ Church), in 1577, that he had given at Oxford lectures on geography, in which he claimed to have been *the first to show " the new lately reformed maps, globes, spheres and other instruments of this art for demonstration in the common schools."* Hakluyt, who was of Dutch origin, had been at Westminster School, the one school in England, apparently, where geography was a distinct subject.[1]

Sir Humphrey Gilbert, c. 1572, proposed for the projected Queen Elizabeth's Academy a second mathematician to teach cosmography and astronomy with navigation at a salary of £66 13s. 4d. In 1615 Sir George Buck, in his *Third University of England,*[2] names geography as a subject of instruction to be obtained within the public colleges in London. Sir Francis Kynaston, in his *Museum Minervae,* 1635, says : " The Professor of Astronomy shall teach Astronomy, Optics, Navigation, Cosmography." Sir Balthazar Gerbier, in his encyclopædic Academy at Bethnal Green in 1648, included geography and cosmography in the course, and himself prepared a lecture on the subject, which he published in 1649. His basis is the Ptolemaic system, and apparently his method is chiefly astrological.

There are indications that geography was coming

---

[1] *See* p. 103 *infra.*

[2] " Or Treatise of all the Foundations of all the Colledges, auncient Schooles of Priviledge and of Houses of Learning and liberal Arts within and about the most famous Cittie of London."

into the people's schools, as well as in the Universities, academies, and private education of nobles. For instance, Comenius (1592–1670) in the Vernacular School requires pupils to learn the chief things in cosmography, " as the rotundity of the heavens, the globe of the Earth hanging in the midst, the movement of the Ocean, the various straits of Seas and Rivers, the chief Divisions of the World, the chief Kingdoms of Europe ; but, above all, the Cities, Mountains, and Rivers of their Fatherland, and whatsoever is memorable therein."

In his *Reformed School* (1650), John Dury requires an outline of geography to be taught in schools.

George Snell, in 1649, requires the pupil in the non-Latin or English school to go on to the " excellent art " of cosmography and the " delightful use " of topography.

There is no evidence to show that Thomas Farnaby taught geography in his Grammar School at Martock in Somersetshire or at his private school in Goldsmith's Rents in Cripplegate, but he was at least well qualified by travelling experience to do so. For in 1595 he accompanied Sir Francis Drake and Sir John Hawkins in their last voyage, and afterwards, it is said, he was a soldier in the Low Countries.

As to public grammar schools I can only find a single definite reference :

"Geography. Westminster School. Laud's transcript of
    Studies 1621–8. 4th and 7th forms.

  "After supper (in summer time) they were called to the Mr's Chamber (spec. those of the 7th forme) and there instructed out of Hunter's *Cosmographie* and practised to describe, and find out cities and counties in the mappes."

The book referred to is the following:

> *Cosmographiae Introductio cum quibusdam Geometriae ac Astronomiae principiis ad eam rem necessariis. MDXXXIII Mense Julio. Venetiis per Jo. Antonium et Fratres de Sabio, sumptu et requisitione D. Melchioris Sessae.* (In prose, with illustrations.)
>
> *Rudimentorum Cosmographicorum Joan. Honteri Coronensis libri III cum tabellis Geographicis elegantissimis.*
>
> *De variarum rerum nomenclaturis per classes liber I Tiguri apud Froschoverum Anno MDXXVIII.* (Four books in verse. With maps.)
>
> *Rudimenta Cosmographica. Tiguri apud Froschoverum.* Anno MDXLVI. (Same as above.)

In an edition printed at Prague in 1595, there appears an index of provinces, mountains, rivers. The combination of text-book and atlas, although the book was in Latin, made it very popular.

Sir William Petty (1647) suggests for his *Gymnasium mechanicum* " the fairest globes and geographical maps of the best descriptions ; and, so far as is possible, we would have this place to be the epitome or abstract of the whole world."

Charles Hoole (1660) in describing the foundation of a Grammar School suggests that : " In the uppermost story there should be a fair, pleasant gallery wherein to hang maps and set globes, and to lay up such rarities as can be gotten in presses or drawers, that the scholars may know them." Now, Hoole had had in hand the writing of his *New Discovery of the Old Art of Teaching School* [1] for many years,

---

[1] Cf. Bacon on *Advancement of Learning*, bk. ii. Address to the King : " We see spheres, globes, astrolabes, maps and the like have been provided (in Colleges) as appurtenances to astronomy and cosmography, as well as books."

and we may safely conclude from the above suggestion that maps and globes were part of the equipment of some of the more progressive and leading schools, both public and private. In the account of Winchester College formerly ascribed to Christopher Johnson,[1] there is a reference to a conspicuous object on the north wall of the school. This is identified with the item in the Bursar's book for **1656-7** of £1 17s. 6d. paid for a Mappa Mundi for the School. In absence of positive knowledge we should not be justified in supposing that modern geography was systematically taught in any English schools until the eighteenth century. In the Mathematical School of Christ's Hospital in **1705**, a good pair of globes were bought at the cost of £5 ; and for a model of a ship **23** guineas were paid.[2] But the case of Westminster, and Hoole's requisition of maps and globes, probably are indications of occasional interest in the teaching of modern geography. Incidentally, no doubt, geography was touched upon, for the geographical interest was in the air. Comenius, for instance, called his realistic language manual the *Orbis Pictus*. Nor must it be forgotten that the Pilgrim Fathers and other

---

[1] Mr. J. S. Cotton in the *Wykehamist*, July, 1899, has shown good reason for believing that this account was written between 1650–1660. The passage quoted above about the map is confirmatory evidence. The date previously assigned by Bishop Christopher Wordsworth on the assumption that the account was written by Christopher Johnson was c. 1569.

[2] Pearce : *Annals of Christ's Hospital*, p. 123.

emigrants from England had brought into the general consciousness some recognition of cosmographical relations in almost every town and village of the land. As to classical geography instruction must have been constantly given to some extent in the schools. Not perhaps as a set lesson, but in the favourite manner of the age, in explanation of classical allusions. In fact, Hoole suggests that any good school should have as a subsidiary book—in its higher form library —*Ferrarius' Lexicon Geographicum, Poeticum et Historicum* (Lond. 1657). Nor was the scholarly schoolmaster ignorant of Pomponius Mela, Solinus and Dionysius. John Milton, in his Tractate, thought the pupil even might read in the original Greek these very treatises of Pomponius Mela and Solinus. But, in addition, he thinks when studying agriculture it will be " seasonable for them to learn, in any modern author, the use of the Globes and all the maps ; first with the ancient, and then with the modern names."

Apparently of the ancient geographers, Pomponius Mela, Strabo, Solinus, there was no Greek text printed in England up to the end of the Commonwealth. But there were numerous foreignprinted editions, and there can be no doubt that these books were more or less frequently sold in England, [1] in Greek and in Latin, Mela probably most frequently in Graeco-Latin editions. It was not till 1587 that Casaubon published the definitive

---

[1] As early as 1520, in the Day Book of John Dorne, a copy of Pomponius Mela is entered as sold at 4d.

text of Strabo, though a Latin translation had been published as early as 1469, and the Greek text had been issued by Aldus at Venice in 1516. There had been, however, translations into English of Pomponius Mela in 1585, and of Solinus[1] in 1590, both by Arthur Golding. The two were published together in 1590 with the following title :

> *The Rare and Singular worke of Pomponius Mela, That excellent and worthy Cosmographer, of the situation of the world, most orderly prepared, and devided every parte by itself ; with the Longitude and Latitude of everie Kingdome, Regent, Prouince, Rivers, Mountaines, Citties, and Countries Whereunto is added, that learned worke of Julius Solinus Poly histor, with a necessarie Table for this Booke ; Right pleasant and profitable for Gentlemen, Marchaunts, Mariners and Trauellers. Translated into Englyshe, By Arthur Golding, Gentleman. London. 1590 (quarto).*

With Dionysius the case is somewhat different. There was a Greek text [2] published at Eton in (?) 1607. An edition claiming closer attention is that of 1658, of William Hill, provided with a complete apparatus of the grammar and rhetorical figures of Dionysius

---

[1] Solinus is a writer on what we call Natural History but he is regarded in this period as a geographer.

[2] With *Dionysius*, also, in England an English translation preceded the Greek text. In 1572 appeared :

> *The Surueye of the World, or Situation of the Earth, so much as is inhabited. Comprising briefely the generall partes thereof, with the names both new and olde, of the principal countries, etc. . . . Now Englished by Tho. Twine Gentl. Imprinted at London by Henry Bynnemann. 1572. (Octavo.)*

together with a voluminous commentary on the geography. William Hill explicitly declares that his work is compiled *ad usum tyronum*. So, here, at last we have a genuine school-book devised for classical schools, containing a Greek text with Latin translation on the opposite page, and of course with the notes in Latin. Hill was a Fellow of Merton College, Oxford, 1639, M.A. 1641, and later on D.D. of Dublin University. He became Head Master of Sutton Coldfield Grammar School, 1640, and afterwards practised medicine in London. At the time of publishing *Dionysius*, he was Head Master of the school of St. Patrick's, Dublin, and after the Restoration, he kept a boarding school for the children of gentlemen. The Regius Professor of Greek in Cambridge, Ralph Widdrington, supplied a prefatory Greek poem to Hill's *Dionysius*. A long poem of Latin hexameters by the scholarly James Duport is also prefixed. William Dugard, the Head Master of Merchant Taylors' School, also furnished a most appreciative Latin poem, in which he says that Mantua boasts of Vergil, Verona of Catullus, the Appulean territory claims Horace and the seven cities, Homer. But the whole world loves Hill. We cannot but wonder if Dugard introduced, at least occasionally, the new " erudite " Geography of *Dionysius*—with its clean-cut, neat, and graphic copper-plate maps to the notice of his higher forms at Merchant Taylors' School. Anthony à Wood says that Hill's *Dionysius* " was used in many schools and by most juniors of the University of Oxford."

ROBERT BURTON ON GEOGRAPHY

The following is the full title of Hill's book:

ΔΙΟΝΥΣΙΟΥ ΟΙΚΟΥΜΕΝΗΣ ΠΕΡΙΗΓΗΣΙΣ

> *Dionysii Orbis descriptio. Commentario Critico et Geographico (in quo controversiae pleraeque quae in veteri Geographia occurrunt explicantur, et obscura plurima elucidantur) ac Tabulis illustrata. Guilelmo Hill, A.M., Collegii Merton, in Academia Oxoniensi olim Socio ; jam vero Gymnasiarcha Dubliniensi.*

> *Textui etiam subjungitur figurarum quae apud Dionysium occurrunt (cum Dialectis et aliis Grammaticis minutiis) systema, in usum tyronum ; ut non modo philologis et Geographicae studiosis verum et scholis inserviatur, in quibus Geographia vetus, Historiae lux, una cum poesi Graeca ex hoc fonte imbibi poterit. Londoni, excudebat R. Daniel.* 1658. Also 1659, 1663, 1679.

A geography of ancient Italy, founded on close study, had been published by Cluverius in 1624, " which has ever since been the great repertory of classical illustration in this subject." [1]

The number of foreign writers on geography, known in England, is amazingly large—probably the best idea can be formed by reading the following passage from Robert Burton's *Anatomy of Melancholy*, 1622 :

Methinks it would well please any man to look upon a geographical Map, *suavi animum delectatione allicere, ob incredibilem rerum varietatem et jocunditatem, et ad pleniorem sui cognitionem excitare*, Chorographical, Topographical Delineations to behold, as it were, all the remote Provinces, Towns, Cities of the World, and never to go forth of the limits of his study, to measure by the scale and compass their extent, distance, examine their site. . . . What greater pleasure can there now be than to view those elaborate Maps of Ortelius, Mercator, Hondius,

---

[1] Hallam, ii, p. 390.

etc. To peruse those books of Cities, put out by Braunus and Hogenbergius ? To read those exquisite descriptions of Maginus, Muster, Herrera, Laet., Merula, Boterus, Leander, Albertus, Camden, Leo Afer, Adricomius, Nic. Gerbelius, etc. ? Those famous expeditions of Christopher Columbus, Amerigo Vespucci, Marcus Polus, the Venetian, Lod. Vertomannus, Aloysius Cadamustus, etc. ? Those accurate diaries of Portugals, Hollanders, of Bartison, Oliver à Nort, etc., Hakluyt's *Voyages*, Pet. Martyr's Decades, Benzo, Lerius, Linschoten's *Relations*, those Hodoeporicons of Jod. a Meggen, Brocard the Monk, Bredenbachius, Jo. Dublinius, Sandys, etc., to Jerusalem, Egypt, and other remote places of the world? those pleasant Itineraries of Paulus Hentznerus, Jodocus Sincerus, Dux Polonus, etc., to read Bellonius' Observations, P. Gillius, his Surveys ; those parts of America set out, and curiously cut in pictures by Fratres a Bry. . . . What more pleasing studies can there be than the Mathematics, theoric or practic parts ? as to survey land, make Maps, Models, Dials, etc., with which I was ever much delighted myself.

It is surprising to find the small number of short treatises on geography until the latter part of the eighteenth century, when scraps of geography teaching and the use of the globes became a recognised subject of teaching in girls' schools. In history we have seen there was a copious supply of scrappy books. The amount of geographical knowledge was, in the mass, considerable. The geographical interest was great, if we take into account the various aspects, of travelling, descriptions or " histories " as they were called of various countries, of the geometrical and astronomical treatment of the " spheres," the " natural history " and " civil history " which were then component parts of geography, or at any rate of cosmography. Perhaps the very diversity of interests of the subject made short treatment difficult. But, on the other hand, the large folios of the current cosmographies were prohibitive in size and price, if for no other reasons, from allowing the fascinating subject to reach the school curriculum. And, further, like other modern subjects, cosmography and geography were " crowded out " by the vast developments of Latin and Greek with their authors, grammars, rhetorics, etc., excepting, once more, in all probability, the " allusive " aspects of classical authors required geographical as they required historical treatment in the class-room.

To the modern mind, it is startling to find the reference to the use of geographical study for the purposes of oratory or composition. But the subject is thus recommended by Erasmus in his *de Conscribendis Epistolis :* " There is a vast body of facts concerning geographical phenomena, some of which are extraordinary, and these are of peculiar value to the scholar ; though even the usual occurrences of nature are not to be passed over. These, again, are partly drawn from antiquity, partly are within our own experience. I refer to rivers, springs, oceans, mountains, precious stones, trees, plants, flowers ; concerning all of which comparisons should be derived and stored away in memory for prompt use in description or argument." [1]

Such natural history as had a geographical bearing was therefore not entirely neglected. One of the books recommended for the sixth form by Hoole was Pliny's *Historiae naturales*. The *Polyhistor* of Solinus

---

[1] *See* Woodward's *Erasmus*, p. 143.

which, as we have seen, had been translated into English by Golding, was largely a collection from Pliny. Of Pliny, there was the well-known translation of Philemon Holland, published first edition, 1601 ; second in 1634. But, again, it is clear that such a book must have been available in necessarily but very few schools, and then probably was chiefly used for the purpose of getting material for the Latin themes, which were required from the school-boys on all sorts of subjects, and regarded as opportunities for collecting all kinds of out-of-the-way information, such as Pliny would supply to the great delight of schoolmasters such as Hoole and Farnaby.

Comenius, in his *Schola Infantiae*, i.e., the education of the child up to six years of age, observes, with the penetration which justifies the title which has been given him of " father of educational method " : " The elements of geography will begin during the course of the first year and thenceforward, when children begin to distinguish between their cradles and their mother's bosom." Then in their early years, " they should discover what a field is, what a mountain, forest, meadow, river." [1] For any advance on this application of psychology to geographical training we should have to pass from the age of the Commonwealth until we reach the age of Locke and Rousseau.

There are rare indications of the beginning of

---

[1] Similarly Comenius suggests : " The beginning of history will be to remember what was done yesterday, what recently, what a year ago."

modern elementary geographical practice, such as *Heimat-Kunde* [1] and the school journeys.

For example, Hezekiah Woodward (1590–1675), one of those private schoolmasters who showed such valuable initiative in educational work in the time of the Commonwealth, clearly has the modern idea of *Heimat-Kunde*. Woodward[2] has a chapter on " Occasional Instructions from observations of things within doors and without." Woodward insists that the most ordinary events and routine of the house may serve as occasions for lessons. For instance, observe the maid " scumming the pot " or scraping the trenchers and washing the dishes. It is true that the lessons on those subjects in which Woodward particularly lays stress are for the purpose of moral inculcations. Still, he has the merit of drawing attention to the observation of objects close at hand, and " near " as Herbart says, to the child. In this way he would have the attention of children called to the hens, to the swine, sheep, the stable with a horse," higher than a lion though not so strong " and the ox. " Go we now to the barn to observe the least grain . . . to the garden now . . . so, in the orchard." In all cases, he is searching for physical objects, in and around the house, as far as the mill and the church with a view to presenting, graphically, moral analogues.

In connexion with the famous school at Mantua in the fifteenth century, Vittorino da Feltre

---

[1] *Heimat-Kunde*. The *Orbis pictus* of Comenius supplies examples.

[2] Chap. vii, *A Gate to the Sciences*, 1641.

instituted a school journey in the summer months to the castle of Goito.[1]

In England, Milton, in the short *Tractate* (1644), which abounds in suggestions which have been felt to soar to the empyrean of culture, far beyond the school-reach, at least touches solid ground in the delightful suggestion of the school journey, which is to be carried out with Miltonic largeness of scale and Miltonic enterprise of patriotism. We must regard his suggestions as falling upon the minds of a generation familiar with the journey[2] of the Grand Tour of Europe as a part of the nobleman's education. Milton applies the idea to a Tour through England, transferring the magnanimity in the continental enterprise to the journey over the Native Land.

In those vernal seasons of the year, when the air is calm and pleasant, it were an injury and sullenness against nature not to go out and see her riches, and partake in her rejoicing with Heaven and Earth. I should not, therefore, be a persuader to them of studying much then after two or three year that they have well laid their grounds, but to ride out in companies, with prudent and staid guides to all the quarters of the land ; learning and observing all places of strength, all commodities of building and of soil, for towns and tillage, harbours and ports for trade. Sometimes taking sea as far as to our navy, to learn there also what they can in the practical knowledge of sailing and of sea-fight. These ways would try all their peculiar gifts of Nature, and if there were any secret excellence among them, would fetch it out and give it fair opportunities to advance itself by, which could not but mightily redound to the good of this nation, and bring into fashion again those old admired virtues and excellencies, with far more advantage now in this purity of Christian knowledge.

---

[1] *See* Woodward's *Vittorino*, p. 66.
[2] *See* Excursus ii to this chapter, p. ▨ *et seqq.*

Footnote 2: the page number should read 128.

REPRESENTATIVE LIST OF ENGLISH
GEOGRAPHICAL BOOKS TO 1660

Map of England. 1520. Folio. Wynkyn de Worde. *See* Ames, *Typ. Antiq.* vol. ii. p. 244.

Mappa Mundi. Otherwise called the Compasse, and Cyrcuet of the Worlde, and also the Compasse of euery Ilande, comprehendyd in the same. B. L. R. Wyer (London, 1535 ?). 8vo.

Cuningham (William), M.D. :
> *The Cosmographical Glasse, conteyning the Pleasant principles of Cosmographie, Geographie, Hydrographie, or Navigation.* (With a map of Norwich and other woodcuts.) J. Day. 1559, fol.

Saxton (Christopher) :
> 35 coloured *Maps of England and Wales.* London, 1579, fol.

Twyne (Thomas), M.D. (Translation of *Dionysius*) :
> *The Survey of the Worlde, or Situation of the Earth, so much as is inhabited ; comprising briefly the generall appearance thereof, with the names both new and olde, of the principal countries, etc., first written in Greeke by Dionese Alexandrine, and now Englished,* etc. London, 1572, 8vo.

P., (D.) :
> *Certaine brief and necessarie rules of Geographie, serving for the understanding of chartes and Mappes,* Collected by D. P. B. L. H. Binneman, London, 1573, 8vo.

Twyne (Thomas), M.D. :
> *The Breviary of Brytane,* 1572.
> *The Wonderful Workmanship of the World.* 1578.

Pomponius Mela. Translater : Arthur Golding :
> *The Rare and Singular Worke of Pomponius Mela, That excellent and worthy Cosmographer, of the situation of the worlde, most orderly prepared and devided every parte by itselfe ; with the Longitude and Latitude of everie Kingdome, Regent, Province, Rivers, Mountaines, Citties and Countries.* London, 1585, 4to, and 1590.

Blunderville (Thomas) :
>   *A Briefe Description of universal mappes and cardes,
>   and of their use ; and also the use of Ptholemy his
>   Tables,* etc. B. L. R. Ward, 1589, 4to.
>   *M. Blunderville, his Exercises, containing Sixe
>   Treatises verie necessarie to be read and learned by all
>   young Gentlemen that . . . are desirous to have know-
>   ledge as well in Cosmographie, Astronomie, and Geo-
>   graphie, as also in the Arte of Navigation,* etc. B. L.
>   J. Windet, 1594, 4to. Also 1597, 1613, 1622, 1636.

Torquemada (Antonio de). (Translated by Ferdinando
>   Walker) :
>   *The Spanish Mandevile of Miracles, or the Garden
>   of Curious Flowers ; wherein are handled sundry
>   Points of Humanity, Philosophy, Divinity and Geography,
>   beautified with many strange and pleasant histories.*
>   London, 1600, 4to.

Abbot (George), Archbishop of Canterbury :
>   *Geography, or a Brief Description of the whole World,
>   wherein is particularly described all the Monarchies,
>   Empires and Kingdoms of the same, with their Aca-
>   demies.* London, 1617, 4to, 1636, 1642, 12mo ; 1664,
>   8vo.

Heylyn (Peter) :
>   *Microcosmus, or a little description of the great
>   world.* Oxford, 1621. Afterwards expanded into
>   *Cosmographie,* etc., p. 125 *et seqq infra.*

Carpenter (Nathaniel) :
>   *Geography delineated forth in two Bookes. Containing
>   the sphaericall and topicall parts thereof.* J. Lichfield
>   and W. Turner. ·. . for H. Cripps. Oxford, 1625,
>   4to. Also 1635. *See* p. 117 *infra.*

Pemble (William) :
>   *A briefe introduction to Geography containing a
>   description of the grounds and generall part thereof,*
>   etc. J. Lichfield for E. Forrest. Oxford, 1630, 4to.

Stafforde (Robert), Geographer :
>   *A Geographical and Anthologicall description of all
>   the empires and kingdomes in this terrestriall globe,* etc.
>   N. Okes for S. Waterson. London, 1634, 4to.

Line 27, under Heylyn: delete *et seqq*

Hues (Robertus) :
>A Learned Treatise of Globes, both celestiall and terrestriall. . . . Written first in Latine. . . . Afterward illustrated with notes, by J. J. Pontanus. And now . . . made English. . . . By J. Chilmead, etc. Printed by the Assigne of I. P. for P. Stephens and C. Meredith. London, 1638, 8vo.

Roberts (Lewis) :
>The Merchants' Mappe of Commerce : wherein the Universal Manner and Matter of Trade is compendiously handled, etc. 3 parts. Printed by R. O. for R. Mabb. London, 1638, fol.

Nassir Eddin :
>Tabulae Geographicae. Arab. Lat. a Jo. Gravio. London, 1652, 4to.

Ferrarius Philippus Alexandrinus :
>Lexicon Geographicum (published first at Milan, 1627), et exactum cum Tab. Long. ac Lat. London, 1657, fol.

Dionysii Orbis Descriptio. Translated by William Hill. 1658. See p. 46.

Further names of authors and books on geography, including maps, globes, dialling, may be found in W. Clavell's *Catalogue of Books*, London, 1675.

EXCURSUS I

TWO GEOGRAPHICAL BOOKS

I NATHANIEL CARPENTER [1]

>Geography Delineated forth in Two Bookes Containing the Sphaericall and Topicall Parts thereof. By Nathaniel Carpenter, Fellow of Exeter College in Oxford,

---

[1] Nathaniel Carpenter was born 1589 and died about 1628. Matriculated S. Edmund Hall, Oxford, 1605. Fellow of Exeter, 1607 ; M.A., 1613 ; D.D., 1626. He became, at Dublin, schoolmaster of the King's Wards in Ireland, i.e. minors with estates left to them from Roman Catholic parents. (*See Dict. Nat. Biog.* under *Carpenter.*)

Ecclesiast. 1. *One generation cometh and another goeth, but the Earth remaineth for ever. Oxford, Printed by John Lichfield and William Turner, Printers to the famous University for Henry Cripps. An. Dom.* 1625. 4to.

The first book is occupied with mathematical Geography, and deals with the following subjects. The matter and form of the terrestrial globe ; the conformity of parts in the constitution of the terrestrial sphere ; the partial magnetical affections in the sphere of the earth ; the total motions magnetical ; the site, stability and proportion of the earth ; the circles of the terrestrial sphere ; the artificial representation of the terrestrial sphere ; the measure of the terrestrial globe ; zones, climates and parallels ; the inhabitants of the terrestrial sphere ; longitudes and latitudes ; distances of places compared with one another.

The interest of Carpenter's book lies in two directions. 1. It gives a valuable and inclusive outlook on the whole field of geographical study in his day. 2. It contemplates geography as a study having a considerable number of points of contact and connexion with other subjects. It is the second of these aspects that the following passages are intended to illustrate.

Navigation necessary for increase of Knowledge as well as of riches. The promotion of religion and sciences . . . cannot well be achieved without sea-voyages or navigation. For the former we need go no farther than the holy Scripture which gives large testimony of such voyages. In the Old Testament as well as in the New, we have recommended to all posterity the industry of the Queen of Saba, who is said to have come from the uttermost parts of the earth to hear the wisdom of Solomon. And how should the Gospel of Christ have been divulged to diverse nations, had not the apostles dispersed themselves, and passed the sea in ships, to convey their sacred message to diverse nations and kingdoms ? neither is it less evident in the propagation of learning and human sciences. First, out of the example of many and famous worthy philosophers, who travelled far to converse with learned men of other nations, to enrich their minds with knowledge. Secondly, out of the first propagation of learning into our parts ; which we shall find (as it were) foot by foot to follow navigation. Hence we see that from the Hebrews and Chaldees it was derived to the Tyrians, from them to the Egyptians ; so to the Romans, and thence to most parts of Europe. [1]

Carpenter's Comparison of East and West in Learning.

Of the happy endowments of Europe, Asia, and a good part of Africa, both in arts liberal and mechanical, state, policy, magnificence, and religion, we have often spoken, and need make no repetition. To this if we compare America, being (as it were) the only portion of this (the Western) Hemisphere, we shall amongst them find few or no Arts either invented or taught, the use of letters scarce ever known ; state and magnificence little regarded, and the light of Christian religion scarce ever seen, or at least through the dim clouds of Roman superstition. He that would know more in this matter let him read Peter Martyr, Cortesius, Acosta and others, of the natural disposition of the people of America. [2]

Carpenter becomes eloquent when dealing with the description of his native county Devon, as illustrating his " theorem " that *mountain people are for the most part more stout, warlike and generous than those of plain countries, yet less tractable to government.*

---

[1] pp. 136–7.   [2] pp. 251–2.

MODERN SUBJECTS IN ENGLISH SCHOOLS

The Praise of Devon. [1]

Who hath not known or read of that prodigy of wit and fortune, Sir Walter Rawleigh, a man unfortunate in nothing else but the greatness of his wit and advancement ? Whose eminent worth was such, both in Domestic Policy, Foreign Expeditions, and Discoveries, Arts, and Literature . . . which might seem at once to conquer both example and imitation. For valour and chivalrous designs by sea, who reads not without admiration of the acts of Sir Francis Drake, who thought the circuit of this earthly globe too little for his generous and magnanimous ambition ? Of Sir Richard Grenvill, who undertaking with so great a disadvantage so strong an enemy ; yet with an undaunted spirit made his honour legible in the wounds of the proud Spaniard : and at last triumphed more in his own honourable death, than the other in his lax conquest ? Of Sir Humphrey Gilbert, Sir Richard Hawkins, Davies, Frobisher and Captain Parker, with many others of worth, note, and estimation, whose names live with the Ocean ?

After citing many further names, and comparing the attractions of the metropolis, a common receptacle of the most selected wits, with the country (affording as it does " estimation sooner than sufficiency "), Carpenter gives his reason for dwelling so long on the delights of Devon and her worthies.

Dialect - speakers may be as keen-witted as townsfolk.

Yet should I not have spun out this theme so long, but to stop their mouths, who being sooner taught to speak than understand, take advantage of the rude language and plain attire of our countrymen, admiring

---

[1] p. 261. (The passage given is only a portion of what Carpenter has to say on this subject.)

nothing more than themselves or the magnificent splendour of their own habitation ; as though all the wit in the world were annexed to their own schools, and no flowers of science could grow in another garden. But a rude dialect being more indebted to custom than nature, is a small argument of a blockish disposition ; and a homely outside may shroud more wit than the silk-worm's industry. I have sometimes heard a rude speech in a frieze habit express better sense than at other times a scarlet robe : and a plain yeoman with a mattock in his hand speak more to the purpose than some counsellors at the bar.[1]

It may be added that Carpenter, overcome by his enthusiasm for Devon worthies, suddenly calls to mind that he is an Oxonian by adoption. He bursts forth into six pages of verse, and bitterly reproaches the University for not sufficiently advancing him.

---

[1] pp. 264–5. The idea was one which finds frequent expression in the seventeenth century. Milton's passage at once occurs to one's mind : " If a linguist have not studied the solid things in the languages he knows, as well as the words and the lexicons, he were nothing so much to be esteemed a learned man, as any yeoman or tradesman competently wise in his mother dialect only." Cf. also Preface to *Phraseologia Puerilis* of John Clarke (1638). " Many witty, smart, and emphatical expressions, drop sometimes out of vulgar mouths in familiar discourse, and daily in ordinary affairs, which a scholar may make excellent use of ; and it is pity they should be lost, or not laid up where he may know to find them again when he stands in need." In a note on *vulgar mouths,* Clarke adds : " Even ploughboys have phrases observable about their cattle, land, pastures, etc. (Clarke lived in the country at Fiskerton, five miles from Lincoln, where he was at one time Head Master of the Grammar School). So Artificers, Tradesmen, Labourers, etc. yea, Women, Servants, have fine significant expressions about household business," etc.

Footnote: line 8, the date is 1638.

Sea-borderers, as a rule, are wittier and have more knowledge than inlanders.

In our days every man can speak how much the industry of the Venetians, Spaniards, Hollanders, English, and Portugals have effected in both Indies, in trafficking with them, deriving together with their merchandize, much of their own knowledge and religion. But as the islanders and sea-bordering people have excelled the inland nations in skill and knowledge, so also in vices: which stands with reason, whether we ascribe it to their natural wit, or condition of life, or education. . . . Arts and sciences turned to the worst use become more dangerous than naked simplicity. [1]

In Carpenter's last chapter he treats " Of the dispositions of Inhabitants according to their Original and Education." By the " Original " he does not mean from the first stock of Adam and from the second stock of Noah (after the flood) because these springs are common to the race, but " the more immediate or special stock, whence they sprang, which is found to have no small power in the nature and temper of posterity."

The Original or First Dispositions.

In this connexion we must remember that:

1. Colonies transplanted from one region into another, far remote, retain a long time their first disposition, though by little and little they decline and suffer alteration.

2. The mixture of colonies begets in the same nation a greater disparity and variety of the inhabitants amongst themselves.

[1] p. 274.

GENERAL EFFECTS OF EDUCATION

Education as an agent in varying Dispositions.

Amongst all external causes of the change of dispositions there is none greater than education. For as a good nature is oftentimes corrupted with evil conversation, so an ill disposition with good institution hath in some sort been corrected. Education hath great force in the alteration of natural dispositions ; yet so as by accident remitted, they soon return to their former temper.

The Force of Institution.

The force of institution hath been so great that by some it hath been thought to equal, if not surmount, Nature ; whence they have termed it a second nature. For as we see all sorts of plants and herbs by good husbandry, to grow better, but left to themselves to grow wild and barren, so shall we find it, if not much more, in mankind ; which, though never so savage and barbarous, have by discipline been corrected and reformed, and though never so polite and civil, neglecting discipline, have degenerated, and grown barbarous.

Neglect of discipline amongst the Americans.

To this and to no other cause can we ascribe the present ignorance and barbarism of the Americans. Their descent being from Noah and his posterity, they could not at first but have some form of discipline, which afterwards, being by long process of time or uncertainty of tradition neglected and obliterated, they fell back into such ways, as their own depraved nature dictated or the devil maliciously suggested. [1]

Discipline renders nations less stout and courageous.

Various causes, but the chief :

I. *Religion* than which there is no greater curb to the courage ; not merely of itself but by accident. Because death being the greatest hazard of a soldier, religion gives a more evident apprehension and sense of the immortality of the soul of man, and sets before the eye of his understanding, as it were the images of Hell-pains and celestial

---

[1] p. 283.

joys, weighing in an equal scale the danger of the one and the loss of the other. Whereas, ignorant people, wanting all sense of religion, lightly esteem of either, holding a temporal death the greatest danger.

II. *The Severity of Discipline*

which, especially in the training up of youth, is mixed with a kind of slavery : without which our younger years are very untractable to taste the bitter roots of knowledge. This fear (as it were) stamped in our affections cannot but leave behind it a continual impression, which cannot suddenly be razed out, such as we find in us of our masters and teachers, whose friendship we rather embrace, than familiarity.

III. *Delight of the studious in contemplative studies.*

For people of knowledge must needs find a greater felicity in gifts of the mind, which is usually seconded with a contempt of external and military affairs.

IV. *Want of use and practice of military affairs in most commonwealths.*

Many states well established continue a long time without wars, neither molesting their neighbours, nor dissenting amongst themselves ; except very seldom, and that by a small army, without troubling the whole state ; whence the general practice being less known, becomes more fearful.[1]

Nevertheless, Discipline is desirable in a Captain or Statesman.

Forasmuch as it more strengthens the wit, than abates the courage of a nation. Neither is it properly said to break and weaken, but rather to temper and regulate our spirits. For it is not valour, but rather rashness or fierceness, which is not managed with policy and discretion. And although it hath sometimes been attended with notable exploits, as that of Alexander the Great, of the Goths, the ancient Gauls, and many other, yet shall we observe such conquests to be of small continuance. For what they achieved by strength, they lost for want of policy. So that it is well said by one : that moderation is the mother of continuance to states and kingdoms.

[1] p. 285.

II PETER HEYLYN. [1]

> *Microscosmus, or a little Description of the Great
> World. A Treatise Historicall, Geographicall, Politi-
> call, Theologicall.* 4to. By P(eter) H(eylyn), Oxford,
> 1621, 1625, 1627, 1629, 1631, 1633, 1636, 1639. In
> 1652 was published the much larger work : *Cosmo-
> graphie, in four Books, containing the Chorography and
> History of the whole World and all the principall King-
> doms, Provinces, Seas and Isles thereof.* [A very large
> folio volume.]   1657, 1664 (?), 1666, 1670, 1674 (?),
> 1677, 1682, 1703.

This book is dedicated to Prince Charles. In the
address to the reader in the third edition Heylyn
remarks that in the former edition he dealt with
" pettie chapmen, pedlers of history and geography."
Now he has read further " merchants of the best
sort." He has expanded all the departments of
the former work, in the " six integral parts " of
history, geography, policy, theology, chronology
and heraldry, and occasionally, too, there are
" diverse philological discourses." The general
Praecognita of geography give some interesting
details of Heylyn's view of geography. Geography
and history are like " the two fire-lights Castor and
Pollux, or like two sisters entirely loving each other

---

[1] Peter Heylyn (1600–1662) was Fellow of Magdalen
College, Oxford ; M.A., 1620 ; D.D. 1630. He relates, in
his Preface to the *Cosmographia*, that, on going to meet
certain charges before a Committee in the Courts of Justice,
on the way, he was taunted by the jeer : " Geography is
better than Divinity." He says that this gibe had its
influence in bringing him back to his younger geographical
studies (which had led to his *Microcosmos*, 1621) of thirty
years before, though in the Preface to the earlier work,
" I had obliged myself to deal no more " with geography.

and not without great pity, (I had almost said impiety) to be divided. So as that which Sir Philip Sidney said of Argalus and Parthenia :

> 'Her being was in him alone,
> And she not being he was none :'

may be as justly said of these two *Gemini*, history and geography."

One of the great merits and attractions of geography to the seventeenth-century was that it was " exceedingly useful " as Heylyn says to the reading of the Holy Scriptures. It helps in " discovering the situation of Paradise,[1] the bounds and borders of those countries mentioned in the Bible. Especially it elucidates the travels of the Patriarchs, Prophets, Evangelists, Apostles, yea of Christ himself, " not otherwise to be comprehended and understood, but by the help of geographical tables and descriptions." It is useful to *astronomers*, who learn " the different appearances of stars in several countries, their several influences and aspects ; their rising and setting according to different horizons. *Physicians* learn from geography the different temper of men's bodies, according to the climes they live in ; the nature and growth of many simples and medicinal drugs. To *Statesmen*, geography shows the "nature and disposition of those people with whom they negotiate : the bounds and borders both of their own kingdoms and the neighbouring countries, with the extent of their respective

---

[1] Cf. the account of Raleigh's *Historie of the World*, p. 60 *supra*.

dominions both by sea and land, without the exact knowledge of which there would be a perpetual seminary of wars and discords." To *Merchants, Mariners and soldiers*, " the several professors of which kinds of life find nothing more necessary for them in their several callings than a competent knowledge in geography which presents to them many notable advantages both for their profit and entertainment."

In his *Praecognita*, Heylyn gives definitions of geography,[1] the earth, continents, islands, etc. ; greater and lesser circles, parallels, and climates. He constructs a table of climates, framed from the commentaries of Clavius on the works of John de Sacro Bosco, and Hues : *On the Use of the Globes*. He then defines the various divisions of water, oceans, seas, straits, lakes, rivers, etc. Heylyn tells us clearly what is meant by cosmography. It is " compounded and intermixed of universal comprehension of natural and civil story, which by a proper distinct name, may be termed cosmography. It draws from natural history, or geography, the regions themselves and their commodities. From civil history, accounts of habitations, governments, manners. From mathematics, the climates, and configurations of the heavens, under which the coasts and quarters of the world do lie." Heylyn has apparently taken this account direct from Bacon, *Advancement of Learning*, Book ii.

---

[1] Geography (following Ptolemy), a "description of the whole earth, imitated by writing and delineation, with all other things generally annexed unto it."

Perhaps the best way of describing Heylyn's cosmography is to say that it is a body of geography in its natural, civil, historical and climatic aspects. He revels in statistics, episodes, anecdotes, and illustrative material. He knows the orders of knighthoods, he is able to compare the cathedrals and public buildings, he knows the names of distinguished dignitaries. In short, the work is encyclopaedic. In its thick folio form, with wide margins, well printed, matterful, 1,100 pages, it is replete with reference-matter in history and geography for all the known parts of the earth. The frequency of reprints is a tribute to its interest and attractiveness in a book of such great length and detail. It was a gentleman's book both from the costliness of its production and the leisure required for reading it.

EXCURSUS II

TRAVELLING AS A PART OF EDUCATION

On the whole, the gentleman of the period was desirous of showing that he was not a " scholar." His parents often declined to send him to a " public " school, and sometimes even to the University. For a youth would sometimes go direct to the Inns of Court from the hands of his private tutor, and though his education might not be so thorough in the classical authors, he would at least have wide knowledge, which would by no means be limited to the classics. Then he would travel. Travelling became an educational institution. The origin would seem to be connected with the scholar, who in the time of the Renascence worked his way to Italy at all costs and sacrifices. Erasmus, More, Grocyn, Linacre, and the other English scholars who visited Italy were, unconsciously, influential in popularising an interest in European countries amongst the cultured and wealthy of our nation. The pilgrimage to Italy was in the first place definitely for the purpose of receiving instruction from the most distinguished scholars. It was a means to an end. The wealthy man who had not been there himself wished his son to go, and sent him with a tutor, who was only too glad to get the opportunity of a knowledge of classical Italy on the spot. It thus became the custom for the young nobleman to travel, and it naturally happened some improved the opportunity ; some neglected to do so. The young noble became more attracted by the courtly arts than by the academic types of knowledge. Sir Thomas Wilson says in his *Art of Rhetoric* (**1553**) writing of any " noble personage " : " I may commend him for his learning, for his skill in the French, or in the Italian, for his knowledge in cosmography, for his skill in the laws, in the histories of all countries, and for his gift of enditing. Again, I may commend him for playing at weapons, for running upon a great horse, for charging his staff at the tilt, for vaulting, for playing upon instruments, yea, and for painting, or drawing of a plat." [1]

---

[1] The mention of drawing may be a reminiscence of Sir Thomas Elyot's *Gouvernour*. *See* p. 137 *infra*.

These pursuits were distinctly those of the nobles, and it was to promote these, that, in the first place, the young noble went abroad, in the wake of the older scholars who had gone for " scholarship " in the narrower sense. It is interesting to compare the above passage with one[1] which appears in Wilson's dedication prefixed to the translation of the *Olynthiacs* of Demosthenes (1570). Speaking of Cheke, Wilson says : " I did call to mind his care that he had over all the English men (when at Padua) to go to their bookes, and how gladly he did read (there) to me and others, certain orations of Demosthenes in Greek, the interpretation whereof I and they had then from his mouth."

We can thus see the two types of noble travellers, the one attracted to the courtly exercises and disciplines, the other inclined to learning. A third type would quickly develop, viz. those who (finding themselves in new surroundings, freed from local and national restraints) would confuse liberty with licence, and become a discredit to themselves and to their country. This type of Englishman would be regarded at home as corrupted by the foreigners, particularly when such degradation became a ground for further attack upon the Church of Rome. At any rate, the danger to morals of the travelling youth, who, for whatever cause, by the fault of himself or his national hosts, broke through moral and religious restraints, seriously raised the question whether foreign travel was educationally sound. Thus

---

[1] Quoted by Prof. J. E. B. Mayor in his edition of Ascham's *Scholemaster*, p. 223.

there is a letter from the Privy Council to Whitgift, in which the Council says : [1] " The Queen's Majesty found the daily inconvenience growing to the realm by the education of numbers of young gentlemen and others her subjects, in the parts beyond the seas ; where, for the most part, they are nourselled and nourished in Papistry." This was in 1580. Ascham, in 1570, in the *Scholemaster* was very decided against the youth travelling in Italy unless with a tutor of undoubted wisdom and " authority." For Ascham quotes the view of the Italians themselves : " *Inglese italianato e un diabolo incarnato*. They remain men in shape and fashion but become devils in life and condition ! " [2]

Richard Mulcaster, in the *Positions* (1581), asks why should we condemn whole nations for " particular misdemeanour," or for some error in some few youths, wish a general restraint ? Mulcaster, however, has doubts as to the necessity of travel. It is not necessary for " learning." " We have in learning (thanks be to God for the pen and the print !), as much at this day as any country needs to have ; nay even as full, if we will follow it well, as any antiquity itself ever had." If young gentlemen would buy libraries of books they could learn far better at home in their " standing studies " than they ever will in their " stirring residence," even if the desire of learning were the cause of their travel. For the youth to be justified in travelling, they must have an educational purpose, and must not let

---

[1] Mayor's edition of Ascham's *Scholemaster*, p. 222.
[2] *Ibid.*, p. 78.

merely wealth " egg them on to wander." The schoolmasters of the period, however, as a class were against travelling, though some teachers would recognise the ground for travelling stated negatively by Shakespere, who might indeed be addressing Ascham and Mulcaster :

> " Cease to persuade my loving Proteus ;
> Home-keeping youths have ever homely wits."

Peacham, in his *Compleat Gentleman*, (1622) is inclined to blame parents for the misjudging which sends the wrong children, or the right children at the wrong time, to serve as pages at court, or " to see the fashions in France and Italy."

A letter from James Howell to Dr. Fr. Mansell at All Souls' in Oxford, dated 5 Mar. 1618, puts the educational side of travel very concisely :

I am returned safe from my foreign Employment, from my three years' Travel ; I did my best to make what Advantage I could of the time, though not so much as I should ; for I find that Peregrination (well used) is a very profitable School ; it is a *running Academy*, and nothing conduceth more to the building up and perfecting of a Man.

Purchas in his Preface to his *Pilgrimes*, 1625, says :

As for Gentlemen, Travell is accounted an excellent Ornament to them. . . . I speak not against Travell, so usefull to usefull men. I honour the industrious of the liberall and ingenuous in arts, blood, education ; and to prevent the exorbitancies of the others which cannot travell farre, or are in danger to travell from God and themselves, at no great charge I offer a *World of Travellers* (his own volumes of the *Pilgrimes*) to their domestic entertainment, easie to be spared from their smoke, cup or butter-flie vanities and superfluities, and fit mutually to entertain them in a better Schoole, to better purposes.

Bishop Joseph Hall, in his *Quo Vadis* (1617), takes an adverse view of travelling for the youth : " I deal only with those that profess to seek the glory of a perfect breeding and the perfection of that which we call civility in Travel : of which sort I have (not without indignation) seen too many lose their hopes and themselves in the way ; returning as empty of grace and other virtues, as full of words, vanity, mis-dispositions." Hall accordingly draws attention to " the dangerous issue of (the travellers') curiosity."

The geographical side of travel was understood by Thomas Morrice, who wrote his *Apology for Schoolmasters* in 1619 :

When they travel, they may see the people, converse and confer with the better sort, perceive their natures, dispositions and manners, know their orders, laws and customs, behold the situations of the Cities, the flourishing Academies, the courses of the Rivers, the Castles, Fortresses and Havens, the fruitfulness and barrenness of the soil : And so further and furnish themselves, not only with the languages but also with the Geographical knowledge of those countries.

In 1642 James Howell published :

Instructions for Forreine Travell shewing by what cours and in what compasse of time, one may take an exact survey of the Kingdomes and States of Christendome, and arrive at the practicall knowledge of the Languages, to good purpose. Post motum dulcior inde Quies. . . . Lond. 1642. 12mo, pp. 284.

There was a second edition in 1650.

MODERN SUBJECTS IN ENGLISH SCHOOLS

Mr. W. B. Rye [1] mentions the following books on " method " in Travel :

> Robert Dallington : *Method for Travell*. 1598.
>
> Thomas Palmer : *Essay of the Meanes how to make our Travailes into Forraine Countries the more profitable and honourable.* Lond. 1606.
>
> *The Traveiler of Jerome Turler devided into two bookes. The first conteining a notable discourse of the maner and order of traveiling over-sea, or into strange and forrein Countreys. This second comprehending an excellent description of the most delicious Realme of Naples or Italy, etc.* (Translated from the Latin.) B. L. Lond. 1575.

Lord Bacon, in his Essay *Of Travel*, gives advice as to what should be brought to the notice of the travelling youth by his tutor. He further describes the profit which " is not to be missed." The youth, in the first place, must learn the language of the country. [2] He must study the " Card " (i.e. the Map) and a " Book describing the country." He must keep a diary. He must seek to associate himself with men of knowledge, e.g. secretaries and ambassadors. When a traveller returns, let him not altogether leave behind him the countries where he has travelled, but let him maintain a correspondence by letters with those of his acquaintance there

---

[1] In *England as seen by Foreigners.* 1865.

[2] This might seem to be sufficiently obvious, but in the sixteenth and also often in the seventeenth century, the really essential language was considered to be Latin, which of course was the international spoken language of the learned. *See English Grammar Schools, Latin-speaking,* chap. xix.

which are of most worth. Then let his travels appear in his discourse rather than in his apparel or gesture. And in his discourse let him be rather advised in his answers than forward to tell stories." Lord Bacon saw that the educational side of travel implied educational aims and methods, and his view held the field " with gentlemen " against the alarmists like Ascham and Mulcaster.

CHAPTER IV

THE TEACHING OF DRAWING[1]

THERE is little reference to Painting as a subject of an educational curriculum. Aristotle's saying that " Painting is silent poetry and poetry speaking painting " is, of course, quoted from time to time by Renascence writers.

In the Middle Ages, drawing and painting may be said to have been important subjects in the education of those who were to be employed in the illumination of manuscripts. In the scriptoria of the monasteries, therefore, such work was carried on and beautiful pictures produced, for which a course of training was clearly necessary. Calligraphy and miniature painting were closely connected, and this connexion, to the modern mind, strange and unreal, was bequeathed to the Tudors and Stuarts, as a survival. The calligraphy was accepted, the drawing and painting, as subjects of instruction, were not ordinarily studied. The fact is, that in the post-Renascence school curriculum there was no room for any subjects which did not bear directly on classical scholarship. The first voice raised in England after the Renascence on behalf of drawing was that of Sir Thomas Elyot in his *Boke called the Gouvernour* in **1531**. He considers

---

[1] e.g. Polydore Vergil, *de Inventoribus Rerum*, 1, 2, cap. 4.

that if a child is inclined by nature "to paint with a pen or to form images in stone or tin," he should receive instruction in those arts. Examples could be cited of excellent princes, who had been equal to actual artificers in painting and "carving" (sculpture). For those who had ability, instruction may be said to be necessary. He pointed out that drawing served for the devising of engines of war, for the survey of the adversary's country, for reconnoitring, for fixing on positions of advantage, and so on. "What pleasure and utility there is in being able to figure out in imagination what new buildings a man purposes to have constructed, and to so think out his plans that there shall ensue no repentance!"

Elyot realises that the pleasure of being able to picture a thing out may be associated with drawing. "When he (i.e. the one who has been trained in the art) happeneth to read or hear any fable or history, forthwith he apprehendeth it more desirously and sustaineth it better than any other that lacketh the said feat: by reason that he hath found matter apt to his fantasy. Finally, everything that portraiture may comprehend will be to him delectable to read or hear. And where the lively spirit, and that which is called the grace of the thing, is perfectly expressed, that thing more instructeth him than the declaration in writing or speaking doth the reader or hearer."

Elyot has seized the import of what modern writers call visualisation. He recognises that the graphic representation appeals with peculiar power

137

to the learner. He is no mere verbalist as it is sometimes asserted the men of the Renascence times were. There is a forecast of Comenius in Elyot's conviction of the importance of realistic teaching. For example, he says, in geometry, astronomy, and cosmography ("called in English 'the description of the world'")—in these studies, "I dare affirm a man shall more profit, in one week, by figures and charts, well and perfectly made, than he shall by the only reading or hearing the rules of that science by the space of half a year at the least ; wherefore the late writers deserve no small commendation which added to the authors of [in] those sciences, apt and proper figures." [1]

A fortiori, the argument proceeds, there will be a great gain to education if the pupil learns to draw for himself. Not that the author wishes to make a nobleman's son a common painter or sculptor, "which shall present himself openly stained or embrued with sundry colours, or powdered with the dust of stones that he cutteth, or perfumed with tedious savours of the metals by him yoten " (melted)—but he thinks drawing, carving, etc., excellences in themselves, in their training of the eye (like music, of the ear), and also because of their " adminiculation " (service) to the other serious studies.

---

[1] The discovery of America (by Columbus) in 1492, Newfoundland (by Cabot) in 1497, and the other Tudor enterprises of sea and land, add a special interest to this passage, written within forty years of those events.

This appreciation of the educational value of drawing and sculpture did not penetrate into the educational practice of the period. It is doubtful whether any instance can be produced of the actual inclusion of drawing in the curriculum of a grammar school in the Tudor period. [1]

Richard Mulcaster, perhaps the most independent and robust of all our English educational writers, is side by side with Sir Thomas Elyot in the recognition of the value of drawing. He went further than Elyot, in that he saw its place in the school curriculum, and boldly advocated that drawing should be a necessary subject for the elementary school. " Pen and penknife, [2] ink and paper, compass and ruler, a desk and a dust-box will set them (i.e. writing and drawing) both up, and in these young years, while the finger is flexible, and the hand fit for frame, it will be fashioned easily. And commonly they that have any natural towardness to write well, have a knack of drawing too." Intellectual judgments are made by the understanding in matters " exempt from sense." But in things perceivable by the senses, in questions of the " proportion and seemliness of

---

[1] *See* p. 148 *infra* as to Peacham in the Stuart period. John Brinsley (1612) saw the closeness of connexion between drawing and writing, but this did not lead him to advocate drawing as a school subject on its own account. He regarded it as an adjunct for the illustration of the writing lesson. *See* his *Ludus Literarius*, chap. iv.

[2] Mulcaster, *Positions*. Quick's Reprint, p. 34.

all aspectable things," "the assured rule" is this "quality of drawing by the pen and pencil." If drawing be thus valuable we ought "to ground that thoroughly in youth which must requite us again with grace in our age."

Mulcaster calls the ancient examples to witness. For he would be blind who "would contemn that principle, which brought forth Apelles, and so well-known a crew of excellent painters, so many in number, so marvellous in cunning, so many statuaries (i.e. sculptors), so many architects; nay (a subject) whose use all modelling, all mathematics, all manuaries do find and confess to be so notorious and so needful." But even if the suggestion were Mulcaster's alone, he urges that the "device" itself would show he deserved "not ill" in suggesting it.

But he can claim the authority of "the great philosopher Aristotle"[1] who "joineth writing and reading under the word γραμματική, with drawing by pen or pencil (as I translate his γραφική) both of one parentage and pedigree, as things peculiarly chosen to bring up youth, both for quantity in profit, and quality in use." Aristotle's argument is that writing and reading minister to "house-holdry," learning and public affairs. So Mulcaster adds that drawing by pen or pencil enables a man to judge what he buyeth of artificers and craftsmen "for substance, form, and fashion, durable and

---

[1] *Politics*, book viii, cap. 3.

handsome or no : and such other necessary services, besides the delightful and pleasant." [1]

So far, Mulcaster develops the educational warrant for drawing, in the *Positions* (1581). In the *Elementarie* (1582) he valiantly urges that the subjects of the *Elementarie* " be five in number " —reading, writing, singing, playing (instruments), and drawing. His reasons for the inclusion of drawing are somewhat different from those advanced in the *Positions*, and the following passage is the first suggestion in England for the universal teaching of drawing. It is therefore an educational pronouncement of high importance :

The plat and method for the principle of drawing.

This done I must teach how to draw. Which drawing because it is not so evidently profitable, nor so generally received, as writing and reading be, I will therefore prove in a pretty, short discourse both how profitable it is, and how it deserveth the learning, even for profit sake, besides many petty pleasures. Then because drawing useth both number and figure wherewithall to work, I will cull out so much numbering from out of Arithmetic, the mistress of numbers, and so much figuring out of Geometry, the lady of figures, as shall serve fit for an elementary principle to the child's drawing, without either hardship to fray him, or length to tire him. Whatsoever shall belong to colouring, to shadowing, and such more workmanly points, because they are nearer to the painter than to the drawing learner, I will reserve them to the after habit, and to the

---

[1] Mulcaster does not insist on including painting in the school course. Still if the child be by nature inclined to it, he " dare not condemn the famous fellowship of Apelles and others." For painting is " anciently allowed " and is so near a cousin (drawing he has stated to be " cousin german ") to the fairest writing, whose cradle-fellow it is.

students' choice, when he is to divert, and to betake himself to some one trade of life. At which time, if he chance to choose the pen and pencil to live by, this introduction then will prove his just friend, as he himself shall find when he feels it in proof. Last of all, forasmuch as drawing is a thing, whose thorough help many good workmen do use, which live honestly thereby, and in good degree of estimation and wealth, as architecture, picture, embroderie, engraving, statuarie, all modelling, all platforming, and many the like : besides the learned use thereof, for Astronomy, Geometry, Chorography, Topography, and some other such, I will therefore pick out some certain figures proper to so many of the foresaid faculties, as shall seem most fit to teach a child to draw, and withal I will show how they be to be dealt with even from their first point, to their last perfection, seeing it is out of all controversy, that, if drawing be thought needful, as it shall be proved to be, it is now to be dealt with, while the finger is tender, and the writing yet in hand, that both the pen and the pencil, both the rule and the compass may go forward together. [1]

Though Mulcaster's suggestion of drawing as a permanent and necessary part of the curriculum of the elementary school was not carried out in the Tudor and Stuart period, [2] it is not to be understood that drawing was entirely neglected as an educational discipline. Three considerations require mention : first, the introduction of illustration in books ; secondly, the flourishes and pen "free"-hand of the writing-masters ; thirdly, the place of drawing in connexion with arithmetic-schools.

---

[1] Mulcaster's *Elementarie*, p. 58.

[2] Drawing was first officially recognised in 1837 in the School of Design, established at Somerset House. The School was transferred to Marlborough House in 1852 and in 1856 to South Kensington, when the name was changed to the National Art Training School.

I. With regard to illustrations.

The printed book at first had no illustrations, though the earliest books were issued with spaces for the initial capital letters at the heads of chapters to be filled in with coloured illuminations. The first book with wood-cut illustrations is said to have been issued in 1467. Amongst the books most frequently illustrated were the *Horae*.

Of educational works Euclid was issued in 1482 by Ratdoft of Augsburg and the Geography of Ptolemy was supplied with maps in 1484 by Holl at Ulm. In England, the school grammar of John Holt called *Lac Puerorum*,[1] brought illustration to the aid of grammar. But the mathematical books were the chief educational books which received early illustration. It was with the teachers of mathematics that drawing was associated, ordinarily, when taught at all.

An epoch-making pronouncement on the importance of illustrations in school-books is hidden away in an *Epistolary Discourse*[2] of Eilhardus Lubinus, before his edition of the New Testament, in 1614. Lubinus says :

Let there be presented (by illustrations) and offered to the eyes, all household instruments, things belonging to smiths' or carpenters' craft, things appertaining to the country, war, shipping, fishing, hunting, tailoring, music, sewing, whatsoever is to be met with in the business of books or study, in man's body, and in all its parts and members ;

---

[1] Printed before 1496. *See* Lupton's *Colet*, p. 23 n.

[2] Translated from Lubinus (1614) by Richard Carew, and included in *The True and Readie Way to Learne the Latine Tongue*, edited by Samuel Hartlib (1654), p. 26.

all living creatures, four-footed beasts, birds, fishes, worms, insects, colours, herbs, trees, fruits, all womenly instruments, and those that belong to weaving, baking, riding, playing and building, etc. Lastly, all those things which are set before the eyes, which if they cannot conveniently be had in things themselves, surely they may be painted. Let younger ones (i.e. children) be brought to these things or to the images of things well known already from the contemplation of the things themselves, depainted in tables,[1] the namings of which things they shall first learn in their own, and then in the Latin, tongue, which will be sooner than one would think, effected.[2]

No doubt Lubinus's plan of teaching the child to learn languages by visualising the objects named from pictures, and thus associating things and words, was the source of the idea of Comenius' *Orbis pictus*.[3] The expression of the educational significance of illustration is Lubinus's own achievement. But the idea was suggested doubtless by the whole series of editions of illustrated Aesop's fables, illustrations to the Bible, and perhaps especially by the many books of emblems, an important class of books, which supplied the sixteenth and seventeenth centuries with much general information and food for reflection.[4]

II. A book like Cocker's *Plumae Triumphus*, or the *Pen's Triumph*, though professedly a text-book for writing, is also a book of free-hand flourishes, completing an intricate system of curves, which outline figures representing the Car of the Sun, with

---

[1] French, *tableaux*, pictures.
[2] The translation into English is that of Samuel Hartlib.
[3] *See* R. H. Quick : *Educational Reformers*, p. 166 n.
[4] *See* p. 198 *infra*.

Cocker as driver, all done in marvellous style and certainty of drawing, by an unbroken stroke of the pen. Old copies of this book show how children have delighted to either colour the figures or insert variations and deviations of Cocker's curves on their own account.

III. The Arithmetic or Cyphering Schools sometimes annexed drawing as a subject of their curriculum. In 1582 Robert Recorde undertook to teach pupils " to draw or reduce any map or card in true proportion from a great quantity to a small, or to bring a smaller to a greater." John Mellis, who edited the second edition of Recorde's *Ground of Arts* in 1607, was a schoolmaster in Southwark. In an epistle to Dr. Robert Forth which is included in the 1607 edition of Recorde's *Ground of Arts,* Mellis says :

The entire love and exercise of this excellent Art (Arithmetic), with drawing of proportions, Mappes, Cardes, Buildings, Plottes, etc., were the only studies whereunto I ever more have been inclined. Touching Drawing, it was only *Dei beneficio*, naturally given me from my youth, without instruction of any man, more than love thereof, delectation, desire, and practice. In this Art, also having great delight, I had no other instruction at my first beginning but only this good author's book, but afterwards I greatly increased the same during the time I served your Worship in Cambridge, in going to the Arithmetic lecture at the common school ; and more furthered since the time that I left your Worship's service, which is about eighteen years past, by continual exercise therein (the mother and nurse of science), during which time my only vocation hath been (thinking it a meet exercise for a commonwealth) in training up of youth to write and draw, with teaching of them the infallible principles and brief practices of this worthy science.

145

Perspective was thus a subject taught in the arithmetic schools and as a part of geometry. About 1572 Sir Humphrey Gilbert proposed to include drawing of maps, sea-charts, and perspective in the projected *Queen Elizabeth s Academy*. In Sir Francis Kynaston's *Musaeum Minervae*, planned in 1635, painting and sculpture were included as optional subjects. In the prospectus of Sir Balthazar Gerbier's *Academy* at Bethnal Green, in 1648, there were to be taught drawing, painting, limning and carving. These projected institutions were for noblemen and gentry, and in this connexion it may be remarked that Locke, in 1690, thought drawing should be studied, after writing, " as a thing very useful for a gentleman on several occasions and especially if he travel." But he is not to take up too much time over it.

In 1641, drawing had its protagonist in Hezekiah Woodward, who suggested that the subject fitted the child's nature and was therefore suitable for the elementary school. The following passage [1] of Woodward might have been written by Rousseau :

Observe him with his little stick puddering in the ashes, drawing lines there, or upon the dirt, where he can make an impression ; and almost as busy he is as one [2] was, who would not be driven from it with the sword. I will tell my observation. I have known some who were not taught to write, yet could draw faces of all sorts, bodies in due proportion ; frame several buildings, castles, ships, and the like. I mention it that parents and masters might be

---

[1] *A Light to Grammar*, p. 49.
[2] i.e. Archimedes.

persuaded to draw forth Nature, as you would do a piece of gold, it will spread and compass itself (as gold will) beyond an ordinary imagination. Let us follow nature here, for this drawing, whether with stick, or pen, is but cosen-german to writing, a pre-cognition or training principle thereunto. These two, (and *drawing* the most children do naturally) are of one parentage and pedigree as is noted by the Philosopher [i.e. Aristotle] and others.

In 1648, Sir William Petty planned his *ergastula literaria* (i.e. schools in which profitable manual labour should be encouraged and required as well as the ordinary school subjects). In his plan of studies he includes drawing as a subject of the curriculum for the elementary school. Petty intended these schools to be open to all, the poor as readily as the richer children. The first place in the education given by the school should be, in Petty's opinion, the cultivation of the observation and remembrance of all sensible objects and actions.

In no case [is] the art of drawing and designing to be omitted, to what course of life soever those children are to be applied ; since the use thereof, for expressing the conceptions of the mind, seems (at least to us) to be little inferior to that of writing ; and in many cases performeth what by words is impossible.

Snell,[1] in 1649, advocates the introduction of limning or drawing in the school, and thinks that time could be won for this and other subjects, if English instead of Latin were used as the medium of instruction.

There was one grammar schoolmaster, viz. Henry Peacham the younger, at one time Head

---

[1] *The Right Teaching of Useful Knowledge.*

Master of the Free school at Wymondham in Norfolk, who both learned drawing himself and apparently taught it to his boys. In the *Compleat Gentleman*, [1] 1622, Peacham says :

> From a child I have been addicted to the practice (of drawing) ; yet when I was young, I have been cruelly beaten by ill and ignorant schoolmasters, when I have been taking, in white and black, the countenance of some one or other (which I could do at thirteen and fourteen years of age, beside the map of any town according to geometrical proportion, as I did of Cambridge when I was of Trinity College and a junior sophister), yet *could they never beat it out of me*. I remember one master I had (and yet living not far from St. Albans) took me one time drawing out with my pen that pear-tree and boys throwing at it, at the end of the Latin Grammar, which he perceiving, in a rage struck me with the great end of the rod and rent my paper, swearing it was the onely way to teach me to rob orchards ; beside, that I was placed with him to be made a scholar and not a painter, which I was very likely to do, when I well remember he construed unto me the beginning of the first Ode in Horace—*edite* set ye forth, *Mœcenas* the sports, *atavis regibus*, of our ancient kings.

Peacham eloquently discourses on the usefulness of drawing and painting, and proudly claims that in ancient times, painting " was admitted into the first place among the liberal arts." He showed proof of his own devotion to drawing and painting by publishing " for the benefit of many young gentlemen who were my scholars for the Latin and Greek tongues," a book entitled :

> *The Art of Drawing with the Pen and Limning in water colours in* 1606. Afterwards this book was styled *Graphice, or the Most Ancient and Excellent Art of Drawing and Limning.* 1612.

---

[1] Chapter xii.

Nor were Petty[1] and Snell the only Commonwealth writers who saw the value of drawing. John Dury in 1650, in the *Reformed School* urged " that in the earliest period of education, i.e. before eight or nine years of age, children should be exercised in taking notice of all things offered to their senses, to know their proper names, to observe their shapes, and to make circumstantial descriptions thereof by word of mouth, and *painting in black and white.*" Petty, Snell, and Dury, therefore, are at the point of view of Mulcaster, but it may be noted that they had in mind rather the education of those who were not predominantly learning the classics, while Mulcaster's *Elementarie* was a course intended as preparatory to the Grammar School.

Christ's Hospital was apparently the first school to establish a department of drawing teaching. It was proposed in 1692 that the teaching of drawing should begin in the writing school so as to save the

---

[1] Wm. Petty (1632–1687) is said to have had a " fine hand in drawing and limning " and to have developed power in caricature. John Aubrey (1626–1697) says at eight years of age : " I fell then to drawing . . . and at nine (crossed by father and schoolmaster) to colours, having nobody to instruct me, [I] copied pictures." Aubrey also relates of Samuel Foster (*d.* 1652) at one time Usher at Coventry School, " in his lodging on the wall of his own hand-drawing is the best dial, I do verily believe, in the whole world." So, too, it is stated, that " the walls of the room in which Sir Isaac Newton lodged were covered with charcoal drawings of birds, beasts, men, ships, and mathematical figures." Brewster's *Life of Newton* (1875), p. 7. Aubrey notes early proficiency in drawing of Francis Potter, 1594–1678 ; Robert Hooke (1635–1703) ; Thomas Hobbes (1588–1679) ; Wenceslaus Hollar (1607–1677).

mathematical master's trouble later. [1] Experts were consulted about the inclusion of drawing. Amongst others, Sir Christopher Wren replied : " Our nations want not [a] genius but education in that which is the foundation of all mechanic arts, a practice in designing or drawing to which everybody in Italy, France and the Low countries pretends more or less."

A drawing master named Faithorne was appointed in 1693, at a salary of £20. He was found inefficient and the project of the drawing school was a failure—though afterwards it was revived.

REPRESENTATIVE LIST OF BOOKS ON DRAWING
TO 1660

> *A very proper treatise, wherein is briefly sett forthe the art of Limning, etc.* B. L. R. Tottil, London, 1573, 4to.

Haydocke (Richard) :
> *A tracte containing the Artes of curious Paintinge, Carvinge and Buildinge written first in Italian by Jo: Paul Lornatius (Lornazzo), painter of Milan and Englished by R. H., student in Physick.* Oxford, 1598.

Caus (Salomon de) :
> *La Perspective avec la Raison des ombres et miroirs.* J. Norton, London, 1612.

Author not named) :
> *The Gentleman's Exercise ; or an exquisite Practise, as well for Drawing all manner of Beasts in their true portraiture, as well as the Making of Colours, for Limning, Painting, Tricking and Blazoning Coats of Arms, etc.* 1630, 1634.

---

[1] *See* E. H. Pearce : *Annals of Christ's Hospital*, p. 159.

Bate (John) :

>   *Mysteries of Nature and Art in four parts, con-
>   cerning water-works, fire-works, drawing, washing,
>   limning, painting and engraving.* London, 1634, 1635.
>   4to. 1638, 1654.

J[ohn] W[ells], Esquire :

>   *Sciographia, or the Art of Shadowes. Demonstrat-
>   ing out of the sphere, how to project both great and
>   small circles, upon any Plane . . . with a new Conceit
>   of reflecting the Sunne beames upon a Diall . . . all
>   performed by the Doctrine of Triangles ; . . . by helpe of
>   Logarithmes.* By J(ohn) W(ells) Esquire, 1635.

Junius (Franciscus) :

>   *The Painting of the Ancients in three Bookes : Declaring
>   by Historicall Observations and Examples the Beginning,
>   Progresse, and Consummation of that most Noble Art.
>   And how those ancient Artificers attained to their still
>   so much admired Excellencie. Written first in Latine
>   by Franciscus Junius F. F. And now by Him Eng-
>   lished with some additions and alterations.* London,
>   1638. 4to.

Dacres (William) :

>   *Elements of Water Drawing,* 1660. 4to.

See also William London's list of *Books of the
Mathematics.* (1658.)

CHAPTER V

THE TEACHING OF PHYSIC AND NATURAL HISTORY

WITH AN *EXCURSUS* ON A MUSEUM OF CROMWELL'S TIME

As Charles Beard said, " We live in so full a sunlight of natural knowledge as often to fail to realise how modern a thing [science] is." [1] The recent triumphs of scientific investigation often dazzle and even blind us to previous efforts in science. Yet the struggle for truth in science was sometimes quite as keen in the earlier centuries as in our own. This will be recognised if we recall the sacrifices made in its search by a Roger Bacon, a Giordano Bruno, by a Galileo, or by a Campanella.

It is difficult to steer a way through the vexed questions arising as to the position of Aristotle in the study of science. Without going into detail it is necessary to realise that during the whole of the Middle Ages, at least portions of Aristotle's *Organum* were known. The *Organum* consists of Aristotle's combined treatises on Logic. It is so called because Aristotle called Logic ὄργανον ὀργάνων. By this expression he evidently intended to imply that it is the instrument of which use is to be made *as the*

---

[1] *The Reformation* (Hibbert Lectures), p. 384.

means to the acquisition of knowledge. Instead of this it was taken to mean, in the Middle Ages, that logic was " the best of all instruments " for the discovery of truth. Aristotle, therefore, was supposed to be opposed to the observation of facts.

Devotion to Aristotle's *Organum*, then, marks the first stage, historically, of Mediaeval Aristotelianism, i.e. it was the authoritative utterance, in accordance with which all theology and all philosophy were discussed. Boethius c. 510 A.D. gave portions of the *Organum* to Europe, in Latin, and Europe intellectually lived on these, as final authority, till about the middle of the twelfth century, by which time the whole of the *Organum* was known. Additional knowledge of the Aristotelian Logic increased its interest and gave it further impetus. Up to this period the basis of all intellectual discipline was logic. That is to say, logic was the basis of all psychological, metaphysical, theological questions. It is not, therefore, surprising to find that it was also the basis of all natural history, and of all subjects which we now call scientific. It is true that there was the term *Physica* [1] which included the formal knowledge of medicine, but this was part of the organic whole of knowledge, which was throughout penetrated by the Aristotelian Logic.

The second stage of Mediaeval Aristotelianism is reached in the middle of the twelfth century up to the first half of the thirteenth, when from Toledo

---

[1] T. C. Allbutt : Harveian Oration in 1900 on *Science and Mediaeval Thought.* This lecture contains an interesting survey of Mediaeval Science in its bearing on Medicine.

153

and other places there were poured forth into Europe Latin renderings of oriental ingatherings from the stores of the Arab physicians and philosophers. Amongst these were numerous MSS., either of Aristotle's writings, or scraps of the great philosopher interlarded with glosses and comments of learned Arabs. Thus after six or seven hundred years of stereotyped authoritative portions of Aristotle, a " new Aristotle " was forthcoming, which included works unknown from the sixth to the twelfth century. Amongst these works, particularly, were his physical writings, including the *Physica, de Coelo et Mundo, De Generatione et Corruptione,* and *Meteorologia,* etc. Along with the physical, or, shall we say, scientific writings of Aristotle, other Arabic forms of Greek writers appeared, e.g. Gerard of Cremona translated the *Almagest* (i.e. Astronomy) of Ptolemy, and some works of Galen and Hippocrates. Michael Scot early in the thirteenth century translated an Arabic abstract of Aristotle's *Historia Animalium.* Thus, then, there was a body of knowledge in questions of natural history, astronomy, and even mathematical and physical knowledge. As far as Aristotle was concerned, his use of observation with regard to natural phenomena was evident. But the Middle Ages were thoroughly ingrained with the idea that all acquisition of knowledge was solely based on dialectics, and ignored the observational side of knowledge.

This vast accretion of new material of thought from the Arabs produced an intellectual stimulus

which almost reached to a " revival of learning."
But the mental energy of the age took the direction
of subjugating the new material to the absolute
monarchy of dialectics. Physics and natural history fell into the old mediaeval discipline of argu-
mentation on generals and particulars, quite apart
from any reference to experience and observation.
The old torpor fell upon an extended territory.
The new Aristotle was absorbed in the old Aristotle,
and the two, with a single face, met the future, with
all branches of knowledge closed up within the
folds of their mantle.

One man, in this second stage, saw the significance
of the " new Aristotle " dealing with nature, and
stood out from his age as an independent thinker.

Roger Bacon is sometimes regarded as the only
English Mediaevalist who can be said to be a scientist at all. This is grounded on his actual original
work.[1] Further, in his *Opus Magnus* (c. 1255), he
says : " There are two ways of knowing, viz. by means
of argument, and *by experiment.*" As to the latter
he says : " If any man who never had seen fire,
proved by sufficient arguments that fire burns
and hurts and destroys things, the mind of the
listener would not by these means be set at rest,
nor would he avoid fire until he had placed his hand
or some combustible object into the fire, so that he
might try by experience what the argument was
teaching, but having gained the experience his mind

---

[1] e.g. the study of gases, a theory of combustion, a
theory of optics, a theory of mechanical locomotion and
the invention of gunpowder.

is made certain and rests in the splendour of truth for which experience, not argument, suffices." This exposition clearly announces the experimental method.

But Roger Bacon in these supreme moments of his work, must not be taken as the type of the Middle Ages. The study of the group of subjects we call science was continued on Aristotelian lines and by mediaeval developments of Aristotelian methods until the Italian Renascence. As mediaevally interpreted, orthodox methods ignored, and even forbade, the methods of observation and experiment, as avenues to a true interpretation of nature.

Turning to the subject-matter of science-teaching, apart from methods of development, it will be sufficient, as far as the Middle Ages are concerned, to take the curricula of the Universities (to which it will be remembered students went at an earlier age than is now the custom) at the end of that period. At Oxford in 1431 the University course consisted of the Trivium and Quadrivium, and the rest of the arts studies consisted of Philosophy, viz., the *Physica*, *Ethica* and *Metaphysica* of Aristotle. The course in Physics was one of the following of Aristotle's works : The *Physica*, *Coelum et Mundus*, *de Vegetalibus et Plantis*, *de Anima* or *de Animalibus*. Substantially the physical teaching at Cambridge was the same.

The third stage of the influence of Aristotle is marked by the Renascence, viz., the return to the Greek Aristotle. Though this in itself was a significant change, it was accompanied on its science side by the introduction of other Greek authors, who wrote on natural phenomena. Professor Woodward has shown that Erasmus found a place for " real " studies. [1] More marked still is the effect of the revival of learning in its bearing on a knowledge of Nature as shown by J. L. Vives. As Vives is all too little known in England, one of the countries of his adoption, and as he writes distinctly with a view to the education of youth in his *de Tradendis Disciplinis* (1523), I will translate here his views on the subject and method of nature study : [2]

Then follows the knowledge of Nature. The youth understands this more easily than practical ethics (*res prudentiae*), because for nature study he only needs alertness of the senses, whilst for ethics he needs experience in life, knowledge of events, and memory. But what we know of nature we learn both from sense and imagination (fantasia) but with the judgment of the mind added, the director of the senses. Therefore we have only accomplished little and that little badly (in science) on account of that darkness which besets and prompts the minds of mortals. All that we pursue, therefore, rather than acquire in this subject should be regarded as probable instead of absolutely true. There are some hard and difficult men who ask in all things for ground either obvious to the senses, or irresistible to the mind ; such as Aristotle and C. Pliny are. These are incredulous as to what has been discovered by others, and in questions of religion, impious. Whilst thus towards other persons they are inexorable, in those things to which they assent, often they ground themselves on the slightest of reasons, and rely on the authority of one man, to whose views they have committed themselves. Nor should anything of this study be taught to those not firmly established in their religious faith, unless also be added, the exact grounds of first philosophy which pertain to divinity.

---

[1] *Erasmus Concerning Education*, p. 139.
[2] Early in Book iv.

Vives proceeds to argue that the study of Nature, if it is to produce its rightful effect, must be of such a kind as to lead to piety. If it does not lead to knowledge of the arts of life and to love and admiration of God, it is idle, superfluous and harmful. For he who trifles subtly *de instantibus* and *de motu enormi aut conformi* is not a philosopher, but he who knows the causes why and how anything happens. Much less should the pupil learn the Arabian lore, unscholarly, insipid, and godless.

And although the writings of the old Greeks and Romans are the opinions of learned men, yet not even all these opinions and judgments are to be accepted. For what useful purpose does it serve that there are those who have contended that snow is black and fire cold ?

So, too, it is better to pass by Aristotle's quarrels and disputes with ancient philosophers. For he does not always quote his opponents exactly, and he sometimes inverts their words and meanings. He is confuted by his own principles, and it is not of great value to know all his details. " In all the philosophy of natural history, the youth is to learn such knowledge as far as he can test it by his own judgment, experience and diligence, and these things it should be his charge to cultivate, for it is *rarely that we can confirm as established (pro certo) that which is stated for truth.*"

Vives next proceeds to describe his method for teaching boys natural history, and names the textbooks on natural science which should, in his opinion, be used.

At first should be shown that which is most easily perceivable by the senses. For the senses are the sources of all cognition. Thus, amongst the knowledge of nature early taught, the first place will be given to an exposition (as it were a picture of all nature) of the heavens, the elements, and things in the heavens and the elements. i.e. in fire, air, water, earth ; so that there may be secured, in a high degree, a comprehensive outline, and description in a picture, of the whole world. Aristotle wrote to this end, his little book *de Mundo* (at least he or some other was the author). Its language is more pleasant than is the wont of Aristotle's gravity. It is written with more clearness than that with which Aristotle usually discourses on Nature, but Justin Martyr and John Picus ascribed the small work to Aristotle : it certainly issued from the Aristotelian school. Apuleius has published it as his own and called it *Cosmographia*. Other books more comprehensive and more accurate, must be explained, such as the *Sphaera* of John Sacrobosco the *Theorica Planetarum* of George Purbach and the second book of Pliny. On geography and hydrography, Pomponius Mela and the four books of Pliny preceding the seventh should be read. There is no need of disputations but only the silent "contemplation" of nature. The scholars should *rather ask and seek what is true* than wrangle and discuss. There are some youths not at all suited for the higher search in these questions, e.g. youths, who are endowed with slow wit and as it were with downcast head, who either will not rise up, or cannot gaze on subjects of such splendour, e.g. the blear-eyed pupils and those not physically equipped otherwise. Such cannot succeed in these nature studies.

Out of the class-room, let the pupil read for himself the *Phænomena* of Aratus ; and the *Coelestis historia* of Julius Hyginus. In the *Astronomicon* of Manilius there is much Chaldaic superstition and vanity. This book must not be read without a guide. It will require discrimination, and the pupil must not learn things which ought to be avoided. Let the pupil study Strabo, the describer of the globe and writer of history. He should pore over the maps of Ptolemy if he can obtain them in a well-produced edition. Let him add what has been recently discovered on the borders between East and West by our (i.e. Spaniards') voyages. Further let him read the treatises of Aristotle *de Animalibus* and his disciples Theophrastus *de Stirpibus* and Dioscorides *de Herbis* with the annotations of Marcellus Virgilius, who translated them (into Latin) and *Corollaries* of Hermolaus Barbarus. Then, let the pupil proceed to rustic studies, Cato, Varro, Terence, Junius, Columella, Palladius, as before, not with a view to a knowledge of books but for the insight into things themselves (*non iam ad verba, sed ad res intuendas*). Peter Criscentius writes in bad style and language, but he cultivates well his fields and property. Oppianus, fellow-countryman of Dioscorides, writes on fishes in all parts. In this topic of nature study we are extremely ignorant, because nature has been almost incredibly prodigal in the supply of fishes. The practice in naming fishes causes difficulty in their study. In every region of the sea, on every coast, are found varieties differing in shape and form. Not only do national languages vary in naming them, but also there is a difference in the local names given to fishes by towns and cities which are quite near each other, and whose inhabitants speak the same language.

Concerning gems, metals, pigments, Pliny has written. He has indeed included all the subject matter which I have just described. Julius Solinus has done the same. Solinus is the imitator, or rather the plunderer of Pliny. Of not less helpfulness in this study is Raphael Volaterranus in the third part of his Commentaries which he called *Philologia*. This author deserves high praise for his industry.

These books must be read by the student who wishes to get a real hold on this part of studies and they must be thoroughly and industriously studied. He who would advance still further must study outward nature by close investigation, and this will be as it were a pleasant recreation. We look for the pupil to be keen in his observation, and sedulous and diligent in it, but he must not be pertinacious, arrogant, contentious. There is no need of altercations and quarrels : all that is wanted is a certain power of observation. So will he observe the nature of things in the heavens, in clouds and in sunshine, in the plains, on the mountains, in the woods. Hence he will seek out and get to know many things from those who inhabit those spots. Let him have recourse, for instance, to gardeners, husbandmen, shepherds, and hunters, for this is what Pliny and other great authors undoubtedly did ; for any one man cannot possibly make all observations without help, in such a multitude and variety of directions. But whether he observes anything himself, or hears any one relating his experience, not only let him keep eyes and ears intent, but his whole mind also, for great and exact concentration is necessary in observing every part of nature, in its seasons, and in the essence and strength of each object of nature. Such students bring great benefits to husbandry, for the culture of palatable fruits, and for remedies and medicines for the recovery of health. For the well-to-do old man, the pursuit of nature study will be a great delectation, and it will be a refreshment of the mind to those who have business affairs of their own, or who conduct affairs of state. For not easily will any other pleasures of the senses be found which can compare with this in magnitude or in permanence, since it stimulates the desire of knowledge, which for every human mind is the keenest of all pleasures. Therefore whilst attention is given to observation of nature, no other recreation need be sought. It is a sauce to appetite. It is in itself a walking exercise (*deambulatio ipsa*), and a study at one's ease. It is at once school and schoolmaster, for it instantly presents something which one can look at with admiration, and at the same time a man's culture (*eruditio*) is advanced by it.

Such is the humanist view and the pedagogic method suggested by J. L. Vives, assuredly an outstanding thinker, by 1523. But it must not be supposed that it was also the academic view. For the statutes at Cambridge of 1549—a quarter of a century later—prescribe for the lecturer in Philosophy the advance on previous statutes (though slight, in comparison with Vives' exposition), of supplementing Aristotle's *Physics* with readings in Pliny or Plato.

Even in 1636, in the Laudian Statutes for the

University of Oxford, the duties laid down for the Sedleian lecturer in Natural Philosophy over a hundred years after Vives· had written his *de Tradendis Disciplinis* are mediaevally Aristotelian : " The lecturer in Natural Philosophy is to lecture in Aristotle's *Physics*, or the books concerning the heavens and the world, or concerning meteoric bodies, or the small *Natural Phaenomena* of the same author, or the books which treat of the soul, and also those on generation and corruption " ; and he is to give these lectures twice every week in full term, that is, on Wednesdays and Saturdays at eight o'clock in the morning. His audience is to be composed of the bachelors of arts, who are also to be the auditors in astronomy.

It was, however, chiefly outside of the liberal arts and philosophy that the development of natural science came. The physicians, as their name implies, were the mediaeval students of such physic or knowledge of nature as was then possessed. And this knowledge of physics in the wide sense of the term was sought by others than those engaged in the medical art as a livelihood.[1] Masters of

---

[1] There is excellent reason for supposing that in the mediaeval times, in the ages of chivalry, the girls in noble families were well skilled in potions, plasters and fomentations. Mediaeval romance frequently regards the young lady as the only doctor to be found, at any rate, in dealing with wounds. Girls, also, in mediæval romances are clearly acquainted with the virtues of herbs, though the treatment of wounds appear to have been particularly their province.

So, too, John Evelyn, speaking after the Restoration of his own earlier times says formerly " virgins and young

Arts in the Middle Ages studied medicine, i.e.
τὰ ψυσικὰ, as a solid part of knowledge " which in
their apprehension was not only a whole but a
manageable whole." [1] Since medicine and anatomy
were taught from books even till the sixteenth
century there was no special difficulty in their
study for the general student. [2]

In 1516 Sir Thomas More wrote his *Utopia* in
Latin. He says he carried to the Utopians amongst
other books Theophrastus, *Of Plants*, but a de-
signedly imperfect copy. His companion took with
him physic books, " certain small works of Hippocrates and Galen's *Microtechne* or *Ars parva*.
The which books they have in great estimation."

Thus Vives, in his *de Tradendis Disciplinis*
(1523), requires his youth to read in Greek amongst
other authors some of Galen's works, such as *de
Tuenda Valetudine*, in the edition with the Latin
translation which Linacre supplied to the Greek text.
He further says if the student reads Pliny he will
not add merely one author but a whole library alike
complete in itself and equally valuable for the

---

ladies made their recreations in the distillatory, the
knowledge of plants . . . and in the virtues of the family
which wholesome plain diet and kitchen physic preserved
in perfect health."

Mrs. Bathsua Makin, in her *Essay to Revive the Ancient
Education of Gentlewomen* in 1673, maintained that girls
should be taught physic and chirurgery, and says unless
she understood those subjects, a woman could not look well
to the affairs of her household.

[1] Allbutt, p. 72.

[2] *Ibid.*, p. 69.

riches of the matter and language. Sir Thomas Elyot, though a man in the service of the state as lawyer and diplomatist, studied medicine. In 1534, he wrote *The Castle of Health*, and had the audacity to write in English. After writing this book, Elyot was plainly told by doctors that he had much better write on matters with which he was better acquainted. They admitted that he was " prettily seen in histories," but denied that he was " learned in Physick." Elyot replies : " For before that I was twenty years old a worshipful physician [supposed to be Linacre] and one of the most renowned at that time in England, perceiving me by nature inclined to knowledge, read unto me the works of Galen . . . and some of the aphorisms of Hippocrates. And afterward by mine own study I read over in order the more part of the works of Hippocrates, Galen, Oribasius, Paulus Celius, Alexander Trallianus, Celsus, Plinius the one and the other, with Dioscorides. Nor did I omit to read the long canons of Avicenna, the commentaries of Averroys, the practices of Isake, Haliabbas, Rasis, Mesue. . . ." This may be taken as a representative list of authors in a good medical education of the time. Elyot once more delights in having written a book in English, and says, with his spirit aroused : " If physicians be angry that I have written physicke in English, let them remember that the Greeks wrote in Greek, and Romans in Latin, Avicenna and the other in Arabic, which were their own proper and maternal tongues. And if they had been as much attacked with envy and covetise, as some now seem to be, they would have devised some particular language, with a strange cipher or form of letters, wherein they would have written their science, which language or letters no man should have known, that had not professed and practised Physick. But those, although they were Paynims and Jews, yet in this part of charity, they far surmounted us Christians, that they would not have so necessary a knowledge as Physic is, to be hid from them, which would be studious about it."

No doubt Elyot read *de Medicinali materia*. This is a description of simples and herbs, and of course in the sixteenth century it was published with well-drawn woodcuts of plants and flowers.

In 1553 Dr. Thomas Phaer wrote the *Regiment of Life*,[1] in which is a very early treatise on the health of children in English. Phaer thus follows Elyot as a pioneer in using the vernacular for a text-book. In his preface the author explains his position : " My purpose is here to do them good that have most need, that is to say, children : and to show the remedies that God hath created for the use of man, to distribute in English to those who are unlearned, part of the treasure that is in other languages, to provoke them that are of better learning, to utter their knowledge in such like attempts." He concludes : " I hope to see the time when the nature of Simples (which have been hitherto incredibly corrupted) shall be read in

---

[1] Which ran through at least six editions by the end of the sixteenth century.

English, as in other languages : that is to say, the perfect declaration of the qualities of herbs, seeds, roots, trees & of all commodities that are here amongst us, shall be earnestly and truly declared, in our native speech, by the grace of God. To the which I trust all learned men (having a zeal to the commonwealth) will apply their diligent industries : surely for my own part I shall never cease during my breath, to bestow my labour to the furtherance of it (till it come to pass) even to the utmost of my simple power."

The problem of memory was treated, chiefly, from the side of the physician. In 1563 was published in England a translation by William Fulwood of the *Castle of Memory* by the physician Gratarolus, a Protestant refugee from Italy, who became Professor of Physic first at Basle and afterwards at Marburg. There are books published in England which deserve mentioning in treating of the connexion of physic with education. Firstly, books on Memory. *Libellus de Memoria, verissimaque bene recordandi scientia. Authore G. P.*[1] *Cantabrigiense. Huc accessit eiusdem Admonitiuncula ad A. Disconum, de Artificiosae Memoriae, quam publice profitetur, vanitate. Londini,* 1584. Both parts are in Latin. The former is divided into chapters, and treats of : 1. De Memoriae facultate. 2. De Memoriae Arte et de Propositione. 3. De Syllogismo. 4. De Methodo. 5. De exercitatione. The Admonitiuncula contains a list of herbs or drugs supposed to

---

[1] Probably Guil. Perkinsus.

preserve the brain if it be (*a*) moist and cold, (*b*) dry and cold. *Mnemonica, Sive Reminiscendi Ars : e puris artis naturaeque fontibus hausta, et in tres libros digesta. Necnon De Memoria naturali fovenda libellus : e variis doctissimorum operibus sedulo collectus. Jam primum in lucem edita, authore Joanne Willisso, sacrae Theologiae bacchalaureo. Omne bonum, Dei Donum. Londini,* 1618.

John Willis's Latin work was translated into English in 1661 with the title: *Mnemonica ; or, The Art of Memory, Drained out of the Pure Fountains of Art and Nature. . . . London,* 1661.

" Maister Willis his book of Memory, called *Mnemonica sive Reminiscendi,* are gathered out of the best who have written thereof : out of which the most profitable things may be selected and used by them who are judicious." So says John Brinsley in *A Consolation for our Grammar Schools* [1] (1622), when he is suggesting text-books to be used in schools. Willis states that the authors who have been most useful in furnishing him with " precepts " for his work are : Theologi : St. Tzegedinus, Guil. Perkinsus. Medici et Philosophi : H. Gualt. Ryff, Guil. Gratarolus, Fernelius, Leon. Fuchsius, H. Ranzovius, D. Brightus. The following are the subjects of the chapters, as given in the English translation : Book i : Of remembering common affairs—Of remembering words—Of remembering Phrases—Of remembering Sentences—Of remembering long Speeches. Book ii : Of remembering

---

[1] pp. 79-80.

without writing—Of remembering by certain Verses purposely borne in mind—Of remembering by *ex tempore* Verses—Of exonerating things charged on Memory *ex tempore*. Book iii : Of Repositories —Of Places—Of Ideas in General—Of the Quantity of Ideas—Of the Position of Ideas—Of the Colours of Repositories and Ideas—Of direct Ideas —Of Relative Ideas—of Fictitious Ideas—Of written Ideas—Of Compound Ideas—Of choosing Ideas— The manner of reposing Ideas—Of the practice of the Art of Memory—Of Dictation and Reposition —Of irregular Reposition—Of Depositing Ideas.

A Treatise of Cherishing Natural Memory : Chap. i : Of such as debilitate Memory—Chap. ii : Of things corroborating Memory—Chap. iii : Of a prescript order of life—Chap. iv : Of restoring a debilitated Memory—Chap. v : How to discern the temperament of the Brain—Chap. vi : Of diet properly convenient to every temperament—Chap. vii : Of diseases of the Brain.

Secondly, Richard Carew in 1594 translated Juan Huarte's *Examen de Ingenios* (written in Spanish c. 1578) from the Italian into which it had been translated from the Spanish by Camillo Camilli under the title, *The Examination of Men's Wits*. This is a comparatively little known, but interesting, treatise on education. The author avows that Galen supplies the " ground-plot " of his treatise, though the particular application to education is the writer's own. An Italian writer, Annibale Romei, in the *Courtiers' Academy*, (translated by John Kepers in 1598), classes physic among the

" liberal arts," which are requisite in the training of the noble.

John Milton considered that medicine was a constituent part of a liberal education. The general student, as well as the physician should read a writer on the Institution of Physic to know " the tempers, the humours, the seasons, and how to manage a crudity." Such knowledge will lead to self-guidance in health and will be of service on many occasions. It may help a man to save an army, when engaged in military movements. Lord Herbert of Cherbury at more length, and with greater detail of medical books, insists that a gentleman should know how to diagnose, to prepare right doses of medicine and prepare his potions himself. John Evelyn in 1645 studied physic at Padua.

William London, the bookseller, shows the general educational view of physic in 1658. After a reference to Luke as a physician and to Christ as the good Physician, followed by a reference to the poets as testimony that the origin of medicine goes back to Apollo, the chief grace of medicine, and Aesculapius " his son, who was a God and a Professor of Physic, and to Mithridates, King of Pontus, the first compounder of mithridate—London proceeds : " It (physic) must needs be a noble science that's of so general a use to mankind, as we see from a well-cut Herball, flourishing with all sorts of foreign and domestic plants, flowers, herbs ; with the virtues of each vegetable, all which demonstrate the usefulness of this art. Of what esteem ought such to be had, that with Galen or

169

Hippocrates, dead many years, yet stand alive to this day by their learned parts and knowledge in mysteries of their art, and the great discoveries of those greater secrets contained in the mysteries of God in nature." Later on, in the seventeenth century, in 1678, in the directions given by J. Gailhard, Gent., in his *Compleat Gentleman*, when discoursing on travelling, it is remarked : " If a traveller hath time, and happens to be in a convenient place, as may be Padua, Montpellier, or other, it would be in him a commendable curiosity to learn something in Physic, not to be a doctor of, or to practise it, only to be able to understand the grounds of it." [1]

In the proposed Academy of Sir Humphrey Gilbert, c. 1572, there was to be a reader of natural philosophy at £40 a year ; a doctor of physic [2] to read physic and chirurgerie at £100 a year.

100*li.* was alotted for the philosopher and physician to have a garden for all kinds of simples.

Hallam [3] is of opinion that a botanical garden was first established by Lorenzo dei Medici, though

---

[1] Gailhard, p. 56.

[2] Gilbert's reason for establishing a reader of physic was thus explained : " The physician shall practise to read Chirurgerie, because through want of learning therein, we have very few good Chirurgeons, if any at all. By reason that Chirurgery is not now to be learned in any other place than in a barber's shop, And in that shop, most dangerous, especially in time of plague, when the ordinary trimming of men for cleanliness must be done by those which have to do with infected persons."

[3] *Lit. of Europe*, i, p. 470.

Euricius Cordus of Marburg is said to have been the initiator of the movement. However, the University of Pisa is supposed to have possessed the first public botanical garden, and the date given is 1545. There were also botanic gardens at Padua and Bologna. Apparently Sir Humphrey Gilbert was the first to propose such a garden in England. In 1632 the Oxford Physic-garden was started. At Cambridge the Botanic Garden was founded in 1762.

It is clear, however, that botany takes its rise from the study of physic by the physician, and that it was differentiated into a separate study slowly. Its development, however, was more marked than that of zoology, for, the " herbals, Dispensatorium and Kräuterbücher were much in advance of the Bestiaries." [1] It is noteworthy, however, that in both botany and in zoology the main advances were made by professed physicians. Gilbert's proposed Academy was for gentlemen, and the study of physic was thus regarded as a part, we cannot say, of a liberal (for that is technically limited to the seven arts of the trivium and quadrivium), but of a generous, or to use the Miltonic term, a magnanimous education. " For," says Mulcaster, [2] in 1581, " which be gentlemanly qualities, if these be not, to read, to write, to draw, to sing, to play, to have language, to have health and activity, nay even to profess Divinity, Law, Physic, and any trade else commendable for cunning ? " Gentlemen, as Mulcaster points out, have most leisure and " best

---

[1] Allbutt, p. 71.   [2] *Positions*, p. 206.

furniture," and so can pursue all these subjects " without any corruption." Indeed, medical studies had received an incalculable impulse from the Revival of Learning, not only for specialists, but for the general student, for had not the Greeks insisted on the necessity of music and gymnastic (of which medicine formed a part) in all sound education ?

It would be going beyond my scope to trace in detail the training for the specialist physician. But it may be permitted to recall the name of Thomas Linacre, in connexion with physic. He was one of that considerable body of Englishmen who graduated in physic at Padua,[1] as he was probably the first Englishman to read Aristotle and Galen in the original Greek. In 1518 the College of Physicians was founded by letters patent by King Henry VIII, on the suggestion of Linacre. Dr. Caius, who endowed Gonville College, Cambridge, so beneficently, was also a benefactor to the College of Physicians. Caius was a student of anatomy under the great Vesalius at Padua. Vesalius's work, the *de Humani Corporis Fabrica*,[2]

---

[1] The names of English students at Padua are contained in the *De Natione Anglica Universitatis Patavinae*, by J. A. Andrich, 1892.

[2] The significance of Vesalius is that his researches on the human frame, wonderful in the extent of the first attempt at an independent inquiry, were founded on dissextions of the human body. Galen had experimented on pigs and apes. On the revival of learning, Mundinus and Berenger and the great Leonardo da Vinci pioneered the movement, in direct studies, recognising the greatest study of mankind is man, and to study him it is necessary to study him directly.

1543, was the meeting place of science and art. For Vesalius, the exponent of anatomy, is one of the giants standing at the portals of modern knowledge, and this book is illustrated with designs said to have come from the hand of the great artist Titian or of one of his pupils. Lord Herbert of Cherbury, it may be mentioned, includes not only medicine, but also anatomy as a commendable study for a gentleman. [1]

That physic and anatomy were permissible or even commendable studies for the gentleman requires the supplementary remark that such studies as law, physic, and military science were recognised as entitling a man to receive a coat and arms, " to be called master and be reputed for a gentleman ever after." [2] The healing of the sick by emperors, kings, brings physicians amongst the ennobled. The religious sanction of saints, " Yea, our blessed Saviour cured the sick," completes the dignity of the study. [3] If physic can make the physician " noble," sixteenth century logic argued on the principle of *noblesse oblige*, the noble ought to know something of physic.

The well-trained noble youth, then, as Vives had said, should read his Galen and his Pliny. These books obtained the reputation of being gentlemen's

---

[1] He adds a reason: " Whosoever considers Anatomy, I believe, will never be an atheist." *See* S. Lee's *Lord Herbert of Cherbury*, 2nd ed., p. 31.

[2] At least so says William Harrison in his *Description of England* (in Hollinshead's Chronicles, 1577).

[3] Peacham, *Compleat Gentleman*, p. 11.

books. This is a consideration of some importance in the development of the " natural history " which springs from these studies. The costly folios with splendid engravings of the " History " of Plants and " Histories " of Animals, or in later periods the beautifully produced Herbals and Book of Animals, could not have found a public to justify publication had it not been for the training in those subjects, in the earlier part of the Renascence, and at least the tradition and sometimes the practice of the teaching of them amongst " gentlemen." Lord Herbert of Cherbury (1583–1648) says : " It is a fine study and worthy of a gentleman to be a good botanic, that so he may know the nature of all herbs and plants, being our fellow creatures, and made for the use of man ; for which purpose it will be fit for him to cull out of some good herball all the *icones* together, with the descriptions of them and to lay by themselves all such as grow in England, and afterwards to select again such as usually grow by the highway side, in meadows, by rivers, or in marshes or in cornfields or in dry or mountainous places, or on rocks, walls or in shady places, such as grow by the seaside, for this being done and the said icones being ordinarily carried by themselves, or by their servants, one may presently find out every herb he meets withal, especially if the said flowers be truly coloured." [1] So too Burton [2] says :

[What greater pleasure can there be than] To

---

[1] Herbert : *Autobiography* (Lee's 2nd. ed.), p. 31.
[2] *Anatomy of Melancholy*, 1621. Partition II, Section 2, Member 4.

see a well-cut Herbal, Herbs, Trees, Flowers, Plants all Vegetals, expressed in their proper colours to the life, as that of Matthiolus upon Dioscorides, Delacampius Lobel, Bauhinus, and that last voluminous and mighty Herbal of Besler of Nuremburg, wherein almost every Plant is to his own bigness. To see Birds, Beasts, and Fishes of the Sea, Spiders, Gnats, Serpents, Flies, etc., all Creatures set out by the same Art, and truly expressed in lively colours, with an exact description of their natures, virtues, qualities, etc., as hath been accurately performed by Ælian, Gesner, Ulysses, Aldrovandus, Bellonius, Rondoletius, Hippolytus Salvianus, etc.

Other kinds of gentlemen's books indirectly led to the reading of the more descriptive characteristics and legendary botanical and zoological lore, and to impress on the imagination, fabulous as well as observed details. Thus it is to be remembered that books of heraldry[1] often contained accounts of animals and plants—for the noble and gentleman to inform himself as to these subjects, so that he could know the physical details on which the emblematical figures of his shield are grounded. Heraldry does not seem *à priori* a probable subject for inclusion in the school curriculum, yet George Snell, in his *Right Teaching of Useful Knowledge* (1649) suggested that heraldry should, in the school course, follow on cosmography, topography, and drawing. This no doubt it commonly did in the nobleman's education. The inclusion of schoolmasters amongst professional men who studied divinity, law and physic, was one of the objects aimed at by Mulcaster in his desire to have a Training College for Teachers

---

[1] e.g. Gerard Legh's *Accedence of Armorie*, 1562, and John Guillim's *A Display of Heraldrie*, 1610.

established. He does not say that he would have a teacher practise physic, but he does say that a gentleman ought to know that subject at least in a general way. The status of a profession was beginning to be attached to divinity, law and physic, and the real significance of Mulcaster's suggestion is probably that he wished the teacher to become a member of a profession through his College of Teachers, so as to qualify as a gentleman. Such a conception if it had been carried out would have been a most effective way of the broadening and modernising of the curriculum, which was the very head and front of Mulcaster's writing. However that may be, the knowledge of physic was, in earlier times, often pursued by schoolmasters. For instance, in Germany, Michael Neander, 1525-1595, was not only a great classical scholar, and conducted what Melanchthon considered was the best seminary in Germany, at Ilfield am Harz, but also was a physician and attended his scholars when ill. In England, there are indications that " physic " was studied by schoolmasters. Thus Christopher Johnson, Head Master of Winchester College, 1560-1571, on leaving Winchester became a practising physician at Westminster. Bloxam in his *Registers of Magdalen College*, mentions several masters of the school attached to the College, who were sufficiently adequate in knowledge of medicine to leave the school and practise medicine.[1] We have seen that

---

[1] The Ordinances of Bristol Grammar School (founded 1533) prescribed that the Master be a Master of Arts or a Bachelor of Laws or Physic of two years' standing.

William Hill the geographer, on leaving the Head-mastership of Sutton Coldfield Grammar School, practised medicine in London.[1] In the Statutes of Camberwell Grammar School, 1615, it is specific-ally enacted that the master shall not practise physic " without the consent of the governors," a restriction which would be meaningless unless this were known sometimes to have happened. We should hardly expect that elementary medical studies were part of a school course, yet the Statutes of East Retford Grammar School, in 1552, prescribe for one of the forms " the Scriptures, Sallust, *Salern*, and Justinian [Institutes] if the School-master and Usher be seen in the same." The ques-tion arises : What is the meaning of *Salern* ? It certainly seems that it was the founder's intention that in his school should be studied the *Regimen Sanitatis Salerni*, the famous treatise on medicine or hygiene composed in 1100 and dedicated to Robert Duke of Normandy as prospective " King of the English." Mr. Hastings Rashdall[2] says of the treatise " many still current pieces of proverbial medicine may be traced to this source, e.g. :

' Sex horis dormire sat est juvenibusque senique
   Septem vix pigro nulli concedimus octo.'

And ' Post coenam stabis aut passus mille meabis.' "
The East Retford Statutes, therefore, seem to show that law, physic, and divinity (the Scriptures) were capable of being regarded as general studies, so far

---

[1] *See* p. 108 *supra.*
[2] *History of Universities*, i, p. 82.

as to be available, in the opinion of the founder, as *school* subjects. [1] Nearly a hundred years later, in 1649, George Snell [2] pleaded for the instruction of schoolboys in hygiene. He says : " The ignorance of any knowledge merely human may better be tolerated than of so much knowledge in physical rules as are needful to preserve the healthful well-being of a man's own person."

Vives (*de Tradendis Disciplinis*, bk. iii) points out, in 1523, a group of writers on natural knowledge, viz. " rustic " authors who should be read. As leaders to be followed for vocabulary in Latin " let the boy read Cato, Varro, Columella, Palladius in rural studies (*de rebus rusticis*) ; and Vitruvius is important for naming with the greatest purity and accuracy most objects of the country. Varro is harsh and accommodated to artisans, Columella more elegant and terser. Vitruvius often quotes Greek and is difficult to understand (unless you have the illustrations of Jucundus Veronensis), because the old idea of building has gone out of use ; not unjustly of him, Budaeus says : ' It is not given to every man to reach Corinth.' To these add Grapaldus, on the house."

Milton, as usual, follows [3] Vives. " The next stage would be to the authors Agriculture, Cato,

---

[1] *See* p. 236 as to " physic " as a school subject.

[2] In *The Right Teaching of Useful Knowledge*.

[3] There are close parallelisms between Milton's *Tractate* (1644) and Vives' *de Tradendis Disciplinis* (1523), e.g. the spacious house and ground away from, though near to, the city, and the union of school and university studies in one institution, together with the lists of text-books.

Varro, and Columella, for the matter is most easy, and if the language be difficult, so much the better, it is not a difficulty beyond their years." Though Milton seems to follow Vives, he brings him up to date. In this case he adds, with true Hartlibian spirit, if the old agricultural authors are read "here will be an occasion of inciting and enabling them hereafter to improve the tillage of their country, to recover the bad soil, and to remedy the waste that is made of good ; for this was one of Hercules' praises."

Important as the study of these ancient Latin agricultural writers was, in the view of Vives and Milton and of the humanists generally, they fell into disuse from the schools, and the nature study with them, after the practical treatises on agriculture of Hartlib and his friends in the time of Cromwell. For these latter gave the impulse to the specialistic and practical side of agriculture. When a subject becomes specialistic the tendency naturally is for it to drop out of school studies.

In the subject of natural history, in the Middle Ages, the chief text-book was that of Bartholomew Glanville, the Englishman, written in the thirteenth century and with a very wide circulation before and after the invention of printing. It is called the *Liber de proprietatibus rerum*.[1] The English

---

[1] Dibden says : "Of all the books printed in England in the fifteenth century this is the most curious and elaborate, and probably the most beautiful for its typographical execution." The book has also the distinction of being the first printed on paper made in England (manufactured by John Tate of Hereford).

translation was made by John of Trevisa and was printed at Westminster by Wynkyn de Worde in 1496. Glanville's work written in Latin was translated into French, Dutch and Spanish. Of the Latin text there were ten printed editions in the fifteenth century. The book took up a new lease of life in 1582 when Stephen Bateman, Chaplain to Archbishop Parker, re-published Trevisa's translation under the title *Bateman uppon Bartholome, his Booke De Proprietatibus Rerum, newly corrected, enlarged and amended*. Bartholomew Glanville's book was the chief, not to say the only, authority on natural history until the end of the sixteenth century in England, and in all probability the numerous references in Shakespere to natural history, are founded, indirectly or directly, on Friar Bartholomew's work of about 1260 A.D., as contained in Bateman's revised edition. Bartholomew's book is an encyclopaedia. The "Properties of Things" are stated for the most comprehensive departments of life. The mediaeval cosmos receives its exposition, and the account is just anterior to Dante, the unravelling of whose cosmical system attracts so many students. "Man" is considered, and Bartholomew is a shrewd observer of boys and girls, and has clear views as to their right bringing up. He shows the contemporary view of the good baron and the good man, and manners of his time, and illustrates copiously the daily life. Medicine and physiology are dealt with and the geographical knowledge of the time is set out in detail. Plants and trees are discussed,

Aristotle and Pliny giving him materials for birds and fishes. Perhaps the most interesting of the subjects is that of the animals, taken from Aristotle and Pliny, of course, as bases, but with additions from the mediaeval *Physiologus*[1] and the *Bestiarium*. It will thus be seen that Bartholomew Anglicus's *de Proprietatibus Rerum* sums up the natural knowledge of the Middle Ages. It deals with the subject-matter in mythological, anecdotal, allusive fashion, and above all is rich in allegory and simile. The consequence is, that since the influence of Bartholomew Anglicus lasted through the Elizabethan era, metaphors and similes came ready to hand to the dramatists in an English form, and settled into the ordinary speech. Besides Bartholomew's book on the *Properties of Things*, from the time of Anselm, at any rate, to Caxton, there were *Elucidarii libri*[2] which gave accounts of a similar kind, (sometimes in the form of a catechism) of animals, plants and other natural objects. These were intended for the purpose of teaching, for they are sometimes thrown into the

---

[1] The *Physiologus* is a compilation of moralities on animal myths, which came into Europe from the East. As a compilation it was in a state of flux. It included the *Bestiarium*. Works of this kind stimulated and widened imagination through symbolism.

[2] Mr. Robert Steele in his delightful little book of extracts (*Mediaeval Lore* from Bartholomew Anglicus or de Glanville) instances " Licked into shape " from Bartholomew's account of the bear. Mr. H. W. Seager in *Natural History of Shakespere's Time* (1896) gives a large number of parallel passages from Bartholomew and other writers on Nature, and the Elizabethan dramatists.

form of questions asked by the child of his master. So, too, the *Hortus Sanitatis* dealt with herbs, animals, birds, fishes and stones. It is thus a very early herbal and compendium of natural science, In its early printed form it was adorned with about 100 woodcuts, boldly drawn and cut, the plants being of distinctly good design. It is medical in origin and intention, but must have been generally known and used by the well-informed man of the fifteenth century. In 1601, Philemon Holland translated *The Historie of the World, commonly called the Naturall Historie of Caius Plinius Secundus*. There had been published in England two editions of abstracts of this book, translated from the French of P. de Changy, one about 1565 and the other in 1587. But Holland's translation was the first complete English Pliny, and apparently no edition of Pliny in the original had been published in England. The natural history is of the encyclo-paedic class and deals with the " antiquities and wonders of the world, with the secrets and mys-teries of nature." It is a " pansophia," to borrow Comenius' term, as to the heavens, the earth, the animal world, plant-life, metals, and natural phenomena of all kinds. Pliny enumerates all authors Latin and foreign from whom he had quoted, and the book may be described as the most comprehensive compilation of universal nature knowledge up to Pliny's own time.[1] Apparently it gathers up the whole of the ascertained, as well as

---

[1] Pliny lived A.D. 23–A.D. 79 ; the date of the *Polyhistor* of Solinus is c. 238 A.D.

traditional, legendary and mythological knowledge of antiquity. It is in thirty-seven books, and Holland's nephew characterised it as being as " full of variety as nature itself." Caius Julius Solinus, whose *Polyhistor* is often mentioned along with Pliny on natural history in the sixteenth and seventeenth centuries, made copious extracts from Pliny, and was known as the " ape of Pliny."

By the time of Holland's translation of Pliny's *Natural History* in 1601 the encyclopaedic natural histories had shown signs of breaking up into histories of plants and of animals. In England had appeared in 1525, an anonymous Latin Herbal ; in 1526, the anonymous *Grete Herbal*; and in 1551 the first part, in 1562 the second part, and in 1568 the third part of Dr. Turner's Herbal. The *Stirpium Adversaria* of Pena and Lobel was published in London in 1570 ; at Antwerp in 1567 Lobel published his *Plantarum Historia*, and in 1578 Henry Lyte's translation of Dodoens. In 1597 the Herbal of John Gerard appeared in London. It was written in English, but largely borrowed from Dodoens, and was adorned with fuller illustrations than any previous English published Herbal. In 1633, Gerard's Herbal was enlarged by Dr. Thomas Johnson, who published accounts of botanical journeys.[1] This was followed in 1640 by the *Theatrum Botanicum* of John Parkinson, a more considerable work than that of Gerard. In 1659 he published *Paradisi in sole Paradisus Terrestris*, which is a

---

[1] One of these is called *Mercurius Botanicus*. Is this the first use of the word *botanicus* in England ?

herbal and also a kitchen-garden and orchard-book, furnished with illustrations. It is perhaps the most attractive of all the old English herbals.

The above list represents the main English plant and herb books up to 1660. The Oxford Dictionary's first reference to the use of the term " Botanic " as adjective and as noun is by Parkinson [1] (1657–8) and of " botany " is in 1696 by John Ray. As I am only dealing with English books as the basis of English school teaching, the list given must show the outside limit of general knowledge. Of professed teachers of the subject there were none. Was there any school teaching of botany, or anything resembling it ? Withals' *Dictionary* [2] in English and Latin, " devised for the capacity of children and young beginners," probably in the period 1550–1660, by far the most widely circulated of all children's dictionaries of Latin-English, was divided into sections, *not alphabetically but according to subjects* ; there are sections on corn, the corn-field, the meadow, trees, parts of trees, names of trees, fruits, vineyards, herbs, gathered by divers men, " especially by Master Linacre," names of herbs, spices, and later in the book medicines, remedies and cures. Each section has words and often phrases and sentences, and

---

[1] In the passage above (p. 74) quoted from Lord Herbert of Cherbury the noun " botanic " is used. Herbert's *Autobiography* ceases at 1624, and as he died in 1648, it must have been written between 1624–1648.

[2] John Withals published the children's *Dictionary* c. 1554. Lewis Evans revised and increased it in 1574. William Clerk re-edited it in 1602.

the sections with vocabulary and phrases would lend itself to explanation when a teacher himself knew the subject. There can be no doubt as to the intention of Comenius to teach children in schools as to trees and fruits, herbs and shrubs. In the *Janua Linguarum*, 1631, a chapter is devoted to each of these three subjects. A certain amount of information is given in complete sentences in the vernacular and in Latin, and the names of plants and trees would imply a very considerable amount of knowledge if the teacher were able to give it. In the *Orbis pictus* Comenius allots a section to each of the following : trees, fruits of trees, flowers, pot-herbs, corn, shrubs. There are also in the *Orbis pictus* copper-plate illustrations of all the different plants, etc., named with a number to identify the name in the text with the plant in the picture. But the practice thus laid down by Comenius can be traced to a much earlier date. At the Friars' School, Bangor, Dean Nowell's Statutes (1563) direct the Master or Usher, besides " ordinary lectures " to teach vocabularies to the scholars. " They shall begin with words that concern the head, reciting orderly as nigh as they can every part and member of the body, after that they shall teach the names of sickness, beasts, herbs, shrubs, trees, and so forth they shall proceed in good order to *such things as may be most frequented and daily used.*"

We have seen that schoolmasters sometimes had studied physic, and that that study included such knowledge of nature as was ordinarily known.

MODERN SUBJECTS IN ENGLISH SCHOOLS

Since dictionaries and nomenclators included references to names of objects in natural history,
it is probable that well-informed schoolmasters
supplied natural history knowledge. For instance,
Philemon Holland, the translator of Pliny's
Natural History, who was an M.D., became headmaster of Coventry Grammar School in 1628.
Who can doubt that from his rich stores of knowledge in physic and natural science, he directly
or indirectly instructed his boys in subjects with
which he was so familiar ? As to the Universities, at Oxford the first Professor of Botany was
Robert Morison in 1669. John Martyn gave the
first course of lectures in Botany in the University
of Cambridge in 1727. The Chair in the University of Cambridge in Zoology and Comparative
Anatomy was not founded till 1866.

The classical writers on agricultural and rural
subjects were sometimes read in schools as recommended by Vives and Milton. Moreover, Pliny
was used in the school, for subject matter, and for
illustrations, in themes and in verse-composition.
Hoole wishes his boys to compare the English of
the translation of Pliny with the original. It should
be also borne in mind that Vergil's Eclogues were
read in schools. They are prescribed by Statute at
Sandwich Grammar School, 1580. Vergil's Eclogues
or Georgics are fixed at Bangor for the Friars' School,
1568. Hoole requires these books to be studied in
the Fifth Form, and desires that Mr. Ogilby's big
book of Translation of the Eclogues be purchased
for the school library, " so that the lively pictures

will imprint the histories in scholars' memories."
The Georgics of Vergil are, with Hoole, part of the
Fifth Form work, and the pupils will require for
their reading, the master's help. Besides the
agricultural writers, and Vergil's Eclogues and
Georgics, in the sixteenth and earlier part of the
seventeenth century, the famous *Bucolica* of Baptista Spagnuoli Mantuanus claimed attention in
many schools. Mantuan's Eclogues are specifically
fixed by Statute for St. Bees Grammar School, 1583,
and by School Orders at the King's School, Durham,
1593, and were in use in Hoole's Grammar School in
1660. The pastoral form of literature necessarily
includes appreciation of nature, and Baptista
Mantuan undoubtedly can be shown to have passages
which imply nature study, though like the other
authors (chiefly) he was read for his Latin verse, in
which even Erasmus thought that Baptista would
in the future rank not much below Vergil. The
Bucolica seu Adolescentia of Baptista Mantuan
were published about 1498. Such lines as the
following show the Mantuan's interest in natural
subjects :

> In my country now
> The lowly brooms, the lofty vines do blow
> Along the banks of Po, the pastures' sides
> Where Mincius with silvered water glides :
> There now the corn is eared ; with blossoms red
> Pomegranate trees now there are all bespread :
> The frondent alder there (this month of May)
> Doth sweet white flowers on each hedge display. [1]

---

[1] Harvey's translation into English verse of the Latin
of Baptista Mantuanus was published in 1656. The book
was read, of course, in the schools, in Latin.

Turning to the zoological side of natural knowledge, the story of theoretical development can soon be told. Again, it comes particularly from the physicians' books. As plant-knowledge took its source mainly from the physicians' study of herbs and simples, so zoology as a theoretical study springs from the physicians' researches into anatomy. The father of modern anatomy was Vesalius (1514-64). Galen had founded his anatomy on dissections of apes. Vesalius, in spite of all prejudices and opposition, achieved the revolution of basing the knowledge of the structure of man's body on direct dissection of the human corpse. In a sense, Galen, by dissecting apes and other animals, was the founder of zoology. But the impulse to the close study of comparative anatomy could only begin, so to say, from the top downwards, and the cause of anatomy was therefore won when Vesalius dared to investigate man's body itself. Vesalius's work *De Corporis humani Fabrica* was published at Basle in 1543. The progress of anatomy in the period with which I am dealing is not an English movement. It is rather Italian. But its effects permeated throughout the civilised countries, and in many directions of knowledge. This will be realised by recalling the names of books in the department of English literature, e.g. John Lyly's *Anatomy of Wit* in 1579 and Robert Burton's *Anatomy of Melancholy* in 1621. The greater the advance in anatomy, naturally the more removed it became from any connexion with the school. Still, it may be noted that the learning of the names of the parts of man's body to which reference was made above in the case of Bangor Friars' School was no uncommon feature of a school-course. Comenius, who often enters into old traditions whilst disclaiming them, gives a chapter in his *Janua Linguarum* on the anatomy of man's body, and his section in the *Orbis pictus* is, of course, accompanied with an illustration which with the numbers attached (in the English editions) refers the pupil to the point in the illustration given in the text.

In the modern sense of the term, up to the time of the Restoration in England, there was no scientific zoology. Comparative physiology and anatomy (particularly the anatomy of animals) have proceeded to a (comparatively) high development in later times, and though differentiated from human physiology and anatomy, the subject has received an impetus from those studies. But in the period under consideration, the most that was attempted was, so to say, an inventory. Interesting descriptions especially of the external characteristics of an increasing number of types of the animal kingdom, reaching downwards to histories of insects became familiar developments in books of natural history and even in special monographs.[1] The great problem of both zoology and

---

[1] e.g. in England the type up to 1660 is represented by such a work as that of Samuel Purchas : *A Theatre of flying insects where especially the nature, worth, and work, wonder, and manner of the right ordering of the bee is discoursed and described with theological, Historicall and Morall observations.*

botany in their earlier stages of differentiation was that of description of different kinds of animals and their classification. To name the English works, Edward Wotton (1492-1555) wrote *de Differentiis Animalium,* but he wrote it, still under the influence of Aristotle, and Turner wrote an *Avium historia* and Dr. Caius, a book on Dogs. Johnston, a Scotchman, published his *History of Quadrupeds* in 1652. Finally, there is Topsell's *History of Four-footed Beasts and Serpents* in 1607–8 republished in 1658. The full title shows the line of treatment (1658 ed.) : *The History of four-footed Beasts, and serpents, their figures, names, conditions, virtues, love and hatred to mankind, the wonderful work of God in their creation, Preservation and Destruction :* *with variety of Historicall narrations from Scriptures, Fathers, Philosophers, Physicians, and Poets, with Divers Hieroglyphicks and Emblems, collected from C. Gesner ; to which is added A Theatre of Insects as Bees, Flies, Caterpillars, Spiders, Worms, by Dr. Moufet.* Here may be mentioned the name of an earlier and foreign writer who transcended all writers of his age in his vast erudition, and summed up all the knowledge of his time, almost as completely though, of course, with much greater bulk, than Pliny summed up ancient natural knowledge. This was Conrad Gesner (1516-65) a Swiss, whom Hallam justly calls " that prodigy of general erudition." His *History of Animals* was published in parts, between 1551 and 1587, and includes volumes on viviparous and oviparous quadrupeds, birds, fishes, serpents, and the book of woodcuts called *Icones Animalium*. In botany Gesner hits upon the idea of classifying plants according to their flowers and not merely by their general appearance. His zeal in botanical observation is typified by having a botanical garden of his own at Zurich. He travelled to observe both plants and animals. The travels of discoverers and explorers and especially of professed naturalists on journeys of observation clearly had direct influence on the development of botany and zoology. Gesner was probably the first naturalist to make a zoological collection. He had drawings made at his own house of what he considered necessary in plants and animals. He was also distinguished [1] in mineralogy.

From Gesner to John Ray (1628–1705) modern zoologists seem to recognise no developments in the *basis* of classification,[2] though the number of animals described is largely increased, and detail

---

[1] Gesner is equally remarkable for his knowledge of literature. He was a great linguist and his acquaintance with books was probably unsurpassed in an age of booklovers. His *Bibliotheca Universalis* 1545, and the *Pandectæ Universales*, 1548–55, were attempts to make books in general knowledge analogous to the Digest of Justinian in Civil Law. It is a bibliographical encyclopaedia, of the greatest value in tracing the knowledge of the learned world of antiquity and the middle ages ; and the Renascence up to the time of Gesner himself. His *Mithridates sive de Differentiis Linguarum*, was one of the earliest treatises in the subject of modern comparative philology. *See* p. 508 n. *infra*.

[2] Ray's first book on Quadrupeds was not published till 1693.

of description is greatly improved. Ray, however, introduced the method of comparative anatomy as the ground of zoological classification. So, too, in botany he established his classification on acknowledged inner affinities, rather than on merely external marks.

It is hopeless to search for the progressive side of zoology in school practice up to the time of the Restoration. The influence of Aristotle still held the Universities in its grip and Aristotle's *de Animalibus* was the zoology which the University schoolmaster learned, if he learned any, from the University Professor of Philosophy. Pliny was the main source of the detail of natural knowledge for the classically trained man. Wotton and Topsell might reach the " gentlemanly " schoolmaster. But if the teacher were an average man, probably the main source of his zoological knowledge was the tradition which Bartholomew Anglicus and the *Physiologus* had created. Yet the religiously-minded schoolmasters, and they were a much more important element than is ordinarily supposed, would draw their notions of animals, not from the progressive zoological writers, such as they were, nor from the old mediaeval sources, but from Du Bartas's *Première Semaine ou Creation du Monde*[1] or John Swan's *Speculum*

---

[1] Joshua Sylvester translated Du Bartas's book under the title : *Divine Weeks and Works* in 1592. Charles Dunster in 1800 wrote a book to prove that probably Milton derived the idea of *Paradise Lost* from Sylvester's translation of Du Bartas. The first subject is the divine work of Creation, and Du Bartas thus deals with chaos,

Mundi, 1635. In these books the six days of the Creation are fully described, and the Biblical account of the Cosmos as developed from chaos takes the place of Aristotelianism, excepting for the filling up of the details. Thus, the fifth day deals with the creatures which live in the waters, and those which live in the air, whilst the sixth day describes those which live neither in the air or water, but on the earth.

The animal world is described by Swan [1] with poetic fervour. Thus he writes of the nightingale :

But do you not hear sweet Philomel ? hark, how she plays the silent world asleep. This is a bird much addicted to watching, for she sitteth all the night singing upon a bough, with the sharp end of a thorn against her heart to keep her waking. Her very throat is able to ravish the dullest ear, and so much the more is her music beyond

---

the elements, the sea and the earth, the heavens, sun, moon, etc., the fishes and the fowls, the beasts and man, the Sabbath. After the Divine Week follow further days and weeks of history, and the author intended to wind up all in the eternal happiness of the Heavenly Sabbath. The significance of this poem, which was undoubtedly very popular in Puritan households, is, in connexion with the present subject, the inclusion of " every ornament of classic literature and scientific knowledge." The method of treatment in natural knowledge is that of the physical, as symbolical of religious import. Thus when Du Bartas speaks of the flowers, Sylvester translates:

"Never mine eyes in pleasant spring behold
    The azure flax, the gilded marigold,
    The violet's purple, the sweet rose's stammel,
    The lily's snow, the pansy's bright enamel ;
    But that in them the *Painter* I admire."

For further account of Sylvester *see* p. 166 *infra*.

[1] p. 395.

compare in that from so small a creature such dainty cries are warbled forth. The Latins called her Philomela, that is, a bird loving to sing, and what stoic but would love to hear her, and to give her thanks for her dainty ditty ? . . . The pretty lark chants with a sugared throat, so doth the blackbird, linnet, the several kinds of finches, the mirthful mavis, red-breast, wren, thrush and starling.

> "But all is nothing to the nightingale,
> Breathing so sweetly from a breast so small."

The schoolmaster, however, would not always limit himself to a book like Swan's *Speculum Mundi*. He and his boys would turn to such a book as Thomas Farnaby's *Index Poeticus* and find the references to classical authors who have described the nightingale, and to Textor's *Epitheta*, and find the epithets, which the great classical poets have judged appropriate to the sweet songsters.

Then, too, the characteristics of animals were brought out in strong relief in the numerous collections of apophthegms and adages. When Shakespere says " Like the poor cat i' the adage," he is speaking to a generation which abounded in allegorical and symbolical literature, which impressed into its service zoological knowledge, tradition, mythology. The *Metamorphoses* of Ovid meant more to Elizabethan and Stuart England than to us, for Ovid took them on the way to the world of magic and the romance of the learning derived from the Arabs of the East, in which they still more than half believed. The Puritans not only read the moralised Nature-poem of Du Bartas and the prose treatise of John Swan, but taught subject-matter on these lines in the schools. The teaching of the sciences of this type certainly was a part of the curriculum in some schools in the first half of the seventeenth century. Thus Hezekiah Woodward, as Charles Hoole tells us, " an eminent schoolmaster in London," wrote in 1641,

> *A Gate to the Sciences, opened by a naturall Key : or a practical Lecture on the great Book of Nature, whereby the child is enabled to read the Creatures there.*

As he says elsewhere, it is the duty of parent and teacher, to enable the child " to spell nature, and by degrees to read the volume of God's works." And again, " There I see herbs, flowers, trees, leaves, seeds, fruits, perhaps now in their winter and withered quarter; or in their spring-time receiving a new life again. . . . There I see the Behemoth (beasts) so called for her greatness; here the little worm, retiring into its hold, and earthing itself in case it feels the least touch. I cannot reckon up what I see ; *but if I do no more but see, the mule and the horse and the ox do as much as I.*" [1] In *A Gate to the Sciences*, Woodward explains his object in science-teaching, viz. by the senses to enfranchise the understanding, and to make the child " a free denizen of the world." He considers that the best way is to lead the child away from

---

[1] *A Child's Patrimonie*, 1640, a treatise on the child's bringing up, an excellent presentment of the Puritan ideas in education. Woodward opened a private school in Aldermanbury c. 1619. Mr. A. F. Leach mentions that a list of books was kept in St. Saviour's Grammar School, Southwark, at the incoming of Hezekiah Woodward as Master there (*Vict. County Hist. of Surrey*).

books and even the school, to see the "creatures" for himself, and to guide him personally in the interpretation of what he sees. But we cannot carry him everywhere from place to place unless we could go as far as it is fabled "Fame claimed she could go, viz. 2,500 miles a day." How then can we keep him? "I know no better way," Woodward affirms, "than by Emblems." Emblem teaching, however, implies representation by pictures. "If we had books (for teaching) wherein are the pictures of all creatures, i.e. herbs, beasts, fish, fowls, they would stand us in great stead. For pictures are the most intelligible books that children can look upon." Woodward, then, intensely appreciates the value of sense-instruction. This is to appeal to the mind by interpretation. And all exercise of senses and of intellect is to lead to the glorifying of God. His books show genuine love of nature, knowledge of Pliny as well as of later writers, but the moral and religious side of interpretation is uppermost in his mind. This side becoming still more emphasised led in a later generation to the extreme form of the *Divine and Moral Songs* (1715) by Isaac Watts (bringing interpretation "to the capacity" of children), after the type of:

> "How doth the little busy bee
> Improve each shining hour;
> And gather honey all the day
> From ev'ry opening flow'r."

Nevertheless, Woodward the schoolmaster is a pioneer of Nature study in the school and in several

196

particulars anticipated in his teaching, principles associated with Rousseau and with Pestalozzi.

Let me here refer to Palingenius's *Zodiacus Vitae*. This book was prescribed by Orders for St. Saviour's School, Southwark, in 1562, St. Bees' Grammar School, 1583, for Durham King's School, 1593, for Camberwell Grammar School, 1615. Its position as a school text-book is, therefore, undoubted. Palingenius taking the Zodiac as his theme, applies the whole system of natural knowledge, in a moralised form, to the practical affairs of life. The book contains, more-over, strong invectives against the Church of Rome, and was, therefore, in a special degree, acceptable to Protestants. There are many poetical passages, though abounding in the fabulous ; there is much imagery which sends the reader to contemporary knowledge of nature, in plants, animals and, of course, to astronomy. But any rational reading of the book implies a nature knowledge as realised in the times, which though difficult for the modern reader must not be ignored in any consideration of the teaching of these ages in matters of nature.

This (to us) strange mixture of the mythological, zoological, and the ethical, together with the glamour of the marvellous, was driven home by devices which have passed away from the modern con-sciousness. One very important class of book used in the school and circulated still more widely outside was, as advocated by Woodward, the Emblem Book. As contributing to the knowledge of all kinds of nature aspects, e.g. animals, it was of particular importance on account of the beauty of the engravings. In these Emblem books we may see charming illustrations of the bee, turkey, falcon, eagle, ostrich, unicorn, phœnix, the hydra, lion, fox, and so on, with characterisations conveying epigrammatic moral instruction. That these written books were used in school, we have the testimony of Thomas Farnaby, who gives the names of thirteen writers of Emblem books, beginning with Alciat, for boys to refer to, and Charles Hoole, who names them as sources to which boys should have recourse, in obtaining suitable matter for their higher themes. The mediaeval moral fiction of the type of Reynard the Fox worked its way into the ordinary consciousness. And for moralised zoology the school course prepared the way early by the inclusion of the animal fable-books of Æsop and others.

Æsop's Fables in Latin were part of the plan of studies drawn up for Ipswich School, 1528, by Wolsey, who says : " Of authors who mainly conduce to form a familiar style, pure, terse and polished, who is more humorous than Æsop ? Fables were prescribed by Statute at Bangor Friars' School and were part of the work of Form II at Westminster School, probably from 1560. They were prescribed at S. Bees' Grammar School, 1583, at Harrow, 1590. They were used in the Third Form at Rotherham School about 1630 and they were part of Hoole's curriculum in 1660 for his Third Form. Hoole regards Æsop's Fables as a book of " great antiquity and solid learning," whose moral apologues insinuate themselves into

every man's mind. The pupil should have an
English-Latin text, so that he may first be delighted
with the English story. Hoole gives a detailed
account of the best method of teaching Æsop.

The books mentioned in treating of the teaching
of botany, viz. the Nomenclators, Withals' Dictionary, and Comenius' *Janua Linguarum* and *Orbis
Pictus*, equally were interested in animals. Hoole
further devised a *Plain and Easy Primer for Children,
wherein the pictures of Beasts and Birds for each Letter
in the Alphabet are set down*. This was prefixed to
the *Orbis Pictus*.

Thus with a small copper-plate Crow we have—
in Latin—Cornix cornicatur ⎱ à à A a
in English—The Crow crieth ⎰

With a similar plate of a lamb
in Latin—Agnus Balat ⎱ b è è è B b
in English—The Lamb bleateth ⎰
and so on through the alphabet (except in two
cases), an animal's cry represents the sound of the
letter, and before the letter is placed a picture
representing the animal. It is from this Primer
that the very first instruction is to be given to the
child.

Samuel Hartlib stood sponsor to an extraordinary
tractate of Dr. Cyprian Kinner entitled *A Continuation of Mr. J. A. Comenius' School endeavours* (1648).
Kinner proposes a system of object-lessons in the
mother tongue. " I shew," he says, " Naturall
Things in the living book of Nature, Things Artificiall
in the shops and Work-houses of their Makers,

and both of them in the Repositories of their figures, and representations which belong to our school, where I shew them either living [1] or carved (yet as near the life as may be) or at least painted." The method of teaching is, he explains, analytical, synthetical, and " syncretically," i.e. by comparing the structure of things together. The production of natural things in their *living* form seems to imply the idea of a school collection of living animals. This idea is not peculiar to Kinner. In 1648, it was advocated by a man who commanded more attention than Kinner.[2] Sir William Petty realised, like Kinner, that, logically, if the school was to make the realistic impulse in education an actuality, then the study of plants and animals must be by direct observation and experience. He would have a gymnasium for practical training.

In connexion with the gymnasium would be the *nosocomium* (lit. : a hospital) *academicum*, which would include : " a complete *theatrum botanicum, stalls and cages for all strange beasts and birds with ponds and conservatories for all exotic fishes ;* here all animals capable thereof should be fit for some kind of labour and employment, and that they may as well be of use living as dead."

---

[1] The dates given for the formation of the earliest zoological gardens are : Ebersdorf, 1552 ; Dresden, 1554 ; San Rossore, c. middle of seventeenth century ; Versailles, c. 1666. The Zoological Gardens of London were formed in 1828. *See Geschichte der Menagerien und der Zoologischen Gärten,* by Dr. W. Stricker, Berlin, 1879.

[2] For a fuller account of Kinner *see* J. W. Adamson, *Pioneers of Education,* pp. 108–11.

NATURE STUDY IN DRAMAS

In 1657 Comenius wrote a school-play which appeared in England in 1664 under the title :

Johan Amos Comenii, schola-Ludus, seu Encyclopædia viva : i.e. Januæ Linguarum Praxis scenica. Res omnes Nomenclatura vestitas et vestiendas sensibus ad vivum repræsentandi artificium exhibens amoenum.

The object is clear. It is to bring the various subject matter of the natural world into a scenic representation.

On the title-page within the *Encyclopaedia Viva* (i.e. a second title-page) appears the description :

JANUAE LINGUARUM PRAXEOS COMICAE. PARS I. IN QUA RES MUNDI MAJORIS QUAE NATURALITER FIUNT, ORDINE IN SCENAM PRODUCUNTUR.

Psalm xlvi. v. 48.

VENITE, VIDETE OPERA DOMINI.

Now this would seem to imply that all the natural products of the earth were to be brought on to the stage, and as far as possible described, and, at the moment of description, some specimen to be produced and shown to the audience. This supposition would seem to be confirmed by the N.B. at the bottom of the second title-page, which reads as follows : " Hi Rerum Naturalium Ludi agi commode non possunt hieme, si ad vivum exhiberi debent Herbae, Flores, Spicae, Siliqua, Fructus Arborum, Muscae, Hirundines, aliaqua hieme mortua."

Professor Laurie says : " Anything more dreary than this sportive *Janua* it is impossible to

201

conceive." He points out, however, that Comenius states that it was most popular and successful with boys and masters. I venture to think that probably the basis of the success was the fact that examples of the objects spoken of and personified were shown to the audience ; and the very ingenuity of representing some of " the things " explains that " just applause " of which Professor Laurie speaks with the surprise in which everyone who examines the almost interminable " play " will participate.

At least it will be evident by the passages quoted from Cyprian Kinner and Comenius that they wished that school instruction should be of *living* forms, and the encyclopaedia should be where possible *viva*. In this respect, viz. in the recognition of the desirability that the pupil should learn the natural form by personal observation and examination, the Reformers of Schools of the time of the Commonwealth were as advanced in their attitude towards science as the experts themselves of botany and zoology and other natural knowledge.

It must be remembered that in the account given above, emphasis is laid on the *progressive* side of Natural Science knowledge and teaching. The *current* knowledge of the particularly well-informed men of the period would certainly reach its upward limit in the types of books given in the following lists. The school teaching, if the subject were included in any form, would not usually be in advance of the accepted text-books.

REPRESENTATIVE
LIST OF WORKS ON NATURAL SCIENCE
Taken from

William London's Catalogue of the most Vendible Books in England. 1658.

(*A*) The books on *Natural Science* from the section of William London's catalogue entitled " Physick and Chirurgery."

NOTE.—This list of natural science books as given here omits from London's list all works on anatomy, physiology, the Materia Medica, medical chemistry, astrological and occult aspects of medicine, books of housewife's simples and herbs, books of cookery, preserving, candying, and making syrups—on all of which subjects the current books are named, and often shortly described.

Ashmole (Elias) :

> *Theatrum Chymicum Britannicum, containing severall pieces of our famous English Philosophers, which have written the Hermeticall Mysteries in the ancient Languages ; by the truly noble Elias Ashmole, Esq.*

Brown (Thomas) :

> *Nature's Cabinet Unlockt ; Or the Natural Causes of Metals, Stones, Precious Earths, Juices, Humours and Spirits ; the Natures of Plants in general ; their affections, parts and kinds in particular, etc.* Lond. 1657. 12mo.
> *Chemicall Collection.* 8vo.

Mr. Glawber :

> *A description of new philosophicall Furnaces, or the art of distilling, in five parts ; of the tincture of gold, or the true Aurum potalile ; with the first part of the Minerall Work.* 4to.

M. de Lobell :

> *Botanographi, sive plantanum Historiæ Physicæ.* fol.

MODERN SUBJECTS IN ENGLISH SCHOOLS

Parkinson :

> *Theaticum Britannicum, or Generall History of Plants.* Fol.
>
> *Paradisi in sole Paradisus Terrestris : or a choice Garden of all sorts of rare flowers, with their nature, place of birth, time of flowering, names and virtues to each plant, usefull in physick, or admired in beauty ; with a Kitchen Garden furnished with all herbs, roots, and fruits, for meat or sauce ; with the art of planting an Orchard for all fruit-trees and shrubs, with the nature of grafting, inoculating and pruning of them, and preserving them and select virtues, all unmentioned in former Herbals.*

Paracelsus :

> *Secrets of Alchemy.*
>
> *A Philosophical and Chymicall Treatise of fire and salt.*
>
> *The Chymists' Key to open or shut, or the true Doctrine of corruption and generation : by N. Nolins. Pub. by Eng. Philalathes.* 8vo.
>
> *Philologia Brittanica, natales exhibens Indigenarum stirpium sponte emergentium.* 8vo.

(*B*) From the section of William London's Catalogue, entitled " History, with other Pieces of Human Learning intermixed. (1658.)"

> *Anthologia or the speech of Birds and Flowers ; partly moral, partly mystical.* 8vo.

Bacon, Francis :

> *The Natural and Experimentall History of Winds for making up of Philosophy ; Of the form of heat ; Of severall kinds of motion or active virtue, to find out the ebbing and flowing of the sea, etc.* 12mo.

Brathwait, R. :

> *Essayes on the five Sences, revived by a new supplement with a pithy one upon detraction.* 12mo.

BOOKS ON NATURAL SCIENCE

Brown, Dr. Thomas :
> *Pseudoxia Epidemica ; or inquiries into very many Received Tene(n)ts and commonly preserved Truths ; with many enlargements, with marginal observations, with a Table folio.*

Comenius, J. A. :
> *Naturall Philosophy reformed by Divine Light ; or a synopsis of Physicks, being a view of the world in generall, and the particular natures therein, grounded on Scripture Principles ; with an Appendix of the diseases of the body and the soul.* 8vo.

Digby, Kenelm :
> *The nature of Bodies and the nature of men's souls, looked into by way of discovery of the immortality of reasonable souls.*

Boate, G. :
> *Ireland's Naturall History, its situation, greatness, shape and nature : of its hills, woods, heaths, bogs, heads of promontories, harbours, roads, and bays, springs, fountains, mettals, minerals ; the nature and temperature of its air and season, etc., by G. Boate, Dr. of Physick to the State in Ireland.* 8vo.

Johnston, J. :
> *An History of the Wonderfull Things in Nature : Of Heaven ; The Elements, Meteors, Minerals, Plants, Birds, Beasts, four-footed ; Things wanting blood ; Fishes, and of Man.* Fol.
> *An History of the constancy of nature ; that the world derives not universally of itself, nor the Heaven's Elements, mixt Bodies, Meteors, Plants, nor Man, etc.* 8vo.
> *Naturall Philosophy, a description of the world and all therein, of Angels, Heavens, Stars, Planets, Elements, their order, nature, and government, of minerall, metalls, plants, stones, with the colours, forms and virtues.* 4to.

Pliny, C. :
> *The History of the World, commonly called the Naturall History.*

The Rich Cabinet of rare inventions. 8vo.

Tradescant, J.
> *Rarities, published by himself.* 8vo.

MODERN SUBJECTS IN ENGLISH SCHOOLS

White, Thomas :
> *Peripateticall institutions, in the way of that eminent person the excellent Philosopher, Sr. Kenelm Digby, the theoreticall part, with a theologicall index of the beginning of the world.*

Maplet, J. :
> *A Green Forest, or Natural History ; wherein may be ssene, the suffereigne virtues of all kinde of Stones and Metals ; next of Plants, or of Herbs, Trees and Shrubs ; lastly of Brute Beasts, Fowles, Creeping Wormes, and Serpents, and that alphabetically.* Lond. 1567. 8vo.

Widdows, Dan. :
> *Natural Philosophy, or Description of the World and several Creatures, therein, viz. angels, Mankind, Heavens, Stars, Planets, the 4 elements, with their Order, nature and government, as also of minerals, metals, plants, and precious stones. With their colours, forms and virtues.* 1621. 4to.

Mr. Nichols :
> *A lapidary, or the History of Precious Stones.*

Mr. Purchas, M.A. :
> *A theatre of political flying-insects ; where especially the nature, worth, work, wonder and manner of the right ordering of the Bee is discoursed and described, with Theologicall, Historicall, and Morall observations.*

Naturall Magick by J. Baptista Porta, a Neapolitan, in 20 Books, of the causes of wonderful things, Animals, Plants, Metals, Gold, Loadstone ; of strange cures, of beautifying women, distillation, perfuming, fires, tempering steel, cookery, fishing, fowling, hunting, invisible writing, strange glasses, statick experiments and pneumaticks ; of the Chaos ; setting forth all the riches and delights of naturall sciences.

To London's list, perhaps, the following book may be added, as disclosing directly and indirectly contemporary views on almost all the subjects of scientific survey, of the sixteenth century.

Agrippa, Henry Cornelius :
> *The Vanity and Uncertainty of Artes and Sciences. Englished by James Sandford.* Lond. 1569, 1575. 4to. 1576, 1684, 1694.

EXCURSUS

A Museum of Cromwell's Time

Charles Hoole wrote in 1660 in the *New Discovery of the old Art of Teaching School* :

London, of all places I know in England, is best for the full improvement of children in their education, because of the variety of objects which daily present themselves to them, or may easily be seen once a year, by walking to Mr. John Tradescant's, or the like houses, or gardens, where rarities are kept, a book of all which might deserve to be printed, as that ingenuous gentleman hath lately done his, by the name of *Musaeum Tradescantianum*, a Collection of Rarities.

This Museum was in South Lambeth. The collection had been formed by John Tradescant the elder, and augmented by John Tradescant the younger, his son. It was the latter who drew up the catalogue in 1656. The elder Tradescant died c. 1637, so the son had the Museum for over twenty years. In his preface to his *Musaeum Tradescantianum*, he apologises for not having brought out his catalogue earlier, as his friends had so often urged him to do. With some pride, he recounts their argument : " that the enumeration of these rarities (being more for variety than any one place known in Europe could afford) would be an honour to our nation." Moreover, it would provoke further inquiries into the " various modes of Nature's admirable works." Having explained the causes of his delay (one was the death of his only son), Tradescant gives his division of his curiosities into : I. Natural ; II. Artificial. In the natural section " some are more familiarly known and named amongst us, as divers sorts of birds, four-footed beasts and fishes, to whom I have given usual English names. Others are less familiar, and as yet unfitted with apt English terms, as the shell-creatures, insects, minerals, outlandish fruits, and the like, which are part of the Materia Medica (encroachers upon that faculty may try how they can crack such shells). The other sort is artificials, as utensils, household-stuff, habits, instruments of war used by several nations, rare curiosities of art, etc. These are also expressed in English (saving the coins, which would vary but little if translated) for the ready satisfying whomsoever may desire a view thereof. The catalogue of my garden I have also added in the conclusion (and given the names of the plants both in Latin and in English) that nothing may be wanting which at present comes within view, and might be expected from your ready friend, John Tradescant."

But not even in this account does the author include everything. There must be added choice pieces in carvings, " turnings," and paintings. Let us go over some of the details of Tradescant's collection. Amongst birds' eggs, he had the cassowary or emu, from Scotland the Soland goose, divers sorts of eggs from Turkey—one, he quaintly notes, "given for" a dragon's egg. But the specimens of eggs, beaks, feathers, birds, beasts, fishes, animals, and fossils are but small and casual, in comparison, even with present-day local museums. He had, however, a stuffed dodo from the Mauritius. This bird has been extinct now over two hundred years.

Amongst the " variety of rarities " were idols of the sheep, the beetle, and the dog, worshipped by Egyptians, which Mr. Sandys, the author of the well-known *Travels*, had presented to the Museum, a trunnion of Captain Drake's ship, and Jews' phylacteries. " On September 17th, 1657," occurs the entry in John Evelyn's *Diary*, ". . . to John Tradescant's museum, in which the chiefest rarities were, in my opinion, the ancient Roman, Indian, and other nations' armour, shields, and weapons ; some habits of curiously coloured and wrought feathers, one from the phoenix' wing, as tradition goes. Other innumerable things there were, printed in the catalogue."

It is not at all unlikely that the boys coming from Hoole's school would be interested in the physic garden (apparently the first in England) as well as in the museum. At any rate, Hoole would wish them to be. In a passage in which he has been advocating the establishment of libraries in schools he adds : " I should desire that towards the better completing of a grammar school there might be a little library well furnished with all sorts of grammars, phrase books, lexicons, dictionaries, orators, poets, histories, *herbals*," and so on. It is true Hoole specially recommends these for the master's use, but so that the master " may be able to inform his scholars in anything that shall be necessary for them to know."

Was Tradescant's collection the first in England ? The father died (c.) 1637. We know that there were raree-shows long before. " Were I in England," says Trinculo, " now (as I once was), and had but this fish painted, not a holiday fool there but would give a piece of silver ; there would this monster make a man ; any strange beast there makes a man. When they will not give a doit to relieve a lame beggar, they will lay out ten to see a dead Indian." Shakespere's *Tempest* was produced about 1610. One cannot help wondering if Trinculo is referring to John Tradescant's beginnings. The catalogue gives the impression that the Tradescants had catered, on the whole, for tastes of a more refined, a more scientific cast than that of Trinculo. But the question whether Tradescant's was the first collection of the kind or not is after all not a vital one. What is more important, viz. the spirit of wondering interest, of sympathetic imagination as to peoples far distant, and as to the curious—even the " anthropophagi, and men whose heads do grow beneath their shoulders "—the origin of all this is clear enough. It dates back to the voyages of Frobisher, Raleigh, Drake, and the great discoverers and navigators. It was emphasised by the physical contact with Spain and the relation of England to Spain's dependent provinces and territories. The wonderment and sense of greatness of the world found literary embodiment in the collections of *Voyages* of Hakluyt and in Purchas's *Pilgrimes*.

So in books like the *Relation of a Journey* (1615) of George Sandys (Tradescant's friend), story, adventure, curious customs, myths, habits, and modes of life filled the air.

ORIGIN OF THE "ASHMOLEAN"

Isaac Walton in the *Compleat Angler* says :

I know we islanders are averse to the belief of these wonders ; but there be so many strange creatures to be now seen, many collected by John Tradescant, and others added by my friend Elias Ashmole, Esq., who now keeps them carefully and methodically at his house near to Lambeth, near London, as may get some belief of some of the other wonders I mentioned.

Elias Ashmole (1617–1692) became acquainted intimately with the Tradescants ; he and his wife lived for a summer in the house with the Tradescants, " during which," says Sir John Hawkins,[1] " Ashmole agreed for the purchase of Tradescant's collection, and the same was conveyed to him by a deed of gift from Tradescant and his wife." Soon afterwards Tradescant died. Mrs. Tradescant, the serious-looking Hester of the portraits, was unwilling to give up the curiosities, and Ashmole filed a bill in Chancery for their delivery. In the end he succeeded. Ashmole removed his collection to Oxford and presented it to the University. The Ashmolean Museum was thus built up from Tradescant's collection as the nucleus.

For further account of Tradescant, *see* (1) in the treatise of Dr. Ducarel, F.R.S., F.S.A., in a letter to Dr. William Watson, F.R.S., *Upon the Early Cultivation of Botany in England, and some Particulars about John Tradescant*, etc. (**1773**) ; and (2) in Dr. Hamel's volume, *England and Russia, comprising the Voyage of John Tradescant the elder*, etc. (**1854**).

---

[1] *Compleat Angler*, 1795, note on p. 109.

CHAPTER VI

THE TEACHING OF EXPERIMENTAL NATURAL PHILOSOPHY

In the fourteenth century Petrarch had boldly said that though Aristotle was a man of vast learning he was after all a man, and liable to err.[1] The Italian Renascence proclaimed Aristotle anew, by the cry back to the original Greek. In the fifteenth century Laurentius Valla claimed that an appeal must be made to *facts*, viz. the facts of grammar as found in the writing of antiquity without regard to the abstractions of the Aristotelian conceptions applied to the study of grammar by the Mediaevalists. In the sixteenth century Vives, as we have seen, took up the same position with regard to the study of nature. It is necessary to emphasise the fact that the Humanists, of whom Erasmus and Vives may be taken as types, were the leaders of the revolt against the domination of *à priori* abstract conceptions, into which all science was to be fitted, without appeal to experience. Vives wrote his *liber in Pseudo-dialecticos*, a powerful protest against the all-absorbing dialectic, which ended in itself. " Who would tolerate," he says, " the painter who occupied all his life in preparing his brushes and his colours. Logic

---

[1] Mullinger : *Cambridge*, vol. i. p. 386.

is a most respectable art, but what are we to think of this cursed *babel* which has corrupted every branch of knowledge ? " This, then, is the position of Humanism, which, in its main current, was not the obstructor of scientific progress, but the very source of its inspiration. It was through the Humanists that the spirit of revolt against "Aristotelianism " was intensified. In 1536, Pierre de la Ramée (Petrus Ramus), the arch-iconoclast, made the astounding challenge, in the very citadel of Aristotelianism, i.e. in the University of Paris, on the occasion of a thesis for his M.A.—of asserting : Whatsoever has been said by Aristotle is false. This thesis Ramus maintained against the learned doctors, and such was his intrepidity that his courage and ability won the day over all obstacles, and he was awarded the degree with applause.

This action of Ramus produced a sensation throughout Europe, and awakened thinkers to inquiry into fundamental positions. Ramus had been led to his revolt, as he says himself, because he recognised that having been trained by disputes and questions in the liberal arts, he had not gained in knowledge, but merely in subtlety of sophisms. So, later, as Charles Waddington the biographer of Ramus remarks, Descartes, on leaving College, declared that he had derived no benefit from his instruction, excepting indirectly he saw how ignorant he was. When it was pointed out to Ramus that he had maintained his thesis by the very logic which he attempted to dethrone—and that his action was base ingratitude to Aristotle, he replied in the words of Aristotle, used on an occasion when he was charged with opposing Plato : " If it should be my own father, who had taught me these errors, I should attack them with no less force and perseverance. Truth would be dearer and more precious than my father himself, and I should count myself a criminal if I put my affection for one person alone, above the well-being of all." [1]

This attitude of Ramus is of vital significance in tracing the development of science It has been said, "What Luther was to the Church, Ramus was to the Schools." And logic, the chief discipline-subject of the University course, was conspicuously reflected in the grammar schools which sent pupils to the Universities. Thus Ramus proclaimed far and wide the position that the logic of Aristotle was an unsuitable instrument for discovering truth in the sciences, that method must be brought to bear in arranging one's own ideas and in analysing those of others, and that every man has the right to think for himself in matters of philosophy. The fact that Ramus perished in the Massacre of St. Bartholomew (1572) gave to such views the halo of martyrdom for science, i.e. amongst Protestant scholars.

It was, therefore, Humanists like Vives and Ramus [2] who shattered the idea of infallibility of

---

[1] Waddington : *Ramus*, p. 30.

[2] I have instanced Vives and Ramus, because of their influence on English thought. Other writers who appealed to observation and experience as methods for the study of natural phenomena were Telesio, Campanella, Caesalpinus, and Giordano Bruno, whilst the experimentalists by word and deed established the new realism.

method of the *Organum* of Aristotle, and who paved the way for Francis Bacon's *Novum Organum*, and later for the *Discours de la Méthode* of Descartes. In 1620, over eighty years after the famous thesis of Ramus, Bacon's *Novum Organum* was published. The attack which Ramus had made on the logic of Aristotle, Francis Bacon pursued on Aristotle's Natural Philosophy in the *Novum Organum*. Bacon maintains that Aristotle corrupted natural philosophy by his logic. He fashioned the world out of categories. He imposed countless arbitrary restrictions on the nature of things, being more anxious to affirm something positive in words than to declare the inner truth of things. In the *Physics* of Aristotle you have hardly anything but the words of logic. Bacon will not even allow any credit to Aristotle, although in his books on animals and other treatises experiments are introduced. For "he did not consult experience as he should have done in the framing of his decisions and axioms; but having first determined the question according to his will, he then resorts to experience, and bending her into conformity with his placets, leads her about like a captive in a procession." Bacon had little to urge against Aristotle which had not already been said. If originality be claimed for Bacon it must be on some other ground. The two main features of his *Novum Organum* are, first, that the student in any subject must abstract himself from all prejudices and preconceived opinions; he must keep clear of the idola of the mind; the tribe, the den, market-place and theatre. Being thus absolutely open-minded, casting books and systems on one side, his business is to come face to face with actual facts. Man is *naturae minister et interpres*. Man perceives the phenomena of nature through his senses. Provided he perceives correctly, the phenomenon in its simplest aspects is itself the outcome of an inward mechanism and action, of which the phenomenon is the result, and its presentation the outward sign which, by interpretation, enables us to understand the operations of Nature. But more than this. He thought the object of science was to penetrate to the essence and form of things—and that causes could be discovered and assigned for abstract properties or qualities. It will be seen at once that such a view, even if it were a practical undertaking, has absolutely no relevance to the greatest of scientific discoveries, e.g. the circulation of the blood, the laws of motion or the law of gravitation. Bacon's method failed as a method of discovery, because he supposed, as Whewell [1] says, that "method could do what must be done by mind, that method could do by rule what must be done by a flight beyond rule."

This collection of instances and facts by observation and experiment, though safeguarded by discrimination of instances, is Bacon's Inductive Method, and it is mechanical. He does not, however, propose "induction by simple enumeration of particulars," which he considers childish and precarious. True induction implies rejections and

---

[1] *Philosophy of Discovery*, p. 151.

exclusions. His idea of method in its basis is a large account book with nature introducing occasional balances of the particulars into a lump sum. On the other hand, however imperfect as showing a philosophy of the natural sciences, it was the most remarkable production of any age, up to his own, showing the recognition of the value of empirical knowledge, the value of particulars of experience, and the methods of observation and experiment. It glorified the single instances and cases, if there were sufficient of them to institute comparisons.[1] It stimulated the idea of differentiation of subjects. It brought all the divisions of knowledge, of natural science, into clearly marked territories for independent pursuit and research, whilst it encouraged the outlook for general principles. Perhaps its greatest service was the hopefulness which it roused in men's minds after the stagnation of mediaeval scholasticism, of the dawn of investigation into the numberless new subdivisions of physics and natural history. Its classifications were indeed magnified reflexions of a Conrad Gesner, but Bacon's encyclopaedic outlook, and hint of a perfected whole of scientific range, made him comparable with no one but Aristotle, to an age waiting with an intellectual impatience hitherto unknown "for the man and the hour" to embody its longings for progressive knowledge in a direction different from the stultifying logomachies of the schools.

---

[1] For the effect of Bacon's inductive method on the teaching of grammar see *English Grammar Schools*, pp. 289–292.

The *Novum Organum* was the new method to reach out to all knowledge, independent of authority. The *Advancement of Human Learning* is a statement of the best means, in Bacon's opinion, of propagating the knowledge already achieved, and of noting and filling up its gaps by determined investigation. In the *Advancement of Human Learning*, 1605, and its continuation *de Augmentis Scientiarum*, 1623, Bacon gives a complete survey of human knowledge as it presented itself to him. The standard to be applied to these books is surely that of a comparison only with anything previously written. The magnificence of Bacon's appeal (such in form it was) to the King for the national recognition of all intellectual inquiry—it must not be forgotten, Bacon included in his treatment the humanistic, as well as the scientific, side of knowledge—takes us back to the Platonic conception of the Prince-Philosopher, and contemplates him as establishing at any rate the conditions for the building up of an *Orbis Intellectualis* which shall excel in its glory " the wealth of Ormus and of Ind," or even the more stable riches of the Americas in the heyday of Spanish supremacy. As Lord Macaulay said of these books of Bacon, however we may view their influence or lack of it on actual discoveries, " we must give to written wisdom its proper meed ; no books prior to those of Lord Bacon carried mankind so far on the road to truth." If this be taken to mean that Bacon was great amongst men in the stimulation to high enthusiasm, by disclosing the possibilities of man in his search for knowledge, it is not ungrounded.

For, in a sense, Bacon is the father of the idea of an intellectual democracy. He holds that his methods level men's wits, leaving the philosophers in a position of mere self-assumed superiority, for every one may with the new methods satisfy himself by certain rules and demonstrations, on equal terms with the philosophers. From the pedagogical point of view it would be impossible to name any man whose direct influence as a thinker was greater on educational writers than that of Bacon in the seventeenth century. With the progress of science, scientific writers have tended to minimise the importance of Bacon, on account of the inadequacy of his methods as a statement of the principles underlying scientific discovery. But of his significance in stimulating scientific inquiry and the propagation of ascertained knowledge, there can be no doubt if we turn to the records of the middle of the seventeenth century. [1] In 1640, Hezekiah Woodward begins his preface to *Of a Child's Portion* by saying : " Our great Advancer of Learning noteth," etc. In 1647, Sir William Petty writes his educational pamphlet under the title *Advice of William Petty for the Advancement of some particular parts of Learning*. In 1649, John Dury writes on *An Agency for the Advancement of Universal Learning*. In the same year John Hall wrote *An Humble Motion to the Parliament of England concerning the Advancement of Learning*. So, too,

---

[1] Even in 1614 W. Holland founded a Grammar School at Steyning in Sussex " for the advancement of learning," and instruction of youth in the town of Steyning.

MODERN SUBJECTS IN ENGLISH SCHOOLS

Samuel Hartlib, in 1651, proposes an *Advancement of Husbandry Learning*. In 1654, John Webster, Chaplain in Cromwell's Army, offered his book criticising academies " to the judgments of those who love *the Advancement of Learning*." In the same year Hartlib edited educational pamphlets (by Eilhardus Lubinus, Richard Carew, and Michel de Montaigne) " for the consideration of those who seek the *Advancement of Learning* in these Nations." In 1661, Abraham Cowley brought forward his " Propositions for the *Advancement of Experimental Philosophy*."

These titles clearly follow the naming of Bacon's *Advancement of Learning*, but the contents of these works show still more emphatically the study and acceptance of Bacon's views, as containing within them the promise of the reformation of the schools of the country. If we compare the devotion to Aristotle in the sixteenth century with that to Bacon in the seventeenth, they almost suggest the inference : *Le roi est mort ; vive le roi.* The change in thought is revolutionary. The demand is made for a complete change in the curriculum and spirit of school-teaching. The direction of the change is towards the dropping of the classical atmosphere of the school, and its replacement by the study of natural and experimental science. The proposals are numerous and almost unanimous, in the reference to the source of their inspiration as the " Great Advancer of Learning."

If we take some passages from the authors named above, we can judge as to the extent of the proposals for the teaching of science in the schools in the first half of the seventeenth century, and at the same time trace the influence of the ideas of Bacon.

Hezekiah Woodward,[1] pleads for the study of Nature. " If we track and eye her well ; if we hound [2] her (as the Noble Scholar [3] phraseth it), she can lead us and must needs do so, from the footstool on earth to the chair in heaven . . . but it is not possible, as the same Noble Scholar saith, for us to make a perfect discovery of the more remote and deeper parts of knowledge, standing the while but upon the flat or level of this natural knowledge." With homely illustration, Woodward insists that mere sense-experience, as a method of teaching children, is not in itself sufficient. Shepherds and husbandmen have the opportunity of looking daily on the open book of Nature. They constantly live in the view of heaven and earth. " Yet experience shows us that the shepherd and the husbandman are the most ignorant people in the world." Woodward adds the comment : "Their senses report no more to the mind, but that they have seen it : no more." Hence Woodward implicitly suggests that object-lessons are inadequate, if they end in sense-experience. Power to interpret and understand Nature must be cultivated. With all the instinct of a modern democrat Woodward says (in 1640) : " For my part had I a child to design to the Plough

---

[1] *Of the Child's Portion*, 1640—a parent's manual for the bringing up of children. p. 94.

[2] *Advancement of Learning*, p. 106 (Woodward's note).

[3] i.e. Bacon.

or the Sea, or to some less stirring trade (in all these cases or courses of life learning is neglected as a thing of no use), I should as faithfully bestow upon him the culture and manurance of his mind first, and as readily, I should think, to very good ends as another parent would do, that had designed his to the College." [1]

As to the method of teaching, Woodward declares : " Nothing comes into the understanding in a natural way but through the senses. . . . And we note the child goes on with ease and delight when the understanding and the tongue are drawn along like parallel lines, one not a jot before another." He adds : " Make the child not an hearer only, but a *party in the business.* . . . *Speaking wholly* (by the parent or teacher) *is lost labour.*" [2] The parent is to help the child how to ask questions.

The subject-matter of instruction in natural philosophy begins with the earth, our mother, our nurse, our table, our grave. First, Woodward teaches the child the earth's figure, its dependence, its magnitude. In these subjects, he gives of the knowledge of his times, but always introduces theological and moral analogies where he can. The Aristotelian authority gave way in the Puritan mind to the authority of the Bible, placing it before the spirit of the new physical discoveries ; and one of the interesting features of Woodward is the attempt to reconcile the new Baconian and other physical teachings with scriptural texts. Thus Woodward

---

[1] *Of the Child's Portion.* Preface, p. 21.
[2] *Ibid.*, pp. 98–9.

says : " It is a good note which the learned Advancer
gives us, ' We see how that secret of nature, of the
turning of iron touched with the loadstone towards
the north, was found out in needles of iron, not in
bars of iron.' " To which Woodward adds that the
power, wisdom, and goodness of God is seen in things
great and small, " mountains and all hills, fruitful
trees and all cedars, beasts and all cattle, and in
creeping things." He then treats of the elephant,
quoting from Pliny, Bacon, and Alsted, [1] and of the
" mite or weevil," quoting Plautus, Vergil and
Bacon. Next, Woodward describes the waters
of the globe, their surface, their bounds and bars,
their weight and the creatures therein and the ships
thereon. Here again comes a quotation from Bacon,
who is associated with the Scriptures, with Grotius
and Scaliger. Next, the air, the winds, the winged
creatures, the clouds, rain, thunder, lightning, snow
and hail. The starry heaven is described, and of
the sun Woodward says : " It is a mathematical
conclusion, and *that hath the certainest grounds of any
art*, that the sun for quantity would make a hundred
and sixty earths, and the least of all those stars is
fifteen times bigger than the earth." Finally, day and
night are described, but the treatment is that of
moralising. Although the titles quoted show the
direct source of their inspiration, much more remarkable is J. H. Alsted's *Encyclopaedia of all the Sciences*
(1630) as an attempt to follow Bacon, not only

---

[1] J. H. Alsted (1588–1638) wrote *Encyclopaedia
Scientiarum omnium* published in 1630.

expounding the contents of all sciences, but also offering an educational method of teaching them. Still, it was Comenius who most thoroughly applied Bacon's treatment of science to school practice. It is Comenius who seizes on the two implicit principles which especially underlie Bacon's work, viz. encyclopaedism through classification and knowledge of all sciences, and what I have called the democratic principle, in Bacon, viz., that men have only to use their eyes properly, collect their instances and particulars, classify them, and build up axioms which make their classes intelligible, and they may intellectually reach heights which no philosophers can reach by intensest application of keenest wits to Aristotelianism. Hence Baconianism is interpreted by Comenius, as meaning that encyclopaedism is the inheritance, or at least within the possibility of acquisition by all. This is the thesis of Comenius in his *Great Didactic*,[1] "setting forth the whole art of *Teaching all Things to all Men*, or a certain inducement to found such schools in all the parishes, towns and villages of every Christian kingdom, that the *entire youth of both sexes, none being excepted, shall quickly, pleasantly, and thoroughly become learned in the sciences*, pure in morals, trained to piety, and in this manner instructed in all things necessary for the present and for the future life."

The Great Didactic evidently is one of the most optimistic educational treatises ever written. It

---

[1] Written in Latin c. 1630. Translated into English (1896) by M. W. Keatinge.

applies to pædagogy that hopefulness which breathes in Bacon, in believing that science can be perfected to embrace all knowledge. Comenius accepts the doctrine, and applies an educational method which he believes is capable of propagating all discovered knowledge. Education, he thinks, can accomplish everything for the child, if its method be sound, and the child be normal.

These views were accepted in England by men like Samuel Hartlib, John Dury, and to perhaps a less extent by Sir William Petty, John Evelyn, and Abraham Cowley, not to mention others.

More remarkable and at the same time more marked by Baconianism is Sir William Petty, who in 1647 issued his *Advice to Mr Samuel Hartlib on the Advancement of some Particular Parts of Learning,* 1647. Like all the educational followers of Bacon he was of opinion that education ought to have closer relation to life. The keener-minded amongst educationists, such, for example, as Charles Hoole, saw that education must be adapted to children's capacities—that education was not merely scholarship, and that the teacher was not merely a scholar. William (afterwards Sir William) Petty wished to satisfy his age that the training of young children could be accomplished without the aid of the classics—without even Latin grammar.

For Petty would have the ordinary school made into a trade or industrial school. *All* children, even those of the highest rank, should be taught some " genteel manufacture " in their minority.

MODERN SUBJECTS IN ENGLISH SCHOOLS

The following are Petty's reasons, in full :

1. They shall be less subject to be cozened by artificers.
2. They will become more industrious in general. 3. They will certainly bring to pass most excellent works, being, as gentlemen, most anxious to excel ordinary workmen. 4. They, being able to make experiments themselves may do it with less charge and more care than others will do it for them. 5. The *respublica artium* will be much advanced when such as are rich and able are also willing to make luciferous experiments. 6. It may engage them to be *Mæcenates* and patrons of arts. 7. It will keep them from worse occasions of spending their time and estates. 8. As it will be a great ornament in prosperity so it will be a great refuge and stay in adversity and common calamity.

Petty then recommends the establishment of a *gymnasium mechanicum*, or technical college, and his *nosocomium academicum*. As to the former he considers that it would attract the ablest of mechanics because it would afford " a market of rare and exquisite pieces of workmanship," for which there would be a ready sale. Teaching, of course, should be realistic, and should consist of observations and demonstrations in all studies of plants and animals,[1] in all kinds of rarities, ancient and modern engines, and buildings, gardens and experimental husbandry, paintings and statuary, knowledge of geography and allied subjects. A child thus made acquainted with " all things and actions would easily understand all good books (afterwards) and smell out the fopperies of bad books." One great text-book will be necessary, to be called *Vellus aureum*,

---

[1] See p. 200 *supra* for similar views of Comenius and Kinner as to the study of plants and animals. The *Nosocomium* is, substantially, a menagerie.

sive Facultatum Lucriferarum Descriptio magna.
In this book should be described every kind
of trade. Its " history "—i.e. a thoroughgoing
account not only of its past but also of its present—
should be given, including a full description of all
manual operations in it, together with an account
of instruments and machines used. Wherever
possible these should be pictured, and colours added
where necessary. Throughout, reasons are to be
given for the different operations, and an entire
theory of the trade to be given.

The compiler, moreover, is to publish all his
conjectures, showing how to improve on all old
inventions, and suggestions as to the invention of
new *desiderata*. All points as to the best way of
producing materials needed in manufacture are to be
explained. A preface must explain how to make
the most use of experiments and how to record
them whether they are (luciferous or lucriferous).
The whole spirit of these suggestions is clearly
derived from Bacon's catalogue at the end of the
Advancement of Learning to which at the end of
his " Advice," Petty refers the reader. The compiler
is to give his life-time to the book. All printed
books are to be collected and examined. The very
experiments described are to be the subject of re-
experiment. The compiler should be as young as
" sufficient abilities will permit," so that he may
" heap up the larger stock of experiments." All
men's interest must be enlisted, both those to whom
the appeal is the *auri sacra fames* and those who
are lovers of real knowledge.

Petty supplies a long list of advantages to be got from this monster book of trades. The last one—the fourteenth—must be quoted : " Boys, instead of reading hard Hebrew words in the Bible (where they either trample on, or play with, mysteries), or parrot-like repeating heteroclitous nouns and verbs, might read and hear the history of faculties expounded ; so that before they be bound apprentices to any trade they may foreknow the good and the bad of it, what will and strength they have to it, and not spend seven years in repenting, and in swimming against the stream of their inclinations." He further suggests that if boys learn the theory of a trade before being bound apprentice, three years will suffice instead of seven. The other four may be spent in *travelling*, "to learn breeding" and the perfection of their trades. The scheme of education, therefore, is organic. Petty believes it is grounded on the nature of the boy and therefore his education will be continuous and suited to his " propensities." " For we see children to delight in drums, pipes, fiddles, guns made of elder sticks, bellows' noses, piped keys, etc., for painting flags and ensigns with elder-berries and corn-poppy ; making ships with paper and setting even nutshells a-swimming ; handling the tools of workmen as soon as they turn their backs, and trying to work themselves ; fishing, fowling, hunting, setting springs and traps for birds and other animals ; making pictures in their writing-books ; making tops, gigs, and whirligigs, quilting balls, practising divers juggling tricks upon the cards, etc., with a million more besides. And for the females, they will be making pies with clay, making their babies' clothes and dressing them therewith ; they will spit leaves on sticks, as if they were roasting meat ; they will imitate all the talk and actions which they observe in their mother and her gossips. . . ."

Petty's conclusion is that since children delight in " things " they will be most capable of learning about them. They have quickness to apprehend and unpreoccupied memories to retain. Their good-will is *to* them, whereas their will is *against* grammar and the ordinary school subjects, and their judgment unripe for them. In addition to proposing a scheme of education for schools, which he believes to be natural, or as we say, founded on psychology, Petty looks to such developments to " make us able (if it be at all possible) to demonstrate axioms in philosophy, the value and the dignity whereof cannot be valued or computed."

John Dury, who gave himself to the task of bringing about a reconciliation of the various divisions of foreign and English Protestantism and other philanthropic endeavours, was in matters of education a follower of Bacon. In 1642, he wrote *A Motion Tending to the Publick good of this Age and of Posterity*. To Dury's mind it was clear that a " reformation " of schools was necessary. The system of things in nature, obvious to the senses must " be insinuated into children's imaginations with the proper names thereof, that they may have a true conceit of the simplest outward things of the world as a crude matter of that whereof they are afterward to receive instructions." They will then be prepared to study the " body of sciences." In addition scientific method must be laid down so that " we may find out by our own industry any truth as yet unknown and resolve any question which may be proposed in nature as the object of a rational meditation." All these views are after the manner of Bacon himself, though applied by Dury to the training of children. In Dury's *Seasonable Discourse* (1649), he insists that in schools, " things necessary and universal must first be taught *universally*. The objects of sense must be taught as the ground of all rational matters." How definitely Dury builds his ideas on Bacon will be seen by the following passage from the *Seasonable Discourse* :

The Advancement of our Learning.

Seeing we are now about a reformation of our ways and necessitated to think upon the public good, even for our preservation from utter ruin and confusion, and seeing some such thing as the advancement of learning hath been oftener and in a more public way at least mentioned in this nation of late than in former times, partly by the publication of those excellent works of the Lord Verulam . . . and chiefly seeing there is a reserve of means purposely kept to be employed for the advancement of religion and learning . . . we ought not to despair of some good issue at last. . . . We shall then, as concerned in the public, use our rational freedom to suggest thus much, that except the bounds of learning be extended beyond the Universities, and be understood equal to the bounds of schools, and to the care of education, incumbent to a well-regulated society of men ; and except the bounds of schools be made as large as the borders of rationality in mankind ; we shall come very far short of that aim which should be meant by the advancement of learning.

The writer then insists that without in any way decreasing the work of the Universities it is high time to increase the number of inferior schools. That to supplement the work of both, an agency of universal learning should be established so that men's spirits should not grow " flat and sluggish and settle on their lees."

These ideas are further applied to the courses of instruction in the schools (which are to be universal) in Dury's *Reformed Schools* published in 1650.

From eight or nine to thirteen or fourteen years of age children are to be exercised ' in observing all things natural and artificial extant in the world, whereunto their imagination shall be led in a certain method to cause them to reflect orderly upon them and observe them in their several kinds, coherences, differences, parts, actions, properties, uses and references unto man by trades and manufactures. From thirteen or fourteen to nineteen or twenty, the things which are to be taught them, and wherein they shall be exercised, are all the useful arts and sciences which may fit them for any employment in church and commonwealth.

Of John Hall, of Gray's Inn, 1627–1656, Thomas Hobbes, the philosopher, said : " No man had ever done so great things at his age." At the age of twenty-two years he wrote *An Humble Motion to the Parliament of England concerning the Advancement of Learning*. Hall's appeal is specially for a " reformation of the Universities." He complains : " We have hardly Professors for the three principal faculties, and these but lazily read and carelessly followed. Where have we anything to do with chemistry, which hath snatched the Keys of Nature from the other seats of Philosophy, by her multiplied experiences ? Where have we constant reading upon either quick or dead anatomies, or ocular demonstration of herbs ? Where any manual demonstrations of mathematical theorems or instruments ? Where a promotion of their experiences, which, if rightly carried on, would multiply even to astonishment ? Where an examination of the old tenets ? " The reference to chemistry is interesting. Bacon had little to say[1] with regard to this subject, but the little is in keeping with Hall a quarter of a century later. Up to Hall's time, Paracelsus and Van Helmont are the only names of note, and the development of chemistry can hardly be said to be differentiated from alchemy, till the foundation of the Royal Society. Mayow published his account of experiments in combustion in 1674 and then there is a gap in the development till Stahl in 1729. A professor of chemistry, however was appointed at Oxford in 1683, and at Cambridge in 1702.[2]

As to the function and position of chemistry,

---

[1] " Some little has been produced by the industry of chemists but it has been produced accidentally and in passing, or else by a kind of variation of experiments such as mechanics use."—*Novum Organum*, LXXIII.

[2] The first Professor of Chemistry (1683) at Oxford was Robert Plot, a gentleman of property, described as an antiquary. He was also in 1683 appointed as first " Custos" of the Ashmolean Museum at Oxford. The first Professor of Chemistry at Cambridge, John Francis Vigani, a native of Verona, who had taught the subject at Cambridge from 1683, was officially appointed in 1702.

Joseph Glanvill [1] in 1668 writes : " As we cannot understand the frame of a watch without taking it to pieces so neither can Nature be well known without a resolution of it into its beginnings, which certainly may be best of all done by Chymical Methods. In those vexatious analyses of things, discoveries are made of their natures, and experiments are found out which are not only full of surprise and information, but also of valuable use especially in the practice of physic. . . . The late cultivators and particularly the Royal Society have laid aside the Chrysopoietick, the delusory delights and vain transmutations, the Rosicrucian Vapours, Magical Charms, and superstitious suggestions and formed it into an instrument to know the depths and efficacies of Nature." [2]

The reference by John Hall to " quick or dead anatomies " leads us to the recognition of William Harvey (1578–1657), whose vivisections helped so largely to establish his theory of the circulation of the blood, announced in 1616. Probably there is no discovery of the seventeenth century of more transcendent triumph in the sphere of experimental science than Harvey's discovery, and, at the same time, none less in keeping with Bacon's scientific

---

[1] In *Plus Ultra : or the Progress and Advancement of Knowledge since the Days of Aristotle. In an Account of some of the most Remarkable late Improvements of Practical Useful Learning*, 1668. This is the best contemporary account of what had been achieved in science up to 1668.

[2] Glanvill, pp. 11-12.

method of discovery.[1] Bacon's lack of insight as to what was happening in his own day (e.g. in the case of Harvey, Gilbert, Galileo, and Kepler) and his lack of observation and reflection on their methods have led to a serious loss of reputation for Bacon in the minds of later scientific thinkers. It was therefore a sign of discrimination on the part of Hall, to appreciate the outstanding genius of William Harvey.[2]

Hall further wishes to see a change in methods of teaching school children. "They should be essayed by most easy trials and those by pleasant pastimes of sense . . . and your children with a pleasant success possessed of all the treasures of real knowledge, ere they could have thought they had entered the gates."

Hall's attack on the Universities in 1649 was followed by that of John Webster (1654). The latter was still more trenchant and copious in his protest against the sway of Aristotle in the Universities : "Aristotle's natural philosophy and his astronomy admit of no reformation. They must be eradicated."[3] As a substitute, it would be better

---

[1] References in the writings of Harvey show that he had intimate acquaintance with the anatomy of more than sixty animals, and had given years of study bearing on comparative anatomy.

[2] For a description of Harvey's treatise on the discovery of the circulation of the blood, *see* D'Arcy Power's *William Harvey*, chapter viii. For Harvey's method *see* Whewell, *Philosophy of Discovery*, chapter xvii.

[3] Seth Ward, Savilian Professor of Astronomy at Oxford, wrote a sarcastic reply to Webster in the *Vindiciæ Academiarum*. But his own disavowal of the authority of the physical views of Aristotle virtually concedes the point at issue.

to introduce Lord Bacon's methods and teaching. "No axioms should be received which are not proved by observation and luciferous experiments, so that they may be recorded in a general history of natural things. So, every age and generation, proceeding in the same way and upon the same principles, may daily go on with the work, to the building up of a well-grounded and lasting fabric. This is the only way for the instauration and advance of learning and knowledge."

In the boys' schools, too, subjects and methods must be changed. Webster follows Hall in the advocacy of chemistry as a subject of experimental study. Youth should be taught pyrotechny and chemistry by "manual operation and ocular experiment so that they may not be sayers but doers, not idle speculators but 'painful' (i.e. painstaking) operators. They must have laboratories as well as libraries, and work in the fire instead of building castles in the air." Webster is not so happy in his treatment of physic. The Galenical way of the medicinal part of physic must not imprison the student. He must enter into the discoveries of Paracelsus and Helmont. Webster was stronger on the negative than the positive side of education. Abraham Cowley in 1661 drew up a plan of a "philosophical" College, which in its spirit was Baconian. There were to be twenty professors, four of whom were always to be travelling, though sending regularly an account of all that bore on learning and especially on natural philosophy. They were to send despatches, books, simples, animals, stones, metals, minerals, etc., and to have considerable grants for this purpose. They were pledged to send only what was tested as true, and if any report which had been forwarded were found untrue, they were to recant. The remaining sixteen professors were to study and teach all sorts of natural and experimental philosophy, viz. " mathematics, mechanics, medicine, anatomy, chemistry, the history of animals, plants, minerals, elements, agriculture, architecture, art, military, navigation, gardening, trades, manufactures, all *natural magic* or divination, and briefly all things contained in the catalogue of natural histories annexed to my Lord Bacon's *Organon.*" Cowley planned not only a college but a school in connexion with it. This was to consist of 200 boys, to enter at thirteen years of age, after having learned Latin grammar, and having read some authors. No fees were to be paid, but parents out of gratitude might present some curiosity to the school. Cowley accepts the reading of Latin authors in agriculture, such as Vives and Milton had named, viz., Varro, Cato, Columella, Pliny, part of Celsus,[1] and of Seneca, Cicero *de Divinatione, de Natura Deorum,* Vergil's Georgics, Grotius, Nemesianus, Manilius. These are chosen, as Milton said, and as Cowley agrees, for the " solid " things in them, though Cowley would prefer that a single book should be compiled of all things in the ancient poets which would " seem for the advancement of natural sciences." He would add

---

[1] The mention of a medical author seems to point to the tradition of physic as a subject taught in schools. *See* p. 177 *supra.* For account of Manilius *see* p. 376 *infra.*

the Morals and Rhetorics of Cicero and like Milton would add (as part of boys' reading) a book of education. Milton's choice was Cebes and Plutarch in Greek and Quintilian (first two or three books) in Latin. Cowley enjoins the Quintilian. Every month or second month the boys are to act a comedy of Terence, or Plautus. They are to read a few Greek works, amongst which are to be Aristotle's *History of Animals*, Theophrastus and Dioscorides, *of Plants*.

With the History [1] of Animals is to be joined anatomy, and modern knowledge is to be applied to correct what is wrong in Aristotle. So with Plants. Other studies are added, but the above gives the chief provision for natural philosophy as in the mind of Cowley. He partakes of the general hopefulness of the age when he adds : " The school will give us the best education in the world (purely *gratis*) to as many men's children as shall think fit to use it. Neither does it interfere with any parties in state or religion, but is indifferently to be embraced by all differences in opinion, and *can hardly be conceived capable* (as many good institutions have done) *even of degeneration into anything harmful.*"

In optics, the use of lenses in magnifying objects was discovered by Baptista Porta in 1560 ; in 1610 Galileo had discovered Jupiter's moons by a telescope, and in 1611 Kepler was using a still better telescope. In 1621 Snellius discovered the law of refraction. In

---

[1] i.e. Descriptive account.

1637 Descartes had said, to quote Glanvill's estimate in 1668, the "most clear useful, and improvable things about optics that ever were extant on the subject."

In 1649 is the first instance I have found of the proposal to introduce optics as a school subject of teaching. It occurs in George Snell's *Right Teaching of Useful Knowledge*. In mechanics in **1583** Galileo found out the principle of the pendulum, and in **1589** the law of falling bodies ; and towards the end of his life he discovered the laws of motion. These, however, were first made available for general knowledge by Sir Isaac Newton in **1687** in the *Principia*. In 1586, Stevinus published his *Statics* and *Hydrostatics*, enunciating the triangle of forces, distinguishing between stable and unstable equilibrium ; and in hydrostatics enunciated the law of fluids on a horizontal surface, and he made other discoveries in hydrostatics. Thus Galileo is the father of dynamics and Stevinus of statics.

It is difficult to determine whether mechanics was in any way taught in the school, as the differentiation of subjects within the terms experimental philosophy and mathematics was not settled. There was, however, a text-book on the subject, which connected the subject with geometry.

Mathematicall Magick. Or the Wonders that may be performed by Mechanicall Geometry. In two books.

Concerning Mechanicall { Powers Motions.

Being the most easy, pleasant, usefull (and yet most neglected) parts of Mathematicks. Not before treated of in this language. By J. W., M.A., 1648.

This book was written by John Wilkins, [1] the first secretary of the Royal Society (1662) and afterwards Bishop of Chester. Wilkins says in his Preface : " Other discourses of this kind are large and voluminous, of great price and hardly gotten. Besides there are not any (that I know of) in our vulgar tongue for which these mechanical arts of all other are most proper." Wilkins makes a good show of ancient authors who have written on mechanics. To these he adds the names of modern writers, including Galileo. The subjects treated include the balance, the lever, and the relation of the natural motion of living creatures to these principles ; the wheel, the pulley, the wedge, the screw. Wilkins next inquires into the magnificent mechanical works of the ancients, the comparison of which with our own, he thinks, implies that decay has taken place in mechanical arts. He next discusses how the balance and lever may be contrived to move the whole world or any other conceivable weight. Next he takes the wheel, by multiplication of which, it is easy to move any imaginable weight. Then he deals with *Automata*, representing the motions of

---

[1] John Wilkins (1614–1672) and John Wallis (1616–1703), both very interesting men, educationally, in the advancement of experimental science, established in Oxford the Philosophical Society, which lasted from 1648-9–1690. For some time the meetings of the Society were held in the rooms of John Wilkins in Wadham College. Amongst those who came were Robert Boyle, William Petty, Seth Ward. This Oxford group were amongst the chief founders of the Royal Society, whose first *Journal Book* began November 28, 1660.

living creatures, various sounds of birds or beasts and some of them articulate. Further, he deals with the possibility of framing an ark for submarine navigations and,—what may surprise the modern reader—several ways of attempting to devise flying machines, and offers suggestions for meeting the difficulties which seem to oppose the possibility of a flying chariot. He describes the attempts at solving the problem of perpetual motion. He discusses subterranean and " perpetual " lamps, and other questions relating to perpetual motion, from the side of chemistry and of magnetism, and of fluid weights.

Amongst the advances made in scientific discoveries of general natural philosophy were the following : In electricity, Gilbert showed that other stones beside amber could by being rubbed produce electricity, but it was not till 1672 that Guericke invented the first electrical machine. Other important advances were made in the theory of musical notes in 1638 by Galileo. In 1646 Pascal proved that air had weight. In 1658 Huyghens made cycloidal pendulums, and in 1661 Boyle discovered the law of compression of gases. The power of steam, in propelling, had been understood by Caus in 1615 and was applied by the Marquis of Worcester in 1663 to an engine. Scientific inventions are especially to be noted as significant of the possibilities of the advancement of knowledge. It is on these inventions that Joseph Glanvill especially bases modern superiority over Aristotle. It may be remarked, too, that the Baconian method was of little or no avail in promoting the discovery of these instruments of progress. Glanvill particularly mentions the telescope,[1] microscope,[2] thermometer,[3] barometer,[4] air-pump.[5] As to the teaching of these subjects in the universities, the time had not come. There was sufficient subject-matter for experimental and descriptive science before 1660, and there was earnest, even vehement, pleading for the teaching of natural philosophy. Reformers were unanimous, as Seth Ward affirms, that " we (i.e. University men) should lay aside our disputations, declamations and public lectures and betake ourselves to Agriculture, Mechanics, Chemistry and the like." But the students who came to the University did not come to study natural philosophy as a special or leading subject. They often stayed only two or three years and then passed on to the Inns of Court, " to become rational and graceful speakers " and to have a good carriage, and superior manners. " I am persuaded," says Seth Ward (that in the

---

[1] It is impossible to say who invented the telescope. In a sense, its origin began with the use of lenses (the use of which was not unknown to Roger Bacon). Galileo was the first effective user of the telescope—of a simple kind, however, such as could now be purchased, probably at a toy-shop for half-a-crown, as Sir Oliver Lodge suggests. (*Pioneers of Science*, p. 97.)

[2] Malpighi, says Hallam, was the first to employ good microscopes in anatomy. This was in 1661.

[3] Drebbel invented the alcoholic thermometer in 1620, but it was not till 1670 that the mercurial thermometer was invented.

[4] Torricelli invented the barometer in 1644.

[5] Guericke invented the air-pump in 1650.

Universities) "not one in many hundreds (if they have their option) will give themselves to be accomplished natural philosophers." Ward wrote [1] in 1654, and though the intention of his writing is to answer attacks on the Universities, yet his admissions show that Aristotelianism was retiring from its citadel, and the supremacy of the old dialectical and philosophical studies was about to give place to the modern discipline of the mathematical order. The old Aristotelian problems were replaced in the disputations by questions in moral and often in natural philosophy [2] and Rohault's Physics, founded on Descartes, became a University text-book in the latter half of the seventeenth century.

The fact remains, however, that experimental natural philosophy was not a recognised academic study in the Universities, even in the second half of the seventeenth century and much of the eighteenth century was barely marking time in the English Universities. It was not till 1783 that a Professorship (the Jacksonian) in Natural and Experimental Philosophy was established at Cambridge. The professor was to be chosen for his knowledge of natural experimental philosophy and chemistry, and the only restriction on the subject-matter of his lectures was that they were to be of an experimental

---

[1] In *Vindiciae Academiarum*.

[2] But even as late as 1672, a candidate for the medical degree, in France, obtained recognition for a thesis concluding that the circular motion of the blood is impossible —showing that the knowledge of scientific discoveries moved slowly in Universities.

character. Isaac Milner was the first Professor. The propagation of the knowledge of natural philosophy gathered together in the first half of the seventeenth century was not that of University teaching, but the work of a voluntary society. Joseph Glanvill [1] discusses the methods of spreading and communicating knowledge, and makes no allusion to universities or schools. The three means of the diffusion of knowledge [2] he names as (1) printing, (2) the compass, (3) the Royal Society. There is no need to follow his argument as to printing. For the reformers of Glanvill's time were rather concerned to show that the printed book was too successful. It absorbed the attention of students away from the book of Nature. The compass, "as the loadstone to navigation, had opened up foreign lands to travellers, had made possible knowledge of the great waters of the sea, and had brought the knowledge of other civilisations to us and had reported ours to them. Thus by the compass [3] the 'history' of Nature was enlarged and knowledge propagated and improved." Glanvill's third agency for the propagation of knowledge was the Royal Society. The Royal Society started from an informal weekly gathering of certain natural

---

[1] *Plus Ultra,* chapter xi.

[2] Glanvill is showing the advantages of modern times over Aristotle, and perhaps he is assumed too readily that academic institutions remained Aristotelian in spite of increasing knowledge.

[3] Said to have been invented by Flavio Gioia of Amalfi in the fourteenth century.

Footnote: line 3, delete "is."

philosophers (largely medical men) in London, in 1645, and from an Oxford group in 1648-9 onwards. In 1662, the gatherings were organised, and the Royal Society was formally recognised. It became the centre of the scientific movement in England, and it was to the Royal Society that the discoveries were announced, of the great succession of distinguished scientists of the latter half of the seventeenth century : Boyle, Hooke, Mayow, Ray, Grew, Malpighi, Huyghens, Halley, and Sir Isaac Newton. The memoirs and transactions of the Royal Society thus virtually are the records of the progress of science.

In the proposals for encyclopaedic colleges, Sir Humphrey Gilbert c. 1572, Sir Francis Kynaston in 1635, do not mention natural philosophy. Nor does Sir George Buck in his Third University of England (1615), in his long list of subjects taught in London, include any branch of natural philosophy, excepting *pyrotechny*. [1] Sir Balthazar Gerbier, in his scheme for a proposed Academy at Bethnal Green, enters into the spirit of the age and includes " Natural Experimental Philosophy " in the curriculum, and in the time-table which he drew up. He also includes *fireworks*. [1]

With regard to school-teaching of natural philosophy, we cannot therefore expect to find the subject

---

[1] *Pyrotechny*, literally, is the use of fire or a furnace in the mechanical arts. *Fireworks* similarly means (1) the work done with a furnace, (2) or a projectile of an explosive nature for use in war as well as for a display.

taught in the grammar schools of the seventeenth century. In individual cases, teachers drawn by the educational fervour of Comenius to teach the elements of the subject cannot be expected to have taught in accordance with the latest developments of the foremost scientists of the age. For in this subject the text-book written by Comenius is permeated with a scriptural, allegorical, and moralising interpretation more in accordance with the spirit of the old Bestiaries than the method of a Galileo or a Descartes. The general import of Comenius's Natural Philosophy may be gathered from its title :

> *Naturall Philosophie Reformed by Divine Light : Or, A Synopsis of Physicks : by J. A. Comenius : Exposed to the censure of those that are Lovers of Learning, and desire to be taught of God. Being a view of the World in generall, and of the particular Creatures therein contained : grounded upon Scripture Principles with a briefe Appendix touching the Diseases of the Body, Mind, and Soul. By the same Author.* London. 1651.

Nor will an idea of the practice of teaching be complete unless we glance at the Aristotelians. There were those, not a few, and schoolmasters amongst them, who believed that Bacon and Descartes were the " idols of a transitory fashion " and that the true wisdom was to stick to that which had stood the test of ages. These writers are naturally passed by in the histories of science, but representatives should be mentioned in a history of educational practice. As a type, perhaps the best of this school of thought, in the subject of natural philosophy is :

> *Peripateticall Institutions in the Way of that eminent person and excellent Philosopher Sir Kenelm Digby. The Theoreticall Part. Also a Theologicall Appendix of the Beginning of the World. By Thomas White.* Gent. 1656.

The object of the book, a small one, and in English (noteworthy facts for their bearing on educational influence), is to maintain Aristotelian method, though showing a willingness to accept conclusions different from Aristotle, when genuine argument compels a different conclusion. But the author maintains that there is *in Nature and in things beyond Nature* " a no less connection of Terms and force of Consequences than in Mathematics." Since all science is in the last resort received into the unity of definition, White trusts that natural philosophy will be " rescued from desperation." He has divided his book into " lessons and very frequent breaks," each of which he thinks will be sufficient " at one sitting to be explicated," for pupils who are novices will require a teacher, and a breathing space should be allowed for. To the auditors or pupils, questioning is to be permitted, but opposition is to be prohibited till they have been through the whole work once or twice. " The work is but short, so for a little while the affection of credulity may be fairly exacted in a learner that he may clearly apprehend the things proposed. When he shall have understood against what he is to object, there will be liberty of disputing."

The superiority of White's book may at once be admitted over the manuals of the school of Bacon in its compactness and the sense of an organic whole, in its recognition of " lessons," all of which are logically suitable in their place, and well connected. As an exposition of Aristotelian principles it compares favourably with the compends of Baconian natural philosophy of the period, which I have seen. Book I contains the " part of Logic which is necessary to Sciences." Book II " contains those things which concern the Nature of Bodies in common." Book III, those things which concern the World and its greater parts. This deals with the Planetary World, the Earth, the Sea, Mountains, Rivers, Lakes, the Air, Clouds, Rain, Snow, Hail, Meteors, Winds, Earthquakes, Comets, Ebbing and Flowing of the Sea, the Motion of the Earth, Motion of the Air, of the Moon, the Primum Mobile. Book IV deals with the essential motions of bodies or Metaphysic. Book V, with the substances abstracted from Matter and the operation of Things.

The production of a text-book, however logical and compact, which ignored the new experimental method of investigating Nature with an open mind, was an attempt to set back the finger of time. The Renascence spirit had brought into existence forms of investigation which had the effect of overwhelming its first intention, viz. the return to antiquity. The Renascence spirit itself provoked voyages of intellectual discovery, and the essence of its gain was not only in the products realised, but also in the process, viz., the enterprising spirit of inquiry, which claims truth as its end whether it be ancient or modern. Yet in tracing the line of continuity of the practice of teaching, the ancient is as important as the modern, and in the light of the most recent theory of science, that of evolution, a recognition of the position of Thomas White [1] and the Aristotelians is complementary to that of Baconianism. Both views have their recognition in any complete modern statement of the thought and practice of seventeenth century school teaching.

It is not however to the specific teaching of the numerous branches of natural philosophy that we are to look for the scientific influence of the seventeenth century. The realistic spirit of teaching, based on the senses, was the main result of the scientific studies, discoveries and inventions, as far as the schools were concerned. This we have seen in the works of Hezekiah Woodward, the schoolmaster, and in John Dury, perhaps the most original educational writer of the Commonwealth. I have not yet mentioned Samuel Hartlib. It was he who wrote a letter of commendation to Dury's *Reformed School* in 1650. In this letter Hartlib says : " The training up of scholars in one school or two though very great and most exactly reformed, will be but an inconsiderable matter in respect of a whole nation and will have no great influence upon the youth thereof, when so many schools remain unreformed and propagate

---

[1] Thomas White (1593–1676) was a Roman Catholic, educated at St. Omer, Valladolid and Douay. He held a post at the English College at Douay, and was afterwards (President) of the English College at Lisbon.

corruptions ; therefore the *propagation of reformed schools* is mainly aimed at ; and to that effect, the training up of Reformed Schoolmasters is one of the chief parts of this design." Hartlib then develops his argument : " The readiest way to reform both Church and Commonwealth is to reform the schools of Education therein, by sending forth Reformed Schoolmasters amongst them." In 1581 we have seen [1] Mulcaster, in his *Positions*, had proposed a Training College for Teachers. Hartlib and Dury proposed a new way for influencing reformed schoolmasters, and others. This was what Dury called 'an Agency towards the Advancement of Universal Learning," or in Hartlib's phraseology, "an Office of Address." The work of the agent will be to animate the professors of all arts and sciences " by a correspondency with all that are of any note, to waken them by one another unto all industry, and to gather up the fruits thereof, to be applied unto all the schools for the advancement of learning therein."

When the reformed schools shall have been established, Dury points out how essential will be this correspondence, this communication of worker with worker. With Commonwealth sanguineness he urges :

" The chief cause of our distractions and most lamentable disorders in learning is this : that there is no concurrence in any common aim, nor in any rules which lead thereunto amongst the professors of the same kind of learning ; which makes every

---

[1] pp. 175–6 *supra*.

one of them walk by themselves differently; solitarily, and without that help which their communications about the conquering of common difficulties would yield unto them. . . . A central object of concurrence is wanting which might make them meet with one another. This centre then should be this agency, which should be employed to discern in every kind the several abilities of men and their undertakings, to acquaint them with other men's endeavours of the like abilities, labouring in the same subjects, either the same or a different way that by mutual acquaintance and conference, their thoughts may be ripened, they may perfect, rectify, and benefit one another, and beat out the hidden paths of truth, which in due time seasonably may be published for the benefit of all." The " correspondence was to be made with foreigners as well as amongst Englishmen, and foreigners were to be brought over when they had special knowledge or experience to communicate. Further, a special printing-press was to be set up to print reports and notices which were desirable to be distributed to the schools and universities, to stir teachers to thoughts " of a public concernment " in their work.

This idea was shared by Comenius and Hartlib with Dury. In a letter written by Dury, he says, in replying to some suggestion : " I will propose the matter to Master Comenius and Master Hartlib, for *we are bound to do things with mutual advice*. This educational triumvirate were the founders of the modern realistic or experimental training in the schools. They are the leaders who, for England, made teaching from sense-experience a prior educational principle to book-learning more than a hundred years before Rousseau and Pestalozzi. Dury pathetically states that through " love " of educational reforms, " we (I mean Mr. Comenius, Mr. Hartlib and myself) are put to a non-subsistence." But in the practice of English schools, through their initiative influence, the appeal to sense-experience in teaching has had advocacy and been in evidence, a revolt against mere book-learning, and as a preparatory ground to the later teachings of a Rousseau and a Pestalozzi. Essentially this development is traceable to the Baconian spirit of the advancement of learning, and to that source, Comenius, Hartlib, and Dury themselves attributed, chiefly, the inspiration of their school endeavours.

I have met with a school in which natural philosophy was systematically taught on the basis of experiment, but it is much later, viz. 1723. This was at the Academy or Accomptants' Office in Little Tower Street, London, in a school kept by Mr. Thomas Watts. The courses in experimental philosophy were " performed " by Benjamin Worster, M.A., and Thomas Watts. These courses had a comprehensive syllabus. The Little Tower Street School proposed to qualify completely young gentlemen for business, after a new and approved method, " free from the interruptions and loss of time in common schools." These two teachers, Watts and Worster, claimed to teach rationally and to the highest perfection writing, arithmetic and book-keeping by double entry as to be found in "real business." "All parts of the Mathematics" were taught; French, and drawing. But the chief feature apparently was the experimental philosophy as taught by Benjamin Worster. The course included the laws of motion, gravitation of fluids, the air as an elastic fluid, the principles of optics (according to Sir Isaac Newton's principles), mechanics (with a full and comprehensive syllabus), hydrostatics, pneumatics, optics (also in detailed syllabus).

The charge of "going the course" was two guineas and a half; one guinea to be paid on subscription, the remainder the third day of the course. Those who were desirous of going over the course again were charged one guinea and a half; afterwards as often as they pleased, *gratis*. Thomas Watts translated from Rohault *A Treatise of Mechanics, or the Science of the Effects of Powers or Moving Forces, as applied to Mechanics, Demonstrated from its first Principles*. The text-book of the course appears to be one written *ad hoc*:

> *A Compendious and Methodical Account of the Principles of Natural Philosophy : As they are explained and Illustrated in the Course of Experiments performed at the Academy in Little Tower Street. By Benj. Worster, A.M.* 1722.

The main point of interest is that here we see Sir Isaac Newton's principles of mechanical philosophy reaching to the school, in a direct manner. The demonstrations seem to have been open equally to pupils of the Academy and to outsiders.

[For further details as to the progress of Experimental Science *see* C. R. Weld's *Hist. of the Royal Society*, 1848, and for the contemporary view *see* Joseph Glanvill's *Plus Ultra* (–1668), Improvements in Mathematics (chaps. iii, iv), in Astronomy (chap. v), in Optics and Geography (chap. vi) ; the use of the Telescope, Microscope and Thermometer (chap. vii) ; advantages of Barometer and Air-pump (chap. viii) ; Experimental Optics (chap. ix) ; improvements in Natural History (chap. x) ; Mr. Boyle's contributions to useful knowledge (chap. xiii). *See* also William Wotton's *Ancient and Modern Learning*, 1694 (chaps. xv–xxvii).]

CHAPTER VII

THE TEACHING OF MATHEMATICS

MATHEMATICS are briefly discussed by Erasmus. "It is sufficient," he says, "to have a smattering of Arithmetic, Music and Astrology,"[1] though he admits that sometimes children have a special bent to them, and such pupils should not be discouraged. On the other hand, J. L. Vives has much to say in their favour.[2] After the pupil has had practice in rhetoric, Vives suggests, with a dash of humour, it will be well to lay upon him the relief of silence which is necessary for mathematics, and transfer him from the use of his ears to the practice of his eyes. For this reason, on the other hand, Ascham[3] condemns mathematics. "Mark all mathematical heads, which be onely and wholly bent to those sciences, how solitary they be themselves, how unfit to live with others, and how unapt to serve the world." Mathematics are described by Vives as "both speculative and practical; the relation between these two aspects being that of sire to son. Light and restless intellects shrink from the continued effort necessary for speculative mathematics. There is a continual bond and series of proofs. They lead, too, away from

---

[1] Woodward : *Erasmus*, p. 145.
[2] *De Tradendis Disciplinis* (1523), bk. iv.
[3] *Scholemaster*, 1570. (Mayor's ed., pp. 14–15.)

the ordinary experiences of concrete life. But mathematics are valuable both for application to life and for philosophy. Plato would not allow the student ignorant of mathematics to enter his classroom, for mathematical examples are bound to arise in philosophical questions. First should be studied arithmetic, for it tests the understanding and sharpens the wit, though it is the simplest mathematical subject. No part of life is devoid of numbers, and writers of sacred and profane history teach many mysteries of nature and of divinity which can only be understood by means of numbers. A certain crass kind of nobleman thinks it high born not to know how to reckon. But he thus makes himself like a lion, or bear, or boar that he wears on his escutcheon. For not to reckon is the part of the whole brute creation ; man alone calculates. Let then young men know the elements of numbers. Let them reckon by algorisms,[1] an Arabic invention, and let them follow arithmetic in its whole inner treatment. In geometry are set forth theorems and proofs which compel and capture us. From geometry spring perspective and architecture, studies which protect our very bodies. By these studies we come to measure fields, mountains, towers and edifices. [2]

Astronomy discusses the number, magnitude and

---

[1] Algorism is the term given to Arabic numerals and the Arabic arithmetic, to distinguish it from the arithmetic of Boethius.

[2] Vives next deals with music, which, in accordance with received tradition, he regarded as a part of mathematics.

motion of the heavens, and constellations, treating of them separately and as a whole, and as compared with one another. This subject must not be carried to the divination of the future or of hidden things, for this pursuit leads to impiety. But astronomy must have as its province the description and limits of seasons to help the country husbandmen, to the determination of longitude and latitude, which is not only of importance to cosmography but is also absolutely necessary for one's imagination. Astronomy requires the astrolabe or quadrant such as that of Ptolemy or our *orbiculare*.

Vives then proceeds to the recommendation of mathematical text-books. Jacobus Faber writes (in Latin) on theoretical and practical arithmetic with sufficient simplicity to be translated by boys in schools, and from him and Jordanus Nemorarius and Boethius Severinus, arithmetic may be learned, together with music from the last-named. For geometry Faber, again, is to be recommended. Faber, further, wrote *Theorica Planetarum*, which was elucidated with commentaries by his disciple Jodocus Chlichtoveus, though the basis of the work was taken from Purbach. Proclus is to be read on the astrolabe, though a better work is that of my friend, John Poblatius, yet even to him the teacher should add notes from John Stoflerinus Justingensis and Ptolemy. The *Margarita Philosophica* is at least to be consulted. Carolus Bovillus has written on geometry, but for perspective[1] John Cantuarensis is better.

---

[1] Perspective, i.e. optics.

Then comes Euclid, who needs careful explanation. The pupil should read for himself Martianus Capella. Petrus Cirvelus has written commentaries on John Sacrobosco. Francis of Capua and Purbach's *Theorica Planetarum* should also be read. There should be no disputations on these matters. Short questions and answers will suffice, showing the work and referring to the diagrams, or using a rod with sand or even an abacus. These studies must be frequently revised. Such equipment will suffice to those whose wits are not Minerva-like, as long as they carry their theory into practice. For more advanced students in arithmetic, Tonstall and John Siliceus should be read ; in geometry, Thomas Bradwardine, in astronomy, Ptolemy and the mathematics of George Valla. No doubt the works of Archimedes are the most finished in this kind of study, but I have not seen them. My friend Juan Vargara has told me that he has read them in Spain with the greatest possible care, and translated them from a secret manuscript. This is the curriculum in mathematics for a youth up to the twenty-fifth year or thereabouts. [1]

Richard Mulcaster, in the *Positions*, 1581, proposes a College [2] for the teaching of mathematics. Mulcaster apparently had felt the attraction towards mathematics when at King's College, Cambridge. Sir John Cheke at the time was Provost, and sought

---

[1] *See* the note at the end of this chapter (pp. 286–7).

[2] The seven Colleges proposed by Mulcaster are for " Tongues," Mathematics, Philosophy, Divinity, Law, Physic, and for the Training of Teachers.

to encourage mathematics in spite of his great learning in other subjects, which were ordinarily supposed to make mathematics of no interest. Mulcaster himself tells us in the *Positions* that Sir John Cheke, in the reign of King Edward VI, brought Buckley, a fellow of the College, to read arithmetic and geometry to the students. Cheke further presented a number of Euclids at his own cost to students. Buckley drew up the rules of arithmetic into verses for easier learning. Mulcaster was the recipient of one of Cheke's Euclids (and had also from the same donor a copy of Xenophon). Mulcaster understood that Cheke had also done the same kindly office to students of St. John's College when he was connected with it. Mulcaster asks : " Can he then mislike the mathematical sciences who will seem to honour Sir John Cheke and reverence his judgment ? " Mulcaster further asks : " How can a man take upon himself to be a master of *arts*, who hath not studied them before he proceeded to his degree ? So that the very University herself doth highly esteem of them (Mathematics) if she would entreat her people to esteem of their mother's judgment." Mulcaster also pleads the usefulness of the subject to many professions and trades. Our life indeed would be " quite maimed without them." It is no " objection of account " to say what should merchants, carpenters, masons, shipmasters, mariners, devisours, architects, and a number such do with learning ? " If they do well without, might they not do better with ? But to learn mathematics they would need to learn

Latin. If so, let them learn Latin, for the " tongues be helps to all trades as well as to learning." Mulcaster admits that mathematics must be " fetched from the Greeks," but they borrowed them from other nations, and were founders only as to method and language. Moreover, in ancient times mathematics followed, as a study, directly on the elementary subjects.

" In time," prophesies Mulcaster, " all learning may be *brought into our tongue and that natural to the inhabitant*, so that schooling for tongues may prove needless, as once (i.e. in Greece) they were not needed : for *it can never fall out that arts and sciences, in their right nature, shall be but most necessary for any common weal, that is not given over unto to(o) to(o) much barbarousness*." [1]

It is not generally realised that Mulcaster planned to write a treatise on Mathematical Teaching, to follow his *Elementarie* and *Positions* (i.e. the " Tongue " School). Unfortunately he did not accomplish this, but sufficient has already been said to claim for Mulcaster the distinction of being the first practical teacher to advise the beginning of mathematical studies in the school, directly after the elementary subjects were acquired. The reasons for the inclusion of the subject as given by himself are :

1. " The Mathematicals," in their very nature, " do work some good thing, sensible even to simple people by number, figure, sound or motion."

---

[1] *See Positions* (Quick's Reprint), p. 24**2**

2. In the manner of their teaching, they induce a habit " inexpung[e]able by bare probabilities and not to be brought to believe upon light conjectures in any other knowledge, being still drawn on by unfallible demonstrations."

3. They supply an antedotal training to false similitudes of rhetoric. For instance, " When ye compare the common weal to a ship and the people to the passengers, the application being under sail, may be out of sight when ye seek for your proof. But in these sciences, the similitudinary teaching is so certain in applying, and so confined by effects, as there is nothing so far from sense, and so secret in understanding, but it will make it palpable. They be taken from the sense, and travel the thought, [1] but they resolve the mind."

Amongst the Elizabethans, no man takes so high a position from his writings on mathematics as Robert Recorde, the physician. He was the most important writer of his times in English on arithmetic, in the *Ground of Artes*, 1551 (probably the first edition was in 1540) ; the first writer on geometry (*The Pathway to Knowledge*, 1551), the first writer in English on astronomy and the doctrine of the sphere (*Castle of Knowledge*, 1556), the first to introduce algebra into England (*Whetstone of Wit*, 1557).

It is important to note that Recorde was not a teacher in an academic institution, though he was a Cambridge graduate. Nor is it only, perhaps not chiefly, to the teachers in the Universities we have

---

[1] *Travel the thought*, i.e. make the thoughts work.

to look up to the end of the sixteenth century for advances in mathematics. The Universities professed to teach the quadrivium, and the quadrivium included arithmetic, geometry, music, astronomy; but such teaching was evidently perfunctory, even when it existed, till the institution of Professors of Mathematics at Oxford in 1619 and at Cambridge, 1664. For two hundred years in the Middle Ages Merton College, Oxford, surpassed even Paris in its teaching of mathematics, but after the Renascence, Cambridge took the leadership. The Tudor mathematicians, though chiefly coming from Cambridge University, pursued their higher mathematical training after leaving the University. They were sometimes physicians, sometimes gentlemen of means, and again men of political affairs, or ecclesiastics. There was, too, a movement of interest in mathematics, outside of the Universities in Queen Elizabeth's reign, when men like Sir Thomas Smith and Sir Thomas Gresham established lectureships in the subject, the former privately, the latter in public lectures.

The cardinal point to be realised in the period previous to 1660 is that in all subjects outside the classical authors, the basis of all mental discipline in all academical institutions was Dialectic. Logic occupied the place which afterwards was won by mathematics as a mental discipline. In the latter half of the seventeenth century, Aristotle's physics gave way at Cambridge to an exposition of the philosophy of Descartes, and this again to the *Principia* of Newton, at the close of the seventeenth century. The first half of the eighteenth century was dismally unprogressive in the Universities. In 1753 was issued the first Tripos list.

In tracing the development of mathematics to the time of the Restoration, for the most part we have to look outside of the Universities. It is thus necessary to notice the contemporary views of mathematics outside of the University, and the methods of propagation of the subject.

In tracing contemporary ideas of the place and function of mathematics, I will take typical representations of what we way call (1) the popular view, (2) the nobleman's and gentleman's view, (3) the philosophical view as represented by Bacon, (4) the view of mathematics at the time of the Commonwealth of educated non-mathematicians.

1. *The Popular View.*

In an interesting and valuable contemporary book in dialogue form, which for shortness' sake we may call *Examination of Complaints* [1] printed in 1581, there are three interlocutors, a capper (i.e. a

---

[1] *A compendious or briefe Examination of Certayne ordinary Complaints, of divers of our Country men, in these our Dayes ; which although they are in some part unjust and frivolous, yet are they all, by way of Dialogues, thoroughly debated and discussed. By W. S., Gentleman. Cum privilegio.* 1581.

Also in the Harleian Miscellany, ed. 1812, vol. ix, p. 139.

This book once had the honour of being attributed to William Shakespere ! In fact, it was once reprinted (in 1751) with Shakespere's name (*see Harleian Miscellany*, vol. ix, p. 139). Anthony à Wood suggested that the author was William Stafford, gentleman.

capmaker), a knight and a doctor of physic. Amongst
other subjects, they discuss the state of learning and
its outlook. We thus get an insight into the attitude
of the representatives of these three classes towards
learning as a whole and mathematics in particular.
The capper thinks it would " make no matter " if
there were no learned men at all. He would have
men " learn to write and read, and to be acquainted
with the Scriptures in their mother tongue, and
even to learn the languages used in countries about
us, that we might write our minds to them and they
to us." But he would have men learn no more. The
knight has hitherto thought there was no other
learning in the world but such as that of doctors of
divinity or law or physic. The doctor of physic says :
" It is time people fall to those sciences which
they see ' in some price ' e.g. to divinity, law and
physic. But they ought (as ordained in Universities)
first to be bachelors and masters of arts ere they
come (say) to divinity. These arts be the seven
liberal sciences : grammar, logic, rhetoric, arithmetic,
geometry, music and astronomy." These, says the
doctor, are in his age " *skipped over.*" The doctor
attempts to show the capper and the knight the
gifts we have by learning. By learning, man
supplies his lacks. For he is short lived and compared with animals often inferior, by grossness of
weight of body. But the learning of cosmography,
for instance, remedies these defects, for we can
" purchase by peregrinations " of learning as well
as we should, if we should flee from our country to
another like birds and yet with less travail and

danger. So through astronomy we know the course of the planets, " as certainly as if we were amongst them." A bird, however agile, could not attain to this knowledge which learning gives us. The reading of Vegetius will give the knight more knowledge than personal experience could alone supply, so (addressing a husbandman) " you, good husbandman [would find] in Columella."

Knight. I say again, might we not have that in our English tongue, and read them over, though we never went to school ?

Doctor. Yea, well enough ; and yet should ye be far from the perfect understanding of them, except ye had the help of other sciences ; that is to say, of arithmetic, in disposing and ordering your men ; and geometry, in devising of engines to win towns and fortresses, and of bridges to pass over ; in the which Cæsar excelled other, by reason of the learning that he had in those sciences and did wonderful feats which an unlearned man could never have done ; and if ye had war over the sea, how could ye know towards what coasts ye be sea driven, without knowledge of the latitude of the place by the pole, and the length by other stars ;

Astronomy.

And you, good husbandman, for the perfection of the knowledge of husbandry, had need of some knowledge in astronomy, as under what aspect of the planets and in the entry of what sign, by the sun and the moon it is time to ear, to dung, to sow, to reap, to set, to graff, to cut your wood, your timber ; yea, to have some judgment of the weather that is like to come for inning of your corn, and grass, and housing of your cattle : yea of some part of

Physic

called Veterinaria, whereby ye might know the diseases of your beasts, and heal them.

Geometry.

Then for true measuring of land, had ye not need of some knowledge in geometry to be a perfect husband ?

Architecture.

Then for building, what carpenter, or mason, is so cunning or expert, but he might learn more by reading of Vitruvius and other writers of architecture ; that is to say the science of building ?

The only other branch of learning mentioned by the doctor is moral philosophy, especially necessary for the rulers of the Commonwealth.

Such are the subjects of knowledge which the representative of learning expounds to his lay audience, trying to explain to them the place of the individual subjects. It is interesting to note that with the exception of veterinary physic and of philosophy, the whole of the subjects which he names as illustrative of learning are what were then called "the mathematicals." A second point to be observed is that emphasis is laid on the practical side of mathematical subjects. This is contrary to the modern educational view, which regards the main value of mathematics as being that of a mental discipline. Let us, then, in this connexion recall the fact that arithmetic, geometry, and astronomy belonged to the arts, all of which in the Middle Ages were regarded as belonging to the sphere of practice. We recognise, of course, that the object of dialectic was practical, i.e. it was for the purpose of the disputation. All mathematical knowledge was given with a view to practical purposes in the idea of the Middle Ages, and continued so in the seventeenth century. Vives strikes a modern note when he speaks of theoretical and applied mathematics.

Partly for this reason (though there are doubtless others), the development of mathematics, instead of proceeding from the universities, came in the first place from those engaged in the practical affairs of life. Taking the names of Recorde, Dee, and Digges as the three most representative English mathematicians of the sixteenth century,[1] we may note that Recorde and Dee were doctors of physic, whilst Digges was a man of affairs, M.P., and later, muster master-general of the English forces in the Netherlands.

II. *The Nobleman's View of Mathematics.*

The view of the nobleman and gentleman with regard to mathematics is clearly laid down in Sir Humphrey Gilbert's scheme for Queen Elizabeth's Academy (c. 1572). " Whereas in the Universities men study only school learnings, in this Academy they shall study matters of action meet for present practice both of peace and war."[2] School learning does not train for practical affairs. The greatest

---

[1] This was the judgment of the late Professor de Morgan.

[2] The preparation of the noble for " peace " is especially the work of readers in divinity, law, physical exercises and modern languages, and heraldry. These, however, are directed to practical ends. Thus the object of teaching law is to enable the gentleman to take up his function of a Justice of the Peace, or Sheriff.

clerks are not always the wisest men.[1] Gilbert's proposed provision in the Academy for mathematics is :

There are to be two mathematicians, one to teach arithmetic and geometry with their applications to millitary science, at salaries of 100*li*. each, an engineer at 100*li*., and two ushers to teach the principles of arithmetic and geometry at 40*li*. per year each, a horseman who is to have due allowance (the figures are all given) for the provision of horses, a " soldier " at a salary of 66*li*. 13*s*. 4*d*. The second mathematician is to teach cosmography and astronomy, with navigation, to be paid 66*li*. 13*s*. 4*d*. There is to be one to teach how to draw maps, sea charts, and perspective at 40*li*.

Gilbert is explicit as to the place of mathematics. Their main function clearly is that of usefulness in such matters as embattling, fortifications, artillery, i.e. for the purpose of war.

Put in more comprehensive terms, the nobleman considered mathematics, as all other subjects, from the point of view of usefulness for his duties in the public service, i.e. in war, in judicial functions, and in the diplomatic service, as well as, though in a subordinate sense, for the management of his own personal estate and affairs. The underlying knowledge serving for practical life was divided into two kinds of arts, the mechanical arts and the liberal arts. Directly even the subjects of the quadrivium, arithmetic, geometry, music and astronomy, became applied to the work of artisans, tradesmen, merchants, or in short to anything of value chiefly

---

[1] Cf. Chaucer : "The grettest clerks beth not the wisest men."

as personal advantage in monetary remuneration, they became mechanical. On the other hand, they were " liberal," if they were not applied to any direct monetary advantage to the person studying them. Thus in John Kepers's translation of Romei's *Courtiers Academie,* 1598, [1] we find such an expression as "leaving apart mechanicall art, as impertinent to a civil man," etc. It was on account of this distinction between mechanical and liberal arts that Sir Thomas Elyot was anxious to show that the advocacy of the practice of drawing and sculpture as an educational discipline need not cause the reader to " scorn him," as suggesting that he is making his nobleman a mason or painter. Modern ideas admit painters as a professional class, but in the sixteenth century the distinction of an artist-painter from a house-painter was not clear, for the recognition of the fine arts was a much later development, though it is traceable in germ. The nobleman must study his mathematics with a view to practical ends in the service of the state. This is thus the distinction of the liberal, as contrasted to the mechanical, aspect. The distinction was a real difficulty to progress in the sixteenth and seventeenth centuries, especially in the applications to experimental science. Even in 1669, Robert Boyle remarks with what diffidence learned men viewed any person addicting himself to an art like chemistry. " They are troubled when they see a man acquainted with other learning, countenance by his example sooty

---

[1] The original Italian text was published at Ferrara, c. 1586.

Empirics. These experiments may indeed be useful to Apothecaries and perhaps to Physicians, but are useless to a Philosopher who aims at curing no disease but *that of ignorance.*" The idea therefore was that learning was academically established as a fixture that could not be moved. Its orthodoxy was impregnable. The influence of the nobleman's view that mathematics should be studied in their relation to practical ends at least had this progressive element, viz. that any new practical invention, of proved service to warfare or the service of the state, must be accepted. Hence this curious result : If we refer to the books on the education of gentlemen, we find that mathematical progress is reflected much more surely than if we look to the ordinances of the Universities. Not that there is an appreciation of the detail of the advance of pure mathematics, but the appreciation of the trend as it affects practical life is definitely seized and used.

There is an interesting account (in 1576) by the Frenchman Louis Leroy of modern knowledge, contrasted with the ancient knowledge, which illustrates in a work written for gentlemen, and not for the Universities, this readiness to note and utilise progress.

Robert Ashley, pupil of the famous schoolmaster Adrian à Saravia, of Southampton, in 1594, issued a translation of the French work,[1] in which is a

---

[1] *Of the Interchangeable Course or Variety of Things in the whole World ; and the Concurrence of Armes and Learning, thorough the first and famousest Nations : from the beginning of Civility and Memory of man, to this Present. Moreover,*

passage which well shows the composite nature of mathematics as ordinarily understood in the Elizabethan age in England as well as in France.

In the Mathematics [we have not at this day such eminent persons as] Euclid, Eudoxus, Archimedes and Ptolomeus : albeit there have been in them very excellent men of this age. For sithence they were extinguished in Egypt, and left off by the Greeks, and Arabians ; they were never more famous than they are at this present : especially Astrology and Cosmography ; for the ancients scarcely understood the one half of heaven, of the earth, and of the sea, knowing nothing in the west beyond the Canaries ; and in the east beyond Catygare. At this day all lands and seas [sic] are known and sailed . . . Cosmography and Astrology are so beautified, that if Ptolemy, the father of them both, were alive again, he would scarce know them, being increased in such sort by the late observations and navigations. Regiomontanus [1] is reputed the best mathematician of this age, and thought to be little inferior to Anaximander the Milesian ; or Archimedes the Syracusan. His master Purbachius, the Cardinal of Cusa, and Copernicus [2] (being Germans all of them) have excelled in these sciences. Also Jovianus Pontanus hath taken great pains in Astrology being no less happy in prose than in verse ; and apt for any kind of writing.

---

whether it be true or no, that there can be nothing said, which hath not been said heretofore : and that we ought by our own Inventions to augment the doctrine of the Auncients ; not contenting ourselves with Translations, Expositions, Corrections and abridgments of their writings. Written in French by Loys le Roy called Regius : and translated into English by R. A. . . . At London. Printed by Charles Yetsweirt, Esq., London, 1594. Fol.

[1] Joannes de Regiomonte (Johann Müller), 1436–1476, native of Franconia.

[2] The Copernican theory had been accepted in England by Recorde in the *Castle of Knowledge*, 1556, and by John Field in the same year in an *Ephemerie* for 1557. Both of these were at work in London. Copernicus's book, the *de Revolutionibus Orbium Cœlestium*, was published in 1543.

To take another instance : De Morgan speaks strongly as to the significance of the Renascence in bringing the old Greek writers on geometry into the range of mathematical studies. For the Greeks, he considers, were the inventors of methods of demonstration. " Had it not been," says De Morgan, " for the writings of Euclid, Ptolemy, Aristotle, Proclus, etc., and judging of what would have been the case in Geometry by the practice which became universal in other branches of exact science, we cannot see how anything like demonstration could have been introduced." This may be too emphatic a statement, but it emphasises the trend of progress in modern mathematics as being particularly centred on geometry. It may be by chance, but it is interesting to find that Peacham [1] writing for gentlemen, emphasises this very point. He says nothing of arithmetic, [2] but devotes a chapter to geometry. It is a subject, he says, worthy the contemplation and the practice of the greatest princes. " It deals with the length, breadth and height of all things, comprised under the figures of triangles, squares, circles, and magnitudes of all sorts with their terms or bounds." Peacham does not give any account of geometry from the side of the content of its scientific scope, but he deals with its practical developments and the use made of its principles by great inventors of ingenious mechanical contrivances.

---

[1] *Compleat Gentleman*, 1622, ch. ix.
[2] Cleland in his *Instruction of Young Noblemen*, 1607, bases mathematical instruction on arithmetic.

Summing up the appeal to the study of geometry by gentlemen, he puts the case thus :

" The use you shall have of Geometry will be in surveying your lands, in building anew, making your mills, bringing water-ducts, the measure of timber, stone, etc. (wherein gentlemen many times are egregiously abused and cheated by such as they trust). Should you follow the wars, without Geometry you cannot fortify yourself, take the advantage of hill or level, fight, order your Battalia in square, triangle, cross (which form the Prince of Orange hath now taken up), crescentwise, level and plant your ordnance, undermine, raise your half-moons, bulwarks, casamates, rampires, ravelins, etc., by fortification." So Peacham confesses he cannot see how a gentleman can do without geometry, though it may not be necessary to study it to the " height of perfection," yet at the least a gentleman " should be grounded in the principles and privy rules hereof."

III. *The Philosopher's View of Mathematics.*

In spite of the defective knowledge of mathematics, which is imputed to Lord Bacon, and his ignorance or suppression of his knowledge as to the progress which the subject had recently made (criticism apparently soundly enough based) it is doubtful whether anyone in his own age had a clearer idea than Bacon himself of the disciplinary value of mathematics, and even of their value for the development of other subjects. Bacon may be wrong when he speaks of mathematics, i.e. pure mathematics, as a branch of metaphysics. Hallam may be right when he protests against Bacon so classing them. Yet Bacon's meaning is clear enough. The idea of quantity abstracted from the material things in which it exists is metaphysical ; the ultimate conceptions of quantity and number, as they reach the limits of zero and infinity, or speculations as to the Pythagorean doctrine of numbers as the principle and originals of things, take us beyond the boundary of natural phenomena. The speculation on such ideas, Bacon would hand over to the metaphysician. But no man was more ready to claim mathematics as the science which is to be applied to interpret with exactitude natural phenomena, on the quantitative side.

" The Mathematics," says Bacon, " are either pure or mixed. To the Pure Mathematics belong those sciences which handle Quantity Determinate, merely severed from any axioms of natural philosophy ; and these are two, Geometry and Arithmetic, the one handling Quantity continued and the other dissevered " (i.e. discrete). The value of the study of pure mathematics in Bacon's view is disciplinary. To Bacon, at the period at which he wrote the *Advancement of Learning* (1605), it appeared that pure mathematics were complete, that there was no deficiency to be noted.[1] If then there was no further scope for

---

[1] His words are : " In the Mathematics I can report no deficience, except it be that men do not sufficiently understand the excellent use of the Pure Mathematics in that they do remedy and cure many defects in the wit and faculties intellectual."

experimental inquiry in them, what were their uses ? His answer was : That they are an excellent discipline with which to exercise and train the mind. The mathematical studies make a man " subtle." " If a man's wit be wandering let him study the mathematics, for in demonstrations, if his wit be called away never so little, he must begin again." [1] And again he says : " If the wit be too dull (the mathematics) sharpen it ; if too wandering they fix it ; if too inherent in sense, they abstract it. So that as tennis is a game of no use in itself, but of great use in respect it maketh a quick eye and a body ready to put itself into all postures ; so in the Mathematics, that use which is collateral and intervenient is no less worthy than that which is principal and intended." [2] There can be no doubt, then, that Bacon saw the value of pure mathematics as mental gymnastic. He afterwards recognised that he had been too hasty in omitting to see that they required further development. He lived before the days of Descartes and Newton. It is easy for us to see that he missed a point in not forecasting that the development of higher mathematics would not only offer a still higher mental gymnastic for the student, but would also be of the first importance in developing mechanical philosophy. But we still recognise Bacon's view by breaking up pure and mixed mathematics into two departments in University studies, and in many of our examinations students are allowed to take pure mathematics apart from mixed mathematics.

[1] *Essay on Studies*, 1625.
[2] *Advancement of Learning* (1605).

The justification for such a course resolves itself to Bacon's view, viz. that it is an excellent training of the mind. But Bacon's interest in pure mathematics was genuine enough when he discovered that they were susceptible of development. This he had done by the time of revising the *Advancement* in 1622, by which time he realised that at least there was a deficiency in pure mathematics in the doctrine of solids and of series in arithmetic. [1]

Accepting, then, the position that Bacon recognised the value of pure mathematics as a disciplinary subject and that he failed to foresee the possibilities of the enormous advance of which the subject was susceptible, an advance which would minister in so high a degree to the progress of that subject in which he was profoundly interested, viz. experimental science, it remains to be said that his main emphasis on mathematics was undoubtedly on mixed mathematics.

" Mixed Mathematics," he says, " hath for subject some axioms or parts of natural philosophy and considereth Quantity determined, as it is auxiliary and incident unto them. For many parts of nature can neither be invented with sufficient subtlety, nor demonstrated with sufficient perspicuity, nor accommodated unto use with sufficient dexterity, without the aid and intervening of the mathematics ; of which sort are perspective, music, astronomy, cosmography, architecture, enginery, and divers others."

---

[1] *See* Spedding's note in *Advancement of Learning* in the section on Metaphysics, bk. 1.

Nor is Bacon out of touch with modern thought when he says : [1] " Inquiries into Nature have their best result, when they begin with Physics and end in Mathematics." He foresees that if this process be developed there will be more kinds of mixed mathematics. " For as Physics advances further and further and develops new axioms, it will require fresh assistance from mathematics in many things, and so the parts of mixed mathematics will be more numerous." [2]

IV. *The Varied Attitude of Scholars towards Mathematics in the first half of Seventeenth Century.*

Lord Herbert of Cherbury (1583–1648) gives in his *Autobiography* a scheme of education for a gentleman. The place assigned to mathematics on the whole is not an important one, but it throws light on the attitude of a more than ordinarily cultivated man in the time of the early Stuarts. The outlook is entirely confined to arithmetic and geometry. These two subjects should be learned " in some good measure." Arithmetic is especially important on account of its usefulness, as, for example, in keeping accounts. Herbert does not think as highly of geometry ; it is not so useful as arithmetic to a gentleman, except as a basis for understanding fortifications, and other branches of military art. Nevertheless, Herbert is aware that

---

[1] *Novum Organum*, Works : Ed. J. M. Robertson, p. 307.

[2] *De Augm. Scientiarum*, Works : Ed. J. M. Robertson, p. 477. 1623.

geometry is a science of much certainty and demonstration. When Sir Henry Savile, in 1619, founded
professorships in geometry and astronomy in Oxford,
the opinions of the gentry were not all so favourable
to geometry as was Herbert. Anthony à Wood [1]
states that " not a few of the then foolish gentry
would not let their sons go to the University to be
" smutted with the black art," mathematics being
" spells " and the professors of them " limbs of the
devil." Peacham, in 1622, we have seen, held a more
liberal opinion.

The comprehensiveness of the territory annexed
by mathematics is scarcely indicated by the terms
arithmetic and geometry. Substantially " mathematics " included the whole quadrivium, and a good
many other subjects. The many-sidedness will be
clear if we look for guidance to Robert Burton
whose *Anatomy of Melancholy* (1621) contains
surely an unique account of studies from the point
of view of book-learning in so many subjects.
In the following passage, I omit his account of
cosmographical studies,[2] which also belong to
mathematics, [3] as he used the term.

" To most kind of men it is an extraordinary
delight to study. For what a world of Books offers
itself in all subjects, arts and sciences to the sweet
content and capacity of the Reader ! In Arithmetick,

---

[1] *Athenæ Oxon.* ii, 2, 836.

[2] For which *see* p. 109 *supra*.

[3] *Anatomy of Melancholy.* Partition ii, Section ii,
Member 4.

Geometry, Perspective, Opticks, Astronomy, Architecture, Sculptura, Pictura, of which so many and such elaborate treatises are of late written ; in Mechanicks and their Mysteries, Military Matters, Navigation, Riding of Horses, Fencing, Swimming, Gardening, Planting, great Tomes of Husbandry, Cooking, Falconry, Hunting, Fishing, Fowling, etc., with exquisite Pictures of all sports, games and what not. . . ." (As Cardan says [1]) : " What is more subtle than arithmetical inventions ? What more pleasant than musical harmonies ? What more sound than geometrical demonstrations ? What so sure, what so pleasant ? He that shall but see that Geometrical Tower of Garisenda at Bologna in Italy, the Steeple and Clock at Strassburg, will admire the efforts of art, or that Engine of Archimedes to remove the earth itself, if he had but a place to fasten his instrument, Archimedes's Cochlea and rare devices to corrivate waters, musick instruments and trisyllable echoes, again, again, and again repeated with myriads of such." [2]

Burton, as is his wont, is not satisfied in stating the subject-matter of mathematics, and their charms. He adds the enthusiastic praise of those who loved the study. These perhaps should be stated, for they were part of the heritage of the age and helped to form the contemporary view of mathematics as a balance to the lukewarm views of nobles and gentry, such as Lord Herbert of Cherbury.

---

[1] Burton gives the Latin.
[2] Cf. Peacham for quotation of Archimedes, p. 76.

Burton continues : " Such is the excellency of Mathematics that all those ornaments and childish bubbles of wealth are not worthy to be compared to them." Leonard Digges says : [1] " I could even live and die with such meditations and take more delight and true content of mind in them than thou hast in all thy wealth and sport, however rich soever thou art." And as Cardan well seconds me : " It is more honourable and glorious to understand these truths than to govern provinces, and to be young."

In the *Catalogue of the Most Vendible Books* issued by Wm. London in 1658, the part devoted to mathematics is described almost exactly in accordance with the subjects mentioned by Burton. " Books of the Mathematicks, viz. Arithmatick, Geometry, Musick, Astronomy, Astrology, Dialling, Measuring of Land and Timber, Gageing vessels, Navigation, Architecture," etc. Other subjects are added as subsidiary, apparently on the verge of being differentiated from " mathematics," viz. Horsemanship, Falconry, Merchandise, Limning, Military Discipline, Heraldry, Fireworks, Husbandry, etc.

Such lists as those of Robert Burton and William London raise the question : What did the writers of the earlier part of the seventeenth century mean by mathematics ? Apparently the answer is given by Edward Leigh, [2] viz. that the mathematics are so-called because they " are not learned without a

---

[1] Shilleto's note : Preface *ad perpet. prognost.* [i.e., " A prognostication everlasting "]. (1556.)

[2] *Religion and Learning*, 1663.

master." They are difficult for all, though formerly
(i.e. in ancient Greece) boys used to learn them before
the rest of the arts." The great amount of learning
required and the need of a master to unravel
the difficulties gave rise to the idea of mystery,
and the study was thus allied to that of
magic. The ancient Pythagorean doctrine of
number as "covering the mysteries of all nature
and even of God Himself, as if all things were
agreeable to number, brought mathematics in the
Middle Ages into the position of a system of secrets,
which required a mastery, open only to the initiate
and supernaturally endowed. It is therefore not
always easy to differentiate subjects such as cheiro-
mancy, or cabalistical and astrological works, from
mathematical books. Alchemy and physics, "secrets" of all kinds were sometimes included. William
London in 1658 passes chemistry over to physic and
chirurgery, but "fireworks" he retains with mathematics, and the astrological and magical books for
the most part, are placed in this same division of
knowledge. When the conception became general
that mathematics, as Leigh, for instance, says, are a
"most accurate and profitable study for the evidence
and certainty of their demonstrations" the province
of mathematics became delimited. It was clearly
the development of geometry, especially, through
the new leading given to it by Descartes, that
established the standard of modern mathematical
demonstration, so that pseudo-sciences and mysteries
fell away from mathematics into their own limbo,
or attempted to join themselves to less exacting

divisions of knowledge, till standards of proof and demonstration placed them outside the scope of scientific standing. The consciousness of the value of mathematics, though combined with but vague knowledge of their definite contents, seems to explain Hezekiah Woodward's remarks in his preface to *A Gate to the Sciences*, 1641. He is aware, as a disciple of Lord Bacon, that he ought to make provision or " preparatory store " in his book for the teaching of all the sciences. He ought, he confesses, to have begun, " in true method," with the mathematics. He recognises the view of Bacon " that if the wit be dull, mathematics will sharpen it ; if too wandering, they fix it ; if too inherent in the same, they abstract it ; so necessary are they." But Woodward shrinks from the attempt of dealing with the subject of mathematics. For when would he be able to leave off ? " For there are a world of disciplines ; I thought it not impossible but tedious and useless to tread such a maze with the child ! "

Milton, in 1644, speaks in very general terms, and is chary as to illustration. " And having thus passed the principles of Arithmetic, Geometry, Astronomy, and Geography with a general compact of Physics, they may descend in Mathematics to the instrumental science of Trigonometry and from thence to Fortification, Architecture, Enginry or Navigation."

George Snell,[1] in 1649, thinks that if Latin were dispensed with, the ordinary school curriculum

---

[1] In the *Right Teaching of Useful Knowledge*.

might include amongst other subjects, geometry, plane and spherical trigonometry, astronomy, optics, the military art. But Snell is much more definite in his attack on the school system in vogue, than in his mathematical suggestions.

John Hall, the advocate of experimental science teaching,[1] in his *Humble Motion to the Parliament of England concerning the Advancement of Learning and Reformation of the Universities* (1649), speaks of the disappointment of the expectations he had formed of metaphysics. "But," he says, "the conduct of reason which I wished for . . . (was) such as might gently sink into younger minds, and be there embraced with no impulsion, but the delight which commonly tickles the soul when she meets with any radiant and pregnant truth. . . . As to the Mathematics, I found them full of excellent variety and harmony, strongly fenced with their own truth, and branched out into many admirable inferences and productions. . . . I found most men employed only in learning those immense heaps of demonstrations left to us by the ancients, but seldom enlarging them or going forward, which made me fear the keys of those sciences were hid." But Hall is reassured, since he has found "two or three great spirits" have set to work and found a way which, if well followed, would "make mathematical reason nimble" and applicable to other sciences.

On the other hand, John Webster, the writer of the *Examination of Academies* (1654), paints a dark

---

[1] *See* pp. 231–2 *supra*.

picture of the state of mathematics. He says :
" The mathematical sciences, the superlative excellency of which transcends the most of the other sciences, in their perspicuity, veritude, and certitude, also in their uses and manifold benefits, yet in the general, they are but either slightly and superficially handled . . . or else the most abstruse, beneficial and noble parts are altogether passed by and neglected." Much is said by Webster in way of attack on University teaching of mathematics, which shows that he had realised some of the mathematical developments of the first half of the seventeenth century, but the praise of arithmetic, geometry, optics, geography, and astronomy is joined with equal, if not greater, enthusiasm for the " noble " science of astrology. The recognition of Copernicus, Kepler and Galileo is joined in the same chapter on Mathematics with the eulogy of Mr. Ashmole, Mr. William Lilly, Mr. Culpepper, etc., for their astrological contributions to mathematics. " For the art (i.e. of astrology) itself is high, noble, excellent, and useful to all mankind, and is a study not unbeseeming the best wits and greatest scholars."

Such inconsistency, common enough in the period, engaged the wrath of Seth Ward,[1] Savilian Professor of Astronomy at Oxford, perhaps the foremost English mathematician of the time. The praise of mathematics by Webster particularly annoyed him. " What have the Mathematics deserved that such a man

---

[1] *Vindiciae Academiarum*, 1654. *See* p. 234 n. *supra*.

and others should render them contemptible by his commendations." Ward's reply discloses the interesting fact that " many boys in the University " at any rate know their mathematics so far as to be able to " resolve a common adfected equation or to give the geometrical effection of it." Arithmetic and geometry are " sincerely and profoundly taught, Analytical Algebra, the Solution and Application of Aequations containing the whole mystery of both those sciences being faithfully " expounded in the schools by the Professor of Geometry, and in many several Colleges by particular Tutors." Ward claims that in optics " instances of more solid knowledge of all sorts of radiation or vision " have been given lately at Oxford than were ever given here or elsewhere before, and such things are ordinary now amongst us as heretofore were counted magical." Ward, a thorough-going Copernican, rouses himself to defend Ptolemy against Webster's attack. " This may be said with justice in defence of Ptolemy, that there is no astronomical book in the world, which may not be better spared than his $Μεγάλη Σύνταξις$. Ptolemy meddled not with the physical part of astronomy, and indeed there is no Mathematical Book in the world more learned or useful in its kind than Ptolemy's Almagest." Ward continues :

The Method observed in our schools (i.e. in Astronomy) is first to exhibit the phenomena and show the way of their observation, then to give an account of the various hypotheses, how these phenomena have been solved, or may be (where the Aequipollency or defects of the several hypotheses are shown). And lastly to show how the geometrical hypotheses are resolvable into tables, serving for tabulating of Ephemerides, which are of quotidian use.

Further, Ward informs us that arithmetic and geometry were taught at Oxford, and taught in the later developments, " in the promotion of the doctrine of indivisibilia and the discovery of the natural rise and management of Conic Sections and other solid pieces ; Optics and Perspective by various inventions and applications on Gnomonicks [i.e. dials] and picture Astronomy, in polishing and indeed perfecting the elliptical hypothesis and rendering it geometrical."

This may be taken as an optimistic sketch of the highest teaching of mathematics in England up to the Restoration. It is, no doubt, the upward limit of Ward himself. The controversy between Webster and Ward in itself shows the unsettledness of the scope of mathematics. The warmth of Ward's reply is also perhaps indicative of the keen need of defence of University mathematics.

William London's testimony (1658) is : " Mathematics is a study of late much engrossed by many of these parts,[1] as well as other places of the Nation. It is somewhat kept under, *for the want of variety of books.*" William London, a Newcastle bookseller, knew his business, as his catalogue shows. He was himself interested in mathematics, and expresses his intention of keeping his catalogue up to date by the inclusion of all new mathematical books. There was, however, another reason for the restricted study of mathematics pointed out by Mr. W. W. R. Ball.[2]

---

[1] London means the north of England.
[2] *Short History of Mathematics*, p. 228.

MODERN SUBJECTS IN ENGLISH SCHOOLS

A knowledge of mathematics was confined to those " who could extract it from the ponderous treatises in which it lay buried." Good advance had been made in algebraical, and trigonometrical notation, but it was not until the end of the seventeenth century that the language of the subject was definitely fixed." Higher mathematics though surely, and even we may say, quickly developing, could not be widely studied even by University students, until good elementary text-books were forthcoming. Such knowledge as was disseminated in the teaching institutions within the period under consideration, viz. in the sixteenth and seventeenth centuries, was substantially confined to the traditional subjects, arithmetic, geometry, and astronomy. A history of each of these subjects separately, especially from the point of view of its teaching, is necessary to complete the account of mathematics in the educational perspective of this period.

NOTE.—Of names of mathematicians given by Vives, pp. 108–10, the following belong to the earlier part of the Middle Ages, viz. Proclus Diadochus (411–485 A.D.), a Platonic philosopher, wrote the *de Sphaera*, " Englished " by W. Salysburye, in 1550. Martianus Capella (before 439) wrote the *de Nuptiis Philologiae et Mercurii*, a treatise on the seven liberal arts and therefore including Geometry (*see* p. 332 *infra*). Boethius (481–525) adapted for the Latin languages Greek material on arithmetic. He is said to have been the first to use the term *Quadrivium* for arithmetic, music, geometry, and astronomy. Jordan wrote an arithmetic in the first half of the thirteenth century, and John Cantuariensis was an English Benedictine monk who lived at the beginning of the thirteenth century. The second group named by Vives belong to the Renascence writers of the fifteenth and sixteenth centuries. Purbachius or George of Peurbach in Austria (1423–1461) was a leading astronomer of the fifteenth century. His *Theorica Planetarum* was edited by Francis of Capua (Franciscus Capuanus, Professor of Astronomy at Padua), who wrote a commentary on Peurbach's book. Pedro Cirvelo (Petrus Cirvelus) lived in the later part of the fifteenth century. He was appointed by Cardinal Ximenes as Professor in the University of Alcala. Joannes Poblatius (Juan Poblacion) came from Vives's own town of Valencia, and lived in the first half of the sixteenth century. Joannes Stoflerinus (Johann Stoeffler) of Justingen (1452–1531) was mathematical Professor at Tubingen. Jodocus Chlichtoveus, anti-Lutheran, died 1543. Carolus Bovillus, i.e. Charles de Bouvilles, lived in the middle of the sixteenth century. Joannes Siliceus (died 1557) was the tutor of King Philip II of Spain. Georgius Valla (c. 1430–1499) of Piacenza, published in 1501 a collection of mathematical tracts. Juan Vergara was Professor of Philosophy at Alcala. He died in 1557. As to Ptolemy *see* p. 353 *infra ;* Tonstall, p. 292 *infra ;* Bradwardine, p. 291 *infra ;* Sacrobosco, p. 356 *infra.*

Margarita Philosophica. Friburg, 1503. Edited by Gregorius Reisch. [1503.] This work is an encyclopaedia of natural and moral philosophy presented in dialogue form and illustrated with a large number of wood-cuts. The twelve books into which it is divided relate to grammar, logic, rhetoric, artificial memory, correspondence, arithmetic, music, geometry, astronomy, cosmography, astrology, natural philosophy, chemistry, alchemy, botany, optics, mental philosophy, theology, and moral philosophy. The numerous editions which were published attest its popularity as a text-book during the early part of the sixteenth century. Friburg, 1503, 1504 [unauthorised Gruninger's reprint of 1503], 2nd ed. 1504, 3rd ed., Basle, 1508 ; Gruninger's 2nd ed. 1508 ; Gruninger's 3rd, 1512 ; Gruninger's 4th ed., 1515 ; 4th ed., 1517 ; 1535, Basle ; Basle, 1583 ; Venice, 1599.

CHAPTER VIII

THE TEACHING OF ARITHMETIC

In the Mediaeval Ages, arithmetic was not a part of either elementary or grammar-school education. The trivium or grammar-school subjects were grammar, rhetoric, dialectic. Arithmetic was usually only learned by higher scholars for the purpose of determining feasts and seasons. In Tudor times, too, arithmetic was not ordinarily part of the curriculum of school training. In the age of the Stuarts, arithmetic began to make its appearance in the course of a London boy's education, but, as a rule, not in the Grammar School, but in the Writing School, a separate private school.

Yet arithmetic was a subject inspiring high respect until the days when it became " common," " vile," " mechanic " as the accomplishment of the class of clerks, artisans, tradesmen and others who bore no signs of heraldry. It is true, noblemen's sons learned arithmetic, one reason being given that it enabled them to check the impositions of those with whom they dealt. The grammar schools were " free " schools for the most part, and open to the poor, the more " gentle " class of the community preferring the employment of private tutors. Nevertheless, the grammar schools excluded arithmetic, probably because the teaching of Latin, together with the knowledge contained in Latin authors exhausted all their energies. There was no ancient classical writer on arithmetic. The introduction of such a subject as arithmetic would have spoilt the symmetry of the school, planned as the grammar schools primarily were, to make Latin and Greek culture live again.

Yet scholars admitted the antiquity of arithmetic, a most important consideration in its favour. In the Middle Ages, arithmetic was honoured as the first of the four quadrivial arts and as necessary as geometry, music and astronomy. Pythagoras was reputed to have been the first to make arithmetic into an art. The Pythagoreans swore *per numerum quaternarium, quo nihil apud nos videtur perfectius.* For there were four elements, four seasons of the year, four qualities of all things (heat, cold, moisture, dryness), four coasts of heaven (north, south, east and west). They might have gone further back, and traced arithmetic amongst the Phoenicians, Egyptians, and the Chinese. But in the Middle Ages, up till the incoming of Arabian arithmetic, the source from which scholars, who went on to the quadrivial studies, derived their notions of arithmetic, was chiefly the scanty account of Boethius, together with the use of the abacus for calculations. Certain mystical speculations concerning number in the abstract seem to have completed the round of arithmetical knowledge.

It was from Spain, a country often overlooked in the history of education, that Arabian mathematics filtered into Europe. Spain had received the great Renascence of the Arab learning in the centuries following Spanish defeat by the Moors. The price paid back by the Moors to Spain for conquest was such as to make that country the most progressive in Europe, at any rate in mathematics and science. The knowledge was passed on as a free gift to the other nations. England was one of the chief countries to avail herself of this new knowledge. Oxford scholars, especially, travelled to Toledo and brought back the Arabian mathematics. The consequence was that mathematics generally flourished at Oxford, and particularly Merton College, Oxford, was for two centuries the leading academic centre in the new subjects, surpassing even the famous University of Paris itself. The country which vied with England was Italy, and it was an Italian, Gerard of Cremona (1114–1187), who translated the Almagest of Ptolemy from the Arabian, and also the works of Alhazen. The greatest change to be recorded in mediaeval arithmetic dates from Gerard's translation of Ptolemy's Almagest, 1136, viz. the earliest use noted in a European work of the Arabic numerals. It was not, however, till 1202 that the *Liber Abbaci* was written by Leonardo di Pisa, in which the Arabic system of numerals was explained, with the nine digits and zero, and advantages of the system were pointed out. Commercial men, in course of time, came to adopt the new system, and a new class of students arose, viz. those engaged in commerce, who needed the best practical course of arithmetic that they could either devise themselves or learn from others. The Arabian system of arithmetic called algorismus was introduced, and entered into competition with that of Boethius. This was used from the middle of the thirteenth century for nearly all mathematical tables, for trade purposes particularly by Italians, for calculations of almanacs, which books generally included an explanation of the system.[1]

Amongst the Mediaeval writers on arithmetic used in England in teaching the subject, were Bede about 730, Alcuin about 760, John Peccam 1260, Simon Bredon 1370, Richard Wallingford 1326, Thomas de Bradwardine 1349, John Killingworth 1360. Boethius Severinus was the source of the old arithmetic, and his treatise on arithmetic was used throughout, alongside of the newer writers.

As a University subject, at Oxford in the Statutes (? about 1408) for determination in arts, the student is required to have " heard " *Algorismus integrorum*, and the method of finding Easter. For licence and inception in arithmetic the student was to have studied Boethius for one term. In the Statutes of 1431, Boethius is still the one prescribed arithmetic. But in Edward VI's Statutes of 1549, Boethius disappeared, and Tonstall and Cardan were substituted. The Statutes no longer required mathematics in the undergraduate's course. The mathematical professor still lectured on Tonstall and Cardan. " There is no evidence, however, to shew that the attendance of students was in any way obligatory, and those who attended appear to have been either sophisters or bachelors of arts." [2]

---

[1] W. W. R. Ball : *Cambridge Mathematics*, p. 5.
[2] Mullinger, ii, p. 402.

Girolamo Cardano (Jerome Cardan) was an Italian, famous in many directions. He wrote *Practica Arithmetice et mensurandi singularis*, Milan, 1539. Of this book de· Morgan says that Cardan shows more power of computation than the French and German writers. The fact is that the Italian and the English writers on arithmetic were for the next century the leaders of Europe in that subject.

After the long reign of Boethius in arithmetic, almost paralleling that of Donatus in grammar, it is surprising to come across his academic successors in two names so little known generally in connexion with arithmetic as those of Tonstall and Cardan. Cuthbert Tonstall or Tunstall (1474–1559) was student at both Oxford and Cambridge, and had also studied at Padua in the Faculty of Law. He was Master of the Rolls and afterwards Bishop of London. In 1522 Pynson published Tonstall's *de Arte supputandi libri quatuor*. De Morgan says : " The book is decidedly the most classical which ever was written on the subject in Latin both in purity of style and goodness of matter. The author had read everything on the subject in every language which he knew, as he avers in his dedicatory letter to Thomas More, and had spent much time, as he says, *ad ursi exemplum* in licking what he found into shape."

Mr. Mullinger speaks of the " remarkable indifference of Cambridge to mathematics during the sixteenth and early part of the seventeenth century," and though Mr. Ball has shown that many mathematicians who rose to contemporary eminence were undergraduates of Cambridge University or migrated thither from Oxford for a time, yet it is evident that for the most part the teaching of mathematics in England was chiefly pursued in London, where the practical usefulness of the subject in its applications to the military art, to business and to mechanical pursuits was most urgent. [1]

The progress in the development of arithmetical science, and in mathematics generally was not always associated with the men who most contributed to the dissemination of the knowledge thus acquired. In other words, the scholars were not always the teachers, though the two functions have perhaps been more closely united in mathematics than in some other subjects. The chief advances made in arithmetic after the introduction of the early Italian algorism are summarised by Mr. Ball [2] as (i) the simplification of the four fundamental processes, (ii) the introduction of signs for plus, minus and equality, (iii) the invention of logarithms, (iv) the use of decimals. As we are chiefly concerned with the development of the teaching of the subject, it must suffice here to mention the chief names associated with these reforms. To an Englishman named Garth is attributed the idea of working

---

[1] Mr. Mullinger quotes from Hearne's *Langtoft*, Pref. p. cxvii, where arithmetic is regarded as a study for " the business of traders, merchants, seamen, carpenters, or the like, and perhaps some almanack makers." Mullinger ii, p. 403 n.

[2] *History of Mathematics*, p. 171.

from right to left, the Arabian method, in addition and subtraction, being to work from left to right, evidently a more difficult and longer operation. The use of multiplication tables was only slowly introduced from Italy. Napier's rods, invented in 1617, were devised for the purpose of effecting complicated multiplications. Division was not fully in use on the present system through Europe (though known in Italy in the fourteenth century) till the eighteenth century. The signs $+$ and $-$ were first used by John Widman in a *Mercantile Arithmetic* (Leipzig, 1489). The sign of equality ($=$) was invented by Recorde[1] (1540). But these three symbols, Mr. Ball states, were not generally employed till the beginning of the seventeenth century. The invention of logarithms was due to John Napier of Merchistoun in 1614. The efforts of Napier, both in the introduction of logarithms and the rods, was peculiarly due to the attempt to simplify multiplication and division. Henry Briggs, the first Savilian Professor of Geometry (1619–1630) at Oxford, made Napier's discoveries known, and in Mr. Ball's opinion Briggs was himself the first to introduce the decimal notation in 1617. The earliest English writer to introduce any plane trigonometry was Thomas Blundeville in 1594.[2] William Oughtred (1574–1660) systematised elementary arithmetic, algebra

---

[1] *See* p. 300 n.

[2] *Exercises, containing six Treatises, viz. on Arithmetic, Cosmography, Description of the Globes, Description of the Universal Map of Plancius, of the Astrolabe of Mr. Blagrave and of the Principles of Navigation.* 1594.

and trigonometry.[1] His *Clavis Mathematica*, 1631, sums up the contemporary knowledge of arithmetic and algebra. His *Trigonometry*, 1657, is the first important English work on the subject and represents for England the knowledge in the subject up till the time of the introduction of Euler's teachings.[2] The Algebra of Thomas Harriot (1560-1621), whose posthumous *Artis Analyticae praxis* appeared in 1631, was the leading text-book on the subject till the time of John Wallis (1616–1703). In 1656 Wallis wrote his *Arithmetica infinitorum*, in 1657 his *Mathesis Universalis*. In 1665 he wrote the first exposition by an Englishman of analytical conic sections. Wallis is regarded as the first systematic mathematician on distinctly modern lines.[3] " His reputation," says Mr. Ball, " has been somewhat overshadowed by that of Newton, but his work was absolutely first class in quality."

The limitations of the acquired knowledge of the times are clearly the upward possibilities of the educational practice. With the above considerations before us, we can proceed to an account of some representative teaching of the subject. It will be noted that algebra and trigonometry arose in connexion with arithmetic, and were often connected

---

[1] Ball, *Cambridge Mathematics*, p. 30. Of William Oughtred it is stated that " he always gave gratuitous instruction to any who came to him, provided they would learn ' to write a decent hand.' "

[2] Leonard Euler (1707–1783). Appointed Professor of Mathematics at Berlin, 1741.

[3] *See* also p. 239 n. *supra*.

both in the text-book and in the teaching methods of the time.

Robert Recorde (1510–1588) taught mathematics at Cambridge and at Oxford. He was a physician, —it is said royal physician to Edward VI and Queen Mary.[1] Recorde was the first writer of an arithmetic in English. This was called *The Ground of artes : Teaching the work and practice of Arithmetike, both in whole numbres and Fractions after a more easyer and exarter sorte than any like hath hitherto been sette furthe ; Made by Mr Robert Recorde, Doctor of Physik, and now of late overseen and augmented with new and necessarie Additions.* J(ohn) D(ee), 1561. The first edition is supposed to have been published in 1540.

The Ground of artes is in the form of a dialogue between master and pupil. Both De Morgan and Mr. Ball quote the passage where the master asks the pupil how old he is and other questions involving number. To which the pupil replies : " Mum." Whereupon the master seizes his advantage, and says : " When number is lacking men are dumb and to most questions, answer : ' Mum.' "

With Recorde's *Ground of artes* before us we are able to get the contemporary answer to the question : Why should arithmetic be taught and learned ?

In the preface to the King Edward VI[2] Recorde adduces the argument of antiquity, but he puts it in a form which must have been strange to his own

---

[1] Mullinger : *History of Cambridge* ii, 403.
[2] This is retained in the later editions.

day, as probably it is ours. Like others, he speaks of the learning, introduced from the Egyptians by Moses into Palestine, by Lycurgus to the Spartans, and by Solon to the Athenians. But clearly Recorde is original in alleging as a title to honour that Dunwallo Molmutius, two thousand years past, brought learning to the old Britons of this realm, and gave them laws which continued " till more perfect reason altered many of them and wilful power opposed most of them." Amongst the arts thus brought to Britain were grammar, logic, rhetoric, " though not so curiously as at this time " (i.e. Recorde's). But besides, there were laws for the just orders of partition of lands, the true using of weights, measure and reckonings of all sorts of bargains, and for order of building. These were the bases of arithmetic and geometry. To these were added astronomy and music. Music was for religious purposes and " for the praise of virtue and discommendation of vice." Songs of evil men were in those days " more abhorred than any excommunication in this time." " The posterity of these musicians," adds Recorde, " continue yet both in Wales and Ireland, called bards from the ancient name of Bardus, the first founder."

The idea of going back to ancient Britain, for the glorious antiquity of learning as parallel to ancient Greece, seems rather like the post-Armada days of pride in the fatherland than nearly forty years earlier. Recorde boasts that in ancient Britain, arithmetic guided buying and selling, assizes, weights and measures, reckonings and accounts,

" yea by proportion of it were the true orders of justice limited," as Aristotle lays down in his Ethics. How essential arithmetic is, from the point of view of the politics of the time, Recorde instances, by referring to the assize of bread and drink. This depended on the standard of the coin of the realm, which had much changed since the time of the statute. This statute, he says, is omitted from the English of the original French of the Statutes, because so few men could understand the reckoning involved.

Recorde has great tact in approaching the delicate political subject of the coinage, for the debasement of the coinage was a crying evil, and one which Recorde gives us reason to suppose was not understood ordinarily, except from the misery which it entailed. The realm, he affirms, is happy in having a King like Edward VI, zealous for learning and desirous of " understanding equity " in all laws. Then follows the remarkable passage : " Many things (in connexion with the statutes of Coinage) are not to be published without your Highness's knowledge and approbation, viz. because in them is declared all *the rates of alloys for all standards from one ounce upward with other mysteries of Mint matters* and also most part of the varieties of coins that have been current in this your Majesty's Realm by the space almost of 600 years last past."

This, therefore, was a political aspect of arithmetic, and Recorde's standing at Court must have been good, for him to venture to give such dangerous information for propagation in an arithmetic. The reason for writing in dialogue form is stated to be that it seems to the author the easiest method of instruction, because in it the master has to meet the difficulties of his pupil.

At the outset, Recorde meets the difficulties experienced by his pupils in undertaking the study of arithmetic at all. He shows it is not " vile " as a study because number is frequently talked about : for the more common the use of it the better and more to be desired " the thing." If it is objected that " it is not clerkly," the answer is the other arts *have* need of it. In music, all perfection " standeth by number and proportion." In physic, besides the calculation of critical days [1] how can any man judge the pulse rightly without number ? As to law, if a judge " delights not to hear a matter that he perceiveth not, or cannot judge for lack of understanding—this cometh by ignorance of arithmetic." Grammar needs number, as in the declinable parts, in quantities of syllables and in all kinds of metres. As for philosophy, Aristotle says he that is ignorant of arithmetic is meet for no science. In Divinity the mysteries attached to number are often of great importance. In army affairs, there is numbering of the host, summing of wages, provision of victuals, viewing of artillery and casting of ground, for the encamping of men. This art is " conducible " for all private " weales " of lords and all possessioners, of merchants and all other occupiers, and generally in all estates of men, besides auditors, treasurers, receivers, stewards, bailiffs, " whose offices without arithmetic are nothing."

---

[1] *See* pp. 367, 387 *infra*.

Recorde's claims for arithmetic may be summarised as :

1. Its antiquity of use in Britain.

2. Its practical value in all departments of experience.

Recorde would also add, even in a summary, that power to deal with the " proportions of numbers " distinguishes a man from a beast. Nor ought to be overlooked in an account of Recorde's, the attitude of the scholar who said after he had heard the exposition of the value of arithmetic : " I to your authority my wit do subdue and whatsoever you say, I take for true." The master replies : " That is too much. It is meet for no man to be believed in all things, without shewing of reason."

There are two kinds of arithmetic, Recorde informs us. There is the arithmetic worked out with the pen, and the arithmetic with counters. Recorde deals with both. As to the pen-arithmetic, Mr Ball [1] says : " Recorde's book is the first English book which contains the current symbols for addition, subtraction and equality.[2] . . . The work is the best treatise on arithmetic produced in that century." De Morgan says : " We heartily wish the *Ground of artes* had been our own first book of arithmetic, seeing that it is better than the miserable compendiums with which the road to mathematics was opened or blocked up, as the case might be."

---

[1] *Cambridge Mathematics*, p. 15.

[2] Recorde explains that the sign = stands for equality, because no two things can be more equal than two parallel lines.

The arithmetic by counters shows the ordinary way of reckoning numbers, a method which, Recorde observes, serves for those who cannot read and write, but also for them that can do both but have not at hand their pens and tables. The method of dealing with counters in its simplest form is as follows. Lines stand for the order of places in pen Arithmetic. Thus the first (i.e. counting from the bottom)—

line stands for units,	—— *1000*	——
the second for tens,	—— *100*	——
the third for hundreds,	——— *10*	——
the fourth for thousands	——— *1*	——

and so on.

Every counter set in the units line stands for one· Thus, with a single line, three counters stand for the figure 3. In the tens line every counter stands for ten. Thus with two lines, with three counters on the lower line (the units line is the starting line), and two counters on the second, represents the figures 23.

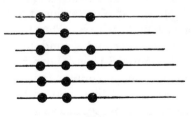

So the third line with four counters represents 400, and the three lines now represent altogether 423. But now comes a difficulty. If 5 has to be represented on any line, this is not done by marking five counters. " You shall remember this," says Recorde (though he confesses he does not know the reason), " that whenever you need to set down, 5, 50, 500, 5000 or any number with 5 as base, you shall set one counter for it in a void place above the line in which it ought to appear, but below the next line." Thus to represent 55 by counters, there will be two lines with a single counter, placed not on, but above the line.

To give a final example, take the number 7965.

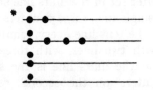

Any figure between 4 and 10 will require the counter in a " void place " above its line, together with a counter for each unit above 5. Thus the 5 in the 7965 goes between the first and second line. The 6 in the tens row requires 5 to go above the second line in the form of a single counter, and the unit over goes on to the second line. So with the 9 in the hundreds row 5 of the 9 goes in a single counter above the third line, and four units are represented by four counters on the third line. The 7 similarly in the thousands row is represented by a single counter above the line for 5 with two counters to represent the remaining two units. A star marks the line for the thousands. The counters-arithmetic is then shown for addition, subtraction, multiplication, division, for money sums, illustrating the contemporary method of " merchants use " in dealing with money-sums by means of counters and the method of auditors' accounts. These methods apparently were employed by the illiterate as well as by educated tradesmen, though Recorde mentions that in keeping accounts by counters " the divers wits of men have invented sundry ways almost innumerable." The intricacy of the normal method described by Recorde is sufficient to show that a good deal of ingenuity and practice was necessary in dealing with large money-sums by counters, at any rate, in multiplication and division. But undoubtedly such a system ingrained by constant practice would tend to become mechanical. At any rate counters-arithmetic needed no ordinary school-teacher, for the language-master clearly would not be so expert as the school-boy's own father if he were in business, and the teaching naturally would be usually a domestic one, if not of the teaching of the boy by the parent, at any rate the training of the apprentice by the master.

Recorde appears to have taught mathematics in Cambridge, to which town he went after graduating at Oxford. He returned to Oxford for a time, but eventually he went to London where in the subjects of mathematics there was greater scope. Financially he was an unsuccessful man ; he died in the King's Bench prison, where he was confined for debt.

Having now explained the system of casting accounts in the sixteenth century, it is necessary to add that this subject was required in some schools, of which the following are examples :

St. Olave's Grammar School, Southwark, 1561.

> The Churchwardens were ordered to receive moneys due from Luke's executory to set up a Free School and choose a schoolmaster sufficient to teach children to write and read and cast accounts.

Minutes of S. Olave's School, 1571–2.

> We have here great number of poor people in our parish who are not able to keep their children at grammar. But being desirous to have them taught the principles of Christian Religion and to write, read, and cast accompts, and so to put them forth to prentice.

Hartlebury, 1565.

> The master and usher shall at least one afternoon every week teach the scholars of the said school to write and cast accounts, whereby their hands may be directed, and so they trained to write fair hands and likewise not ignorant in reckoning and accounting.

Northampton Grammar School, 1596.

> That there be one Scholemaster and Minister to teach the Latin, and to teach to read, write, and cast accounts, or otherwise that there be one schoolmaster to teach the Latin tongue and one other distinct school-master to teach to read, write, and cast accounts.

1597. Aldenham [1] (Herts).

> Founder : Richard Platt. For the free instruction of 60 scholars in purity of life, manners, and religion, and in Latin, English, writing, *cyphering* and *accounts*.

---

[1] This reference and the names of the remainder of the Schools in this list have been arranged from Howard Staunton's *Great Schools of England*, 1869.

1613. *Lady Alice Owen's School, London.*
Under Brewers' Company. For 24 poor children of Islington and 6 of Clerkenwell, [Latin], grammar, writing and *ciphering.*

1614. *Little Thurlow (Suffolk).*
Founder : Sir Stephen Soame. English and Latin, writing and *cyphering,* till sent to the University or apprenticed.

1617. *Stratford-le-Bow.*
Founder : Sir John Jolles. For 35 boys. Grammar and Latin, to write and *cypher.*

1624. *Kirkby-Ireleth (Lancs).*
Founder : Giles Brownrigge. Grammar, writing, *cyphering* and *accounts.*

1636. *Coggleshall (Essex).*
Sir Robert Hitcham for 30–40 poor children of *Framlingham, Debenham and Coggeshall* at Framlingham. Established by ordinance of Cromwell, 1653, which provided for a separate school at each of the above places for 20 or 30 or more of the children of the poorest inhabitants in reading, writing, *accounts* or grammar learning, and also for apprenticing boys and maintaining scholars at Cambridge.

1639. *Grimston (Norfolk).*
Rudiments of grammar, writing and *cyphering.*

1653. *Beachampton (Bucks).*
Founder : W. Elmer. Date of will, 1648. Subjects : English, Latin, writing and *accounts.*

1654. *Aynhoe (Northants).*
Founder : Mary Cartwright. For 25 free scholars to be taught reading, writing and *arithmetic,* and afterwards Greek and Latin.

1659. *Arkingarth-Dale (Yorks).*
Founder : John Bathurst, M.D. For all children of the tenants of the manor of Arkingarth Dale in writing, reading, and *accounts,* and also in the rudiments of the Latin Grammar.

1659. *New Forest (Yorks). Helwith School.*
Founder : John Bathurst, M.D. Writing, reading and *accounts,* as well as the rudiments of Latin grammar.

Until I saw Recorde's arithmetic of counters I could not understand the meaning of these Statutes in prescribing "accounts." But the "casting of accompts" probably was not the arithmetic of numbers, but of counters. The term used for teaching the arithmetic of numbers was "cyphering"[1] which at first sound seems pedantic. If, however, this explanation is correct, it was necessary to differentiate between the teaching of arithmetic by the use of counters and that of figures. Thus, probably, casting of accompts and cyphering were the technical terms for the two types of arithmetic, and they continued side by side for at any rate the sixteenth and seventeenth centuries.

The number of Grammar Schools in which "Arithmetic with the pen," as Recorde calls it, "was taught," must have been comparatively few. I will now name the few notices of School Arithmetic I have come across, only premising again that they must be taken as typical of a comparatively small number of Grammar Schools up to 1660.

The enterprising views of Mulcaster with regard to mathematical teaching have already been quoted.[2] One of Mulcaster's arguments, viz. that from the antiquity of the teaching of the subject, is similar to Recorde's argument, Mulcaster substituting the antiquity of Greece for that of Britain. "The ancient school did begin at the Mathematical

---

[1] At one of the schools to which the writer of this book went, arithmetic was usually called "cyphering" by the Head Master.

[2] See p. 258 *supra*.

after the Elementary while they minded sound learning indeed, and sequestred their thoughts from other dealings in the world." Of the influence of mathematics on Greek literature, Mulcaster's words would have pleased Erasmus. " He that marketh but the ordinary metaphors in the eloquentest Greek writers, shall easily bewray wherein the ancient discipline (of mathematics) travelled." [1] But energetic as Mulcaster's advocacy of mathematics was, there does not seem to be any evidence that he introduced even arithmetic into Merchant Taylors' School. The outstanding distinction of Mulcaster's views on mathematics may be gauged by comparing them with those of John Brinsley, more than thirty years later. At the end of a chapter on : How the scholar may be taught to read English speedily,[2] Brinsley gives directions for numbering. He says numbers can easily be learned, but yet they are often neglected. Boys are to learn the numbers by letters (i.e., Roman numerals). Then he explains, *in a single paragraph*, numbering by figures. " This will perform," says Brinsley, " fully as much as is needful for your ordinary Grammar Scholar." He explains why so much is desirable. " You shall have," he says to his fellow schoolmaster, almost ready to go to the University, scholars who yet can

---

[1] *Positions*, 1581, p. 246. " The authority," he continues, " of the Mathematical must be fetched from the Greeks, though they themselves borrowed the matter of other nations, and were founders onely to language, method, and those faculties, which serve for the direction of language."

[2] Chapter III, *Ludus Literarius*, pp. 25–6.

hardly tell you the number of pages, sections, chapters in a book," the places of which they wish to find. " Without the perfect knowledge of these numbers, scholars cannot help themselves by the indices or tables of such books as they should use for turning to anything of a sudden ; although it be a matter whereof they should have use all their life long."

There was indeed one Grammar Schoolmaster, besides Mulcaster, who had advocated the introduction of the school-teaching of some arithmetic and geometry, viz., William Kempe in the *Education of Children in Learning* in 1588. He says that the scholar can easily pass through these arts of arithmetic and geometry in half a year, and so before " the full age of sixteen years be made fit to wade without a schoolmaister through deeper mysteries of learning, to set forth the glory of God, and to benefit his country."

Moreover, Kempe, who was headmaster of Plymouth Grammar School, made the following translation :

> *The Art of Arithmeticke in Whole Numbers and Fractions. In a more readie and easie method than hitherto hath been published. Written in Latin by P. Ramus ; and translated into English by William Kempe.* 1592. 8vo.

Kempe dedicates his translation to the Right Worshipful Sir Francis Drake. In this dedication Kempe asks who is there that can attain to a knowledge of his art, whatever it is, without arithmetic ? It is useful in divinity, in civil polity, and " in the seat of judgment the golden rule of proportion is the law of equity." In physics, in astronomy it is clearly necessary.

What is music [he goes on], in sounds, in harmony, and in their spaces, concords, and diverse sorts, but only arithmetic in hearing ? Take away arithmetic, ye take away the merchant's eye, whereby he seeth his direction in buying and selling ; ye take away the goldsmith's discretion, whereby he mixeth his metals in due quantities ; ye take away the captain's dexteritie, whereby he embattaileth his army in convenient order ; finally ye take from all sorts of men, the faculty of executing their functions aright. Arithmetic then teacheth unto us matters in divinity, judgeth civil causes uprightly, cureth diseases, searcheth out the nature of things created, singeth sweetly, buyeth, selleth, maketh accompts, weigheth metals and worketh them, skirmisheth with the enemy, goeth on warfare, and setteth her hand almost to every good work, so profitable is she to mankind.

Kempe, however, crude and far-fetched as his notions of the functions of arithmetic may seem to the modern mathematician, must be regarded as exceptional in giving a place in the school curriculum to a book like Ramus's arithmetic, in the sixteenth century. The ordinary limit of teaching where any was attempted, is more likely to have been that covered by Coote's *English Schoolmaster* which, however, was not published till 1596. As the large circulation of this book belongs to the first half of the seventeenth century, it probably represents the work in arithmetic of a number of the lower type of grammar schools such as those named above, whilst in the higher type of grammar schools arithmetic was not taught at all, at any rate inside the walls of the school itself. It was, like writing or French, an extra subject learned in a specialised private school, to which the grammar school pupils out of school hours, or to which a boy went for a short continuous period after he had left " school." Coote's account of arithmetic is limited to numeration, and occupies a single page. He names the nine figures together with the figure O called a " cipher." He emphasises the place of a figure : " Mark that thou call that which is next to the right hand, the first place, and so go (as it were) backward, calling the next unto him towards the left hand, the second place, the next the third place, and so forth. The further any figure standeth from the first place, the greater he is," etc. It is necessary, says Coote, to be perfect in these numbers as far as the fourth place, so as to be able to understand chronology as for instance to know that the present year (my edition of Coote is 1656) is 1675 years from the creation. The chronology is a long list of isolated dates with events attached. The pupil was to learn numeration so as to be able to acquire chronological information.

For one of the Free Grammar Schools mentioned above, a text-book was prepared as follows : *An Idea of Arithmetick, at first designed for the use of the free-school at Thurlow in Suffolk, by R. Billingsley, schoolmaster there.* London ["and are to be sold by W. Morden, bookseller, in Cambridge."] 1655.

The following are further instances of the introduction of arithmetic teaching into grammar schools in the seventeenth century (up to 1660) :

Charterhouse (Orders), 1627.

> It shall be his care (i.e. the master's), and the Usher's charge, to teach the scholars to cypher and cast an accompt, *especially those that are less capable of learning, and fittest to be put to trades.*

This Order is interesting as requiring both " cyphering " and " casting an accompt " and for the implied contempt of the very subject the Order is introducing into the Grammar School.

Ashford Grammar School, Kent, 1632.

> Master appointed by the Knatchbull family. The school was open to Ashford boys free of expense as far as relates to Latin and Greek, but fees were to be paid for writing and arithmetic.

Carlisle in his *Endowed Schools* (1818) mentions that at

Cartmel, Lancashire (founded before 1619)

> A charge per quarter was made upon the parents of those children who learned to write or cypher, the poor not excepted.

The fee payable for writing and arithmetic in " free " Grammar Schools shows that these subjects were regarded as extras.

The following is perhaps an instance of the clear acceptance of Arithmetic as an obligatory subject of the curriculum of the Grammar School.

Blechingley Grammar School Statutes, 1656.

> For a Free Grammar School the master to " teach freely and without gift or reward whatsoever in the English and Latin tongue, and to write and cast accounts according to the rules of arithmetic, 20 male children of the poorest inhabitants of Blechingley and born in the parish."

There can be no doubt that after the Restoration arithmetic began to be looked upon more favourably.

MODERN SUBJECTS IN ENGLISH SCHOOLS

At least twenty-five new Grammar Schools had Arithmetic prescribed by the founders as a subject of the curriculum in the period 1660–1700. Probably schools of the older foundations also introduced it.

Speaking of schools, of free schools (i.e., grammar schools), generally in 1678, Wase [1] would not have a separate room for writing, "yet there should be equipment of proper instruments, and so more solemn, and also there should be general work of numeration."

Soon after the Restoration, in 1673, was the foundation of the first mathematical side of a school, viz., at Christ's Hospital, for forty boys. The boys were to be competent in grammar and common arithmetic, and were to be taught the art of navigation and "the whole science of arithmetic." Then the boys were to be bound apprentices for seven years to captains of ships. Books, globes, maps and other mathematical instruments were ordered for the instruction of the boys, who were to remain at school till sixteen years of age. This "Mathematical School" of Christ's Hospital must be regarded as a landmark in the history of the development of school subjects in England. The Mathematical School was endowed by Richard Aldworth with £7,000. It was under royal patronage. "In fact it had everything in its favour—endowment, a plentiful supply of scientific instruments, a complete set of class-books—everything except the requisite personal impulse which can only come from settled and sympathetic instruction. The history up to

---

[1] Christopher Wase : *Considerations Concerning Free Schools*, 1678.

the latter half of the eighteenth century is one long story of inefficient, ineffective teachers, and one may add of a good deal of incompetent management." [1] The association in various ways with the " Mathematical School " of Pepys, Sir Jonas Moore, Flamsteed, Halley, Sir Isaac Newton, adds greatly to its historic interest. But it failed, nevertheless, to become a great Mathematical School, through the pretentiousness of its curriculum, inefficient teachers, and the neglect of the principle of *Festina lente*. We must look elsewhere and earlier, therefore, for the main currents of mathematical influence.

There is an *Autobiography* [2] of one of the school teachers of mathematics, which gives details in his own case, not forthcoming of the teachers of mathematics of the time generally. In the time of the great Civil War, Adam Martindale was a schoolmaster at Rainford in Lancashire. He wrote a book on arithmetic after the models of Recorde, Hill and Baker. He attempted to shorten their methods, and added an original appendix on the extraction of the roots of fractions. He confesses that he knew nothing of decimals, logarithms, or algebra. The MS. was lost. In 1644 Martindale was appointed to the Free School at Over-Whitley in Cheshire. He tells us he had his name written over the door of the school, had a full school and a pretty store of rich men's sons. Moreover, he added to his income by

---

[1] See the very interesting account in E. H. Pearce's *Annals of Christ's Hospital*, pp. 98–134.
[2] *Chetham Society : The Life of Adam Martindale. Written by himself.* Edited by Canon Parkinson. (1845.)

" making writings " i.e. writing letters and documents for his neighbours. Martindale next became a minister, though continuing his teaching. In 1662 he was ejected from his living of £60 a year. The following is his account of his study of mathematics :

I bethought me of the study of some useful parts of the mathematics ; and, though I was now almost forty years old, and knew little more than arithmetic in the vulgar way, and decimals in Jager's bungling method, [1] I fell close to the study of decimals in a more artificial manner, logarithms, algebra, and other arts, since by me professed, in which work I was encouraged and assisted by noble Lord Delamer.

Martindale was still keeping school ; but the Conventicle Act made him throw it up, and with it the 20s. or 25s. a week on which he lived. He removed to Preston and commenced school again. Then he went to Manchester as a teacher of mathematics. The headmaster of the free school [i.e. the Manchester Grammar School] sent to him for instruction in that subject some of his best boys. Still he had his difficulties.

One that was a teacher in the town, and some others that thought themselves fit for such work, that knew nothing of decimals, logarithms, or the new species way, contemned and assaulted me, sending me questions, which I quickly returned answered and propounded another to every one that had sent any to me, and then I had done with them. But I had much ado to keep in my scholars from revenging my quarrels too far ; for when they, by skill in logarithms, could in an hour answer such a question as these professors could not solve in a month (as, for example, such as this : What is 5d. 3qs. a day to continue 300 years worth in ready money at £6 12s. 6d. per

---

[1] Canon Parkinson's note : " Robert Jager's *Artificial Arithmetic in Decimals*, Lond. 1651, 8vo."

cent.?), it was next to impossible to keep my pragmatical youths from running down these old soakers with their Record's Arithmetic. As for old Richard Martinscroft, who had more true skill in him than they all, though he was a Papist, he never opposed nor contemned me, but was always civil to me and communicative.

Martindale wrote *The Country-Survey Book; or Land Meter's Vade Mecum* (1682) and *A Token for Shipboys; or plain sailing made more plain and short than usual* (1683). They both bear inscriptions, the one " By Adam Martindale, a friend to mathematical learning," the other " A lover of the mathematics."

In the first half of the seventeenth century there were those who saw the importance of arithmetic and advocated its development and the extension of its teaching. In 1623 Bacon in the *De Augmentis Scientiarum*, without noting what had been accomplished by men like Napier in his own time, says : " In Arithmetic there is still wanting a sufficient variety of short and compendious methods of calculation, especially with regard to progressions whose use in physics is very considerable." In 1632, Comenius in his *Didactica Magna* requires arithmetic to be taught as a subject of the curriculum in the vernacular schools. The boy is to learn to count with cyphers and with counters as far as is necessary for practical purposes. When the boy comes to the Latin schools he is to continue his Arithmetic.

In 1644 Milton, in his *Tractate*, prescribes arithmetic. Petty (1647) recommends that the elements of arithmetic be required from all. But he also makes geometry obligatory. The ground on which he requires arithmetic and geometry he states, to be not only for great and frequent use in all human affairs, but also as sure guides and helps to reason, and especial remedies for a volatile and unsteady mind. He urges the teaching of arithmetic also as being the best grounded parts of speculative knowledge and of so vast use in all practical arts. He particularly advises Mr. Pell's three mathematical Treatises.

In Dr. Cyprian Kinner's *Thoughts concerning Education*, given to the press by Samuel Hartlib in 1648, we read: " Because arithmetical cyphers are numbering words I teach to write and pronounce them also, and to tell the value of many of them placed in an order, which we call numeration."

George Snell, in 1649, considers that everyone above an artificer should learn arithmetic. " Though a scholar be fully qualified and thoroughly furnished with all other science, yet if he be ignorant how to work skilfully in numbers and accounts, he stands utterly incapable to execute any good plan, or office of charge of importance." In the same year, in the *Reformed School*, Dury provides from 8–9 years to 13–14 years of age a course in Arithmetic " to include the Four Rules, the Reduction of Fractions, the Rule of Proportions, and no further." Samuel Hartlib's *London's Charity Enlarged*, 1650, contains a plea for orphan schools, in which children should be trained up to " become apprentices, scholars, or accomptants " according to their wits. " Accomptants " implies the learning of arithmetic, either by cyphers or counters ; in Hartlib's time, probably by cyphers.

In 1660, Charles Hoole requires as a part of the qualifications of the teacher of a *Petty School* that he write a fair hand and have good skill in arithmetic, and " so let him teach *all his scholars* (as they become capable) to read English very well and afterwards to write and cast accounts." This is, as far as I can discover, the first distinct statement of the curriculum of the three R's for the " Petty " elementary school by a responsible educationist.

With regard to the education of nobles and gentry, in the " Academies " proposed for their benefit, arithmetic was not included by Sir Humphrey Gilbert (c. 1572) nor by Sir Francis Kynaston (1635), but it is specifically named by Sir Balthazar Gerbier in 1648. The latter also includes : " The true method of keeping Books of Account by double parties as is practised in Italy and other parts of Europe." In 1615, Sir George Buck mentions arithmetic as one of the subjects taught in London Colleges.

The learning of arithmetic by all classes, therefore, was mainly outside of the academic system.

Some scholars were self-taught at a somewhat mature stage of life; thus Adam Martindale began the systematic study of decimals when he was forty years old, and Hobbes was the same age when he began geometry. Many men even in public affairs did not know the principles of arithmetic, at any rate more than was implied in casting an accompt by counters. For instance, Samuel Pepys was made clerk of the Acts of the Navy (at a salary of £350 a year) in 1660, and to this was added the office of a clerk of the Privy Seal in the same year.

Yet it is only in 1662 that he engages a mathematical teacher and begins to learn his multiplication tables. Yet Pepys had been at St. Paul's School, and was at University of Cambridge from 1650–3, when he took his degree. On July 9, 1662, we read " Up by four o'clock, and at my multiplication-table hard, which is all the trouble I meet withal in my arithmetique." He was then thirty years of age. It may be of interest to show here the Multiplication Table as it occurs in Cocker [1] (or Hawkins') Arithmetic (? 1677).

MULTIPLICATION TABLE

1	2	3	4	5	6	7	8	9
2	4	6	8	10	12	14	16	18
3	6	9	12	15	18	21	24	27
4	8	12	16	20	24	28	32	36
5	10	15	20	25	30	35	40	45
6	12	18	24	30	36	42	48	54
7	14	21	28	35	42	49	56	63
8	16	24	32	40	48	56	64	72
9	18	27	36	45	54	63	72	81

[1] For an account of "Cocker's" Arithmetic *see* de Morgan : *Arithmetical Books*, p. 56.

The Table only goes up to the 9 times. The reader must judge for himself whether it is surprising that Samuel Pepys found it " hard " to learn. Yet there were private schools in which arithmetic was taught as part of the curriculum.[1] Thus when Sir Ralph Verney wished to send his boy to a school he mentions a school at Uppingham, and one at Barn Elms in Surrey. He sends his son Jack Verney, thirteen years of age, to the latter, a school kept by the Rev. Dr. James Fleetwood, who reports of the boy : " He is very ingenious and quick in understanding Arithmetic, wherein he hath made very good progress." [2]

Parents who themselves had studied mathematics sometimes taught them to their children. These instances were probably rare, but there is the case of Thomas Fuller's Oxford tutor, Edward Davenant (M.A. 1618), of whom Fuller said that " he had excellent notes of his father's in mathematiques as also in Greek, and 'twas no small advantage to him to have such a learned father [3] to imbue mathematical

---

[1] *See* p. 321 *infra*.

[2] *Verney Memoirs*, vol. iii, p. 356.

[3] The same is said of William Oughtred (1574–1660) by Aubrey : " His father taught to write at Eton and was a scrivener ; and understood common arithmetic. 'Twas no small help and furtherance to his son to be instructed in it when a school-boy." So, too, it is stated of Seth Ward, Savilian Professor of Astronomy at Oxford (1649–1661) : " His father taught him common arithmetic." Edmund Halley (1656–1741), the mathematician and astronomer, was taught arithmetic at nine years old by the apprentice of his father (a soap-boiler).—Aubrey's *Lives* (ed. Clark), vol. i, p. 282.

knowledge unto him, when a boy, at night times, when he came home from school" (Merchant Taylors'). Aubrey says of Davenant : " He was my singular good friend. . . . He did me the favour to inform me first in Algebra. *His daughters were algebrists.*" Mrs. Bathsua Makin was so bold as to advocate arithmetic and other " sciences " for girls. Her *Essay to revive the Ancient Education of Gentlewomen* was written in 1673, but she had apparently kept school at Putney, some years before. Her plea is on very practical grounds : " To buy wool and flax, to dye scarlet and purple requires skill in Natural Philosophy. To consider a field, the quantity and quality requires knowledge in Geometry. To plant a vineyard, requires understanding in Husbandry. *She could not merchandise without Arithmetic,*" etc. At another girls' school earlier still, viz. in 1643, a Mrs. Perwick kept school in Hackney. Her own daughter, Miss Susanna Perwick, was a pupil, and it is said of her that she was an *accountant* in which " her skill was more than ordinary women have."

Though arithmetic was only taught to a comparatively slight extent in the ordinary schools, and though a man like Samuel Pepys might have gone to St. Paul's School, London, and afterwards have taken his M.A. at Cambridge (1660) without knowing even any arithmetic, there was a separate class of arithmetic teachers, apart from the public schools. The usefulness of the subject demanded a supply of teachers of arithmetic. Accordingly, voluntary supply was forthcoming, in private teachers and private arithmetic schools.

EXCURSUS ON SOME PRIVATE TEACHERS OF
ARITHMETIC

1. In 1562, Humphrey Baker wrote his *Wellspring
of Sciences which teacheth the perfect work and practice
of Arithmetic*. This ran through several editions.
De Morgan describes it as one of the books which
break the fall from the *Grounde of Artes* to the commercial arithmetics of the next century. In the
edition of 1562 (the book appears to have been issued
in a slighter form in 1546) appears the prospectus
of Baker's School for the teaching of Arithmetic,
the first specialistic school[1] for arithmetic in England,
as far as is known. It runs : " Such as are desirous,
eyther themselves to learn or to have theyr children
or servants instructed in any of these Arts and
Faculties heere under named : It may please them
to repayre unto the house of Humphrey Baker,
dwelling on the North side of the Royall Exchange,
next adjoyning to the signe of the shippe. Where
they shall fynde the Professors of the said Artes, etc.,
Readie to doe their diligent endeavours for a reasonable consideration. Also if any be minded to have
their children boorded at the said house, for the
speedier expedition of their learning, they shall be
well and reasonably used, to theyr contentation."

2. John Mellis, editing Hugh Oldcastle's *Brief
Instruction and Maner how to Keep Books of Accounts*,
says to the reader :

I am but the renewer and reviser of an ancient old copy
printed here in London the 14 of August, 1543. Then
collected, published, made, and set forth by one Hugh

---

[1] Unless Oldcastle deserves this place. *See* next page.

Oldcastle, Scholemaster, who, as appeareth by his treatise, then taught Arithmetic and this book in Saint Olave's parish in Mark Lane. . . . And if any lack instructions herein, or in any part of arithmetic, either in whole or broken numbers incident hereunto, with also to teach them, their children, or servants, to write any manner of hand usual within this realm of England ; Pleaseth them to repair unto the Mayes Gate nie (nigh) Battle Bridge in S. Olave's parish in short Southwark, where, God to friend, they shall find me readie to accomplish their desire in as short a time as may be. *Vale.*

JOHN MELLIS, Scholemaister.

Dr. Robert Recorde's *Grounds of Arts.* Second edition, by John Mellis, 1607.

At the end of the book Mellis adds a different advertisement :

Finally the author giveth intelligence, That if any be minded to have their children or servants instructed or taught in this noble Art of Arithmetic, or any brief practice thereof. Whose method is such by long custom of teaching, that (God to friend) he will bring them (if their capacities be anything) to their desire therein in a short time. As also to learn them to write any manner of hand usual within this realm of England.

It can also after reasonable understanding of Arithmetic, if any be minded to have them taught the famous account of Debitor and Creditor, they shall find him ready to accomplish their desire. More also, to further such as are desirous that way, in the principal of Algebra or Cossick numbers. Lastly, to learn to draw any manner of demonstration, devise, or portion. Or to learn them to draw either white or black capital letters. Or to draw or reduce any Map or Card in true proportion from a great quantity to a small, or to bring a smaller to a greater. Of all or any these things rehearsed, you shall find the Author (according to his small talent) ready to accomplish the same for a reasonable reward : whose dwelling is and hath been these sixteen years within the Mayes-gate in short Southwark nigh Battle Bridge.

3. Henry Lyte describes himself as *Gentleman* in his book *Art of Tens*, 1619, 12mo.

His keen interest in mathematics is shown by a paragraph in his address to the reader, where he says:

And those who are willing to have conference with me whilst that I am in London, let them repair to Mr. Griffin's, the Printer of this Book, and there they shall learn whom I am, who will be very willing to explain anything that is contained within this Book.

4. John Speidell, " *An Arithmeticall Extraction ; or Collection of divers Questions with their Answers. Most useful and necessary to all Teachers of Arithmetick, for sufficient and speedy instruction of all such persons as desire to be made quicke and ready therein. Most carefully composed, collected, written, overgone, and corrected by the Author himselfe. Jo. Speidell, Professor of the Mathematiques, in Queene Streete. London*, 1628. 12mo."

Speidell says to the reader that he has been these twenty years and more a professor of mathematics.

At the end of address :—

Thus (gentle Reader) hast thou heere a small entrance into arithmetique, which if thou wilt but once passe over, I doubt not but it will make thee sufficient for any Merchant or tradesman's use ; and if anything be too hard for thee herein, if it please thee to repaire to my house in Queen's Street, I will not only assist thee herein with the best and the briefest wayes, but in all the other Rules of Arithmetique and the Rule of Cosse or Algebra ; as also in all other parts of the Mathematiques, as Geometrie, Astronomie, Navigation, and Fortification, with the making of all kinds of Sunne-dyals, and the doctrine of the Triangles, both right lines and sphericall, with the use of the logarithms, etc.

There also may you have this Treatise.

Also a Geometricall extraction and the logarithms by me set forth.

There is also to be had of the best Mathematicall paper.

5. Robert Hartwell, teacher of the mathematics, *Mr. Blundevil: His Exercises, contayning Eight Treatises. 7th edition, corrected and somewhat enlarged by R. Hartwell, Philmathematicus*, 1636.

Last page :

Arts and Sciences Mathematicall.

Taught in Fetter Lane, neare the Golden Lyon, or privately abroad at convenient houses, by Robert Hartwell, Teacher of the Mathematicks, viz. Arithmetick, Geometry, Astronomy, Cosmography, Geography, Navigation, Architecture, Fortification, Horologiography, etc.

Measuring of Land.

The doctrine of Triangles, plaine and sphericall ; the use of the Tables of Sines, Tangents, Secants, and Logarithms. Accompts for Merchants by order of Debitor and Creditor. *Fide sed Vide.*

Vivat Rex.

In 1650, appeared the second edition of the *Arithmetique made Easie* of Edmund Wingate, Esq., who had been English tutor to Princess Henrietta Maria (afterwards wife of Charles I). The second edition of his Arithmetic was edited by John Kersey, who takes the opportunity to insert his Prospectus as a private Teacher of Mathematics.

6. 1650. John Kersey's Prospectus :

Arts and Sciences, Mathematicill, taught at the corner house (opposite to the " White Lion ") in Charles Street, neare the Piazza in Covent Garden, or at the lodgings of such as are desirous, viz. :—

Arithmetique.

1. In whole numbers.
2. In fractions $\begin{cases} \text{Vulgar.} \\ \text{Decimall.} \\ \text{Astronomicall.} \end{cases}$

3. The extraction of the roots, viz. of the
$$\begin{cases} \text{Square} \\ \text{Cube} \\ \text{Biquadrate} \\ \text{Quadrato-cube,} \\ \text{etc.} \end{cases}$$
By rules naturally arising from the genesis of powers.

4. Merchants' accompts, in the Italique methode of debitor and creditor, according to the modern practice.

Algebra.

1. In numbers and characters according to the ancients.
2. In species or letters of the alphabet, according to the modern analysts.

With the use thereof in the invention of theoremes and resolution of subtile questions and problems in arith. and geometry.

Geometrie, viz. :—

The Works of Euclid, Archimedes, Apollonius, Pergæus, Paphus, and other Geometricians, as well ancient as modern, explained and applied unto

1. Divers wayes of Construction, Mensuration, Reduction, and Division of superficiall Figures, viz. of Land, Board, Wainscot, Glasse, &c. Also of Solids, as Timbers, Stone, &c., with the gaging of Cask.
2. The Projection of Plani-Sphaeres, Maps, Charts (universall or particular), Plots of Land, Architecture, &c., with the augmenting or diminishing of them, according to any proportion assigned.

The Doctrine of Triangles, viz. :—

1. Plain

With their use in finding of altitudes and Distances, in measuring of Land, Fortification, Dyalling, Navigation, Theories of the Planets, etc.

2. Sphericall

With their use in the resolution of the usuall propositions of the Celestiall and Terrestriall Globes, Dyalling, Navigation, etc.

Navigation, viz. :—

In either of the three principal kinds of saying, viz. :—
By the Plain Chart, by Mercator's Chart, by Great Circle.

Dyalling, viz. :—

1. Geometrically
2. Instrumentally
3. Arithmetically

⎱ With the inscription of the Almi-canthus, Azimuths, Parallels of Declination, etc. Also the making of reflexive Dyals, showing the house without any shadow.

The Construction and Use of Mathematicall Instruments,
viz. :—

1. The Canon of Sines, Tangents, Secants, and Logarithms.
2. The Quadrant, Sector, Crosse-staffe, plain Table, Rule of Proportion, Instrumentall Dyalls, etc.

Chirographie, viz. :—

The Art of accurate and exact Hand-writing, in the English and best Italique formes, by genuine Principles and plain Demonstration.

By

JOHN KERSEY,

Philomathet.

Vox audita perit, litera scripta manet.

Jack Verney, in 1655, went as a pupil to John Kersey. Kersey told Sir Ralph he did not profess to give a commercial education. If the boy were fitted to be a merchant or other trade the best and readiest way was to put him to board with a business man. " But if his design is only to learn something in the Mathematics I shall do him what service I am able if he can be conveniently lodged and dieted near my house." The terms to be paid for tuition in mathematics were 12*s.* a week, each pupil.[1]

So, too, Edmund Verney, who was twenty-one years of age, in 1657 was " seized with a desire to continue his education." He writes : " J'ai pris Kersey pour m'enseigner la Richmetique, à 20*s.* par

---

[1] *Verney Memoirs*, iii, p. 358.

mois, et il ne me vient que 3 fois la septmaine ; les arts et les sciences sont bien cheres icy, ils ont besoing d'estre bonnes." [1] There was one way of providing for instruction in arithmetic without introducing it into the curriculum of the Grammar schools, viz. to send the boys to a writing school in which the master was competent to teach both writing and arithmetic. This was the method adopted by Charles Hoole in the time of the Commonwealth. Writing in 1660 Hoole says that for twelve years the boys had gone from his (private) Grammar School to Mr. James Hodder, from whom most of them had not only learned to write a " very fair hand " but also arithmetic and merchants' accounts, " which they gained by his teaching at spare moments." This method of receiving instruction in arithmetic outside the Grammar School probably explains the fact that later arithmetic was sometimes charged for as an extra, [2] the payment for teaching being retained, after the subject was taken into the intra-mural curriculum.

Here is Mr. Hodder's advertisement :

The author hereof [3] keepeth a school in Lothbury next door to the " Sunne," where such as are desirous to learn the art of Writing, as also Arithmeticke in whole numbers and fractions, with Merchants' Accompts and Shorthand, may be carefully attended and faithfully introduced by James Hodder.

---

[1] *Verney Memoirs*, iii, p. 305.

[2] *See* p. 311 *supra*.

[3] The advertisement occurs in a writing copy-book : *A Penman's Recreation, containing sundry Examples of Fair Writing, of excellent use for all such as aim at perfection therein.*

There is in the British Museum a copy of " *Hodder's Arithmetick : Or that necessary Art made most easie, Being explained in a way familiar to the capacity of any that desire to learn it in a little time.* By James Hodder, Professor thereof, as also of the Art of Fair Writing, who finding it helpful to his own scholars hath now published it for the general good of the kingdom, 1661."

In his preface to the reader Hodder [1] says : " For the better completing youth as to clerkship or trades, I am induced to publish this small treatise of Arithmetic." From which it appears that arithmetic was taken up for the most part simply by boys going into commercial pursuits, and that the master of a writing school was commonly the teacher of arithmetic to those boys who wished to learn it. Another writer on arithmetic of the period is Noah Bridges. His book is styled *Vulgar Arithmetique* (1653), and is described as " peculiarly fitted for merchants and tradesmen, made useful for all men, familiar to the meanest capacity ; and for the public good laid down in a school method." His preface throws some light on the arithmetic teaching of the period :

" I did long since," he says, " digest Vulgar Arithmetique into a school method, distinguish the rules into papers apart, and affix variety of examples

---

[1] De Morgan says of Hodder's book : " Had this work given the new mode of division it must have stood in the place of Cocker."

carefully wrought to each rule, as concerns it, a course much conducing to the improvement of youth. . . . Though that way seemed in some measure to reach the end I aimed at yet (arithmetic, like green wood, will quickly extinguish without a constant blowing) some by neglect, after they had quitted my care, lost great part of what they had gained, for prevention whereof I contracted my method to fewer examples, and (qualifying those under my charge with fair hands fit for entries) caused them to understand and work over the several examples in each rule in the same order I had done, and then from my papers to make their entries ; conceiving, as in reason I might, that course would put them into a capacity to retain what they learned, or when they came to a loss to beat about and retrieve it.

" But boys will be boys. Such was the indisposition of some to their own good (notwithstanding my care and pains for their advantage) that by their careless transcriptions, they committed many errors both in the rules and examples, and by that means became sometimes unserviceable to themselves likewise. Many times since I have (as some other masters do) entered the rules and examples into the books of learners with great regard to the operation of the questions ; and yet I have met with scholars from some of those masters (probably they with others from me) who after a short time of discontinuance were only accompanied with full books and empty heads." Bridges thinks that his newer " Arithmetic " will make it impossible for youth to relapse in such a way. De Morgan [1] praises Bridges' book as giving what Hodder did not give—an explicit account of the modern mode of division.

Bridges dates : " From my house at Putney in the county of Surrey, April 25, 1653. Where is taught the Greek and Latin Tongues ; also Arts and Sciences Mathematicall, viz. Arithmetique, fair Writing, Merchants' Accounts, Geometry, Trigonometrie, Algebra, etc." His school, therefore, approximates to the later style of private school, in which every subject was taught.

Such a curriculum shows that private grammar schools' teachers were sometimes an evolution from the writing school teacher. A teacher establishes a writing school. He adds to his function the teaching of arithmetic and other commercial subjects. He begins to take in boarders, and then undertakes the whole education. Such private schools as those of Farnaby and Hoole, however, are simply modelled on the grammar schools, and are to be classed with such, except that they set themselves to improvement in method. That these writing masters and their private schools were successful in many instances is seen in Massey. [2]

Teachers of arithmetic in the early part of the eighteenth century became numerous. An indication

---

[1] De Morgan's book gives a full and interesting bibliographical account of *Arithmetic Books from the Invention of Printing to the present Time* (1847).

[2] A biographical account of the old Writing Masters of England is given in William Massey's *Origin and Progress of Letters* (1763).

of this may be seen in the fact that in **1743** Thomas Dilworth, before the text of his *Schoolmaster's Assistant*[1] (in arithmetic), gives the names and addresses of over fifty schoolmasters in London and in the provinces who recommend the book for use in schools in general.

---

[1] In the eighteenth century this was a well-known and often-reprinted book. It may possibly have suggested the title of Miss Edgeworth's *Parents' Assistant*.

CHAPTER IX

THE TEACHING OF GEOMETRY

THE dignity of the study of geometry in the Middle Ages was secured by its position as one of the subjects of the quadrivium, but the actual scope of the study was very limited. Thus, in Martianus Capella, an author whose allegory *de Nuptiis Philologiae et Mercurii* was one of the main early text-books[1] in the Seven Liberal Arts, geometry is included, though it is largely founded on geography gathered from Pliny. It contains a short account of lines, plane figures and solids. In the Ordinances of the University of Oxford in 1431 geometry includes Euclid, Vitellio's *Perspectiva* and Alicen or Al-Hazen. Vitello or Vitellio, was a Pole, who lived in the thirteenth century. He wrote a treatise in ten books on optics. It is a collection of what had been previously known, especially from Arabian sources. Alhazen was an Arabian collector of writings on optics, of an earlier date, from whom Vitellio is supposed to have freely borrowed. It is thus clear that in the middle of the fifteenth century the subject of geometry included Euclid's *Elements* together with optics. A translation of Euclid had been made by Adelhard[2] of Bath early in the

---

[1] It was written before 439 A.D.

[2] Adelhard " disguised as a Mahommedan student got into Cordova about 1120 and obtained a copy of Euclid's Elements. This copy translated into Latin was the foundation of all the editions known in Europe till 1533."— W. W. R. Ball : *History of Mathematics* (p. 158).

twelfth century and in the next age by Campano, both versions, of course, being from the Arabic into Latin. We have seen [1] that Vives recommended the reading of Bradwardine, whose *Geometria Speculativa* was published at Paris in 1496.

The Revival of Learning with its introduction of Greek texts had as stimulating results in mathematics as in other subjects. We begin to hear of the wonderful proficiency of the Greek youth who knew mathematics, particularly arithmetic, geometry and astronomy, to a degree not attained even by the Renascence scholar in his maturest years. Thus we get in Mulcaster the advocacy of the teaching of mathematics to boys, and later in Commonwealth times the suggestion, that if everything were taught in the vernacular and if the burden of the teaching of classics were removed, there would thus be room made for the inclusion of mathematics for the English boy, so that he would be put upon an equal footing with the Greek boy. Moreover, an atmosphere was created in which it became familiar to quote such Platonic expressions as

$$\text{Μηδεὶς ἀγεωμέτρητος εἰσίτω}$$

and

$$\text{ὁ θεός ἀει γεωμετρεῖ.}$$

Mulcaster, in his plea for mathematics in the *Positions* [2] in 1581, seems especially to have had geometry in his view. Naturally, the geometry he

---

recommended was Greek. He urges that Aristotle cannot be understood without a knowledge of geometry. It was for the very purpose of the understanding of Aristotle that Bradwardine over two hundred years earlier had gathered together two books of Euclid. Mulcaster especially advises the study of Proclus : his four books on Euclid, either in Greek or in Latin. Still, it was not till 1570 that the first English translation of Euclid[1] from the Greek appeared.

> *The Elements of Geometrie of the most auncient Philosopher Euclide of Megara. Faithfully (now first translated into the Englishe toung, by H. Billingsley, Citizen of London. Whereunto are annexed certaine Scholies, Annotations, and Inventions of the best Mathematiciens, both of time past, and in this our age, With a very fruitfull Praeface made by M. I. Dee, specifying the chiefe Mathematicall Scieces, what they are, and whereunto commodious : where also are disclosed certaine new Secrets Mathematicall and Mechanicall, untill these our daies, greatly missed. Imprinted at* London by John Daye. (Dee's Preface, February 9, 1570.)

This was the first translation into English. It was not a translation merely of the Latin text of Campanus (which was taken from an Arabic text) but from the Greek.[2]

---

[1] Euclid lived in the time of the first Ptolemy (B.C. 323–283), and was thus a younger contemporary of Aristotle. There is an interesting account of Euclid and his works in Sir William Smith's *Dictionary of Greek and Latin Biography*. The article was written by the late Prof. Augustus de Morgan.

[2] De Morgan : *British Almanac and Companion*, 1837, p. 38.

The importance of this English Euclid, in the words of de Morgan, is due to the fact " that it forms the first body of complete mathematical demonstration in our language." Arithmetic tended to become dogmatical, to teach rules without demonstration. " Our ancestors [1] throughout Europe did not fall into the error of admitting arithmetic and algebra (such as they then were) to the name of mathematics and the rank of geometry. So long as they continued to be only methods without rigid investigation, they were arts not sciences, and the science of arithmetic was sought in the seventh and following books of Euclid. . . . Had it not been for the writings of Euclid, Ptolemy, Aristotle, Proclus, etc., and judging of what would have been the case in geometry by the practice which became universal in other branches of exact science, we cannot see how anything like demonstration could have been introduced." The Renascence of Greek, therefore, was directly stimulative to the study of mathematics, especially of geometry.

As to John Dee, who (if he was not the translator) at any rate was the introducer of the first English Euclid, it should be mentioned that he was Fellow of Trinity College, Cambridge, M.A. 1548 (when twenty-one years of age). He studied at Louvain, and lectured at Paris in Euclid in 1550. He was an astrologer, and joined a society for seeking the philosopher's stone and for invoking angels. He

---

[1] De Morgan : *British Almanac and Companion*, 1837, p. 39.

practised crystallomancy and was " prone to the mystical love of what were termed the occult sciences." [1]

The conjunction of mathematical with magical studies was therefore a natural association of the Elizabethan age. As a mathematician, de Morgan pronounces Dee, " no mean proficient." In fact, de Morgan places Dee with Recorde and Leonard Digges as the three names to be associated with the " real advancement " of English (mathematical) science in the sixteenth century. To the general public Dee, who lived till 1608, was the great magician and sorcerer. Hence one of the greatest and probably the best known of the English mathematicians gave credence to the supposition of the alliance of the clearest and most exact of the sciences with the most secret and occult arts. Dr. Dee, for instance, wrote a *Treatise of the Rosie-Crucian Secrets*. The absence of mathematics from the curriculum of the ordinary grammar school thus had some compensations, and it may be seen that objections to their introduction may, in some cases, reasonably have been grounded upon dangers evident enough in the Elizabethan age. Even in the middle of the seventeenth century, the philosopher Hobbes remarks that the Universities had only just given over thinking geometry to be " art diabolical." Dee's Euclid of 1570 is the starting point of the geometry which was to develop so greatly within a hundred years. But it was not the

---

[1] Isaac d'Israeli : *Amenities of Literature.*

earliest English work on geometry. This distinction belongs to a book of Robert Recorde :

> *The Pathway to Knowledge containing the First principles of Geometrie, as they may moste aptly be applied unto practice, bothe for instrumentes Geometricall and Astronomicall and also for projection of plattes in everye kinde, etc.* (*The second Booke . . .*) *containing certaine Theorems, which may be called approved truthes . . . wherfor the practicke coclusions of Geometry are founded. Whereunto are annexed certaine declarations by example, for the right understanding of the same.* 2 pts. R. Wolfe, London, 1551.

This contains practical geometrical problems and the way of working them, and in the second part it is to be noted Recorde simply contains " descriptions, not demonstrations " of the theorems (Euclid, bks. i–iv).

Leonard Digges, the third of de Morgan's trio of the leading mathematicians of the sixteenth century, was a man of means and position, " of ancient family," who followed mathematics as an amateur. He was said to be the best " architect " of his age " and excellent at fortifications." [1] He wrote :

> *A geometrical Practise, named Pantometria, divided into three books, Longimetra, Planimetra, and Stereometria, containing Rules manifolde for mensuration of all lines, superficies and Solides . . . framed by L. D. . . . lately finished by J. Digges his sonne who hathe also thereunto adjoyned a Mathematicall treatise of the five regular Platonicall bodies,* etc. 1571.

In **1578**, William Fulke, a Cambridge graduate and Puritan divine, chaplain to Leicester and

---

[1] *Dictionary of National Biography*. Art. : " Leonard Digges."

afterwards Master of Pembroke Hall, Cambridge, published Μετρομαχία sive Ludus Geometricus; and in 1587:

> A Mirror for Mathematiques: a Golden Gem for Geometricians. . . . Contayning also an order howe to make an Astronomicall instrument, called the Astrolab, with the use thereof, etc.:

a title which shows that geometry was not entirely differentiated from other subjects of study.

Thomas Hood, a fellow of Trinity College, Cambridge, and afterwards a physician in London, is noteworthy as the first lecturer in mathematics in London. Hood held at one time what was apparently a private lectureship established by (Sir) Thomas Smith, Merchant and Governor of the East India Company and of the Virginia Company, who had lectures on mathematics delivered at his own house. Thus there is extant:

> A Copie of the Speache made by the Mathematicall Lecturer (I. H.) unto the . . . Companye present, at the house of . . . M. T. Smith, dwelling in Gracious [Gracechurch] Street: the 4 of November, 1588.

Mr. Ball [1] thinks that Hood's books, which include a translation of Urstisius' [2] Arithmetic and Ramus's Geometry, and books on the use of the Globes and Surveying, are transcripts of the lectures thus given by Hood. Thomas Hood was the first to present to

---

[1] *Cambridge Mathematics*, p. 24.

[2] Christianus Urstisius, a Swiss geometrician (1544–1588), published his *Elementa arithmetices* at Basle in 1579. This is the arithmetic which John Milton used in his school.

English readers, in 1590, the Geometry of Ramus (which was written in Latin and first printed in 1569). Ramus's Geometry was founded on Euclid, though he was not regarded as orthodox. Hence the spread of his book throughout Europe is an indication of the growing interest in, and study of, geometry.

A further translation of Ramus appeared in 1636 :

> *Via Regia ad Geometriam. The way to Geometry. Written in Latine by P. Ramus and now translated and . . . enlarged by . . .* W. Bedwell (edited by J. Clarke).

Bedwell was one of the translators of the Bible, 1604–11, and specially an Arabic scholar. He is an instance of the workers in mathematics in the period, who are comparatively numerous, who were not specialists, and who were outside of the direct University influence.

The name of Ramus carried great weight in England, and particularly at Cambridge, as an opponent of the Aristotelian supremacy in logic and philosophy. The advocacy of geometrical teaching, therefore, gave a positive turn to Ramism, and the dissemination of geometry on Euclidian lines paved the way for the new Cartesian mathematics which exercised such an influence on Cambridge, until the great days of the teaching of Sir Isaac Newton, who established for England and for Europe a mathematical system which by its disciplinary claims replaced the old Aristotelian supremacy of logic.

Among the remarkable men of the age of Shakespere, Sir Henry Savile (1549–1622) in England holds perhaps the first place as a scholar. He was a fellow of Merton College, Oxford, and in 1570 lectured on mathematics in that College, throwing his lectures open to members of all colleges. The subject he chose was Greek geometry. " I explained," he wrote, " the definitions, postulates, axioms, and the first eight propositions of Euclid's Elements. Wearied by the time spent, I am giving up the art of circles." Savile was tutor in Greek to Queen Elizabeth, then Warden of Merton College, Oxford, translator of Tacitus, Secretary of the Latin tongue to Queen Elizabeth, and held the Provostship of Eton College, whilst retaining the Wardenship of Merton College. His highest claim to remembrance as a scholar is his edition of St. Chrysostom's writings, and for the printing of it he set up a press of his own at Eton, buying magnificent new type and securing the services of the Queen's Printer, John Norton. The production of the Chrysostom is said to have cost Savile £8,000. Other distinctions attaching to Savile's name are his assistance to Bodley in the establishment of the great Library at Oxford and his appointment as a translator of the " authorised " version of the Bible. As Provost of Eton he is said to have been particularly severe on clever boys who did not work hard. " Give me the plodding student," is one of his repeated sayings ; " if I would look for wits, I would go to Newgate ; there be the wits." [1]

---

[1] Maxwell Lyte : *Eton*, p. 196.

Savile's interest in mathematics was not confined to his lecturing on geometry, since the University standard of work in that subject comprised the most " beggarly elements," a type of teaching with which he had utter impatience. In 1619 he established in the University of Oxford two mathematical professorships, one in geometry, the other in astronomy. The occupants of these chairs have been men of high distinction, so that probably Savile's own great achievements in many directions have less contributed to his popular reputation than has the association of his name as founder of the chairs, from which the subjects of geometry and astronomy have received at once effective exposition and noteworthy development.

The first Savilian Professor of Geometry was Henry Briggs, Fellow of St. John's College, Cambridge. In 1596, Briggs was appointed Professor of Geometry in the newly founded Gresham College in London. In 1619, he was called to the Savilian Chair in Oxford. This he held till his death in 1630. Thus Briggs was the first professor in each of the first two chairs in mathematics in England.

The progressive state of geometry may be seen by a comparison of the ordinance of the University, 1431,[1] and the regulations drawn up by Sir Henry Savile in 1619. The Professor of geometry, it is prescribed in Savile's Statutes, " must understand that it is his proper province to expound publicly the thirteen books of Euclid's elements,

---

[1] *See* p. 332.

the Conics of Apollonius, and all the books of Archimedes ; and to leave in the University archives his notes and observations on the same books after he has reduced them to writing. . . . As to undertaking or not, the explanation of the spherics of Theodosius and Menelaus and the doctrine of Triangles, as well plane as spherical, I leave the option at large to both professors. It will, besides, be the duty of the Geometry professor to teach and expound arithmetic of all kinds, both speculative and practical ; land-surveying and practical geometry ; canonics or music and mechanics." Savile left with the professor a free choice as to the books he should explain to his classes on the above subjects.

Savile not only endowed the chairs of Geometry and Astronomy, but he also made provision for a mathematical library and a mathematical chest. He further insisted that once a week each Professor should receive students privately and resolve questions for them in practical logic or arithmetic, "which is best communicated without any formality, and in the vulgar tongue if he thinks fit. And also, that at convenient seasons, he shall show the practice of geometry to his auditors (who choose to attend him) in the fields or spots adjacent to the University." [1]

The importance of geometry was soon realised by some of the writers on the education of nobles. For

---

[1] G. R. M. Ward : *Oxford University Statutes*, vol. i, pp. 273-4.

example, it was emphasised by Peacham[1] in 1622. Peacham refers the beginning of geometry to Egypt, where the overflowing of the Nile forced the owners of property to find out, " by the rules of geometry," the safeguarding of their own limits.   From this beginning, geometry "grew to that height from earth it reached up to the Heavens, where it found out their quantities as also of the Elements of the whole world beside." Thales brought it into Greece, where it developed to " that perfection we see it now hath."

Peacham gives a full account of the scope of geometry, and supplies the contemporary view as follows :

By Geometry[2] are found out " the forms and draughts of all figures, greatness of all bodies, all manner of measures and weights, the cunning working of all tools; with all artificial instruments whatsoever.   All engines of war, for many whereof (being antiquated, we have no proper names ; as Exosters, Sambukes, Catapults, Testudoes, Scorpions, etc., Petards, Grenades, great Ordnance of all sorts. By the benefit likewise of Geometry, we have our goodly ships, galleys, bridges, mills, chariots, and coaches (which were invented in Hungary, and there called ' Cotzki '), some with two wheels, some with more, pulleys and cranes of all sorts.   She also with her ingenious hand rears all curious roofs and arches, stately theatres, the columns, simple and compounded, pendant galleries, stately windows, turrets, etc. ; and first brought to light our clocks and curious watches (unknown unto the ancients) : lately, our kitchen jacks, even the wheelbarrow.   Beside whatsoever hath artificial motion either by air, water, wind, sinews or chords, as all manner of musical instruments, water works and the like.

---

[1] Peacham :   *Compleat Gentleman*.   *See* Chapter IX.
[2] *Ibid.*, p. 73.

The authors recommended by Peacham[1] for geometry were :

" *In English :* Cooke's Principles and the Elements of Geometry, written in Latin by P. Ramus (translated by Dr. Hood sometime Mathematical Lecturer in London). Mr. Blundeville's *Euclid* translated into English.

" In *Latin* you may have the learned Jesuit Clavius, Melanchthon, Frisius, Valtarius, his Geometry Military. Albert Dürer hath excellently written hereof in high Dutch, and in French, Forcadell *upon Euclid*, with sundry others."

Next in the history of geometry happened an event of European importance, the publication by René Descartes at Leyden, in 1637, of the

> *Discours de la Méthode pour bien conduire la raison, et chercher la verite dans les sciences, plus la Dioptrique, les Météores et la Geométrie, qui sont des Essais de cette Methode.*

This book together with the *Meditationes*,[2] 1642. and the *Principia Philosophiae*,[3] 1644, give Descartes' philosophical system, and are regarded generally as the beginning of the modern epoch in philosophy. From the point of view of scientific knowledge, he presents a definite mathematical method. From the title of his book on Method, it will be seen that he claimed to have applied his Method to Dioptrics, Meteors and Geometry. He was therefore strong where Bacon was weak, for it was at once recognised that Descartes was a scholar in mathematics, pure and applied, whereas at most it can only be suggested that Bacon saw the value of mathematics,

---

[1] Peacham : *Compleat Gentleman*, p. 77.
[2] Containing Descartes' metaphysical ideas.
[3] i.e. Descartes' mechanical theory of the Universe.

without being himself accomplished in them. In the vague and indefinite state of science of the time, there was no need so acute as that of introducing some standard of exactitude, just the service which mathematics could yield. Hence Descartes, and following him, Newton, in applying mathematics to science, came on to ground thoroughly prepared for their labours. It may be justly claimed that Descartes showed the purely mechanical nature of physical processes, and paved the way for the introduction of standards of mathematical measurement. Since his time, all science has aimed at the application of mathematical methods[1] into every branch of study, attempting even to apply them to so-called mental sciences, on pain of denying the term " science " if these methods should prove inapplicable. So much for the success of Descartes' method in science. Besides this, however, he showed that in the application of the mind to the examination of Nature, there was a problem beyond the scientific, and gave the starting point to a new direction of philosophical development. Moreover, the negative attitude of Bacon, whereby all prejudices of the mind (the idola), of tradition, training, philosophical catch-words and all other hindrances to absolute open-mindedness were in Descartes consummated by the demand for absolute

---

[1] Thus it is claimed that the knowledge of the physics of the heart has brought physiology into at any rate almost an exact science, and the mathematical data of Harvey in presenting his theory of the circulation of the blood are regarded as an especially admirable part of his proof.

345

scepticism as a basis for starting *de novo* and building from a foundation which at least shall not be false. Without attempting to state the steps whereby Descartes satisfied himself as to his philosophical basis, it is sufficient here to say that he came to the conclusion that mathematics came closest to a true metaphysical system, by furnishing the most self-evident axioms. Further, he came to think that *extension* is the only quality in things that can be conceived clearly. This is just the aspect of the world that can be dealt with by mathematical treatment. Hence, geometry appealed to Descartes as the most certain of sciences, and the best measure of all other sciences. He was able to unify his philosophy and his science, and to proclaim a common standard of certainty in the one subject and exactness in the other. After twenty years of meditation with a patience, force and fruitfulness of genius seldom equalled in the history of the world,[1] he produced his *Method* in accordance with which he based the new subject of analytical geometry. Then, in the *Principia Philosophiae* he brought the aid of mathematics to the solution of questions in physical science, especially to the laws of motion and the theory of vortices,[2] thus

---

[1] Prof. Veitch : Descartes' Method, etc., p. xi.

[2] *See* W. W. R. Ball : *History of Mathematics*, p. 246. "In spite of its crudeness and defects Descartes' Theory of Vortices marks a new era in Astronomy, for it was an attempt to explain the phenomena of the whole universe by the same mechanical laws which experiment shews to be true on the earth."

establishing the starting point of mathematical physics.

The effect of the introduction of Descartes' views was, as Mr. Mullinger[1] says, to " carry almost by storm the leading intellects of Europe." The combination of a scientific method and a metaphysical system carried with it the two classes—the philosophers and the scientists. It is clear that Bacon had little to offer the metaphysicians in place of the Aristotle whom he attacked. But Descartes supplied a resting-place in his metaphysics for the Cambridge School of Platonists, whilst he met the needs of the scientific descendants of Bacon. Accordingly Cartesianism flourished in England from several sides of thought, affording a great stimulus to various types of thinkers without leading to the establishment of an exclusive school of thought. In physics the Cartesian text-books in the Universities, from the second half of the seventeenth century, held the field till about the beginning of the eighteenth century, when they were replaced by Newton's *Principia*.[2]

With regard to Descartes' influence on education in its broadest sense, it is not sufficient to point out the dissemination of his positive views. His

---

[1] *Cambridge in the Seventeenth Century*. Chapter iv deals with the Cartesian (i.e. Descartes') Philosophy, especially in Cambridge.

[2] The *Principia* was published in 1687. Dr. Samuel Clarke made Newton's views the basis of his Notes in his translation of Rohault's *Physics* (in 1697), the Cartesian text-book in use at Cambridge which the *Principia* replaced (Peacock's *Observations*, p. 69).

scientific contributions assisted, in an almost unique way, the development of mathematics and also of science and philosophy, and eclipsed Bacon, in the advancement of learning in these directions. But the result of a criterion of certainty and exactness such as was associated with the idea of Descartes and his followers was that the relatively uncertain became suspect and less attractive of attention or interest. Thus in the extremely interesting account of his mental history in the *Discourse on Method*, Descartes shows how, in himself, the search for a certain method in scientific matters led him to distrust the pseudo-sciences, " to be proof against the promises of the alchemist, against the predictions of the astrologer, the impostures of the magician, the artifices and *vain boasting of those who profess to know more than they actually do know.*"

This attitude of Descartes became the attitude of the scientist, as such, and necessarily there resulted a modification of the contemporary attraction towards occult " sciences," as each descending layer of the community came within the scientific influence. Thus the University student, who came into the recognition of the Cartesian point of view in his undergraduate days, if he took up the work of school-teaching indirectly would bring an educational influence in connexion with these subjects which would tend to dispel the popular credence in such mysteries and untestable studies.

The Lucasian Professorship of Mathematics was established in the University of Cambridge in 1663. The first Professor was Isaac Barrow and the second, Isaac Newton in 1669. Barrow left the Chair of Greek to take the new post in mathematics. This fittingly marks the era of a new development in the importance of mathematical studies. The old Greek knowledge was absorbed as far as mathematics was concerned, and Barrow was the herald of the Conqueror of the combined old and new sources of mathematical learning, Isaac Newton, who was the author of the *Principia* which will ever, to quote the eulogy of the mathematician Peacock, be regarded as the greatest single triumph of the human mind.[1]

The direct influence of these great changes in University teaching upon the schools, was not felt till after the seventeenth century. Yet, in connexion with the teaching of geometry, there were anticipatory suggestions of the inclusion of the subject in the school curriculum. The proposed inclusion of geometry in the school curriculum by Milton in 1644 and by Snell in 1649 has been mentioned. In 1647, Sir William Petty[2] says the elements of arithmetic and geometry should be studied by *all*, " being not only of great and frequent use in all human affairs, but also *sure guides and helps to reason*," and again because " they are the best grounded parts of speculative knowledge and of so vast use in all practical arts. We can but commend deeper inquiries into them." Petty contents himself with referring his reader to Master Pell's " excellent " ideas on the subject

---

[1] Peacock *Observations on the Statutes of the University of Cambridge*, p. 69.

[2] *Advice of W. P.* to Mr. Samuel Hartlib.

in his letter to Mr. Hartlib. In 1649 John Dury in the *Reformed School* includes geometry as a subject in the stage between 8–9 years of age up to 13–14 years. In Abraham Cowley's *Plan of a Philosophical College*, 1661, he inserts geometry in the scheme as a subject for the school attached to his College.

These instances occur after Descartes had written his books. In the earlier part of the seventeenth century, geometry cannot be said, in England,[1] to have come within the field of recommendation as a school subject. In so far as it was learned, it was learned outside of the grammar schools.

Two instances of its private study may be cited. In the account[2] of Evelyn's little son who died at a little above five years of age Evelyn says of the child : " Being much affected with the diagrams in Euclid, he did with great facility interpret to me many of the common postulata and definitions which he would readily repeat in Latin and apply them."

The second instance is the story told of Hobbes. " He was forty years old before he looked in geometry, which happened accidentally : being in a gentleman's library, Euclid's elements lay open at the 47th prop. Lib. i. He read the demonstration which referred him back to another, which he also read *et sic deinceps*, that at last he was

---

[1] Rabelais, however, in France, recommended the elements of geometry for the boy of six years of age, onwards.

[2] Epistle Dedicatory to the translation of *Golden Book of St. John Chrysostom concerning the Education of Children*, 1659.

demonstratively convinced of that truth. This made him in love with geometry.[1] This, perhaps, may be taken as indicative of the state of geometry-learning until after the first quarter of the seventeenth century. It had no established position, and its teaching and learning in the Universities were casual ; in the school, nearly non-existent.[2]

---

[1] Prof. Croom-Robertson *Hobbes*, p. 31.

[2] There is the instance of the suggestion of geometry as a school subject by a schoolmaster in William Kempe's *Education of Children* (*see* p. 308 *supra*), 1588.

CHAPTER X

THE TEACHING OF ASTRONOMY

To earlier ages, astronomy was one of the most practical of arts. Without clocks, watches, the compass, measurements of time everywhere and all questions of direction at sea were determined by personal acquaintance with astronomical data. The absence or inadequacy of artificial lights made the light of day more precious and the dark of night more terrifying ; and the regulation of getting up and going to rest by the natural day and night brought the realisation of the outer universe, its changes and signs, into greater prominence in life.

Hence astronomy was a wide-spread study, such as the well-educated man and even the uncultured man could not neglect on account of its practical guidance. The art was more important than the science, but the intelligent man was impelled to know both, as far as ascertainable.

The treatises on the quadrivium (i.e. arithmetic, music, geometry, and astronomy) on which the studies in the early Middle Ages were based (viz. by Boethius, Cassidorus, Isidore and Martianus Capella [1]) contained the scantiest elements of knowledge. The value of arithmetic and astronomy was chiefly for the practical purpose of finding the

[1] *See* p. 332 *supra*.

right dates for Easter. It was the introduction of the Arabian knowledge which gave the real impetus to astronomical knowledge and this was joined with astrology. Hallam says : " Nor was astrology without its beneficial effect upon the observation and registering of the planetary motions." The Astronomy of Ptolemy (Claudius Ptolemaeus) is contained in the " Almagest."[1] It may be borne in mind that the Greek text of Ptolemy's " Almagest " was first printed in 1538,[2] and that the knowledge of his Astronomy was mainly based on the Latin texts translated from the Arabic. The " Almagest " contains within it trigonometry plane and spherical, together with a table of chords, and the table itself to half degrees for the whole of the semicircle, i.e. of natural series, as to which de Morgan says : " This morsel of geometry is one of the most beautiful in the Greek writers." Ptolemy deals with the spherical form of the earth and explains the motion of the planets and sun round the earth and by his excentrics[3] and epicycles.[4] These are necessarily introduced to

---

[1] The name of Ptolemy's Astronomy in Greek was Μεγάλη Σύνταξις τῆς Ἀστρονομίας. The Arabs called it μεγίστη—the greatest—for which the Arabic was Almagest, and this was the term by which Ptolemy's Astronomy became generally known.

[2] This was also the date of the first printed appearance in Greek of Euclid's Elements.

[3] These are the " revolutions in a circle which has the spectator out of its centre."

[4] Epicycles are circles the centres of which revolve on other circles.

explain the apparent direct, stationary and retrograde motions of the planets due to the different rates of motion of planets at various times, relatively to the annual motion of the sun in its orbit round the earth. Ptolemy supposed that the planets did not keep the exact circumference of their orbits but moved about an ideal centre which itself moved in the orbit. The orbit of a planet was not therefore a circle but a series of circles which combined into a series of uninterrupted waves, called epicycles.

Ptolemy explained the obliquity of the ecliptic and propounded a theory of eclipses. In addition he made a catalogue of fixed stars. Ptolemy, in short, may be said to be to astronomy what Pliny was to natural history. He was the man who summed up the whole of the ascertained knowledge of antiquity as to mathematical astronomy. With regard to the mathematical astronomy of Ptolemy, de Morgan has said[1] that the theory of epicycles was " probably at least as good a theory as their instruments and capabilities of observation required or deserved." It was a convenient method of expressing accepted astronomical opinion, but did not represent sufficiently the actual phenomena. But

---

[1] Again, de Morgan says : " With regard to Ptolemy as an astronomer, it must be said that the history of the science, for a long train of centuries, presents nothing but comments on Ptolemy's writings ; to treat the history of the latter would be so far to write that of astronomy itself." Yet de Morgan affirms that Ptolemy was even better known by his *Tetrabiblon* book of Astrology than by his *Almagest*. *See* article on Ptolemy by Augustus de Morgan in Smith's *Dictionary of Greek and Roman Biography*.

from the thirteenth to the seventeenth century it may be safely said that Ptolemy was more widely known for his astrological work :

Tetrabiblon or Quadripartitum de Apotelesmatibus et Judiciis Astrarum. Edited by John Camerarius. *Greek and Latin.* · Nuremberg, 1535 :⁋ edited with a preface by Melanchthon. Basle, 1553.

The pre-Copernican system, expounded by Ptolemy, consisted of a series of heavens in which were the orbits of the planets, etc. In addition to the orbits of the Moon, Mercury, Venus, Sun, Mars, Jupiter, Saturn, there was the crystalline heaven of the " Firmament," in which were the Fixed Stars, and the Primum mobile, from which was derived the motion which stirred the whole of the globes into motion. Outside of the Primum mobile was the vast immovable heaven, pure, immense, clear, the habitation of God and his angels. In other words the Universe, it has been said, was conceived of in the form of an onion with its rinds all fitting one over the other, and the earth in the centre.

The influence of the heavenly bodies thus encircled the earth. They brought the wind, rain, storm. The rays of the sun brought modifications of heat and cold, which mingled with moisture and dryness. The emanations of the heavenly bodies penetrated to the earth, and man was therefore under their direct physical influence. These affected man's body ; thence they influenced his mind. Thus, the astrological was founded on the astronomical system.

In the Ancient Statutes [1] of the University of Cambridge dated 1303 a new statute was introduced concerning the mathematical sciences. It was thought " not improper to give support to the mathematical sciences, now somewhat in danger." Students were required to attend in the first year, arithmetic and music ; in the second year, geometry and perspective ; in the third year, astronomy. This meant that every student was to attend a course mainly of astrological astronomy of six weeks' lectures.

Speaking of the whole period up to 1550, the study of Greek authors substantially included the whole of what was known in mathematics, and, says de Morgan, " except in astronomy and very much for the sake of astrology, there are but few original writings."

About the middle of the thirteenth century John de Holywood, [2] known as Johannes de Sacro-bosco (Holywood), wrote his *Sphaera Mundi* [3] (made known 1256). This was studied not only in England but throughout Europe. It was the most popular book in astronomy until 1496, when the writings of Ptolemy in Greek were brought to light again. In 1496, John Müller of Königsberg (Regiomontanus) had printed at Venice a Latin epitome of the Μεγάλη Σύνταξις of Ptolemy. [4] The mediaeval Arabic

---

[1] James Heywood : *Early Cambridge Statutes*, p. 87.

[2] De Morgan calls him John of Halifax.—*British Almanac*, 1837, p. 24.

[3] Sacro-bosco also wrote *de computo ecclesiastico* and *De astrolabio* and an introduction to Arithmetic.

[4] Ptolemy died in 168 A.D.

version of Ptolemy was, so Regiomontanus declares, hardly such as the Greek writer would have recognised as his own. It is worth noting that Regiomontanus published immediately afterwards a book on astrology. De Morgan places Aristotle, Euclid, and Ptolemy as the greatest names in science that Greece communicated to modern Europe. The essence of Ptolemy's contribution is the application of geometrical treatment to astronomy.

It is not, however, to be supposed that Ptolemy's mathematical treatment of astronomy was generally understood, any more than the highest development of mathematical physics to-day is generally followed by the ordinary " well-educated " man. In the sixteenth and seventeenth century the average man who was not a specialist in mathematics, probably held the view founded on a mixture of Platonism, together with Biblical allegory, a view of which the origin may be traced to Philo. There had risen up, moreover, "a vast reservoir of mystical doctrines " which the renewed Platonic studies of the Renascence intensified. Yet the Renascence, with its determination of research into the " causes of the corruption " of the sciences, as Vives terms the accretions of the Middle Ages, eventually produced the attitude towards truth in every direction which made modern science possible, and one of the earliest directions, in which physical science developed in the later stages of the Renascence was in astronomy. Copernicus, the initiator of the theory of the solar system on which modern astronomy is based, was a student at one time in Bologna in the Faculty of Law, and Galileo afterwards was a student in the same University in the Faculty of Medicine. Bologna, thus closely connected with the rise of modern astronomy, was, in the Middle Ages, specially interested in Astrology. There was a faculty in the subject, and a Professor, one of whose duties was to supply astrological " judgments " gratis to students.[1] One professor in the fourteenth century was Cecco d'Ascoli, whom Mr. Rashdall describes as the Prince of Mediaeval Astrologers. Mr. Rashdall cites an instance at Oxford in the sixteenth century of a scholar admitted to " practise in Astrology," and quotes a general grace for Regents, early in the sixteenth century, granting permission to any one of them, who has studied astronomy, to practise in the same.[2]

The close connexion of physic with astrology explains the number of doctors who were devoted to the study of astronomy on either the mathematical or the mystical side.

The teaching of Astronomy in the first half of the seventeenth century in the University of Cambridge was at a low ebb, as can be seen from the case of Jeremiah Horrox, who was a young man of remarkable ability in mathematical astronomy, but who died at the age of twenty-three.   In 1635, he wrote of Cambridge : " There was no one who could instruct me in the art, who could even help my endeavours by joining me in the study."

---

[1] Rashdall, *History of the Universities of Europe*, i, p. 244.
[2] *Ibid.*, i, p. 459.

SAVILIAN PROFESSORSHIP OF ASTRONOMY

Astronomical study was more progressive at Oxford, for in 1619 Sir Henry Savile had founded the Professorship in Astronomy. Savile's statute regarding the professor will show the state of astronomy in the University at the time.

The Professor of Astronomy is to explain " the whole mathematical economy of Ptolemy (usually called the Almagest), applying in their proper place the discoveries of Copernicus, Geber,[1] and other modern writers ; and to leave his notes reduced to writing with the University. He may lay before his auditors by way of introduction to the arcana of the science, the Sphere of Proclus, or Ptolemy's hypothesis of the planets, and teach, either publicly or privately, the arithmetic of sexagesimal fractions. It will also be his business to explain the whole science of optics, gnomonics, geography, and the rules of navigation in so far as they are dependent on mathematics. He is, however, debarred from professing the doctrine of nativities and all judicial astrology without exception." In optics, gnomonics (i.e. the art of dialling), geography, etc., he is free to choose his books, on which to lecture, similarly to the Professor of Geometry.

Still earlier, in 1575, Sir Thomas Gresham, the founder of the Royal Exchange, had established

---

[1] Geber, who died at Cordova towards end of the eleventh century, was born at Seville. His book on Astronomy was translated into Latin by Gerard of Cremona, and published at Nuremberg in 1533.—W. W. R. Ball : *History of Mathematics*, p. 158.

lectures in divinity, astronomy, music and geometry in his mansion in Bishopsgate Street, and also founded lectureships in law, physic, and rhetoric. Each of the lecturers was to receive £50 a year. It was contemplated that a lecture should be given daily throughout the year by one of the seven lecturers. This endowment, however, was contingent on the life of Gresham's wife. She died in 1596 and professorships were at once instituted in the above subjects. In Gresham College the best-known professors of astronomy were Edward Brerewood (1596–1613), though his name is rather associated with philology than astronomy ; Edmund Gunter (1619–1626), a well-known mathematician, who invented the sector and wrote on mathematical instruments ; Henry Gellibrand (1626–1636), who applied trigonometry to the systems of Ptolemy, Copernicus, Tycho and others. Laurence Rooke (1652–1657) made observations on a comet and the eclipse of the moon, and Christopher Wren [1] (1657–1660), the great architect. It

---

[1] Sir Christopher Wren is said to have " loved the classics, but mathematics and astronomy were his favourite pursuits." At one time he was a pupil of William Oughtred, who assuredly must have been one of the greatest stimulators of mathematical study and teaching in the seventeenth century. For fifty years Oughtred was rector of Albury, in Surrey, where he welcomed all who wished to study mathematics, foreigners as well as Englishmen. Amongst those who are stated to have been his pupils besides Wren are : John Wallis, the Savilian Professor of Geometry at Oxford (1649–1703) ; Seth Ward, Savilian Professor of Astronomy (1649–1661), and his friend, Sir Charles Scarborough, M.D. The last named two are said to have

may be noted that eight of the professors were Oxford men and three Cambridge, the proportion not unreasonably to be ascribed to the influence of the Savilian Chair in Oxford. These professors were pre-eminently mathematical, and the occupants of the chair after the foundation of the Royal Society were ordinarily in close communication with it, so that, on the whole, Gresham College sustained its position as a leading institution in the progress of the popularisation of the subject, though it can hardly be claimed that the professors greatly advanced the scientific side of astronomy.

Side by side with the mathematical treatment of the subject proceeded the study of physical astronomy. Undoubtedly, in the sixteenth century, the astrological aspect loomed largest in the popular view. It must also be stated that astrology claimed the attention of some of the most distinguished men of the times, men who for want of a better term must be called the " scientists " of their age. To take an instance of the trained astrologer, Girolamo Cardano or Jerome Cardan (1501-1576) was by profession a physician. Soon after he was nine

---

returned to Cambridge (where they both then lived) and to have introduced Oughtred's *Clavis Mathematica* there. Laurence Rooke, mentioned above as a Professor of Astronomy in Gresham College, was apparently a pupil of Oughtred. Aubrey testifies to Rooke lecturing " admirably well on Chap. vi of the *Clavis Mathematica*." Oughtred " taught all free," and refused to take from Seth Ward " a farthing for his diet " when he stayed half a year at Albury to study mathematics.—Aubrey's *Brief Lives*, ed. Clark (1898), vol. ii, p. 108.

years of age, his father, a Milanese lawyer, instructed him in astrology. Eventually Cardan became the greatest physician of his age, and at the same time the greatest astrologer. He was invited to England from Scotland, where he was treating professionally the Archbishop of St. Andrews, and was requested to calculate King Edward VI's nativity, as there was considerable desire to know how long he was likely to live. Cardan's astrology served him to prognosticate a fairly long life with illnesses at twenty-three, thirty-four, fifty-five years of age. The King died almost immediately after Cardan had left England. Cardan was not shaken in his astrology by his failure, but wrote a dissertation, " What I thought afterwards upon the subject." He said that his calculation had not been complete. He had pre-dicted a whole life from a single horoscope. This ought not to be done in the science of astrology as laid down by Ptolemy. In any case, Cardan[1] was in a dangerous dilemma. For prophesying evil astrologers had gone to execution ; in prophesying long life or any other desideratum they were liable to have their predictions falsified by events and thus to be discredited. Such failures were regarded by many not as due to astrology in itself, but to careless or fraudulent practice.[2] The genuineness of the astrological art itself was generally regarded as beyond dispute.

---

[1] The story is told at length in Henry Morley's interesting *Jerome Cardan*, vol. ii, p. 138 *et seqq.*

[2] It was legitimate to be an astrologer but not to be a wizard or sorcerer.

THE CASTING OF HOROSCOPES

To take an instance of the amateur astrologer, Sir Thomas Smith (1513–1577) was Doctor of Civil Law in the University of Padua ; Public Orator, Regius Professor of Civil Law and afterwards Vice-Chancellor of Cambridge University. As a statesman he was Secretary of State to Queen Elizabeth and the writer of *De Republica Anglorum*. His friend, Sir John Cheke, 1514–1557, was Professor of Greek and Provost of King's College, Cambridge, and later, in exile, taught Greek in Strassburg. Both Smith and Cheke were interested in a reform of phonetics, both for the Greek and for the English language, and may be described as two of the most eminent men of the time, who united in themselves the humanistic learning with activity in affairs. Yet Sir Thomas Smith was an expert in astrology, and Sir John Cheke a believer in it. Smith in all seriousness cast the nativity[1] of Cheke. Astrology, therefore, was not regarded as a delusion of the ignorant. It was a serious art, the science and art of which were earnestly pursued by the leading intellects of the time, in their search for truth.

---

[1] Anthony à Wood describes Robert Burton (1577–1640), the author of the *Anatomy of Melancholy*, as " an exact mathematician, a curious calculator of nativities, a general read scholar, a thorough-paced philologist, and one that understood the surveying of lands well." (*Athen. Oxon.*) Aubrey gives indications as to the horoscopes of many well-known men, e.g. Erasmus, John Dryden, John Dee, Sir Kenelm Digby, and eight " coelestial schemes " for the Danvers-Williams family. Aubrey actually reproduces the drawings for the full casting of the horoscopes for Sir Wm. Petty and Thomas Hobbes. *See Aubrey's Brief Lives* (ed. Clark), vol. ii, plates v and iii at end.

Amongst educational writers, Erasmus was an advocate of the study of astrology, though to his mind the appeal was mainly on account of its usefulness in explaining allusions in classical authors. Vives (1523) says : " Joined to Astronomy is divination which is called Astrology completely sprung from love of show and frauds." " But," he adds, " not that I do not believe that the stars have great influence over our bodies." [1] Or to take a later writer, the learned and pious physician Dr. Thomas Browne, who even in 1650 writes : " We deny not the influence of the stars but *often suspect the due application thereof.*" He does not reject " a sober and regulated Astrology." [2] There is more truth in it than there often is in the astrologers who practise the art. There is in wise men " a power beyond the stars, and Ptolemy encourages us, that by fore-knowledge, we may evade their actions."

Tycho Brahe and even the great Kepler [3] cast nativities, and the astronomer who did not practise his art in the sixteenth century would have been as unintelligible as the trained physician who prescribed for no one. In the Great Civil War both sides tried to get presages of the issue by appeals to astrology. With these facts before us, it is not

---

[1] Vives' objection to the astrologer is that he does not keep his attention fixed on the vast celestial bodies, nor even pretend to do so, but upon their powers (*vires*) and efficient causation (*efficientiam*).

[2] *Vulgar Errors,* 2nd ed., p. 195.

[3] H. Morley's *Cardan,* i, 291.

surprising that the writer of the first text-book on astronomy in English was a believer in astrology.

This was Robert Recorde (1510 ?–1558), whom Mr. Ball describes as " certainly the most eminent English mathematician of his age." Recorde puts the case for the study of astronomy almost entirely on practical grounds, and Copernican [1] as he was, he was, still more, an astrologist. In the preface to Recorde's *Castle of Knowledge*, 1556, he says : " Though many saw the star in the East as well as (the Wise Men), yet few or none knew the signification but they : yet did God at the beginning ordain the stars to be as signs or tokens of Time's alteration, and namely of such strange effects as seldom come in use, and therefore are known but to few men. These works, the more strange they be, the more ought men to esteem the fruit of them. . . . Before the Flood of Noah, though God, by special revelation uttered his mind to his servant Noah, yet did he also by wonderful signs and strange conjunctions express the same to the whole world, for all the planets were in conjunction in watery signs . . . sith all nations might see the heavens, and the tokens in it, although but few in every nation could skill of them. . . . There was never any great change in the world, neither translations of empires, neither scarce any great change in the world, neither scarce any fall of famous princes,

---

[1] *See* Mr. Ball (*Cambridge Mathematics*, p. 18) and de Morgan, *Companion to Almanac*, 1837, quotes a definite passage from Recorde affirming the new teaching of Copernicus. *See* p. 36.

no death and penury, no death and mortality, but God by the signs of heaven did admonish men thereof, to repent and beware betime, if they had any grace. The examples are infinite, and all histories so full of them, that I think it needless to make any rehearsal of them now, especially seeing they pertain to the judicial part of Astronomy."

As Manilius said : *Nunquam futilibus excanduit ignibus aether.* It is desirable to be able to read and interpret the signs of the times so as to " avoid many inconveniences" on the one hand, and on the other to " achieve many unlikely attempts." The wise man will be a governor and ruler of the stars. To quote Ptolemy : *Sapiens dominabitur astris.* [1]

The judicial part of astronomy, then, is the application of astronomical data and knowledge to the unravelling of the inner meaning of signs in the heavens. Physical astronomy describes the heavens, the constellations, the planets, and so on, and gives a connected view of the movements of the spheres, and the harmony of the whole cosmic system. All physical facts and relations can be studied in Ptolemy, but the earth as the centre receives the signs and portents amongst the movements of the heavenly bodies, as phenomena, which can be interpreted, if men but attain the astrological discipline, for the guidance of human life. There is no higher knowledge for mortals ; there is no keener mental discipline for the man of science.

---

[1] Recorde's translation :

" The wise by prudence and good skill
May rule the stars to serve his will."

The aims of even the sixteenth and seventeenth centuries in education cannot be completely understood without grasping the idea of the astrological art as the highest practical development of astronomical science.

But apart from judicial astronomy, Recorde claims that astronomy is "the most necessary study that can be." He points out the usefulness for husbandry and for navigation. "In physic the use of it is so large in judging duly of complexions, in prescribing right order of diet and conversation, in governance of health, for just ministrations of medicines in times of sickness, and in right judgment of the critical days, that without it, physic is to be *accompted utterly imperfect.*" Recorde, it must be repeated, was not only the greatest mathematician of his age in England, but also a practising physician. After dwelling on the necessity of astronomy for sowing of grain, growing and planting, at the right times and seasons, Recorde asks : "Who can shew himself so mad as to deny the necessary use of Astronomy in due keeping the times of the years. Ecclesiastical history testifies that great controversy hath been in the Church, for the right observation of Easter, which controversy could never be decided, but by the knowledge of astronomy." He then shows its necessity in grammar, logic, and rhetoric, and for the "vulgar arts," e.g. for mariners and agricultural industries. For law, physic and divinity Recorde considers he has shown it is "exceeding necessary." "But above all other things, the testimony of

Christ in the Scripture doth most approve it, when he doth declare that signs of his coming and other strange effects, shall be seen in the Sun, Moon and Stars."

I have dwelt at length on the practical aspect of astronomy because it is perhaps the best example in history of the claim to inclusion in the educational curriculum of a subject *on account of its usefulness.* Given the state of knowledge of the times, the test of utilitarianism was never applied with greater cogency than to the inclusion of astrological astronomy. The consequences in the history of education were very marked. For instance, in the University of Bologna " the faculty of Astrology absorbed into its domain the whole of mathematics, which were made to minister to its practical aims." When the old Greek geometry came to the modern world, in the time of the Renascence, Euclid, Ptolemy, and the other geometers were seized upon with avidity, chiefly because of the light they threw upon the doctrine of terrestrial and celestial spheres, and their relations and measurements. So, too, the theories of dynamics and statics, dealing with bodies in motion and at rest, found their background of fascination in the preparation which had gone on for centuries in the studies called astronomical and astrological. It was largely because of the bearing of geometry (plane and spherical) on astronomy that the subject became distinguished as the mathematical subject *par excellence.* The path was then paved for its development.

One of the chief popular writers on natural knowledge of the first half of the seventeenth century was John Swan. Swan bases astrology on Moses' [1] words, " Let them (i.e. the stars) be for signs." He quotes Melanchthon as establishing this interpretation as scriptural. But the stars are not only signs of future events ; they are also causes. Job (xxxviii, 31) says : " Canst thou bind the sweet influences of Pleiades ? or loose the bands of Orion ? " It is expressly testified (Judges v, 20) in the Song of Deborah : " The stars from heaven, the stars in their courses fought against Sisera." The causation of seasons by the sun, the terrible accidents that succeed eclipses, the tides of the sea varying with the moon ; thunder and lightning, at the meeting of Mars with Jupiter, Sol or Mercury ; the variation of marrow, blood and humours in the body with the changes of the moon ; the rotting of wood if not cut for timber after the full moon ; the bearing of fruit by the pomegranate no longer than just as many years as the moon was days old at the first setting of the plant ; the critical days of the sick person, according to the ruling of the moon ; the early death of children born in the new moon, as in the time of an eclipse, Saturn or Mars in a bad aspect to the moon—all these facts are, Swan [2] thinks, proved by experience.

---

[1] Genesis i. Cf. Jeremiah, Chap. x, 2.

[2] *Speculum Mundi*, 1635, 2nd ed. 1643. Printed by Roger Daniel, Printer to the University of Cambridge. *See* pp. 327–346. For Swan's views on Nature Study *see* p. 193 *supra*.

He therefore concludes that as herbs have their natural qualities and operations, so the stars likewise work on this inferior world by their qualities and natural virtues. The influence of the stars, however, does not work on man's will but on the temperament and material organs of the body. Hence there is no necessity in their influence but only an inclination. So, too, there is no reason for a man to " curse his stars." If we walk by reason, the stars cannot compel ; if we respond simply to sense, we succumb. *Agunt, non cogunt.* [1] Had man not fallen, the stars could not have influenced him. Melanchthon gives this consideration as a clear proof of the grievousness of sin, by which our temperatures are made brutish. Evil proceeds from man, not from the stars, for man's fall has lost him his purity and strength of will. The operation of the stars is not in their own power, but according to the capacity and aptness of the patient, like " as fire hurteth sore eyes but warmeth cold hands."

Swan concludes from Scripture that it is lawful to search out the nature and influence of stars, though it needs Argus's eyes to do it rightly and safely, but the signs of heaven must not be abused. Magical spells and incantations must not be employed. Nor does Swan approve of the use of

---

[1] Robert Burton, *Anatomy of Melancholy*, puts it : " They do incline but not compel . . . and so gently incline that a wise man may resist them ; *sapiens dominabitur astris* : they rule us but God rules them."—(Part i, Sect. ii, Mem. i, subs. iv.)

astrology for finding things which have been lost.
Moreover, it must be remembered " the stars were
never made to justify the dangerous practices of
wicked imposters or causeless curiosities of
superstitious demanders."

The view of the cultured nobleman of the first
half of the seventeenth century may be gathered
from Lord Herbert of Cherbury, who thus expresses
his opinion on astrology : " It will be necessary
at the same time (as the study of geography is
undertaken) to learn the use of the celestial globe,
the studies of both globes being complicated
and joined together. I do not conceive yet the
knowledge of judicial astrology so necessary, but
only for general predictions : particular events
being neither intended nor collected from the stars."[1]
Even still more emphatically Lord Herbert writes: [2]
" When Astrology is rightly understood and applied,
it be not only a lawful but a most necessary art for
a wise man."

The influence of Lord Bacon on education was
great and his view must therefore be included.
He holds that astrology should be purified, not
rejected. The doctrines of *nativities, elections,
inquiries* are refuted by physical reasons. Let the
greater revolutions be retained but the smaller
revolutions of " horoscopes and houses " be dis-
missed. " The wiser astrologists consider there is
no fatal necessity in the stars, but think they

---

[1] *Autobiography* (Lee's edition, p. 27).
[2] *Dialogue between Tutor and Pupil.*

rather incline than compel. What is wanted is a sane astrology."[1] Bacon, however, is of opinion that the study of the stars enables us to predict natural events such as floods, frosts, droughts, earthquakes, etc., and also wars, seditions, schisms, transmigrations of peoples, and " in short all commotions or great revolutions of things natural as well as civil."

Writers on education of the period are divided in opinion as to the place of astrology. It is noticeable that the theological bias led one set of writers to consider that all study of natural phenomena, " the observation of the creatures," is a necessary study to rightly glorify the Creator, whilst another division of theological educationists began to see " danger " in inquiring into the " secrets of God." The latter class of writers became more and more prominent with the growing intensity of Puritanism. However, Laurence Humfrey, in his treatise on the education of Nobles in 1560, shows the attitude of the earliest Puritans :

Astrology, I see so ravened, embraced, and devoured by many, as they need no spur to it but rather a bridle from it, no trumpeter to encourage them, but a chider to restrain their vehement race . . . I condemn not universally the art, but thereto get they me nor counsellor nor favourer ; it hath plenty enough of praisers.

We come now more definitely to educational practice—the school text-books which have an astronomical teaching. Within the sixteenth and

---

[1] *De Augmentis Scientiarum*, bk. iii, chap. 4.

seventeenth centuries they are, without exception, as far as I have found, Ptolemaic in theory. The book cited, it may be said, are not school text-books entirely devoted to astronomy. This criticism would apply equally to arithmetic and geometry. The text-books in mathematics were not ordinarily designed to be put into the hands of the mere school-boy, except perhaps late in the first half of the seventeenth century in the subject of arithmetic. But the books quoted in the following account, except in the case of Comenius, are actual school-books of the period incidentally showing the preva-lent astronomical views brought before the boy in his studies. Two short passages may serve as samples of the astrological views of Palingenius [1] in the *Zodiacus Vitae*. Every good thing, he says, proceeds to the earth from the heavens. " Therefore no one can be wise and happy who is born with the heavens unfavourable and the stars adverse. [2] Or again, " There is a force in every star. The stars rule the earth, and change all things. The stars produce everything on earth, and govern everything." [3]

But it is not merely passages such as these which show the astrological teaching of Palingenius. Astrology breathes throughout the book, from the

[1] *See* p. 197 *supra*.

[2] *Zodiacus Vitae*. Capricornus, 74–76. "Esse igitur, sapiens et felix nemo potest qui nascitur adverso coelo, stellisque sinistris."

[3] *Ibid*. Aquarius, 428–430. "Est vis omnis in astris. Astra regunt orbem terrarum, atque omnia mutant : Astra creant cuncta in terris et cuncta gubernant."

title *Zodiacus Vitae* to the last chapter. No boy could read the book [1] without having the view clearly brought before him of the " signs " which attach to stars, and portents of physical phenomena such as eclipses of the sun or moon, the significance of comets and meteors and so on, and as we have seen, the idea of nativities. Palingenius esteems the career of a physician very highly. [2] For the physician it is especially necessary to be an astrologer. Medicine needs occult knowledge; it discloses the secrets of flowers, herbs, gems. It closely observes the force (*vires*) of whatsoever earth hides in its entrails and regards astrologically the parts of the human body.

Even a *Dictionary in English and Latin for Children and Young Beginners* [3] contains in the section : " the four Elements," a nomenclature founded on astrology, e.g. " Summer, *Aestas*. That humour of the body which is called choler, cholera. That age of man that is called Childhood, Pueritia. That region of the sky which is called East, Oriens, and the Eastern Wind, Eurus. Whereunto be

---

[1] For definite Statutes of schools in which Palingenius was to be read *see* p. 197 *supra*.

[2] In the epigrammatic manner, Palingenius specially enjoys, he says : "Egregius medicus mendicus non erit unquam." The physician needs to know the " critical days," i.e. the times of influence of the stars on his patient, so that his remedies may be applied at the right junctures of the stars. For references to " critical days " *see* p. 299, p. 367, and p. 369 *supra*.

[3] By John Withals. It was first printed c. 1556, afterwards re-edited by Dr. Evans, by Abraham Fleming, and in 1634 by William Clark.

added three of the twelve signs, which be Cancer, Leo, Virgo, that do govern in June, July, August ; these be of that element, fire."

Next follows in the enumeration, Spring, with the humour, blood ; the age of youth ; region, South ; the three signs, Aries, Taurus, Gemini, which govern in March, April, May. Element : air.

Then Winter, with humour, phlegm, the time of old age ; region, West ; the three signs Capricornus, Aquarius, Pisces, which govern in December, January, February. Element : water.

Finally, Autumn with humour, melancholy ; age of man, decrepit or crooked ; region, North ; the signs, Libra, Scorpio, Sagittarius, which govern in September, October, November. Element : earth.

Thus astrological conceptions were taught even through the teaching of the Vocabularies. Withal's *Dictionary*, as already mentioned, was the children's Latin Dictionary of widest circulation in England.

What Ptolemy was in the Mediaeval and Renascence times to the mathematical side of astronomy, Manilius was to the physical side, when the Revival of Learning made him known. The astrological work, called the *Astronomicon of Manilius*, a book of far higher estimation in the sixteenth century than now, was recommended for school use by Vives in 1523 amongst works of poetry ; elsewhere for its astronomy, Vives prescribes Manilius for the pupil's private reading. He adds, however, that Manilius had taken many matters from Chaldaean superstition, and on that account his book requires direction as to what should be omitted. In another place, Vives

mentions Manilius along with Catullus, Tibullus and
Propertius. Manilius' book is in the opinion of Vives
serious, but διδασκαλικὸν. In style Vives considers
Manilius sometimes rises to considerable eloquence
and ardour.

Abraham Cowley,[1] in 1661, proposed Manilius,
Cicero *de Divinatione*, and Virgil's *Georgics* (all of
which have astrological aspects) on account of the
solid and learned matter in them. A brief description
of Manilius's *Astronomicon* will show the irretrievably
astrological bearing of the work throughout.

Manilius, in verse, describes opinions as to the
origin of the world. The universe has a circular
motion round the earth. The universe is round, and
therefore infinite. God governs and sustains the
universe, of which the earth is the centre. Manilius
describes the zodiac and states the various influences
of the chief constellations. He traces the history of the
study of the stars by kings and priests, who cultivated this great science by divine gift. He treats of the
movable and immovable circles. As to the milky
way, so thick it is, there seems some ground for
believing it consists of white-robed souls of the just.
All heavenly bodies, natural or supernatural, are
never without effect on mankind. Meteors and
comets presage events. He inquires to what
sign each part of man's body is appropriate, and
shows the various aspects of the planets in the
signs. He describes the twelve celestial " houses "
and assigns to each its proper planet. Earth and

[1] *Plan of Philosophical College* (treating of the school
in connexion with the proposed college).

heaven are not dissociated nor is the human altogether distinct from the divine. Guardian influences are described for all periods of life. He gives
the rules for finding the horoscope. He discusses
the astrological causes of the differences between
children of the same parents, and describes the
advantages of being born under one heavenly body
rather than another. He introduces legends such as
those of Deucalion and Phaëthon, Andromeda and
Perseus. He regards the whole world as animate,
and every part as having its special influence.[1]

Professor Jebb, in his account of Bentley,[2] says
that Scaliger was of opinion that Manilius was
" ' equal in sweetness and superior in majesty to
Ovid,' a verdict which Bentley cites with approval."
To have had two such editors as Scaliger and
Bentley is a distinct tribute to so little known a
classic as Manilius. Mr. Mark Pattison's *Essay on
Joseph Scaliger* shows that the aim of Scaliger was
in this case scientific rather than philological[3] and

---

[1] Thomas Creech, in his translation of Manilius (1697)
says : " It is confessed that Manilius shews no great exactness in the Astronomical part of this book, but *the Astrology
is perfect, and, may for the most part be applied to the most
correct Astronomy.*" This shows that the acceptance of
the theory of Copernicus in Astronomy by no means carried
with it the rejection of Astrology. Copernicus's book was
published in 1543, one hundred and fifty-four years before
Creech's translation.

[2] " Men of Letter Series," p. 143.

[3] Bentley's, of course, was on the other hand mainly
philological and textual. Mr. Pattison's *Essay on Joseph
Scaliger* (*Essays*, Series I, No. 5) is a fascinating study in
the history of scholarship, showing the method of research
pursued by Scaliger in establishing ancient chronology.

that he made Manilius a peg on which to hang a representation of the astronomical system of the first century A.D. Scaliger's edition of Manilius was published in 1579.

Great names, therefore, cluster around the Manilian astronomy, or rather, astrology. Another name may be mentioned. When we think of John Milton it is ordinarily as the writer of *Paradise Lost*. That great poem was published in 1667, but it must be remembered that from 1639–46 Milton was the private schoolmaster of that "wonder-working Academy " (as Samuel Johnson called it) in Aldersgate Street. In that school, as Edward Phillips (himself a pupil) tells us, Manilius was one of the Latin authors read by the boys between ten and fifteen or sixteen years of age. Now this was a hundred years after Copernicus's book (1540). Mr. Mark Pattison has summarised Milton's view (as gathered from *Paradise Lost*) of the contending Ptolemaic and Copernican theories in Astronomy by the judgment : " The ordinary habitual mode of speaking of celestial phenomena is Ptolemaic (*see Paradise Lost*, vii, 339 ; iii, 481). The conscious, or doctrinal exposition of the same phenomena is Copernican (*see Paradise Lost*, viii, 122)." Still, it must be observed that though Milton states, in the latter passage, the Copernican theory clearly, he by no means identifies himself with it. The exposition is made by Raphael to Adam but it is accompanied by the remark that :

> " Whether Heaven move or Earth,
> Imports not, if thou reckon right."

Yet Milton in 1638 had visited Galileo, and in the *Areopagitica*, he says, with indignation, " the famous Galileo grown old had become " a prisoner to the Inquisition for thinking in astronomy otherwise than the Franciscan and Dominican licensers thought."

It is therefore particularly interesting to find that after his visit to Galileo, Milton taught astrological lore from Manilius. It may be urged that he included Manilius in his curriculum for the same reason which afterwards induced Bentley to undertake a recension of the text of Manilius, viz. the philological aspect. But we recall Milton's own dictum in the *Tractate* that " tongues should be read for the solid things in them as well as for the words." However, Milton's teaching of astronomy was not limited to Manilius. Phillips informs us that Milton further taught his pupils Geminus's astronomy and Joannes de Sacro-Bosco: *De Sphaera*. Dr. Masson states that Geminus was a Greek mathematician of the first century A.D. who wrote on the *Sphere*, and de Sacro-Bosco was, as already stated, the great English mediaeval exponent of Ptolemaic astronomy. Thus, as a schoolmaster, there is no doubt that Milton taught the Ptolemaic theory to his boys, and this was after he had given himself the opportunity of becoming a Copernican by direct contact with Galileo.

It seems justifiable to conclude that if Milton taught in his school the Ptolemaic system of astronomy, it is not improbable in the other schools in which astronomy was in any way treated, that it would be from the same point of view.

MODERN SUBJECTS IN ENGLISH SCHOOLS

Besides the Latin and Greek books directly bearing on astronomical subjects, the treatises on antiquities, mythologies, phrase-books, rhetorical books, etc., bore the impress of the old astronomy, when they dealt with the subject. Books of reference such as Farnaby's *Index Rhetoricus* (ed. 1659) for instance, under *Astronomia* referred the pupil to Manilius, Ovid, Lucan, Buchanan, Barlaeus, giving a cross-reference *vide Causas cognoscere rerum*. Farnaby also under *Astrologi* refers the boy to passages of Lucan, Juvenal, Thomas More's Epigrams. And for *Astrologiae defensio* bids him consult Micyllus Conrad. Lycosthenes includes in his *Apophthegmata*, written in 1555 (in first form but often added to afterwards), a small collection of quotations on *Astronomia vel Astrologia*. Natalis Comes,[1] an author of constant use in the first half of the seventeenth century, in the English as well as European grammar schools in his *Mythologiae, sive Explicationis Fabularum Libri decem* claims to deal with "almost all the teachings of Physical and Moral Philosophy." This incidental teaching of subjects, in books of ordinary use for the explanation of allusions in the translations of authors, and in the pursuits of epithets and elegant expressions, is certainly to be taken into account in considering the nature of the teaching in schools of a subject like astronomy. I therefore add here a passage translated from Natalis Comes. Natalis

---

[1] The instances of books of Farnaby, Lycosthenes, and Natalis Comes are chosen because they were authors of very wide circulation in schools.

Comes says that " the philosophers of old believed that according to the first temperament of the air which was drunk in when children were born, they also drew in morals, fortune, actions and the vigour of life, all which things in their happening or issue, they called Fata or Parca." To this Juvenal (Satirae) bears testimony: "Certainly I should not deny that it is for the most part the effective form in air (which we drink in at birth) which the hidden influence of the stars imprints upon us so as to induce strength of our body, temperament, and benignity of fortune and still more that which leads to the goodness of our morals and magnanimity of our mind, which we have also expressed in our book *de Venationibus*.

> 'Scilicet et multum refert ad corpora, vires,
> Et mores genitale solum quae sidera spectent.'

" Yet we think that no influence of the stars can be so great as to be able to exercise power over us against our will, or to overwhelm the power of our reason or judgment, if indeed the body obeys, and is tempered by, the curbs of the mind, and not *vice versa*. Nor does it escape me, that as happens with what is commonly called fate by a crowd of wise men, so it is with what others call fortune, when they should at least see that everything is governed by some divine order, and nothing happens by chance nor without some antecedent beginning, i.e. from the stars."

Comenius was the greatest educational writer and schoolmaster of the first half of the seventeenth century. Whilst he advocated the teaching of Latin and Greek, he turned away from the classical writers in those languages because he did not find in them the real knowledge, in which he conceived the modern world had far surpassed the ancients. Accordingly he framed his text-books on what he took to be the undoubted teaching of the science of his age. It is therefore of unusual interest, in any account of contemporary views on the school teaching of " real " knowledge, to consult the text-books which he wrote. Moreover the *Janua Linguarum* and the *Orbis Pictus* were written for the use of the pupils themselves. Comenius, in the *Janua Linguarum* (ed. 1650) chapter lxxviii, on astronomy, says : " An astronomer considereth the motions of the stars. An astrologer (Prognosticator, i.e. Stargazer) their powerful working, influence and effect." The *Orbis pictus* (translated by Charles Hoole into English in 1658) is a reading book in Latin and English, intended to be used directly after an elementary Latin Grammar had been learned. Chapter cvi deals with the Aspects of the Planets. I give here the English only.

" The Moon ☽ runneth through the Zodiack every month ; the Sun ☉ in a year. Mercury ☿ and Venus ♀ about the Sun, the one in a hundred and fifteen, the other in 585 days. Mars ♂ in two years. Jupiter ♃ in almost twelve. Saturn ♄ in thirty years.

"Hereupon they meet variously among themselves, and have mutual Aspects one towards another. As here the ☉ and ☿ are in conjunction :

" ☉ and ☽ in Opposition.
" ☉ and ♄ in a Trine aspect.
" ☉ and ♅ in a Quartile.
" ☉ and ♂ in a Sextile."

In chapter cix Comenius describes the Terrestrial Globe, in which he remarks that the earth is " but a prick compared with the World (i.e. Universe) whereof it is the centre." To show the slow progress of astronomy in comparison with other subjects, it may be remarked that Comenius's book was first used in England over a hundred years after Copernicus had written. To make the case still worse, in 1777, when a new editor revised the *Orbis Pictus*, he inserted a chapter on Botany, and altered another chapter so as to bring it into accord with the discovery by " our Harvey " of the circulation of the blood ; yet 230 years after Copernicus, in a book which is professedly brought up to date in scientific knowledge, he retained the old Ptolemaic conception which Comenius had originally favoured, of the Earth as the *centre* of the solar system.

Again, we may see a more uncompromising attitude towards Copernican astronomy in another schoolmaster, the Headmaster of Southampton Grammar School (from 1616 onwards, died 1654), Chaplain to King Charles I and Vicar of Carisbrooke, by name Alexander Ross. Ross was a doughty Aristotelian, a man who wrote in opposition to Bacon, to Hobbes, to Sir Thomas Browne, to William Harvey, Sir Kenelm Digby, and indeed to progressive scientific and philosophical ideas generally.

MODERN SUBJECTS IN ENGLISH SCHOOLS

On the other hand, he was renowned for his school text-books, some of which, for instance, were praised and adopted by Charles Hoole and William Dugard.[1] We may not accept his diatribes as intrinsically valuable, but at any rate they exhibit great learning of a distinctly conservative kind, and what is of importance, in judging of his contemporary influence, he was widely known (e.g. Pepys and Evelyn each made a point of seeing him), and he had the ear of a very considerable public. His books, which were very numerous, in various instances, ran through a number of editions. One of his works, as already stated, was the continuation of Sir Walter Raleigh's *History of the World*. He epitomised and translated the *Christian Divinity* of Wollebius (who was one of the chief authors from whom, as Phillips tells us, Milton used to dictate to his pupils in his school). Perhaps the simplest way to summarise Ross is to say he was a stubborn, successful orthodox clergyman and schoolmaster. For this very reason, as representative of an important class, attention is due to his view of astronomy. It will be clear if we quote the title of his work :

> *The New Planet no Planet ;*[2] *or, the Earth no wandering Star ; except in the wandering heads of Galileans. Here out of the Principles of Divinity, Philosophy, Astronomy, Reason, and Sense the Earth's immobility is asserted ; the true sense of Scripture in this point cleared ; the Fathers and Philosophers vindicated ;*

---

[1] Headmaster of Merchant Taylors' School (1644–1650).

[2] De Morgan speaks not altogether unfavourably of Ross's book, in view of the available proved knowledge of his time. *Brit. Almanac and Companion*, 1836, p. 6, *et seqq.*

divers Theological and Philosophical points handled, and Copernicus his opinion as erroneous, ridiculous, and impious fully refuted. In answer to a Discourse that the earth may be a Planet, 1646.

It must not, however, be assumed that the acceptance of the Ptolemaic system in astronomy, necessarily involved the acceptance of Ptolemy's Judicial Astrology. For instance, Alexander Ross himself in his *Mystagogus Poeticus*, 1648, says : " Astronomers and such as will undertake to foretell future contingencies, or will take upon them such things as pass human power, are like Icarus ; they fall at last into a sea of contempt and scorn."

In 1679, a book appeared which upheld the Ptolemaic theory though it disowned astrology. In the *Indiculus Universalis*, or the *Universe in Epitome*, a book first composed by the learned F. Pomey in French and Latin for the use of the Dauphin of France, with an English translation added by A. Lovell, published in London. It is an encyclopaedic school text-book after the manner of Comenius' *Janua Linguarum*. It gives an account of the " World " and its parts, the Heavens, Angels, Hierarchies, the Saints, the Firmament and Stars, the fixed Stars and Constellations, the Planets. Later on there is a fairly full description of the use of astrological terms, such as " Houses," " Dignities," " Aspects," " Influences," with sub-divisions. The author, however, tells the pupil that the " science " is " vain and made up of mere lies," and says he describes the terms used in astrology " rather to decry than praise it."

On the other hand, a man might be a Copernican and still advocate astrology. John Webster (1654) published the *Examination of Academies*, with " expedients proposed for the Reforming of Schools." In dealing with astronomy, he condemned the current University teaching with Ptolemy as text-book and advocated the substitution of Copernicus, Kepler, Tycho Brahé and Galileo. At the same time he says he must defend astrology as an art " high, noble, excellent and useful to all mankind, a study not unbecoming the best wits and greatest scholars." It is the " ignorance, knavery and imposturage of many Sciolists which should be condemned." Webster was answered by Seth Ward that if any astrologer (such as Mr. Ashmole, for whom Ward has " very good respect ") will show him upon the grounds of reason or constant experiment, any one rule of Judicial Astrology, he will turn proselyte. Seth Ward was Savilian Professor of Astronomy [1] at Oxford 1649-61, and a man of highly progressive scientific spirit. Another critic of Webster probably had a much wider following than Ward, viz. Thomas Hall, of King's Norton, who, in his *Examen Examinis* in 1654, urges against astrology that godly and learned men like Calvin, Beza, Perkins, Gataker, etc., condemned it as a " dangerous " study. He reminds his readers that Judicial Astrologers were formerly excommunicated by the Church. For it is an art which leads men to the Devil. *Astrologers usually are wizards*, and with venom he says Mr. Webster " seems to know more of this art *than honester*

---

[1] *See* pp. 234, 283, and 360 *supra*.

men do." The view of Thomas Hall is not that astrology is false but that it is damnably true. Thomas Hall was, like Alexander Ross, a schoolmaster, Puritan and Aristotelian, a strong advocate of a " learned ministry," but a determined opponent of any changes in educational methods and subjects. He was perpetual Curate and Master of the Grammar School, King's Norton, and in 1662 was ejected from his living.

Milton might urge, on intellectual grounds : " Be lowly wise " in astronomical questions. But the decadence of astrology in the seventeenth century does not seem to have arisen from humility, or from loss of belief in horoscopes, in " critical days," and in signs and portents of the heavenly bodies, of meteors and comets, or of earthquakes. The diminution of open profession of the art of astrology was largely due to the horrible punishment of the wizard or sorcerer, who was supposed to obtain influence over others by being in league with the devil and evil spirits. It was only too easy for the astrologist to be confused with the wizard, and extremely difficult to extricate himself from the confusion. Mr. Lecky has asserted, with much store of illustration, that Puritanism predisposed men to see Satanic influence in life, and thus produced the phenomena of witchcraft.[1] The man

---

[1] W. E. H. Lecky : *Rationalism in Europe.* Mr. Lecky says : " During the few years of the Commonwealth there is reason to believe that more alleged witches perished in England than in the whole period before and after." i, p. 107. (1873 ed.)

in league with the devil was *par excellence* the enemy of God. The right attitude towards such the Puritan believed to be that of the old Testament, where the shedding of blood in the service of God seemed a pledge of piety. The more intense the religious fervour of the Puritan, the more pitiless he became. The Puritan in power suspected the slightest sign of evil influence. It was perilous to run any risk of accusation, for cases of suspicion of witchcraft soon gathered strength from the most ordinary occurrences. Hence the wisdom of the Commonwealth astrologist in avoiding the appearance of evil.

Calvinism, by the time of the Commonwealth, unconsciously probably *tended* to the acceptance of Copernicanism, and this factor is an important one in the struggle between the two astronomical theories. The Ptolemaic theory exalted the dwelling-place of man, by making the earth the centre of the universe, and thus indirectly magnified man, and led to the doctrine of the dignity of man, a favourite Renascence theme. Pico della Mirandola wrote : " I have set thee," says the Creator to Adam, " in the midst of the Universe, that thou mayst the more easily behold and see all that is therein. . . . Thou bearest within thee the germs of a universal life." But Calvinism insisted that the " universal life " was that of God alone ; that man with his original sin was a sink of iniquity, a being who loved darkness rather than light, who of himself could do nothing that was right, and that he was in the meanest degree, through the Fall, insignificant. The

Copernican theory which made our earth a " point " in the universe, brought a physical basis much more in accord with man's depravity and helplessness. And so the attempt to read the stars was a presumption on the part of man to pry into the secrets of his Master. Success in this pursuit must surely mean the strong suspicion of assistance from supernatural diabolic agencies. If this interpretation of Calvinistic Puritanism be correct, it explains the decadence of the astrological " science," since undoubtedly in the Commonwealth period, the theological autocracy of Puritanism in its fiercest form, was almost a Renascence of the old Hebrew theocracy. It was a power that scrupled at nothing to suppress what it conceived to be contrary to the will of God.

The non-committal attitude of Milton, with regard to the rival astronomical theories, was probably closely considered the scientific point of view, for the strict demonstration mathematically based, was not forthcoming till the outstanding genius of a Newton produced his *Principia* and placed astronomical science on its own basis outside of the relevancy of theological support or antagonism.

Mr. Lecky points out that after the Restoration a reaction against Puritanism set in, the writings of Hobbes and the institution of the Royal Society, bringing about the rationalism which eclipsed the idea of the occult sciences.[1] These forces, at the

---

[1] Lecky, i, p. 109 n. *See* also p. 348 for the influence of Descartes' writings.

same time, prevented the return to the old prevailing Judicial Astrology, because the enterprising spirits of the new age centred rather on the speculations of the nascent experimental science of the times. A consideration of a few dates will show how unreasonable it would be to expect astronomy on modern lines to be taught in the school up to 1660. Copernicus died in 1543 ; Tycho Brahé in 1601 ; Kepler in 1630 ; Galileo in 1642. Newton's *Principia* was not published till 1697. Kepler had discovered that the planets moved in elipses with the sun in one focus, and he had established the mathematical relationship of the distances and the periodic times of the planets, that is, he proved that the cubes of the distances were proportional to the squares of the times of describing the orbit in the case of the six primary planets, and he had worked out the same relationship for the satellites of Jupiter. But the question why this should be so had to be resolved. Galileo added his contribution of the laws of motion, which were re-presented by Newton, and are now known as Newton's Three Laws of Motion. He further showed that to explain the motions of the planets in their elliptical orbits, there must be a force exerted by the sun, in each case varying inversely with the square of the distance from it. With the labour and insight of genius he reached so far, and together with the laws of motion explained the orbit of the moon round the earth, and similarly the earth and other planets round the sun. But let it be remembered that even after the idea that this was possibly the solution, it took Newton sixteen years to work out the mathematical detail.

With the establishment of natural law mathematically based, Newton gave a realistic present-ment of the Platonic θεὸς ἀεὶ γεωμετρεῖ and finally overthrew the Ptolemaic conceptions, and made impossible the supposition that the separate, isolated influence of the planets controlled human affairs by bringing all the heavenly bodies under the still more marvellous law of motion and of gravitation.

At the end of the seventeenth century, it should be added, schools came into closer touch with both mathematical and observational astronomy.

We have seen that the Mathematical School in Christ's Hospital was founded in 1673, and that the Court ordered books, globes, maps and other mathematical instruments for the boys' instruction with a view to a sea-faring career. Boys were encouraged to remain in the school up to sixteen years of age. From about this time may be dated the rise also of private navigation schools, especially at seaside towns, in which frequently the mathematical education given was relatively to the times, progressive and reasonably good.

Astronomy was taught in the Mathematical School of Christ's Hospital, and was taught in a practical manner. For the story is told of Mr. Peter Perkins, who was appointed mathematical teacher in 1679, that he quarrelled with the " assistant nurse to the forty" boys, and the dispute was referred to the school authorities, who decided " that Mr. Perkins should give notice to the nurse what night he intended the children which he shall name *shall sit up to make their observation of the rising and going down of the moon and stars.*" The nurse can then see that the children go to bed " in due order." If the night " shall prove cloudy, he shall give timely notice to the said nurse that he will not use the said children, that so they may go to bed in due order with the rest." [1]

One word more. I have tried to show that there was in the first half of the seventeenth century in the English schools, a reflection of the prevailing astronomical and astrological doctrines of the age, since some astronomical teaching was thought necessary for the elucidation of the recognised aim of the grammar school—the teaching of the Latin and Greek classics. Can we claim, in our own age, that we have an equal interest in the inclusion of physical (not to say mathematical) astronomy in the modern curriculum ? For the unique universal outlook of astronomy is probably the most inspiring of introductions to the idea of Natural Law—the very conception which most distinguishes our generation from the seventeenth century. If we neglect the school-teaching of such a subject, do we not admit that our ancestors brought the heritage of their cruder views into the schools, whilst our more wonderful Copernican-Newtonian conceptions are

---

[1] Quoted from the minutes of Christ's Hospital School by Rev. E. H. Pearce : *Annals of Christ's Hospital,* p. 110.

deprived of their educational use ? For there is no subject which so enlarges the scope of imagination, and none which more stirs the reasoning powers and trains an idea of vast perspective, than the study of the heavenly bodies which we constantly look upon, when we attempt to enter into an understanding of the system of which the earth is a part.

CHAPTER XI

THE TEACHING OF MODERN LANGUAGES

I. French

When the Renascence writers spoke of "the languages," they meant Latin, Greek, and the Northern writers usually included Hebrew. They looked on the vernaculars with less respect than we regard provincial dialects. From the scholarly point of view, vernaculars were hindrances to the universal adoption of the one learned language which scholars recognised for communication, viz. Latin. The philological interest which afterwards engaged the scholar in modern languages was pre-occupied in the ancient languages, and until a vast body of philological knowledge had accumulated in connexion with them, fixed material of comparison was not forthcoming for weighing and judging the unstable phenomena of the national languages. The growth of national literatures gave the element of fixity, in some degree, to the current vernaculars, which were too fluid, as well as too barbarous, to detain attention, when compared with the classical languages, which gathered no new elements, and gave a standard, which was established objectively when once there had been a recovery of all the old MSS. texts. It is uncertain how far Erasmus in later years knew his native Dutch, the French of the Paris where he had lived for ten years, the Italian, where he had travelled, and the English of the England where he found a hospitable home.[1] But it is certain that he habitually used Latin in conversation with his friends. " He was dominated," says Professor Woodward, " by the ideal of a universal culture, within which racial differences would sink into due subordination." Vives, as we have seen,[2] realised the value to a teacher of a real study of the vernacular. Mulcaster was the first in England to speak strongly of the value of English as an instrument in education for the English child. This was not till 1582. When the slow progress of the introduction of English into English schools is borne in mind, it will be seen how improbable it would be to find an easy entrance for other modern languages.

The Humanist ideal of Latin as a universal spoken language for scholars was the ideal of the English schools, at any rate, to the end of the Commonwealth. There is probably not a single case of the provision for the teaching of a modern language by school statutes, up to that date. The grammar schools never included even French as an authorised subject, even of an optional nature, in that period. There is one case in which a foreigner (a " Brabander ") won respect as a master. On the tablet (in St. Albans Abbey) of the first known Master of St. Albans Grammar School, John Thomas Hylocomius, written in 1624, is the epitaph in Latin,

---

[1] For a discussion of these points *see* Woodward's *Erasmus,* p. 60, *et seqq.*

[2] *See* p. 1 *supra.*

stating : "After various fortune, here at last he
settled, ruling as Master the School in the town of
St. Albans. Frenchmen, Irishmen, Belgians rever-
enced him as master, to whom he gave his famous
writings of grammar." [1] There may be a few other
instances, in which, owing to exceptional circumstances, French was taught in a grammar school.
The headmastership of a grammar school held by a
foreigner is an interesting incident in the history of
school education in England, but one or two cases
must not be taken as in any sense typical of the
period.

Joshua Sylvester, the translator of Du Bartas [2] :
Divine Weekes and Workes, was at the school of
Adrian à Saravia, at Southampton. He stayed
there three years, 1573–6, and acquired a sound
knowledge of French. Then, as he regretted, he
was removed from "arts to marts," i.e. from
school to business. Robert Ashley (1565–1641),
who became a proficient linguist, the translator
of Leroy's *Interchangeable Course*, [3] was also
a pupil at the same school. In MSS. memoirs
which Ashley left, it is stated of Saravia's
school : "It was a rule all should speak French ;
he who spoke English, though only a sentence,
was obliged to wear a fool's cap at meals, and to
continue to wear it till he caught another in the
same fault." Saravia was a refugee, a noteworthy
man who took part in drawing up the Walloon

---

[1] *Vict. County Hist.* Herts, vol. ii, p. 60.

[2] *See* p. 192 *supra*

[3] *See* p. 269 *supra*.

confession of faith, and also in 1607–11 was one of the translators into English of the Bible. Saravia was Head Master of the Southampton Grammar School in 1576 when he received, xxs. for "his charges paiens in his tragedie," i.e. for the acting of his boys. Adrian's father was Christopher De Saravia, who is described as a Spaniard. He was a religious refugee. In 1570, the wife and servant of Monsieur Mestre Adrian Saravia are recorded as among those admitted to "the Supper" in the French Church established in Southampton. In 1571 Saravia is described as a witness at a baptism, and as "minister," and in 1572, two of his French scholars' names are similarly included. These are the indications of grammar school teaching of French, of which I have found notice in the period.

In spite of the facts that Latin was the universal language of the instructed man in the Middle Ages, and that but little attention was given to the definite teaching of the English language itself, yet there had been a constant succession of Englishmen who had learned French—outside of the public grammar schools. It is necessary to trace, in its general features, this knowledge of French by English people. Though the English Court had been influenced by Norman ideas before the Conquest [1]

---

[1] Edward the Confessor had lived long in France ; his mother was French, he spoke Norman French, and even introduced Norman barons into high positions in his Court and in the Church. *See* for early French influence on England, E. A. Freeman, Norman Conquest, vol. v.

the intimate influence of the French language on England necessarily dates from the Norman Conquest in 1066. The ruling classes in England in and about the Court, spoke French, and the Englishman desiring to obtain an influential position, and to be acceptable to the Court, had to learn French and speak French. To the ambitious Englishman, hoping for advancement, a knowledge of French became desirable, at least as a proof of loyalty to his foreign King. The development of feudalism made an inroad of foreign terms to signalise new conditions. Bishop and abbots, barons, even the industrial and trading classes introduced themselves and their language into the country and French colonies were established in the larger towns.

The organisation of the Law Courts within 100 years of the Conquest gave the French language a hold, which carried with it the knowledge of French of all who practised law, or learned law in the Inns of Court, and, generally speaking, all official posts required the knowledge of French. After the Norman dynasty, the Angevins continued the domination of the French language. By the time of Edward III, c. 1336, political and social changes had brought the French and English into unity as a nation and the French in coalescing with the English, ceased to speak their French and began to adopt the English. Close as the relation had been between the upper classes, even bi-lingualism gave way for the most part to a new English, in which compromises had been made on a basis essentially English, but with an expansive ingathering of French, which gave a wealth of material to the new organism of the English language.

Looked at from the side of literature, Mr. Kingston Oliphant[1] shows the effect of French on the chroniclers starting at once in 1066 up to 1120. In that year appeared Philip de Thaun's works in French (reprinted in Wright's *Mediaeval Treatises on Science*). Mr. Oliphant gives a list of sixty French words unused before the Conquest, domiciled in English writings within 100 years. The French influence becomes apparent in Homilies, and still more marked in the *Ancren Riwle* of about 1220. The thirteenth century was the time of greatest inroad of French into English. With few exceptions from about the middle of the twelfth century till c. 1250 the literature in England, as extant now, was French. French influence was shown in the language of the noble, and of ladies ; in French terms of dress, in the discourse of Franciscan friars, of military terms, of feasts, hunting, cooking, law, medicine, science, architecture. This process of fusion of words, and intimacy of relation—without entering into any question of philological advantage or disadvantage—was leading, pedagogically, to a great ease of the Englishman in learning French, wherever there was need or desire for knowing that language. The reaction set in about the middle of the fourteenth century. " Let Frenchmen," says Chaucer (1340 ?–1400), " endite their quaint terms in French, for it is kindly to their mouths ; but let us show our fantasies in such

---

[1] *Old and Middle English*, chapter vii.

words as we learned of our dames' tongues." Chaucer himself marks the period when a national literature begins, founded mainly on the old tongue, but sufficiently composite to admit the terms and phrases which introduce European thought and civilisation through the medium of French influence.[1] It was c. 1357 that Ralph Higden wrote his *Polychronicon*, and the state of the language is reported by him at that date to be : " Children in scoles against the usage and maner of all other nations beeth compelled for to leve ther own language, and for to construe their lessons and thinges in Frenche. Also gentylmen children beeth taught to speke Frenche from the time that they beeth rokked in ther cradel. And uplandish men (i.e. country people) will lyken hymself to gentylmen and soundeth with great besynesse for to speke Frenche to be told of."

As to the classes of the people who did not belong to the Court, Professor Cunningham [2] shows that Flemish weavers settled in England (and were assigned a district in Pembrokeshire by the King) and merchants from Rouen and Caen, Norman builders, came into residence in England. There were French artisans, burgesses of Shrewsbury and Norwich, and the weavers of Winchester, Oxford, Beverley, etc., were probably foreign. The artisan settlers were absorbed into the English towns, so that the lower

---

[1] The French of English people in the fourteenth century was held up to ridicule. *See Romania*, XIV, p. 279, *et seqq.*

[2] *Growth of English Industry and Commerce*, p. 173 *et seqq.*

classes in the larger towns must have been, to some extent, influenced by new ideas, and at least have become acquainted with the meaning of a foreign language. The presence of foreign children in the schools, if they were not provided for in some special trade-guild of foreign workers, would open up an interest in school use of French. But on this point, no details are forthcoming.

Ralph Higden wrote in Latin and John of Trevisa translated the Latin into English in 1387 —thirty years later. He adds the following note of correction to Higden's *Polychronicon :*

This maner (the use of the French language) is now some dele ychaungide : for John Cornwaile, a maister of gramer, chaungide the lore in gramer scole and construction of French into English, and Richard Penriche lerned that maner of teaching of him, and other men of Penriche ; as that now the yere of oure Lord a thousand three hundred foure score and fyve, of the secunde King Rychard after the conquest, in alle the gramer scoles of England, children leveth Frensch, and construeth and lerneth in Englisch and haveth thereby avauntage in one side and desavauntage in another. Their avauntage is that they lerneth their gramer in lasse tyme than children were wont to do ; desavauntage is, that now children of gramer scole knoweth no more Frensch than knows their left heele ; and that is harm to them, if ther school passe the see and travaile in strange landes, and in many other places also : also gentylmen haveth now myche ylefte for to teche ther children Frensch.

The Court as a judicial body had become wholly French-speaking by about 1166. It continued so till 1362. In that year a statute was enacted in French, declaring that as the French tongue was but little understood, all pleas should be pleaded, shown, defended, answered, debated and judged in the English tongue. It is worth notice that this statute is passed between the date of Higden's original *Polychronicon* in 1357 and Trevisa's rendering in 1387. With regard to the Statutes, these had been stated in Latin, till about the end of Edward II's reign (1327) when French displaced Latin for this purpose. The transition from French to English in the Statutes occurs at the time of the accession of Richard III (1482). About 1425 the Parliament Roll begins to show English in the operative parts of Statutes, but until 1503, the formal parts were still written in French and Latin.

The earlier legal literature is in Latin. By gradual stages civil lawyers came to write in French. It was not till the latter half of the fifteenth century that English law began to be written and commented upon for the purpose of study in the English tongue. Even to the present, almost all words of definite legal import are, in some degree, old French. The old formula of enactment *le roi le veult*, is a standing instance of the retention of the whole expression. The question of the training of the young lawyer to speak French is clear up to 1362; for Higden explains that French was taught in the schools, but assuming that the lawyer was of good family, it was probably spoken at home, by at least some members of the family. Sir John Fortescue, writing c. 1463, says only sons of noble and gentle families went for their education in the liberal arts and in the law to Inns of Chancery and Inns of Court. He does not mention the teaching of French, so that it would appear that, by this time, formal preparation in French had become unnecessary for the lawyer. In earlier times, too, in the King's Court, to which the lawyers went, the barons and prelates, courtiers as well as lawyers all spoke French, and the succession was probably maintained by the very atmosphere of the Court, without formal institutions; without other than private teachers. At any rate, French was effectively known and continued to be known, long after the pleadings in Court ceased to take place in French. The readings in the Moots [1] were printed in French as late as 1680, as a volume entitled *les cases de Grays Inn* shows, though the readings are of an earlier date.

A well-trained lawyer, of course, knew Latin as well. Sir John Doderidge in his *English Lawyer*, 1631, says that " no one will deny that the knowledge of the Latin tongue is right necessary for the English Lawyer." " For writs ought to be framed in true and congruous Latin." The Magna Carta, and old statutes are in that language, together with the law treatises of Randulph de Glanville, Henry de Bracton, the Fleta, Randulph de Hingham and Sir John Fortescue, *de laudibus Legum Angliae*.

The Universities as well as the schools required construing in French. Mr. Anstey gives an enactment at Oxford to the effect that the masters of grammar " shall teach the boys to construe in English and in French, so that the latter language be not forgotten (in a statute " probably of the thirteenth

---

[1] i.e. Discussions on difficult legal cases.

century "). Mr. Hastings Rashdall[1] says also of Oxford : " There were, it appears, certain persons who taught and others who learned ' the art of writing and composing and speaking the Gallic idiom ' as also the art of ' composing charters and other scripts and of holding lay courts or the English mode of pleading '—an indication of the purpose for which French was in demand." Mr. Rashdall,[2] also relates that at Cambridge, Pembroke College is remarkable as " the only College in an English University in which a preference was accorded in the election of scholars to students of French birth."

On the other hand, English students were evidently in Paris in the twelfth century. Dr. Furnivall quotes the instances of John of Salisbury who was twelve years studying at Paris, Thomas à Becket, Giraldus Cambrensis (born 1147), Alexander Neckham (died 1227). To these may be added the names of Edmund Rich of Abingdon, Roger Bacon, William of Ockham. The University of Paris had four Nations, or guilds of students, of the French, Normans, Picards and English. The English Nation included the Germans, together with students from the north and east of Europe. The English Nation was at one time, divided into the English and non-English and, c. 1440, was re-named the German Nation. Besides the students from the French provinces belonging to England, e.g. Poitou,

---

[1] Rashdall : *Universities of Europe*, ii, p. 459.
[2] *Ibid.*, ii, p. 565.

Guienne, it included the English, Scotch, Irish, Poles, Germans, etc. Dr. Rashdall calculates that the average academic population of Paris may be put at about 3,500. He further states that the proportion of the Nations may be computed on the basis that " candidates were usually sent to be licensed in batches of eight, each of which contained three Frenchmen, two Normans, two Picards, and one Englishman or German." This would make the average number of the " English from about 400 to 450." But a " Nation " which includes so many different kinds of foreigners, as Britons, Poitevins, Poles and Germans, may at different times, within itself have varied greatly in national composition. Yet, on any computation, the English students on their return to England must have constituted an element of French tendencies of some importance. How far they would have acquired French by residence in Paris is a difficult question. But the weight of evidence goes to show that the principal language used academically would be Latin, and the chief effect was probably that they got more into the current of European learning than they would have done under English training, rather than that they greatly served as propagandists of a knowledge of the French language on their return. Robert Henry, [1] in his *History of England*, says that the English in the University of Paris, " were in particular, so numerous that they occupied several schools or colleges ; and made so distinguished a figure by their genius

---

[1] Quoted by Dr. Furnivall, *Manners and Meals* (E.E.T.S.), p. xl.

and learning, as well as by their generous manner of living, that they attracted the notice of all strangers."

The English academic element, whether at home or in Paris, together with the professional classes, especially of the Church, were a considerable conservative force, negatively on the side of the vernacular, since Latin, not French, was essentially the language which they used for their work. The ecclesiastical academic influence was all absorptive amongst the professions ; it was centred on Latin, and at least this had the negative effect of not furthering the progress of the French language to any monopolist position amongst the upper classes. Even of the lawyers, only the civilians used French, the ecclesiastical lawyers remained faithful to Latin. With the ecclesiastical element, Latinist mainly, though usually able to deal with either English or French, or both, and the masses of the people only slightly affected by the foreign element in their midst, the resumption of the mother tongue, with a *modicum* of French influence, was never in doubt. The extraordinary change between the account of Higden in 1357 and his translator, Trevisa, in 1387, indicates that the final die had been cast within those thirty years. The revulsion of feeling against French had been consummated by the French Wars of Edward III, and, as Mr. de Montmorency plausibly suggests,[1] the Great Death of 1348–9 had led to a dearth

---

[1] *State Intervention in English Education*, p. 19.

of priests. In this dearth, it was probably " the foreign priests, Norman or French by birth and instinct," who mainly disappeared from the scene. " If any priest remained it was an English priest, speaking the tongue of his people, writing and reading the language of his people, thinking their thoughts and knowing their aspirations." Moreover, the courtly elements of barons and the military class, the specially French-speaking class, were abroad, many being killed by their French-speaking enemies, and the remainder coming back to an England more than decimated by the Great Death, but now, with the mass of the people aroused to national hatred of France, and invigorated with an anglicised national spirit, able to assert itself triumphantly through its unanimity in itself, and the falling off, in such large numbers, of its opponents.

The great Hundred Years War, together with the Wars of the Roses, consolidated the English people whilst they annihilated the non-English elements amongst the nobles. So from the Tudor period onwards, the French language was a foreign language. Even its " survivals " only indirectly gave a preference to its study, and it ranked as a foreign language, with claims that came *de novo*, not always superior in its vogue to Spanish, as for instance, in the Court of Queen Catharine of Aragon, nor to Italian, as for instance, with Roger Ascham and the Humanists.

Still, the very proximity of England to France led to connexions and relations, which would have been established, had there never been a Norman

Conquest. The marriage of Henry I's daughter with Geoffrey of Anjou and the accession of their son, Henry II, to the English throne, and the coming of the Angevin followers, the marriage of Edward II with Isabella of France, of Edward III with Queen Philippa of Hainault, of Henry V with Catharine, of Henry VI with Margaret of Anjou, in each case led to a stimulus of a knowledge of French at Court. Thus in the household education of nobles either in the Court or in other noblemen's houses, French frequently, if not continuously, held a place in the studies. Thus in the Court of Edward IV, the henxmen or young nobles were by ordinance to study " sundry languages " of which French was doubtless one. Dr. Furnivall has pointed out that Walter de Biblesworth wrote his French vocabulary for the Lady Dionysia de Mounchensy, whom Dr. Oelsner identifies with a lady who died in 1304. Generally speaking, we may take it that ladies at Court, and within the reach of the manners and fashions of the Court, learned French, as well as the men. We are told, for instance, of Margaret Countess of Richmond, born 1441, that she was a " perfect mistress of the French tongue." Still more general was the acquisition, in earlier times, of French, by ladies, to judge by its place in the romances which constituted so great a portion of the reading of the courtiers and knights. Dr. Furnivall quotes the Romance of *Blonde d'Oxford*,[1] in which Jean of Dammartin is an *escuier*. " After waiting at table on the knights,

---

[1] Written by Philippe de Remi (edited by Gaston Paris).

squires, and inferiors, the ladies keep him to talk French with them." As to romances, Vives (1523) made a strong protest against those of Spain, France, Flanders and England indifferently. Yet they had stirred and trained the imagination, and undoubtedly stimulated the knowledge of foreign countries, and, to some extent, of other languages.

In Ellis : *Original Letters*, [1] Series iii, vol. i, p. 341, there is a letter from Gregory Cromwell's tutor to the father of the Earl of Essex, where he says that Mr. Southwell has devised an order of studies for the youth in the French tongue, writing, playing at weapons, casting of accounts, pastimes of instruments. Mr. Southwell daily hears his pupil read in the *English* tongue, and corrects his pronunciation, and expounds " the etymology and native signification of such words as we have borrowed of the Latin or Frenchmen, not evyn so commonly used in our quotidiene speche." Mr. Vallance instructs young Gregory (with two others) in a " wonderesly compendious, facile, prompt and ready way, not without painful diligence and laborious industry."

The book of manners, called the *Lytylle Chyldrenes Lytil Boke* was printed from a later MS., with an interlinear French version by Wynkyn de Worde in *Here begynneth a lytell treatyse for to lerne Englisshe and Frensshe* (printed before 1499).

With regard to the manuals used for the teaching of French up to the time of printing, an exhaustive

---

[1] Quoted by J. A. Froude : *History of England*, vol. i, pp. 49–50.

account has been written by Dr. H. Oelsner.[1] He is of opinion that Trevisa is exaggerating when he says that English peasants ever endeavoured to learn French, though he thinks the class just above them at the chief time of flourishing of the French language in England, knew that language well enough to read the *Contes moralisés* of Bozon. He agrees that after the Great Death in 1349, English was completely reinstated in the schools. The treatises for teaching French are divided by Dr. Oelsner into four classes—I. Vocabularies and kindred works. II. Grammars and portions of grammars dealing with orthography, pronunciations, flexions, etc. III. Model Letter Writers. IV. *Manières de Langage* or model conversation books chiefly for the use of travellers.

The Vocabularies consist chiefly of lists of useful things, such as afterwards were known as *Nomenclators*. The chief of these are the *de Utensilibus* of Alexander Neckham (1157–1217), written in Latin and glossed in French; the *Dictionarius* of John de Garlande (c. 1225) in Latin with English and Latin glosses; and Walter de Biblesworth's vocabulary (probably written before 1304), written for children, and a book which is to

---

[1] In a paper to the Philological Society, Feb. 1905, of which a lengthy summary was given in the *Athenæum*, February 11, 1905. From this paper I have freely borrowed in the text. The writings of P. Meyer in *Romania ;* Stürzinger in his edition of the *Orthographia Gallica,* and E. M. Stengel, *Chronologischer Verzeichnis französischer Grammatiken* (Oppeln, 1890), are the sources to which the reader must look for further information.

be edited by Mr. Aldis Wright for the Roxburghe Club, beginning : *Liber iste vocatur Femina, quia sicut Femina docet infantem loqui maternam (linguam) sic docet iste liber juvenes rhetorice loqui gallicum prout inferius patebit.*

The Grammars include *Orthographia Gallica*, c. 1300 ; the *Tractatus Ortographiae Gallicane*, c. 1400, of T. Coyfurelly, of Orleans ; a *Donait François*, c. 1400, written at the expense of Johan Barton.

Model Letter Writers : " There are five of these, all still in MS. (three at the British Museum, one in the Cambridge University Library, and one at All Souls'). They range from c. 1327 to 1415, and contain interesting allusions—to the kings of the period, to Avignon and the Popes, to the rising of Owen Glendower, etc. The private letters are no less valuable in their way, and are full of quaint touches."

Travellers' Conversation books, or *Manières he langage* : The first of these was written about 1396, probably by T. Coyfurelly, who wrote the grammar before mentioned. It gives an account of Orleans and its University, together with the troubles there in 1389. The second *Manière* is Coyfurelly's " Petit Livre pour enseigner les enfants de leur entreparler comun François." This must belong to *c.* 1399, Richard II.'s captivity being given as a piece of news. A third mentioned by Dr. Oelsner " was written *c.* 1415, as it contains interesting references to Agincourt. Like all the other works of this class, it is full of valuable data concerning contemporary life and manners, and of rare words. The scene is laid in England (mostly at or near Oxford). A fair at Woodstock and the articles bought and sold there form a feature ; thus divers cloths, etc., from Abingdon, Witney, Castlecombe, Colchester, and Salisbury are specified."

Coming to printed books, we have the two further *Manières* :

Dialogues in French and English, adapted from a fourteenth century book of dialogues in French and Flemish, were printed by William Caxton, 1483; and the *lytell Treatise*. From 1400 there is no trace of a French Grammar published in England until 1521, when Alexander Barclay's *Introductory to write and pronounce French* appeared.

The study of French in the Tudor and Stuart periods may be divided into two currents. I. The Court and Commerce. II. The Religious unity of English and French Protestants.

With regard to the conjunction of Court and Commerce, the French teachers who came over to England in the first place looked to the nobles and gentry for their clientèle, but later included those of " mean " estate, which would seem to point to those engaged in international trade and commerce.

I. *Teaching of French in Court and Commerce,* 1528–1660

Giles Dewes or Du Guez, Du Wes or de Vadis, " the singular clerk " as Palsgrave calls him, was librarian first to Henry VII and then to Henry VIII, and teacher of French to Prince Arthur, later to

Henry himself, and afterwards to Princess Mary (i.e. Queen Mary I). It was for her use he wrote in 1528 *An Introductorie for to lerne to rede, to pronounce and to speke French trewly.*

John Palsgrave wrote *Lesclarcissement de la Langue Francoyse, compose par maistre Jehan Palsgraue, Angloys, natyf de Londres et gradue du Paris,* in 1530.

Mr. Thompson Cooper, in the *Dict. Nat. Biog.,* life of Palsgrave (Vol. XLIII, p. 171), remarks that " the book was originally intended to be a kind of dictionary for the use of Englishmen seeking to acquire a knowledge of the French tongue," but that it has now a special value as one of the " best depositories of obsolete English words and phrases." Dr. Furnivall has published (Lond., 1868) a copy of the Agreement between Palsgrave and his publisher, Richard Pynson ; in the Indenture between them (second draft) it is agreed that—" the sayd Rycharde, his executors and assignes, shall Inprynt, or cause to be Inpryntyd, oñ boke callyd ' lez les Clarcissmentt de la lange Francoys,' contay[n]ing iii sondrye bokes, where in ys schewyd howe the saide tong schould be pronownsyd in reding & spekyng, and allso syche grammaticall rules as concerne the perfection of the saide tong, with ii vocabulistes, oone begynnyng with Englishe nownes & verbes enpowndyd in frenshe, and a general vocabulist contayning all the wordes off the frenshe tong expownd in Englishe."

John Palsgrave, who died in 1554, was chaplain to Henry VIII and tutor to Henry VIII's sister, Queen

Mary of France. He says he wrote the book, "desirous to do some humble service unto the nobilitie of this victorious realm, and universally unto all other estates of this my native country."

In 1531 Sir Thomas Elyot in the *Gouvernour* says : "What doubt is there but so (i.e. by family households using Latin to the boy in their 'familiar' speech) may he (i.e. the boy of seven years of age) as soon speak good Latin as he may do pure French, which *now is brought into as many rules and figures, and as long a grammar as is Latin and Greek.*" This evidently refers to Palsgrave's *Eclaircissement* of the previous year. Elyot presents a critical attitude to this new-fangled grammar, and his criticism implies that the ordinary method, in his own experience of learning French was the direct method, of mixing with people who spoke French. To a man who had been on diplomatic missions, and lived in foreign countries, this was simple enough, but he does not explain how the ordinary boy could get the French environment. Probably, however, he only advocated the learning of French by those who had missions or business abroad, and never contemplated its study by children.

In 1539 Cranmer [1] wrote to Thomas Cromwell, making suggestions as to the establishment of a College in the Cathedral Church of Canterbury by means of sequestered funds. He proposes provision for forty students in the "tongues, in sciences and French," and a sufficient staff for teaching these

---

[1] *Remains and Letters*, Parker Society, p. 397.

subjects. This is the first mention I know of any institutional teaching of French in England since the time of school-teaching of French, spoken of by Higden in 1367. Cranmer's scheme was a very large one, the above item being only a detail. Unfortunately, other purposes than this educational project of Cranmer appealed more strongly to Cromwell and to Henry VIII, and the scheme came to nothing.

Under the Stuarts, members of the Court and noble families learned French, more frequently than Italian and Spanish, in the later part of the period ; but it is extremely doubtful whether there was preference for French in the time of the Tudor monarchs. The well-instructed ladies who came under the Renascence influence often knew a fair amount of Latin (sufficient for instance to converse in Latin) and some Greek and even Hebrew, but in the list of their accomplishments French is, surprisingly, omitted. Lady Jane Grey, it is said, spoke French. So, undoubtedly, did Queen Mary I and Queen Elizabeth, but it would seem probable that they knew more Italian than French. Queen Mary I, it is often over-looked, was, before her accession, a zealous Bible student, if Nicholas Udall is to be believed. In his preface to the Princess's own translation into English of Erasmus's Paraphrase on the Gospel of St. John, Udall says : " It is now no news in England to see young damsels in noble houses and in the Courts of princes instead of cards and other instruments of idle trifling to have continually in their hands either psalms, homilies, or other devout meditations, or else Paul's epistles, or some book of Holy Scripture matters, and as familiarly both to read or reason thereof in Greek, Latin, French or Italian, as in English."

" Truly," says Harrison,[1] " it is a rare thing with us now to hear of a courtier which hath but his own language. And to say how many gentlewomen and ladies there are, that beside sound knowledge of the Greek and Latin tongues are thereto no less skilful in the Spanish, Italian, and French, or in some *one* of them, it resteth not in me." Whether the one language hinted at by Harrison as known by ladies would necessarily be French is an open question. One of the daughters of Sir Anthony Coke, Ann, who married Sir Nicholas Bacon, knew Italian well (all the daughters studied Latin and Greek), but there is no mention of a knowledge of French. The learned Elizabeth Jane Weston, who settled at Prague in Bohemia, " understood many languages." But her pride was in Latin, on her know-ledge of which she was complimented by Scaliger, and " Mr. Farnaby ranked her amongst the best Latin poets of the sixteenth century." Catharine Phillips, the " matchless Orinda (born 1631)," was a " perfect mistress " of French, and Margaret Duchess of Newcastle, who wrote on Experimental Philosophy in 1668, knew the French language.

Instances, therefore, are readily forthcoming of the knowledge of French in the precincts of the Court by the ladies as well as the men. But more significant in the history of education than the cases of private

---

[1] Hollinshed's *Chronicles*, vol. i, (1577).

instruction are the attempts to include French as a part of organised instruction. These attempts were associated with the projected Academies :

1561. In the Articles devised by Sir Nicholas Bacon for the bringing up of her Majesty's Wards :

From two to three o'clock each day they are to be with the French Master.

French was a subject to be taught in the following projected institutions :

In **1572.** In Sir Humphrey Gilbert's Queen Elizabeth's Ac(h)ademy.

In **1636.** In Sir Francis Kynaston's Museum Minervae.

In **1648.** In Sir Balthazar Gerbier's Private Academy at Bethnal Green.

In 1615, Sir George Buck described the educational institutions of London under the title *The Third University* of *England*. He deals with the various subjects which are taught in London colleges and schools. Unfortunately, he becomes vague in dealing with the teaching of languages. " There be also," he says, " in this City, Teachers and Professors of the holy or Hebrew Language, of the Chaldean, Syriac, and Arabic Languages, of the Italian, Spanish, French, Dutch and Polish Tongues. And here be they which can speak the Persian and Morisco, and the Turkish and the Muscovian Language and also the Sclavonian Tongue, which passeth through seventeen Nations. And in brief divers other Languages fit for Ambassadors and Orators and Agents, for Merchants, and Travellers, and necessary for all Commerce or Negotiation whatsoever."

In 1619, Thomas Morrice wrote on the subject of French. His views are contained in :

> *An Apology for Scholemasters, tending to the advauncement of Learning, and to the vertuous education of Children.*

Particularly Morrice discusses the question whether Frenchmen should be employed to teach English children, or whether they should be taught by Englishmen knowing French. He decides against the Frenchman : " If he speak broken, and not pure and perfect English, with the right accent distinctly pronounced, and truly write it, there is danger lest he hurt the children's English, being far more necessary for them than the French, and so pull down with one hand, more than he can build with the other. I have had conference with divers Frenchmen, whom I like and love ; I have not heard any one of them to speak and pronounce English, as perfectly as an Englishman doth."

The following passage is interesting, for it shows that the question of the position of French, in an educational course for the nobility, at any rate, had consciously arisen, and Morrice approaches the subject with an evident desire to be as fair as he can be : That French should be learnt rather than Latin is a " most absurd Paradox, seeing that the Latin, being the Catholic or universal language of Christians, who are learned, is commonly taught, both privately in houses, and publicly in Schools and Universities, throughout all Nations in Christendom. A good thing, the more general it is, the better it is. There are but three learned tongues, the Latin, the Greek and Hebrew. The French was never reckoned to be any. It is peculiar to that particular country, as English is to England, Irish to Ireland ; so French to France. The French themselves, especially the nobility and gentry, disburse large expenses for the training up of their children in the study of the Latin. Who hath the knowledge thereof, may travel therewith throughout all Christian Kingdoms. In this tongue all learned Books, for the most part are written, wherein the conferences, disputes and exercises of the Learned are performed. . . . (Latin) is of that sacred estimate by the laws of our Land, that the very reading thereof saveth many Malefactors from untimely death. I do not discommend the French but for the causes before mentioned, I prefer the Latin before it by many degrees."

This was as far as a typical classical man could be expected to go, and marks a stage of concession which (with the decadence of Latin speaking) became necessary for those who recognised travelling as an important part in a nobleman's training. [1]

Here may be recalled the pathetic story of the Princess Elizabeth, second daughter of King Charles I. It is probable that a tutoress was appointed for her in 1641, in the person of Mrs. Bathsua Makin.

---

[1] John Cleland, however, in *The Institution of a Young Nobleman* (1607) went further than Morrice. He says : " I wish *rather (than the teaching of Latin)* that parents were willing to have their sons taught, by frequent usage and custom, the French language, which is so pleasant, common, and spread through the whole world at this day."

In that year the Princess was six years old. From 1642 onwards the little Elizabeth had to live in separation from her mother and father, who were hurrying about the country in all the uncertainty of civil war. The child was a great lover of books, and it is said that before she was eight years old " she read and wrote " French, Italian, Latin, Greek and Hebrew. Again, we see that French occupies no isolated position of marked pre-eminence even in girls' education. Princess Elizabeth died in 1650. Mrs. Bathsua Makin then established a school, first at Putney and afterwards at Tottenham High Cross. In her *Essay to Revive the Ancient Education of Gentlewomen* (1673) she acknowledges with a sense of humour, that it is objected against women as a reproach that they have too " much tongue," but she rejoins, " It's no crime if they have many tongues " (i.e. languages). Indeed, it is admitted as a concession to their natural disposition to be " talkative " that they *may* acquire languages, but may not pursue sciences requiring solid judgment. Mrs. Makin replies to the argument expressed in the question, " What need have women to learn tongues ? there are books enow in English," by saying : " Was all learning in English, *as it is now in French*, I think those dead languages would be of little use, only in references to the Scriptures." [1]

---

[1] Sir William Petty had used almost the same words with regard to boys. Francis Osborn says : " For the statesman, French authors are best, as most fruitful in negociations, and memoirs, left by public ministers and by their secretaries published after their deaths."—*Advice to a Son*, 1656, p. 5.

There is a new ground for the school-teaching of French, which first appears to have become prominent about the time of the Commonwealth. It was a revolutionary opinion to suppose that French contained the best learning of the age, how revolutionary may be perhaps best realised by remembering that Mrs. Makin was a contemporary of John Milton, who had only a few years previously written his tractate to show the need of classical education, on the ground that all really scientific knowledge was locked up in the ancient writers of Greece and Rome, and that the absorbed study of ancient languages, could alone provide the key. The only modern language, by the way, named by Milton in his tractate was the Italian,[1] so Mrs. Makin's argument for French was particularly unorthodox.

It is from Mrs. Makin's school we may date the establishment of private schools for girls of what we now call the High School type, with modern languages as an important part of the curriculum.

---

[1] Though Milton knew French. In a Latin poem addressed to his father in later years, Milton says: "You then advised me [in addition to Latin and Greek] to add the flowers which are the pride of Gaul," and Masson supposes that "Milton could read French by the end of his school-days." After the Restoration the recognition of the importance of the French language became far more marked. Thus John Locke, in 1677, at Paris, bought for Lord Shaftesbury's grandson the best French and Latin school-books. Further Locke says of the French: "Polishing and enriching their tongue is no small business among them, and there is raised among them a just ambition and emulation of writing correctly."

There had been an earlier girls' school at Hackney, kept by a certain famous Mrs. Perwick in 1643. This school was taught, to a large extent, by specialist masters, but the main subjects were music and dancing, which, in some instances, were carried to high perfection. There is no mention of foreign languages as part of the school-teaching.

The educational writers of the Commonwealth were curiously divided as to the teaching of foreign languages. For instance, John Dury, in 1650, in his *Reformed School*, proposes a class of special schools " for the tongues " which should teach boys either for learning, when they should be taught the classical languages, *or* for commerce, when the schools should teach boys French, Spanish, Italian.

On the other hand, Sir William Petty urged the needlessness of children studying " languages " in any early stage. For such knowledge " judgment " is necessary, more than the child possesses. " There be books enough for their present use in their mother tongue. So that, at any rate, ' languages ' should be deferred to a later stage, if learned at all."

More negative still is John Webster, in his *Examination of Academies* (1654). " It is evident, that if a man had the perfect knowledge of many, nay all languages, that he could give unto man, beast, bird, fish, plant, mineral, etc., their distinct and proper names in twenty several idioms or dialects, yet knows he no more thereby than he that can onely name them in his mother tongue, for the intellect receives no other, nor further notion thereby. For the senses receive but one numerical species or ideal-shape from every individual thing, though by institution and imposition, twenty or one hundred names be given unto it, according to the idiom of several nations. Now for a carpenter to spend seven years' time about the sharpening and preparing of his instruments and then have no further skill how to employ them were ridiculous, so for the scholar to spend divers years for some small scantling and smattering in the tongues, having for the most part got no further knowledge, but like parrots to babble and prattle, whereby the intellect is no way enriched, is but toilsome and almost lost labour." So impressed is Webster with the futility and waste of various languages that he fell back on the dream of a mystical universal language of Nature, whereby all men might understand each other, to whatever nation each belonged, not perceiving that was precisely the reason Erasmus advocated the universal teaching and learning of Latin.

Comenius (1592–1671) recognised all these difficulties and objections. His position was that children required a knowledge of things their properties, qualities, and uses—and, as far as possible—a knowledge of all things. If they had the " thing " realistically before their eyes, what was there to hinder them from first learning the name of the thing in the vernacular, and then proceeding to learn other names in other languages for the same thing ? Thus might three or four languages be acquired, and what was more, a knowledge of the thing in its physical properties be impressed on the senses.

But the public schools were unprepared to consider

the inclusion of modern languages in their curriculum. What could not be accomplished with all the power and resources of authority behind these projects was undertaken, to some extent, by private voluntary enterprise. We have seen that noble families engaged private tutors for the teaching of French and other languages. But as the necessity or desirability of learning French became more apparent, French teachers appeared in England and established schools, in the first place for the higher classes of society, and gradually widened their scope.

It does not seem improbable that these schoolmasters in the first instances were French Protestants, who found a favourable home in England in periods of stress, exiles from their own country. After Giles Dewes (1528), Pierre du Ploiche was the next writer, in 1553, to publish a French text-book " for all young children." This is entitled : *A Treatise in English and Frenche (of the Catechisme . . . of the Letanie . . . for to speke at the table . . . with the manner of . . . speaking to all men, etc.) right necessary and proffitable for all young children.* Richard Grafton, London ; 1553, 4to.

The inclusion of the Catechism and the Litany suggests that the text-book is the work of a French Protestant refugee in England. The English is on the left and the French on the right, in parallel columns. The Catechism, the Litany and the suffrages, a series of prayers, conversation at table, asking the way, and buying and selling make up the six sections of the book. Du Ploiche makes a pupil say that he goes to [French] school " in Trinytie

Lane, at the sign of the Rose." Apparently, therefore, Pierre du Ploiche was a teacher of French to children at that address. [1]

About 1566 Claude Holyband (or De Sain Liens or a Sancto Vinculo, his French and Latin synonyms) published his *French Littleton*. It would seem, from the name of the book, Holyband hoped to appeal specially to lawyers and the students of the Inns of Court. Published by Vautrollier, one of the most interesting publishers of his time, himself a Huguenot refugee, Holyband announced himself as teaching in St. Paul's Churchyard " by the sign of the Lucrece," and his book as a " most easy, perfect and absolute way to learn the French tongue." Apparently Holyband had previously (c. 1565) published his *French Schoolmaster* (of which the first edition known is 1573), which had been "liked of by the nobility and *mean* (i.e. middle) estate of this flourishing nation." But the *French Littleton* is an " easier way." He explains the title of the book : "As every student applying himself to the knowledge of the laws of this realm doth commonly travail in the book called Littleton's *Tenures* to learn at his first entry the ground of the law," so, this *small* volume may be learned for French (" that it may be easier to be carried by any man about him ").

I have suggested that Holyband was, like his publisher Vautrollier, a Huguenot refugee. At any rate, this would be in keeping with the book, which advises the learner to read half a score chapters

---

[1] *See Schools, School-Books, and School-Masters,* by W. Carew Hazlitt, pp. 258–261.

of the New Testament, and then the works of Mr. de Launay, " the most eloquent writer of our tongue." The pupil on reaching the end of the book is expected to learn in French, the Lord's Prayer, Articles of the Faith, graces before and after meals, and chapter v of the Acts of the Apostles. The secular portion of the book consists of dialogues of travellers on the inn, weights, merchants' conversation, proverbs, golden sayings, and there is a vocabulary of fourteen small-sized pages.

> 1573. *The French Schoolmaster. Wherein is most plainly shewed the true and perfect way of pronouncing the French tongue, to the furtherance of all those which would gladly learne it.*

First collected by Mr. C. H(olyband) and now newly corrected and amended by P. Erondelle, professor of the said tongue. London, 1612.

(Contains rules for pronunciation, for syntax, verbs, and then follow dialogues, and some proverbs, the Lord's Prayer, Ten Commandments, graces, prayer on rising, and for the evening, and other religious pieces and a vocabulary.)

The dialogues are on such subjects as :

Familiar talk on getting up in the morning. Two neighbours meeting in a morning. Welcoming any one to a house. For to ask the way. To ask lodging. To go to bed. Rising in the morning. To buy and sell. Then follow : Proverbs, Creed, Ten Commandments, etc., graces, vocabulary.

From time to time the religious element is introduced. There is, moreover, much interesting information as to the studies and manners of the times.

Claudius Holyband,[1] in the *Treasurie of the French Tongue* (1580), says he has set forth *De pronunciatione linguae gallicae* and the *French Littleton*.

In 1593 the *Treasurie of the French Tongue* developed into a *Dictionarie French and Englishe*. Palsgrave and Dewes had included vocabularies in their French text-books. In 1552 Jean Véron, a Frenchman, rector of St. Martin's Church, Ludgate, had added an English rendering of the words in the Latin-French Dictionary of Robert Stephanus: *Dictionariolum Puerorum, Latino-Gallicum nuper aediderat Robertus Stephanus ; cui Anglicanam interpretationem Joannes Veron adjecit.* This was published by Reginald Wolfe. In 1573 John Baret's *Alvearie or Triple Dictionarie in Englishe, Latin, and French* was published. As a purely French and English Dictionary, if not the first, Holyband's Dictionary[2] appears to be the most important. Miss Farrer quotes from the *Stationers' Registers*, (edited by Prof. Arber), the entry that in 1608 Holyband's Dictionary was already augmented or altered by Randle Cotgrave. In 1610 the copy was handed over to Adam Islip, and in 1611 " Cotgrave's " famous French-English Dictionary was published by Islip. Thus Holyband was a pioneer in the compilation of French-English Dictionaries

---

[1] *See* also *Campo de Fior*, by Holyband, p. 461 *infra*.

[2] Miss Lucy E. Farrer, who has written a comprehensive monograph on *La Vie et les Œuvres de Claude de Sainliens alias Claudius Holyband,* says that Holyband's *Dictionary* is founded on that of Nicot (1573).

as well as in the teaching of the French language, and his work was the basis of Cotgrave's great *Dictionary*.

Holyband was followed by G. N. de la Mothe, 1592 :

> *The French Alphabet, Teaching in a very short time, by a most easie way, to pronounce French naturally, to read it perfectly, to write it truly, and to speak it accordingly. Together with the Treasure of the French Tongue, containing the rarest Sentences, Proverbs, Parables, Similies, Apothegmes, and Golden sayings of the most excellent French Authours, as well Poets as Orators. The one diligently compiled, and the other painfully gathered and set in order, after the Alphabeticall manner, for the benefit of those that are desirous of the French tongue. By* G. D. L. M. N. London.

(The above is the title-page of 1647 edition.)

De la Mothe offers the important advice : " When you are prettily furthered in it (his book) get you acquainted, if it be possible, with some French man, to the end you may practise with him, by daily conference together in speech and talk, what you have learned." He further makes the valuable suggestion : " And if you be in place, where the Frenchmen have a Church for themselves, as they have in London, get you a French Bible or a New Testament, and every day go both to their Lecture and Sermons. The one will confirm and strengthen your pronunciation, and the other cause you to understand when one doth speak."

For the rest, De la Mothe suggests the purchase of a hard French book and a French dictionary. Translate the book, or at least read it and note in a paper-book the hardest words and the best phrases.

He says it is not enough to have lived three or four years in France, unless the stranger has mixed with those who speak good French, i.e. with courtiers, gentlemen, ladies and the learned, who *have the true propriety of the tongue*. The common sort of the people are not a model, for they are as far from the true French as the Italian is from Latin. Better stay at home than learn from such. " I know some English ladies, some gentlemen who never went out of England, and yet without comparison they speak much better than some others that I know which have been in France three or four years. . . ." If those who learn are taught by one who " hath a good method of teaching they cannot choose but learn in a short time. What they learn is known better than the French learned in France by rote." It is not a question of learning to speak eloquently like a book, but to speak *purely*, and that cannot be learned from the French of the common people. He continues : " Nevertheless those that go into France have a very great advantage over those that learn here, because being there and hearing nothing but to speak French, they cannot choose but learn in a short time. It helpeth them much if in addition they learn by reading books. But if they do not, I can assure you that one can learn as soon to speak it here *being taught*, as they to understand it there *not being taught*."

De la Mothe deals with the wrong pronunciation of French by the English He refers to the learning of French by the study of the old French texts of English laws, and says that such learners pronounce the French thereof according to the English, so that it is impossible for a Frenchman to understand them. He proceeds : " If we pronounce a stranger's tongue according to the letters of our mother tongue we take away from a language not only his natural pronunciation, but also his grace. That is the only reason why there be as many pronunciations of the Latin tongue as there be nations which speak it. Every one pronounceth it according to his own language [1] and all pronounce it not well, except the Italians which have kept in their tongue the nearest pronunciation to Latin letters, to which their tongue cometh nearer, whatever be said to the contrary for the Spanish tongue. . . ." The reason is clear : " It was at Rome and through all Italy where they spoke Latin ; it is now at Rome and through all Italy they speak Italian."

De la Mothe discusses letters, syllables, pronunciation, divisions of the letters, vowels, consonants and passes on to general rules of pronunciation. He again emphasises the fact that all Frenchmen do not speak French well, and discusses whether Frenchmen speak faster than Englishmen. He deals with the following points :

"It is impossible to learn to speak true French without rules.

"The Difference there is amongst Frenchmen in purity of speech.

"The Difference there is between those who learn French in France and in England.

"The Difference there is between true French and the Law French."

---

[1] Milton says : " To smatter Latin with an English mouth is as ill a hearing as Law French."

He gives familiar " speeches " regarding kindred, time, number, day, week, month, weather, seasons, meat and drink, to buy and sell ; the tailor, shoemaker, barber ; play, music, night and going to bed, rising of men, rising of women, the inn, travelling.

It is to be noted that throughout the book all observations on language teaching and learning are in English on one side of the open book, and in French on the other. De la Mothe promises a *French Tutor* to follow his Alphabet, to teach the parts of speech and syntax. " The promise is great but the performance shall not be less." His *French Tutor* is unknown. The title of *Alphabet* is no doubt borrowed from the elementary text-books for Latin, Greek, Hebrew, etc. A more pretentious-sounding but less valuable book is that of :

1605. Peter Erondell.

> *The French Garden : for English Ladyes and Gentle-women to walke in. Or, A sommer dayes labour. Being an instruction for the attayning unto the knowledge of the French Tongue : wherein for the practise thereof are framed thirteene Dialogues in French and English, concerning divers matters from the rising in the morning till Bed-time. Also the Historie of the Centurion mencioned in the Gospell : in French verses. Which is an easier and shorter Methode than hath been yet set forth, to bring the lovers of the French tongue to the perfection of the same. By Peter Erondell, Professor of the same Language.* London, 1605.

1604. J. Sanford.

> *Le Guichet Francois, sive Janicula et Brevis Introductio ad Linguam Gallicam.* (Oxford, 1604.)

This was written in Latin and was followed in 1605 by *A briefe extract of the former (Latin) Grammer, done into English for the easier instruction of the learner.*

1611. In this year appeared Randle Cotgrave's *Dictionary of the French and English Tongues.*

. . . (Another Edition.) *Whereunto is also annexed a . . . Dictionarie of the English; set before the French,* by R. S(herwood) L(ondoner). 1632, fol.

. . . (Another Edition.) *Whereunto are added the animadversions and supplements of J. Howell.* London, 1650, fol. 1660, 1672–73, fol.

The following book appeared in 1679 :

A dictionary of barbarous French ; or a collection . . . of obsolete, provincial, mis-spelt and made words in French taken out of Cotgrave's Dictionary, with some additions. By G. Miege. Lond. 4to.

1625. John Wodroephe.
The Marrow of the French Tongue. 2nd ed. 1625.

1634. C. Maupas.
A French Grammar and Syntax, containing most exact and certain rules for the pronunciation, orthography, construction, and use of the French Language. . . . Translated by W. A(ufield). 1634.

Maupas, who was a native of Blois, was regarded by Robert Sherwood " as the learnedest and most expert teacher " of French of the time, and Sherwood acknowledges that his own book was founded on that of Maupas and his own experience.

1634. Robert Sherwood.
The French Tutour : By way of Grammer exactly and fully teaching all the most necessary rules for the attaining of the French tongue. 2nd ed. 1634.

ROBERT SHERWOOD'S FRENCH SCHOOL

Sherwood's School was in S. Sepulchre's Church-yard. The second dialogue on the Exercises of Nobility and Gentry includes graceful carriage, dancing, dice and card playing, fencing and hand-ling weapons, riding horse, vaulting, mathematics (especially arithmetic), cosmography, astrology and geography, military art, hunting, hawking.

1652.
The True Advancement of the French Tongue. By Claudius Mauger, late Professor of the French Tongue at Blois, and now teacher of the said Tongue here in London, 1652.

Dedicated to Mrs. Margaret Kelvert, of whom he says : "I have now a good while since had the happi-ness to be called by you to teach those many gallant young gentle women who are of the most noble families of England, that are committed to your safe, prudent and religious education." Mauger says : "The intestine distempers forced me to quit Blois where I had the honour to instruct the flower of all Europe in the French Tongue." Mauger names as many as forty-three of his lady pupils. He asserts that his own town Blois is regarded as purest in pro-nunciation and phrase. In one dialogue an inter-locutor says : " I will go on Sunday to the French Church." The other replies : " You shall do well."

In another dialogue :

"Is it requisite that he be a good scholar that teaches the French tongue ? "

"He cannot possibly do it otherwise."

"What do you give your French Master a month ? "

" Forty shillings, he comes three times a week."

"How does he teach you ? "

"He teaches me to read the language, to tell a story in French, and to pronounce it right."

In one of the dialogues a daughter conversing with her father states that she learns at school reading, writing, singing, dancing, speaking French and Italian. The question is asked :

" Do you know a good and excellent writer (i.e. teacher of writing) ? "

and answered :

" I know a young man of Blois named Monsr. Festeau who excelleth in this Art."

Mr. Mauger's French Grammar, second edition, 1656, has in the Preface : " I have therefore conformed myself to the most skilful writers and will give you nothing but what they all approve, and the other masters of the languages ; amongst the which I reckon Master Penson and Master Festeau who are good masters and many others."

The elements of French Grammar are given in Latin (48 pp.) as well as in English. There is a chapter of Anglicisms " to be avoided," such as Qu'est es vous en faisant, for, What are you doing ? There is also a collection of French phrases and dialogues on the state of France, ecclesiastical, civil, and military, " as it flourishes under King Louis XIV."

1676.

Claudius Mauger's French and English Letters upon all subjects, mean and sublime. 2nd edition, 1676.

" You may hear of the authour at Master Keyser's, a Dutch gentleman and picture-drawer in Long Acre, between the Maidenhead and Three Tuns Tavern, or in Shandors [i.e. Chandos] Street over against the Three Elms at Master St. André, where he lives now."

II. *The Religious Unity of English and French Protestants.*

Between 1555–8, the English theologians who fled from the Smithfield fires which Queen Mary threatened to all who would not conform to the Roman Catholic faith, found refuge, sooner, or later at Geneva. This brought about a *rapprochement* between the English and French Protestants, which had great consequences in the reign of Queen Elizabeth. In Scotland the knowledge of the French language and the interchange of students and visitors was closer than in England, and the French language was systematically taught and learned there to a greater extent than in England.[1] Still, the hospitable reception of the English exiles brought about an attitude of good-will and sympathy which eventually led to a learning of French by English Protestants, partly, no doubt to read French theology and other serious Huguenot works. This tendency was further quickened when after the Massacre of St. Bartholomew, Queen Elizabeth permitted the French refugees to make their home in England, they settled in London, in Norwich, in Canterbury and other places where they were received with the reciprocity of the welcome which the English Protestants in their time of trouble had received at Geneva and elsewhere. Nor should it be overlooked that the Protestant movement amongst

---

[1] M. Michel has written a most comprehensive book in two volumes on *Les Ecossais en France, et les Français en Ecosse.*

French speaking people had not only intensified the love of the French for their own language, but had largely developed the resources and literary exercise of the language itself, there had been earlier writers advocating the use of the vernacular French in teaching French youth, but no influences had been so profound in producing an interest in French as compared with Latin, than Huguenot writers such as Corderius's *De corrupti sermonis emendatione Libellus*, 1530, and no man did more than Calvin himself to build up a standard of French in the translation of his Latin *Institutio Christianae Religionis* (Basle 1535–6) into French as the *Institution Chretienne* in 1541. Professor Saintsbury, with his avowed prejudice against Calvin, regards this work as probably " the greatest literary book of the early Reformation." In its raising of French as an instrument of expression he regards it as not seldom " approaching the still greater achievement of Rabelais himself." Apart from comparisons, Calvin and his followers brought all their powers— and they were highly intellectual powers—to educating the French to the recognition of a difficult theological standpoint, and brought the language itself through a gymnastic of exercise which largely helped to mould it into its recognised position as an instrument of the clearest and most logical kind for the expression of thought. For in spite of the unique position of Latin in France as well as elsewhere, where the propaganda of theology was concerned, it became practically necessary to use the mother-tongue in the propaganda of religion—

hence Calvin's translation. This development, to which the French Protestants largely contributed, constituted a claim on foreign Protestants for the study of French. This was probably unconsciously recognised, in an indirect way, as the reason given by some in England for its study, viz. that the " best books " were written in French. Moreover, the scholarly and noble followers of Calvin gave French in the eyes of English Protestants a *prestige* which attracted attention to their language. Of the English translation of Calvin's *Institutes* in the British Museum there are editions in 1561, 1562, 1574, 1578, 1587, 1611, 1634. The translator was Thomas Norton. It is to be noted that Thomas Norton was the translator of Alexander Nowell's Catechism. This is another illustration of the inter-relations of English and French Protestants, for Nowell's was the authorised larger Catechism of the English Church, and the *Institution of Christian Religion* was the distinctive document of Calvin's theology.

It is to be remembered that the Genevan Bible was the chief Bible of the English in the time of Queen Elizabeth. That is an objective sign of the common ground between English Protestantism and the Genevan theological system of Calvin. As Mr. G. W. Child [1] has shown " almost all the prominent Elizabethan bishops and divines were Zwinglian or Calvinist, and were at much pains to declare themselves at one with the leading Swiss Reformers,

---

[1] In his too little known *Church and State under the Tudors*, 1890.

especially with Bullinger and Peter Martyr." The number of translations into English of religious and theological works by the Swiss and French Protestants shows an incoming interest in the subject-matters of French writers from the religious side, which had a strong influence in stimulating interest in the French language. This, again, is typified in the translations of foreign Catechisms, and the widespread use in England of the *Dialogues* of Corderius and Castellion, which, introduced for the purpose of acquiring Latin—and their educational excellence was undoubted—were equally acceptable to the English Protestant schoolmasters and parents, for the religious teaching embodied in them. We have seen, too, that it is not improbable that the Elizabethan and later French teachers engaged in the teaching of the nobility and men of commerce, were Huguenot refugees.

Nor is there lacking evidence that instruction in French was carried on in England by the schoolmasters by profession whom the Huguenots brought with them. Apparently in 1622, there were sixteen foreign Protestant schoolmasters in London, and as Messrs. R. E. G. Kirk and E. F. Kirk say in their *Returns of Aliens in London*,[1] " The . . . schoolmasters must have been in excess of the demand created by the strangers." At Canterbury the Walloons were granted the crypt of the Cathedral for their services and for their school. In a petition to the Town Council of Canterbury, 1567, the refugees ask

---

[1] *Publications of the Huguenot Society*, 1900.

for authorisation for their schoolmaster to instruct
their children " as well as those who would wish to
learn the French language." And even in the period,
1785–1816, a scholar of the King's School, Canterbury, writes : " We could learn French privately
as several did. . . . I sought the aid of M. Miette,
one of the French refugee congregation." [1]

The bonds of unity of faith existing between the
English and French Protestants survived even the
differences within the English Church itself. In
other words, the sectaries and dissentients from the
Church of England in the time of the Commonwealth were impressed in most cases with the
fascination of the name of Calvin, as had been the
Elizabethans, Cartwright, Whitgift and the rest.
The supposition that the Church of England was
distinguished by its intermediate position between
Rome and Geneva, however correspondent to fact
in details of organisation, did not prevent the English
and French Protestants from closer approximations
in the essentials of doctrine. A good Churchman
and royalist like Sir Ralph Verney, an exile from
England by the Commonwealth troubles, could take
his family to one of the stoutest of French Protestant
centres, accept the French pastors, without a recognition of distance or difference, and could proceed
to have his children educated through the French
language. He writes to his friends, giving them advice
and details on the subject of their children being

---

[1] Woodruff and Cape : *History of the King's School,
Canterbury*, p. 179.

sent to France, for the same purpose. Sir Ralph says of France, enthusiastically : " For that's the fittest place in the world to breed up youth." Sometimes boys were sent with tutors, to live for some months in a town, to learn the language ; sometimes they were boarders in private families, especially with Protestant pastors. Sometimes a boy educated abroad in a good French family would have a tutor in Latin and Greek, together with specialists for mathematics, dancing, fencing, riding, music, modern languages. Sir Ralph Verney tells one correspondent that if all is done fittingly the total expense is about £200 a year, all told. Of the years 1650–54, Sir Ralph Verney says of his son Edmund[1] : " His breeding costs me more than you imagine and I would save money in anything but that." The tutor reports of the boy, Mun [i.e. Edmund], aged eleven : " Il faict merveile. . . . Je luy raconte une histoire en Français, il me la rend (ex tempore) en Latin." Lady Verney writes on this subject, dealing with the period about 1645–6 : " At this moment of intolerance in England and before the Revocation of the Edict of Nantes there was more religious freedom to be found in France, one reason perhaps why English families were sending boys abroad for education." Rouen is " very unfit " for the purpose, wrote Sir Ralph, in answer to an inquiry about a boys' school, for " there most men speak worse French than the poor people do English at [in] Northumberland, and there are no Protestant

---

[1] *Memoirs of the Verney Family,* vol. iii, chap. iii,

masters allowed to keep a school here. . . . There are divers Universities at Sedan, Saumur and Geneva and other fine places, at no unreasonable rate, and not only Protestant Schoolmasters, but whole colleges of Protestants. Mr. Testard, the Protestant pastor at Blois, takes pupils."[1] Sir Ralph and his family were at Blois, a town renowned for the purity of the French there spoken. As for boys, so too for girls, a training in French began to be considered as desirable by Puritan families. To quote again from Sir Ralph Verney, who, in 1652, wrote to a young girl in England : " In French you cannot be too cunning for that language affords many admirable books [2] fit for you as romances, plays, poetry, stories of illustrious (not learned) women, receipts for preserving, making creams, and all sorts of cookeries, ordering your gardens and in brief all manner of good housewifery."[3]

The fact is that Puritan household education was not only strictly religious but was also guided by enlightened studies in various directions, and not least in the subject of foreign languages. The training of Milton's daughters in Latin, Italian and French is a typical instance of the usage of the best families. Mrs. Lucy Hutchinson says : " I was taught, by my nurse, a Frenchwoman, to speak French and English. About seven years of age I began with private tutors in languages." Another

---

[1] *Memoirs of the Verney Family,* vol. ii, 231.

[2] Cf. Mrs. Makin, p. 420 *supra,*

[3] *Memoirs of the Verney Family,* vol. iii, p. 74.

441

instance will directly illustrate the French Protestant influence, in inducing the learning of French by English Puritans.   Mrs. Elizabeth Bury, born 1644, " diverted herself with philology, philosophy, history, ancient and modern ; sometimes with music, vocal and instrumental ; sometimes with heraldry, globes and mathematics ; sometimes with learning the French tongue (*chiefly for conversation with French refugees to whom she was an uncommon benefactress*), but especially in perfecting herself in Hebrew ; which, by long application and practice, she had rendered so familiar and easy to her, as frequently to quote the original in common conversation, when the true meaning of some particular texts of scripture depended on it."

CHAPTER XII

TEACHING OF MODERN LANGUAGES

II. ITALIAN

It has already been stated that the predominance of the study in England of French over other foreign languages did not declare itself so markedly in the earlier Tudor as in the later period, and that a powerful factor in the change of position of French was developed in the approximation of English Puritanism to French Calvinism. It is not usually recognised [1] that the same factor was present, in a considerable degree, even in the Italian influence in England and in the learning of the Italian language. The period of its influence in this respect was reversed. The religious influence of Italy was in the

---

[1] Though it is worked out by Mr. Lewis Einstein, in his *Italian Renaissance in England*, a work to which I am indebted for some of the facts of this section. The introduction of Italian ecclesiastics into English posts, e.g. the Italian Bishops of Worcester in the sixteenth century (*see* Creighton : *Hist. Essays*, pp. 202–235) had no significance educationally for the Italian language in England. Nor did the Lombard merchants in the thirteenth century affect the position of the Italian language as a subject of teaching. Italians working at the Mint or the workmen under Giacopo Acontio, engaged in reclaiming the Plumstead marshes, left no linguistic interests behind. (On these incomings of the Italians into England *see* Cunningham : *Alien Immigrants*, pp. 116, 181.) The Italian literary influence on Chaucer, of course, was real and deep, but even this was not continuous in its tradition up to the Italian revival of the Tudor Period.

time of the early Tudors, whilst that of France on England, as we have seen, came later.

Colet's lectures on 1 Corinthians and 1 Romans at Oxford were influenced by his residence in Italy 1493–6. The Italian Humanists in their collecting of materials and weighing of evidence on literary matters, together with their openness of criticism on scriptural matters, gave an impetus to Colet on one side, whilst the fiery zeal and singleness of aim of Savonarola and the austere and profound piety of St. Francis and his followers, and the stories of other saints of Italy no doubt attracted Colet. In short he learned the lesson of *going to the sources*, to the primitive church for his theology. He also was enthralled in Neo-Platonism of Ficino and Pico.

This appeal to sources was essentially the idea which, logically, brought the Northern Renascence to the examination of the Scriptures, and the necessity for their dissemination. In this sense, Italy was first in the field in the Reformation. Nor was Italy without its early religious Reformers, as in the case of Savonarola and Baptista Spagnuoli Mantuanus. Indeed, at one time Calvin himself turned his eyes hopefully towards Italy as a centre of Protestant propaganda, for when Renée, the daughter of Louis XII of France, in 1528, married Ercole II, Duke of Ferrara, Ferrara became in the course of years, under Renée, a Mecca for Protestant refugees, Calvin himself visiting it, though in disguise. Clement Marot, the Huguenot translator of the Psalms, whose translated work became the great spiritual song-book of France, also visited Ferrara.

Renée's Court is associated with the Protestantism of Olympia Morata, and Vittoria Colonna. Olympia's writings were collected and were dedicated by a well-known Protestant, Celio Curione, to Queen Elizabeth of England. Dr. Sandys mentions the Italian poet, Marcantonio Flaminio, who frequented the Court of Ferrara, who speaks (in Latin) of distant Britain as likely to do honour to the Latin muses and " foretells that even in the *New World* the Latin poets will be studied by the western Nations." [1] But Renée, however sympathetic with Protestantism, dared not openly unfurl the standard of Calvinism, and in her fear of the powers of the Roman Church and the civil authorities, dared not, in the end, personally incur the risks and horror of the taint of loyalty to heretical opinions.

The establishment of the Inquisition in Italy in 1542, is a sign that Protestantism had made itself felt. It was also the cause of the departure of some of the marked champions of the Protestant cause. Some of these refugees made their way to England, and found a welcome, years before the arrival of the Huguenot refugees. To take two instances, Bernardino Ochino of Siena, and Peter Martyr Vermigli arrived in England in 1547. Ochino had been Vicar-General of the Capuchins. Cranmer secured for Ochino a crown pension, and he was appointed minister of the (Protestant) Italian Church in London. Ochino was a preacher of great eloquence. His language was, of course, Italian. Six of his sermons on the

---

[1] Sandys : *Harvard Lectures on Revival of Learning*, p. 82.

use of the Scriptures for attaining a knowledge of God were translated, with the hope that " his native language thereby may be made ours." Lady Anne Cooke (Coke [1]) translated twenty-five sermons by Ochino, " now an exile in this life for the faithful testimony of Jesus Christ." The sermons attracted great attention and their writer was held in high esteem. He was made Prebendary of Canterbury in 1548. On the accession of Queen Mary in 1553, he went as an exile from his adopted country of England, and was for a time pastor at Zurich, and then drifted away from his connexion with England.

Peter Martyr Vermigli, in 1547, had accompanied Ochino to England, also on Cranmer's invitation. He is more closely connected with English theological development. He, too, was granted a crown pension and was made Regius Professor of Divinity at Oxford, 1548, and was first Canon of Christ Church, 1551. But more than this, Peter Martyr was one of the four who drew up the *Reformatio Legum Ecclesiasticarum*, and Cranmer conferred with him in the various steps of the Reformation. There were a number of translations of Peter Martyr's works, chiefly from the Italian. One of his works was translated by Nicholas Udall. He was accounted one of the stalwarts of Protestantism in England. He, too, left England in 1553, and never returned.

Mr. Einstein gives the names of other Italians who came to England for the sake of religious liberty, and concludes that " England then became a home

---

[1] The daughter of Sir Anthony Coke.

and refuge for Italian reformers, just as in the nineteenth century it was one for political refugees." This is at least indicated by the establishment of the (Protestant) Italian Church in London, to which at one time, as already said, Ochino ministered. In 1550 Michel Angelo Florio became minister of this church. He also engaged in the work of teaching Italian. Here again, we see the connexion of Protestant refugees with the work of language-teaching, though it may be repeated that the Italian Protestant influence was earlier than that of the Huguenots. The Italian refugee influence, however, gave way to that of the Huguenot refugee, after the reign of Queen Mary had drawn the English bonds tighter to Calvin and his Geneva. But we have seen that the Italian Church had given the first distinct public teacher of a modern language to London, before the days of Claude Holyband, chief of the Huguenot pioneers of schools for teaching French in England.

Michel Angelo Florio, pastor and teacher [1] published apparently in London, a Catechism and a life of Lady Jane Grey. [2] The Italian Church, of which

---

[1] Einstein mentions an MS. in Cambridge University Library by M. A. Florio : *Regole della Lingua Toscana* (never published).

[2] *Catechismo, cioe forma breve per amaestrare i fanciulli Tradotta di Latino in lingua Thoscana* (1553 ?).

Historia de la vita e de la morte de l'illustriss. Signora G. Graia, gia Regina eletta e publicata d'Inghilterra ; e de le cose accadute in quel regno dopo la morte del re Edoardo VI. Nella quale secondo le divine Scriture se tratta dei principali articoli de la religione Christiana. . . . Lettere e ragionamenti de la Signora G. Graia, 1607.

Florio was pastor, is referred to in Ascham's *Schole-master*. " Men Italianated abroad cannot abide our godly Italian Church at home : they be not of that Parish, they be not of that fellowship : they like not the preacher : they hear not his sermons. Except sometimes for company, they come thither *to hear the Italian tongue naturally spoken, not to hear God's doctrine truly preached.*"   Roger Ascham, sound Protestant as he was, found the Italian Church in London commendable for its doctrine, and the agreement in religion no doubt was a ground of satisfaction for ladies, who, like Lady Anne Coke, liked Italian and professed Protestantism. The elements for still further development of Italian in London were present when the Marian persecution drove away from England, at any rate, the prominent members of the Italian Church in London, along with English Protestants, and those who remained probably relapsed into the old Roman faith.

It was M. A. Florio's son who established the teaching of the Italian language in England. John Florio entered Magdalen College, Oxford, in 1581. It is probable that his earlier education had been abroad, away from Mary I's England. It is certain that he combined a sound knowledge of Italian, French and English, and was an accomplished propagandist of linguistic knowledge. Florio stands out as the leading Italian teacher as Cotgrave was later the leading French teacher in England. Florio is said to have taught modern languages, especially Italian, when at Oxford. Afterwards, he was in the service of Lord Southampton. He married the daughter of Samuel Daniel the poet. He was teacher of languages to the young Prince Henry (son of James I) and then private secretary to Queen Anne (wife of James I). Florio was the translator into English of Montaigne's Essays in 1603. His books of instruction in Italian are :

> *First Fruites, which yeelde familiar speech, merie proverbes, wittie sentences, and golden sayings, also a perfect Introduction to the Italian and English tongues.* London, 1578.
>
> *Second frutes to be gathered of twelve Trees of divers but delightsome tastes to the tongues of Italian and Englishmen.* To which is annexed his *Gardine of Recreation, yeelding six thousand Italian Proverbs.* Ital. and Eng. *London,* 1591.

The latter part was published alone in Italian as :

> *Giardino di Recreatione nel quale crescono fronde, fiori, e frutti, vaghe, leggiadri, a soave, sotto nome di sei mila, Proverbii, e piacevoli riboboli Italiani, colti e scelti da Giovanni Florio.* T. Woodcock, Londra, 1591.

The " familiar speech " introduces dialogues. He tenders advice that English children should learn modern languages and deprecates the custom that " when they have learned two words of Spanish, three words of French, and four words of Italian, they think they have enough ; they will study no more." And, again, what a shame it is, that an Englishman " in the company of strangers, should be unable to speak to them and should then stand dumb, mocked of them and despised of all. What a reproach to his parents ; what a loss to him." [1] The object of

---

[1] Quoted by Mr. Einstein from one of the Dialogues in Florio's *First Fruites.*

the collection of proverbs was to facilitate colloquial and idiomatic speech. Moreover, proverbs brought modern languages into line with the classical languages, for text-books in the latter frequently included apophthegms, and adages. It was fitting that the classical equipment of phraseological compilations should have its analogue in the phrase-books of Italian and French. Proverbs supplied finished examples, and the proverb-literature itself became a cult, the best instance of which in English was John Ray's famous collection. [1]

But Florio's crowning work as an Italian teacher was his Italian Dictionary :

> *A Worlde of Wordes : a most copious and exact Dictionarie in Italian and English, Collected by John Florio.* Lond. 1598.

And in 1611 the second edition entitled : *Queen Anna's New World of Words.*[2] The third edition was revised by Giovanni Torriano and published in 1659 as *Vocabolario Italiano e Inglese,* adding an English-Italian part to the Italian-English.

In this work Florio, as he says himself, attempted to do for Italian what Sir Thomas Elyot and Bishop Cooper had done for Latin and what the Estiennes (the Stephani) had done for Greek (i.e. the Graeco-Latin Dictionary), and he performed his task successfully.

---

[1] *Collection of English Proverbs,* Cambridge, 1670.

[2] This is a " much augmented edition whereunto are added certain necessary rules and short observations for the Italian tongue " (over 500 folio pages).

To the influence of Florio's Italian Proverbs was probably due Charles Merbury's :

> Brief Discourse of Royal Monarchy . . . *Whereunto is added by the same . . . a Collection of Italian Proverbs.* T. Vautrollier, London, 1581.

Besides enlarging Florio's *World of Words*, Torriano also wrote :

1640.

> *The Italian Tutor, or a new Italian Grammar, to which is annexed a display of the Monosyllabic Particles of the language, by way of alphabet. As also, certain dialogues made up of Italianisms or Niceties of the Language with the English to them.* 2 parts. London, 1640.

1649.

> *Select Italian Proverbs : The most significant, very usefull for Travellers, and such as desire that language. The same newly made to speak English, and the obscurest places with Notes, illustrated, useful for such as happily aim not at the Language, yet would see the genius of the Nation.* By Gio. Torriano, 1649.

1657.

> *Della Lingua Toscana-Romana. Or, an Introduction to the Italian Tongue. Containing such grounds as are most immediately useful and necessary for the speedy and easie attaining of the same.* Lond. 1657

(From W. C. Hazlitt's *Collections*.)

When Sir Ralph Verney sought an English school for his son, he found one which satisfied him —a private school at Kensington, kept by Mr. Turberville. This gentleman is described as " a very good schoolmaster." We have seen that the boy Verney had learned his French at Blois, and that he showed progress in that language is a tribute to Mr. Turberville's knowledge of French. Mr. Turberville is stated to have been " master " of Italian [1] also. This is the only instance I know of the school teaching of Italian in a boys' school, though the language was probably taught in the private girls' school of Mrs. Makin, in the time of the Commonwealth. But there is no doubt that, after the Restoration, the pre-eminence of French as modern language was established in those schools where a modern language found a footing. The Puritans, however, of the seventeenth century did not always leave out Italian from their sympathies. Milton,[2] in dealing with prosody, requires his student to know more than what is ordinarily contained in the rudiments of grammar-teaching. He desires them to learn " that sublime Art which in Aristotle's *Poetics*, in Horace, and in the *Italian Commentaries of Castelvetro, Tasso, Mazzoni* and others, teaches what the laws are of a true Epic poem, what of a Dramatic, what of a Lyric, what Decorum is, which is the grand masterpiece to

---

[1] The curriculum apparently consisted of French, Italian, Greek, Latin and music. Amongst the pupils were two sons of the Vicar of Kensington and a son of Baron Steele.

[2] Milton himself, in the Latin poem already referred to (p. 421 n.), speaks of his father as advising him to learn (as well as French) " the speech which the new Italian, attesting the barbarian inroads by his diction, pours forth from his degenerate mouth." There is little doubt, however, of Milton's preference for Italian over French.

observe." Milton had previously suggested that the Italian language " might have easily been learned at any odd hour." It is quite clear that this would not be through a grammar text-book method of learning.

It is not without interest to notice that Thomas Farnaby in his lists of Emblem-books to which he refers boys in the *Index Rhetoricus*, includes one by Paulus Maccius, published at Bologna in 1628.

The *Emblemata* of Maccius contains eighty-one interesting engravings of the emblematic order with descriptive text in Latin and Italian verse. Farnaby can hardly have expected pupils to read Italian, and yet the presence of such books in the school to some extent explains Milton's suggestion of the picking up of Italian at odd hours. The engravings are very finely executed. The subjects are attractive, at any rate in the illustrations. For instance, Emblem No. XLVII shows three boys spinning a top, with the motto : " Vir fortis stat motu."

Or to take a more difficult emblem. Emblem LXXII has the Latin : " Jungendam eloquentiae probitatem. Arist. Rhet." The engraving represents the Italian *pazzo colla spada*. Underneath is written :

" Che l'huomo eloquente deve esser buono."

On the next page to the engraving are short quotations in Latin from St. Augustine, Statius, Juvenal, Quintilian, bearing upon the subject of the emblem.

MODERN SUBJECTS IN ENGLISH SCHOOLS

The following Italian verses explain the significance of the engraved emblem:[1]

> "S'avvien, c'huom giusto, e di virtute amante
> De l'eloquenza il nobil don posseda,
> Virtù non è, che l'eloquenza ecceda.
> Ma se si trouvi in pessimo Oratore,
> Non è cosa peggiore.
> Col ferro ignudo in mano
> Talhor vedesti furiar l'insano ?
> Pensa in lingua perversa egual furore.
> Ma te ciascuno ammira
> Saggio Annibal, che placido, e facondo,
> Sei qual puro nel cor, nel dir giocondo."

The corresponding Latin verses are :

> "Insigni pietate viro, virtutis amanti
> Si des, flexanimo nil prius eloquio.
> Moribus at pravo, atq : in honestae crimine vitae
> Si des, nil ipso nequius eloquio.
> Vidisti gladio insanum saevire micanti ?
> Impia, dic, saevit lingua furore pari.
> Hinc te miramur, puro quod pectore mirus
> Annibal, es miro dulcis ab eloquio."

---

[1] The late Mr. Henry Green said : " The Emblem writers of the sixteenth century and previously made use chiefly of the Latin, Italian, and French languages." (*Shakespere and the Emblem Writers*, 1870.) Green sketches the history of Emblem-book literature up to 1616 A.D., and gives copious quotations to show that Shakespere had diligently studied foreign Emblem-books. Green divides the subject-matter of Emblems into Historic, Heraldic, Mythological, Fabulous, Proverbial, Emblems, together with Emblems from Nature, and particularly animals (*see* pp. 197–8 *supra*), Emblems from Poetic Ideas and Moral and Æsthetic Emblems. Whitney, in his *Choice of Emblems*, 1586, dedicates an Emblem to William Malim (1561–1571, Head Master of Eton ; 1573–1581, Head Master of St. Paul's) ; and to the "very learned " Stephen Limbert, Head Master of Norwich School (1570–1602). He also dedicates an Emblem to the youth at the Grammar School of Audlem in Cheshire.

It does not seem improbable that emblem-books were used for learning Italian. At any rate, the Italians produced delightful books of emblems, and if the Italian in those books were sufficiently modern, there might even to-day be produced from them an attractive elementary Italian reading book, if English were substituted for Latin, or supplied in those cases in which in the emblem-books only Italian is given.

After his Italian visit of 1638 Milton wrote a long letter in Latin to Benedetto Buommattei, who was compiling a treatise of Tuscan Grammar. He says : " With other authorities in your tongue hitherto the intention seems to have been to satisfy only their own countrymen, without care for us. In my opinion they would have consulted both their own fame and the glory of the Italian tongue much more certainly had they so delivered their precepts *as if it concerned all mankind to acquire the knowledge of that language*, yet so far as has depended on them, you Italians might seem to regard nothing beyond the bounds of the Alps."

Milton's daughter Deborah, it will be remembered, could read Italian, Spanish and French. There was a succession of linguistic women outside of the courtier class (women were not amongst the travellers to Italy), such as Elizabeth Lucar, born in 1510, who was " complete mistress " of the Latin, Italian, and Spanish languages ; Elizabeth Legge,[1] born 1580, and Catharine Fowler (Mrs. Phillips),[2] born

---

[1] Ballard : *Memoirs of English Ladies*, 1775, p. 25.
[2] *Ibid.*, p. 243.

1631, the " matchless " Orinda. The Italian language seems, too, later on, to have found a place in the best of the girls' private schools. Thus, throughout the time of the Tudors and in the Stuart period, up to the Commonwealth, there had been sympathetic relations on the Protestant side between the two countries, which helped to maintain the learning of Italian in England. When the great trouble of the Protestants of Piedmont came, the relations between Puritan England and Italian Protestantism intensified the exigencies of political interference, and reached a climax.

" In the spring of **1655**," says Lord Morley, of Blackburn, "the massacre of the Protestants in the Piedmontese valleys stirred a wave of passion in England that still vibrates in Milton's sonnet, and that Cromwell's impressive energy forced on Europe." [1] It is not perhaps generally known that afterwards Cromwell had no difficulty in bringing the Council of State to make the following grants to Piedmont : [2]

To the chief schoolmaster of the valley	£20
To the ten under-schoolmasters of the valleys	£6
And to the three under-schoolmasters in Perosa Valley	£3
Per annum	£89

In addition, an annual grant of £350 was made to ministers ; and to a physician and surgeon, £35 ; to students in divinity and physics, £40.

Court and Travellers. In the opinion of Castiglione, in *Il Cortegiano* (over the writing of which he had

---

[1] *Oliver Cromwell*, p. 441.
[2] *Cal. State Papers. Dom. Series.* May 18, 1658.

spent twenty years), published at Venice in 1528, translated into English by Sir Thomas Hoby in 1561, the courtier " should be more than indifferently well seen in learning in the Latin and Greek tongues," but in addition, he is to be provided with Italian, French and Spanish.

This is an important pronouncement, for it is the recognition of the value of foreign languages, as supplementary to the knowledge of Latin and Greek. Castiglione presents to his readers the ideal of a gentleman and a scholar. His demands, therefore, are great, because he wishes to forego nothing of what is desirable in the one or the other. He is a contemporary of Erasmus, and wide as are the ideals of Erasmus, Castiglione is still more comprehensive. Erasmus wanted Latin to be the universal language. Castiglione was a practical man of the world, and as such he recognises facts as they are. Different Courts speak different languages. The courtier, in his travels, as a dictate of politeness, as far as possible should present himself to others with all respect to *their* outlook, with due regard to *their* customs, manners, and naturally, since *their* language is part of their order of things, he should speak to them in it. This point of view tends to the diffusion of a knowledge of the languages of important nations, and, therefore, Castiglione's claim to recognition as an advocate, particularly on the side of a speaking knowledge of modern languages, is undeniably great.

For Castiglione's *Courtier* is one of the most influential books of the sixteenth century, influential in the extent of its circulation in Italy, France, Spain and England, being translated into the vernacular of those countries as well as into Latin, finding a passport amongst nobles and scholars everywhere. The tri-lingual form of *The Courtier* (Italian, French, English), produced by Sir Thomas Hoby (1588), is as significant from the educational advance of modern languages, as it is for the interest of the subject-matter of the Courtiers' Education in manners.

For generations *The Courtier* was, so to say, the classic of the courtier's life. It was a book for which it was worth while for the nobleman to learn Italian. Probably many have learned what they knew of Italian from its perusal. At any rate, in 1727, A. P. Castiglione, who proudly boasted himself as of the same family, published in London a text with Italian and English side by side.

Roger Ascham, although the protagonist of those who hated the Italianate Englishman, says in the *Scholemaster* (1570) : " To join learning with comely exercises, Conte Balthasar Castiglione in his book, *Cortegiano*, doth trimly teach : which book, advisedly read, and diligently followed, *but one year at home in England*, would do a young gentleman more good, I wisse, than three years' travel abroad spent in Italy." [1] On the subject of physical exercises, all that Castiglione had to say fell on good ground in reaching England, for in the following centuries, the very exercises recommended by

---

[1] *See* Mayor's edition of Ascham's *Scholemaster*, p. 61.

Castiglione were the ambition of the young English noble, and many of them took care to have the training from Italians, who established themselves in London as trainers in horse-riding, in fencing, and in many other directions of the courtier's arts.

Italian naturally appealed to the courtier not only through Castiglione's book and the other Italian books of courtesy, but also through the knowledge of the various Courts of Italy which had become famous as centres of high breeding, such as Mantua, Urbino and Ferrara. As early as 1549, William Thomas, clerk of the Council to King Edward VI, published :

> *The historie of Italia ; a boke excedyng profitable to be redde ; Because it intreateth of the estate of many and divers common weales, how they [have] been and now be governed.* T. Berthelet. London, 1549, and in 1561.

" The avowed purpose of his *History of Italy*, written after five years of residence there, was to enable Englishmen to see how a nation had been enriched through peace and concord and made poor by strife. . . . Its real interest and merit lay in the fact of its being a guide to Italy. . . . It was unquestionably the best English account of any foreign nation written before the seventeenth century." [1]

The instances of English courtiers who learned Italian are numerous. Mr. Einstein mentions in King Henry VIII's Court, the King himself, Lord Rochford, Lord Morley, the Earl of Surrey, Earl of Wiltshire, Sir Thomas Wyatt, and the Princesses Mary

---

[1] Einstein, p. 118.

and Elizabeth. In Queen Elizabeth's Court : The Queen " delighted to speak to Italians, and her courtiers Burghley, Walsingham, Robert Cecil, the Earl of Rutland and Countess of Bedford, and the Earl of Leicester followed her example. Hubert Languet says in a letter to Sir Philip Sidney : [1] " It seems to me quite absurd that your countrymen should make such a point of speaking Italian well."

The following are text-books extant :

1550. William Thomas.
> *Principal Rules of the Italian Grammar, with a Dictionarie for the better understandynge of Boccace, Petrarcha, and Dante.* 1550, 1562, 1567.

Of the 1550 edition T. Berthelet was the publisher. This is interesting as an indication of some attention to the great Italian writers. William Thomas considered that Italian had as much ground for study as Latin and Greek, and might become in the early future as " plentiful " in literature as any of the other."

1578. David Rowland.
> *A comfortable ayde for schollers, full of variety of sentences, gathered out of an Italian author (intituled in that tongue, Specchio de la lingua Latina),* by D. Rowland. Lond. 1578.

In the preface Rowland says : " Once every one knew Latin, and from the Latin, Italian was learned, and now the Italian is as widely spread."

1575. Henry Granthan.
> *La Grammatica di M. S. Lentulo . . . da lui in Latina lingua scritta, e hora nella Italiana e Inglese tradotta da H. Granthan.* T. Vautrollier. 1575 and 1587.

---

[1] Einstein, p. 99.

This was translated by Henry Granthan as a text-book for the daughters of Lord Berkeley.

1575. Claude Holyband (or Desainliens or à Sancto Vinculo).
The pretie History of Arnalt and Lucenda (translated from B. Maraffi's original version of the Greek original, together with the Italian version) with certen Rules and Dialogues set foorth for the learner of th' Italian tong. By C. Holyband, etc. Lond, 1575.

In 1597, the order of contents is reversed on the title-page and the name of the book becomes :

The Italian Schoole-maister ; Contayning Rules for the perfect pronouncing of the Italian tongue ; with familiar speeches. . . . And a fine Tuscan historie called Arnalt and Lucenda, etc. London, 1597.

The change of title was probably made to bring it parallel to the same author's *French Schoolemaister*.[1]

1583. Claude Holyband.
Campo di Fior or else The Flourie Field of Foure Languages of M. Claudius Dessainliens, alias Holiband : For the furtherance of the learners of the Latine, French, English but chieflie of the Italian tongue (Vautrollier, 1583).

This contains a prefatory Latin poem by Richard Mulcaster, in which he highly praises Holyband and his book. He says :

> famam
> Anglia tam pleno personat ore tuam.
>
> Quanta etiam populi nostratis gloria, lingua
> Praeter maternam triplice posse loqui ?
> Quod quia nostra tuis sudoribus Anglia debet,
> Ingeminat laudes officiosa tuas.
> Macte igitur virtute tua, doctissime Claudi :
> Cui labor in nullo claudicat officio.

---

[1] *See* p. 426 *supra*.

Another point of interest is that Holyband takes the following dialogues from Vives [1] (though without acknowledgment), and renders them in parallel columns into the four languages named in the title-page : The Rising out of Bed in the Morning, The First Salutations of the Day, Conducting to School, Reading, Coming Home and Children's Plays, School Meals, Prattlers, The Journey on Horseback, Writing, Dressing, and The Morning Walk.

The first dialogue contains a contemporary account of the private Modern Languages School.

After the salutations, a father tells an interlocutor to bring his son to school to learn to speak Latin and French, for he has lost his time, and it were better for him to be unborn than untaught. The school is by the sign of the Lucrece in Paul's Church-yard. The teacher a Frenchman who teaches both the tongues, in the morning till eleven, the Latin tongue, and after dinner, the French. He is not like " some " who take money, and care not very much if their pupils profit or no. That is a kind of theft. The teacher's name is Claudius Holyband, a man with wife and children. His terms are a shilling a week, a crown a month, a real a quarter, forty shillings a year. Is not that dear ? Not if the son learneth well, but if he doesn't it would be dear to pay a groat a month. A boy in the school relates

---

[1] From the *Linguae Latinae exercitatio*, translated into English, by the present writer, under the title of *Tudor School-boy Life*, 1908. Holyband gives ten out of the twenty-five of Vives' Dialogues.

that Holyband reads Terence, Vergil, Horace, Tully's *Offices*, with others, Cato, *Sententiae pueriles*, accidence, grammar, according to their capacity. The boy who gives this information, adds : " As for me, I only learn French and to read and write." The boys provide their own satchel, books, ink, quills, and paper, inkhorn, penknife. The boys played at dice and cards for points, pins, cherry-stones, counters. The terms of complaint of a boy, rendered in French as well as English, are : " Ah, little fellow, you pravell, brabell, cakell, play the vice ! " Holyband administers corporal punishment with a rod. The boys leave at five o'clock in the afternoon, after evening prayers. In winter, they go home with lanterns and torches.

Holyband advises them how they may learn " without book " : " Rehearse after supper the lesson which you will learn to-morrow morning ; and read it six or seven times : then having said your prayers, sleep upon it : you shall see that to-morrow morning you will learn it easily and soon, having repeated the same but twice."

The above text-books belong to a type, i.e. they attempt either in the text or in the preface to approach Italian as on the same ground with, or as analogous to, Latin, as a subject of learning. This is well in keeping with the spirit of the greatest of the Italian books of the sixteenth century, the *Cortegiano* of Castiglione.

In connexion with the teaching of the Courtier and Noble class, it only remains to mention the institutions proposed for the teaching of Italian. Sir Nicholas Bacon would have French taught to the Queen's wards, but did not include Italian as a subject. On the other hand, Sir Humphrey Gilbert proposed Italian for Queen Elizabeth's Academy—the teacher to have £26 a year, with an usher at £10, the same as for French. Italian was on the same footing as French in Sir Francis Kynaston's proposed *Musaeum Minervae*, 1635, and in Sir Balthazar Gerbier's *Academy* in 1648.

Italy was *par excellence* the country for the young noble to visit and to study in his travels. The journeys of the Scholar-groups of Duke Humphrey, of Beckynton, of the early Oxford group, Free, Fleming, Tiptoft, etc., of Grocyn, Linacre and Colet, have little or no import for the study of Italian in England. The first description of Italy by an Englishman is in 1506, when Sir Richard Guylforde wrote his diary.[1] He was followed by Sir Richard Torkington in 1526. William Thomas, with his five years' residence in Italy, was the closest observer who had gone from England to Italy. He returned from Italy in 1548. Sir Thomas Hoby went in the same year to Italy and stayed there a year, at Venice and Padua, with occasional expeditions to Mantua and Ferrara, and then travelled to Florence and Rome. "I applied myself," he says, "as well to obtain the Italian tongue as to have a farther entrance into the Latin." When Italian travel became still more general as part of the noble

---

[1] Einstein, p. 115.

youth's educational equipment, it took the guise of dilettantism and worse. There was a danger that the youths brought up with the careful rigour of parents and tutors, especially those of Calvinistic mould, once free and on their own resources, would run to extremes. Italy, after the Renascence, was a decadent country in its morals and principles. To become " Italianated " in the bad sense was a calamity which experience proved to be only too probable.

There was another danger, scarcely to the Puritan mind to be counted second to that of frivolity and dissoluteness. There was the possibility that, absorbed in the fascinating atmosphere of Italy, and overwhelmed by the subtle machinations of the Roman priests, the young man might be perverted to Roman Catholicism. This was not merely an imaginary fear. The warning instance was that of Sir Tobie Matthew, whose name became a by-word of horror. Born of Puritan parents, he was educated at Christ Church, Oxford, from which he took his M.A. in 1597, was entered at Gray's Inn, and M.P. for Newport, Cornwall, and afterwards for St. Albans. For two years (1604–1606) he travelled in Italy, against the desire of his parents. He was converted to Roman Catholicism, and took priest's orders. At one time he was imprisoned for his religion ; at another he was sent to Spain to advise Charles and Buckingham, 1623. Later he was Secretary to Strafford in Ireland. Throughout he was mistrusted by the Puritans. He was the intimate friend of Lord Bacon, and translated

Bacon's Essays into Italian. He was regarded as the type of the Italianated Englishman. His identification with the interests of Charles I and Strafford, and his reciprocation of hatred of the Puritans, led his enemies to the verge of detestation of Italy on his account. But, on the other hand, with the young man of steady mind and character, " whom all the siren songs of Italy " could never entice from the path of self-control and self-development, Italy became a noble training ground. Such names occur at once : John Milton, the poet ; Henry Wotton, the ambassador ; and James Howell, the historiographer royal.

The preparation for Italian travel was an intellectual exercise. To read of the country, to gather " relations " or descriptions of parts of the country, to understand the theory and art of travel, to prepare for keeping a diary—were the methods adopted rather than to learn the language before starting. In the case of serious youths, to go on the Italian tour meant to learn the language there. Hence, the fewness of books of travel-talk and conversations for Italian published in England. Hence, too, the value of a good dictionary like that of Florio, if Italian were to be kept up on the return home.

Actual teaching of Italian and the text-books used were entirely outside of the school system, or even the University system.[1] But the Court and

---

[1] There are a few Italian poems in collections of Oxford Poems on events such as the Marriage of King James I's daughter Elizabeth.

literary influences of the time included some reflexion of the culture from Italian sources, and formed a vital part of the educational atmosphere of the Tudors, for such men as Sir Thomas Wyatt, the Earl of Surrey, Edmund Spenser, Sir Philip Sidney, and shall we not say also, in a certain measure, of William Shakespere ?

CHAPTER XIII

TEACHING OF MODERN LANGUAGES

III. Spanish

When Erasmus was asked to declare himself a German he said he was a Netherlander by birth, but if there were any pride of country in him he would wish " that each and every nation and city might go into the strife for Erasmus." This was the spirit of the Renascence. The whole world of learning was their country, and the limitation of citizenship in that commonwealth was bounded by neither time nor clime. Hence we cannot logically class Erasmus, in his culture, as a Dutchman, except in the accident of birth. If ever men broke through the narrowness of mere locality, it was the men of letters of the Age of the Renascence. In the case of Juan Luis Vives, it would be difficult to say that his native country was more influenced by his life and writings than France, Holland, and England. In the record of human achievement in the revival of learning Spain contributed no Spaniard of equal importance with Vives. As we passed by almost the whole of the names of the Italian and French Renascence writers in treating of Italian and French teaching, so we must pass by even Vives, as far as the *teaching of Spanish* is concerned, for he wrote all his books in Latin, and the translators into English of his works translated from that language.

Leaving on one side the Renascence learning of Spain, so especially centred in Vives, the next obvious source from which influence on the teaching of Spanish in England might be anticipated is the presence of Spaniards in the English Court, and the attraction of the English Court towards their language. This influence, however, was not nearly so great as might be expected. For there was no continuity of Spanish influence in the English Court. Henry II's daughter Eleanor had married Alphonso VII of Castile. Edward I married Eleanor of Castile. The Black Prince had fought in Spain on behalf of Pedro the Cruel. The daughter of John of Gaunt, Catharine, married the Spanish Crown-Prince Henry, and Prince Arthur, son of Henry VII, married Catharine of Aragon, and on Arthur's death Catharine was married to Henry VIII. But before the time of Catharine of Aragon, all these inter-relations of the Courts of England and Spain had been spasmodic. There was no permanent Spanish influence created and developed as a survival of its original cause. Every effort was made by Spain in Catharine's case, that there should be a strong Spanish interest and party created in the English Court. In some ways, this was apparently successful, for Catharine brought Spaniards to the Court, and English ambassadors and diplomats from time to time appeared at Madrid. But a snap came to the relations when Henry VIII put Catharine aside. The marriage of Philip of Spain with Mary seemed calculated to bring the Courts together again. But again there was failure. So, too, the effort to bring about a marriage between Philip and Elizabeth collapsed. All these connexions of the Courts of the two countries led to no organic setting in of communications. The need of Spanish in the English Court, as a language, was only occasional. It became no part of permanent political equipment. Spanish, therefore, was only at times necessary for the English courtier. The passage of Englishmen to Spain, and Spaniards to England, was intermittent. Even the amount of Spanish spoken at the English Court has been exaggerated.[1] For instance, Queen Mary I could not speak Spanish when Philip came over to England though she could understand what was said to her. Much of the knowledge of Spanish literature was due to Italian translations as Mr. Underhill points out.[2] Here may be expressed the opinion that the Englishmen who went to Spain, or who studied Spanish, were not of the same type as those who studied Italian. They were not learned men, nor was their interest in Spanish connected with culture, as was much more decidedly the case on the whole with the English learners of Italian. The aim was much rather political, commercial, and in the wider sense of the term, practical. When we

---

[1] See Mr. J. E. Underhill's *Spanish Literature in the time of the Tudors* p. 19. To this book, I am indebted for some of the facts in this chapter.

[2] As an instance may be quoted one of the most original of Spanish pedagogical works : Juan Huarte's *Examen de Ingenios para las Ciencias* (1557). In 1582 Camillo Camilli translated this book into Italian. In 1594 Richard Carew published in London a translation *The Examination of Men's Wits* which he states he had made *from the Italian* of Camilli.

remember the political relations between Spain and England in the sixteenth century, the questions of international expansion not only in Europe but also in the Indies and in the Americas, the contests in the seas, the struggles for treasures, for lands, for imperial supremacy in wealth, as well as subject-territories, the conflict of Catholicism (in which Spain made the highest bid for power) and Protestantism ; the watchful and sympathetic eye of England on the Netherlands, the internecine struggles of the Armada exploit, we see that the knowledge of Spanish from one important side, the national side, was for the most part the natural prudence of diplomacy for the ingathering of information as to the enemy and his movements. Any other motive pales into insignificance. So, too, after the defeat of the Spanish Armada, the interest in Spanish as a language was not that of reverence and respect for Spanish literature (the great age of Spanish literature of Lopez de Vega, Calderon and Cervantes only came at the beginning of the seventeenth century, and any English appreciation considerably later); the English attitude towards Spain was predominantly contempt for the more serious side of Spain, and a recognition, too often on the literary side, of the more superficial, frivolous, or pompous products of its literature. Three aspects of Spanish literature, omitting Romances, [1] however,

---

[1] Such as the history of *Arnalte and Lucenda* translated by Holyband (*see* p. 461 *supra*) from the Italian, and taken by Maraffi from Hernandez de San Pedro. It is to be observed the Spanish romances often came to England by way of France as well as from Italy.

struck home to Englishmen. I. Such books as the *Familiar Epistles* and *Golden Epistles* of Guevara, the former translated into English by Edward Hellowes, 1574, and the latter by Sir Geoffrey Fenton in 1575 ; the *Dial of Princes*, North's translation from Guevara, 1557 (these three however were taken by the English translators from French versions). The group may be called the Courtly Group. II. Chronicles and histories which again are largely a courtly group. III. Commercial and practical books on geography, navigation, voyages, discovery, or the military art. This third group is of great interest as it furnished material for the great collections of Hakluyt and Purchas.

The roots then, of the Spanish influence were mainly practical. The consequence was that, once attaining the information wanted, the English reader of Spanish passed on his interest to the result. Thus, to take the case of geography, Hakluyt took his Spanish material with the keenest interest and readiness, and no doubt made excellent use of his Spanish in doing so, but he just as readily took material from Peter Martyr, the Italian, and all other sources that came to hand. One courtier, however, stands out for special notice from his knowledge of Spanish—Endymion Porter. His knowledge of Spanish was probably still more intimate than that of Sir Tobie Matthew of Italian.[1] Endymion Porter (1587–1649) was brought up in Spain and for a time was page in the household of the

---

[1] *See* p. 465 *supra*. One accuser of Endymion Porter said : " In all his actions he is in nothing inferior to Sir Tobie Matthew."

well-known Spanish minister Olivarez. He accompanied Charles I and Buckingham to Spain in the matter of the Spanish match, and was, like Matthew, one of Charles I's trusty agents. He went through a chequered career, and though no one can better represent the cultured courtier with a thorough knowledge of Spanish, the influence of his knowledge of the language was absolutely of no importance except for his own and his King's aims, and could not be, on account of the hatred of England for Spain, and later for Endymion Porter's master, King Charles I.

We have seen that Protestant France and Protestant Italy influenced the teaching of French and Italian in England. The Protestantism of Spain was a feeble plant, or at least found itself in a somewhat barren soil. Yet there are signs that, slight as was the Protestant clientèle in Spain, it was a means of bringing the Spanish language into the teaching arena of London. It is, again, the story of religious refugees. The Spanish Inquisition was instituted in 1558, and fugitives began to arrive in 1559, and one of the first, Rodrigo Guerrero, was, in spite of the King of Spain's protest, promptly offered a Chair at Oxford.[1]

A house belonging to Bishop Grindal was, says Mr. Underhill, placed at the disposal of the Spanish refugees, who preached there "with the approbation of Queen Elizabeth no less than three times a week." The Queen, of course, was only tolerant to spite King

---

[1] Underhill, p. 184 *et seqq.*

Philip. But we have seen that the French Church and the Italian Church were places which afforded opportunities for Londoners to hear a foreign language spoken, and this opportunity was apparently to be extended to the Spanish language. Mr. Underhill says that the Spanish " heretics " were heartily welcomed by the English Reformers. Two of these Spanish reformers, Antonio de Corro and Cipriano de Valera, wrote religious books which were acceptable to English readers. Valera took his Cambridge degree of M.A. (and became Fellow of Magdalene College, Cambridge), and was afterwards incorporated in that degree at Oxford. He wrote his books in Spanish, and these included Spanish translations of the Catechism, the *Institutes* of Calvin, and the translation of the Bible. Valera, therefore, identified himself with the theology of the English Puritans. For, as Mr. Mark Pattison says : " Before the rise of the Laudian school, the English Church and the Reformed Churches of the Continent mutually recognised each other as sisters." The bond of religious sympathy drew the Protestants together more than the differences of their languages created a distance. The religious refugees thus helped to spread their language, through finding acceptable ground for its teaching. Antonio de Corro was pastor of the Spanish flock in London. This he soon left for higher preferment at Oxford. His chief writings were commentaries on the Scriptures, but the fact of most importance for us is that this Protestant pastor in London, like the Huguenot Holyband and the Italian Florio, produced a grammar of his own language for teaching Spanish to English people. The title was :

> *Reglas grammaticales para aprender la lengua espanola y francesca, confiriendo la una con la otra, segun el orden de las partes de la oration Latinas.* Oxon., 1586.

In 1540 a translation was made of de Corro's Spanish Grammar.

> *The Spanish Grammer ; with certeine rules teaching both the Spanish and French tongues. . . . Made in Spanish by M. Anthonie de Corro (Translated) with a Dictionarie adioyned unto it, of . . . Spanish wordes . . . by* John Thorius, Lond. 1590. 4to.

John Thorius was the son of John Thorius, a physician who came originally from Flanders. The younger John Thorius was at Christ Church, Oxford, at the time that de Corro was *Censor Theologicus* at Christ Church. As Mr. Underhill suggests, the fact of de Carro and Thorius being in the same college probably led to their acquaintance, and Thorius's interest in Spanish. John Thorius, however, died in 1593.

There was a group of English scholars interested in Spanish at Oxford,[1] as Mr. Underhill suggests, under the influence of the Spanish Protestant refugee Valera. There was one man in whom this bore the fruit of an attempt to spread the teaching of Spanish, viz. Thomas D'Oyley of Magdalen

---

[1] The University interest in Spanish at the time seems to have been particularly associated with Oxford. De Corro was there 1578–1586. Valera seems to have come there still earlier, viz., in 1566 and to have lived there, and published books up to the end of the century.

College, Oxford.   In October, 1590, Thomas D'Oyley took out a licence for a :

> *Spanish Grammer, conformed to our Englishe accydence. With a large dictionarye conteyninge Spanish, Latyn and Englishe wordes with a multitude of Spanish wordes more than are conteyned in the Calepine of X languages or Neobrecensis dictionare set forth by Thomas D'Oyley, Doctor in physick, with the conference of Natyve Spaniards* (Arber : Transcripts of the *Stationers' Registers,* quoted in *D.N.B.*)

Like Thorius's father, the Fleming D'Oyley was a physician and had travelled in the Low Countries. Thus the influences under which he had acquired Spanish were those of the Protestant antagonism to Spain.   Whilst preparing his book, D'Oyley passed over his MSS. to Richard Perceval [1] (1550–1620), who was engaged in the same work.   Perceval had lived for years in Spain and in 1588 placed his Spanish knowledge at the disposal of Lord Burghley, for the purpose of deciphering packets containing the first intelligence of the coming Armada.   Perceval's book, with the incorporation of D'Oyley's studies, was published in 1590 :

> *Bibliotheca Hispanica, containing a Grammar with a Dictionarie in Spanish, English and Latin, gathered out of divers good authors, very profitable for the studious of the Spanish tongue. By Richard Percyuall, Gent. The Dictionarie being inlarged with the Latine, by the advise and conference of Master Thomas D'Oyley, Doctor in Physicke.* Lond. 1591.

---

[1] *See Dictionary of National Biography* for an account of Richard Perceval.

PERCEVAL'S SPANISH TEXT-BOOKS

In 1599, the Grammar part of Richard Perceval's *Bibliotheca Hispanica* was revised and enlarged by John Minsheu, and then bore the title :

> Richard Percyvall. *A Spanish Grammar, first collected . . . by R. Percivale . . . Now augmented . . . by J. Minsheu. Hereunto . . . are annexed Speeches, Phrases, and Proverbs, etc. . . (Pleasant . . . Dialogues in Spanish and English,* etc). 2 parts. London, 1599. Fol.

Whilst the Dictionary appeared as :

> *A Dictionarie in Spanish and English, first published by R. Percivale. Now enlarged by J. Minsheu, Hereunto is annexed an ample English Dictionarie with the Spanish words adjoyned,* etc. Lond. 1599. Another edition, 1623.

The significant change which has taken place is that the Latin on which D'Oyley had laid stress has been dropped, showing that the public to whom the Spanish Dictionary would appeal would not particularly need or wish for Latin synonyms. Mr. Underhill says that Minsheu, who was a teacher of languages in London, received help " from preachers, merchants, fencing-masters or what-not."

Next Minsheu published the following :

> *Vocabularium Hispanico-Latinum et Anglicum copiosissimum, etc. A most copious Spanish Dictionarie, with Latine and English (and sometimes other languages) and enlarged with divers thousands of words,* etc. Lond. 1617.

(Probably an enlargement of D'Oyley's work.)

The *Stationers' Registers* contains mention of the following (quoted by Mr. Underhill) :

> *The Spanish Schoolemaster conteyninge 7 dialogues . . . proverbes and sentences, as also the Lorde's prayre, the articles of our belief, the X. Commaundementes, with divers other thinges necessarie to be knowen in the said tongue.*

As far back as 1568–69, the ten commandments were licensed to be printed in the Spanish language. Mr. Underhill mentions, also, *A New Copie booke*, Lond., 1591, as containing the Spanish hand, amongst others. This was, he supposes, an enlargement of Jean de Beauchesne's *Trésor d'escripture*, published at Paris in 1550 and in London, 1570. The point of interest is that the Spanish hand is only introduced into the later editions of this book.

So far, in the series of Spanish text-books mentioned, the main influence is that of the Spanish refugees, de Corro and Valera. In all, both those mentioned and those which remain for naming, the writers are anti-Catholic. This is marked to a violent degree in Lewis Owen, who employed his undoubted attainments in Spanish, like Perceval, to the services of the government of the day, acting as a spy. Owen published a Spanish Grammar :

1605.

> *Key of the Spanish Tongue or a plaine and easie Introduction whereby a man may in a very short time attaine to the knowledge and perfection of that language.* Lond. 1605. Hazlitt, Bibliog. Coll. 2nd series. p. 439.

His grammar contains rules of grammar and pronunciation, a short dictionary of Spanish and English words, and a parallel translation of the first epistle of St. John.

John Sanford.

> Προπύλαιον, *or an Entrance to the Spanish Tongue*. Lond. 1611.

Probably this is the John Sanford of Magdalen College, Oxford, who wrote *Le guichet françois*, 1604, and the *Italian Grammar*, 1605. He also wrote Latin poems and Mr. Madan notes Sanford as *corrector typographicus*. To have produced grammars in French, Italian and Spanish, shows an unusual interest in the teaching of modern languages, but, apparently they were slight performances.

Cæsar Oudin.

> *Grammatica Hispanica*, translated into English by J. W., Lond. 1622. 8vo.

1662. James Howell.

> *A new English Grammar prescribing as certain rules as the language will bear, for forreners to learn English.* There is also another *Grammar of the Spanish or Castilian tung, with som special remarks upon the Portugues dialect. Whereunto is annexed a discours or dialog containing a Perambulation of Spain and Portugall which may serve for a direction how to travell through both countreys, etc. For the service of Her Majesty whom God preserve.* London, 1662.

The reference in the title page of " Her Majesty " is explained by the dedication of the work to Queen Catharine of Braganza by Don Diego Howell.

Possibly there were some who learned their

foreign languages without masters and without grammar books. For instance, Lord Herbert of Cherbury says in one part of his life (c. 1600) that he attained the knowledge of the French, Italian and Spanish languages, whilst in the University or at home, *without any master or teacher*. The method he adopted was to take some Latin or English book translated into one of these languages and to study it with the help of a dictionary. His intention, he says, in learning languages, was to make himself a citizen of the world as far as possible.

To take another instance. " I know not," says Peacham,[1] " whether not only Essex but England can show a young gentleman of fifteen years more accomplished than John Lucas who not only understandeth and speaketh the Latin, French, Italian and is entered into the Spanish . . . yet never troubled or saw University, but by his father for the languages, . . . *intra domesticos parietes*."

No doubt it was recognised by some that the best method of all was for the youth to learn foreign languages by journeys into the countries themselves. Nor were there lacking those who saw the educational advantages of first having learned Latin, and then realising that common element in the antecedents of French, Italian, and Spanish. Thus Thomas Morrice [2] says : " There hath been an

---

[1] *Compleat Gentleman* (1622), p. 207.

[2] *An Apology for Schoolmasters*, 1619. The work of the Schoolmaster on this view, is to prepare beforehand the youth to the best profit of foreign travel as an opportunity for learning languages.

ancient and laudable custom still observed by the
wiser and better sort, that after their sons can
understand the Latin perfectly, and speak it readily,
to send them to travel into France, Germany, Italy
and Spain, to the intent that they may there
learn their languages, which they shall sooner,
with more facility and judgment accomplish
and obtain unto, having the Latin tongue before :
because the Italian, French, and Spanish borrow
very many words of the said Latin, albeit they
do clip, chop, and change divers letters and syllables
therein."

As to the teaching of Spanish, the instances of
private schools are not so clearly marked as in the
case of French and of Italian. It is improbable
that any of the early writers of Spanish books (except
Minsheu) kept school, or even intended their grammars for school use. Spanish was mainly learned, we
have seen, for practical uses and emergencies. No
doubt servants or officials in noble houses were occasionally, in times of Spanish influence, taught the
language by direct contact with Spaniards. Some
few Englishmen married Spanish ladies, and no doubt
Spanish was, in individual cases, taught by them to
their children. George Ballard in his *Memoirs of
English Ladies*, mentions Elizabeth Lucar, born 1510,
as mistress of Latin, Italian, and Spanish, but this is
taken from a monument inscription, and is only a
small part of the numerous accomplishments of a
lady who died at the age of twenty-six years. He
also mentions Elizabeth Legge, born 1580, who is
said to have been well-skilled in the Latin, English,

French, Spanish and Irish tongues, but there is nothing to show how thorough this knowledge was, or where acquired. The nobles on the grand tour only comparatively rarely included Spain in their itinerary, though the marriage of Charles II to Catharine of Braganza, in 1661, seems to have induced Howell in the book mentioned above to give help to travellers including the Spanish peninsula in their route.

Sir Nicholas Bacon did not place Spanish in his proposed curriculum for the Queen's Wards. Sir Humphry Gilbert provided one teacher of the Spanish tongue for the projected Queen Elizabeth's Academy at the same salary as the teacher of Italian and French, viz. £26, but without the usher at £10, which he suggested in each of those languages. Kynaston in 1635 and Gerbier in 1648 put Spanish in the same position as French and Italian, in their projected Academies.

In 1647 an anonymous " Lover of his Nation " proposed a University of London.[1] He would have children learn Latin as they do English by having no other language within their hearing for two years, and similarly the Greek, Hebrew, Italian, French and Spanish. But all these are " projected " institutions. The only institution in which we can infer that Spanish was taught was the private language school of Mr. John Minsheu. If the teaching of languages was his occupation, we can

---

[1] W. C. Hazlitt, *Schools, School-books and Schoolmasters*, pp. 166–169.

hardly suppose he would re-edit grammars and dictionaries of Richard Perceval, without teaching the language for which he had provided the teaching equipment.

Howell's command of languages [1] naturally led him to wish to utilise his unusual linguistic acquisitions. Teaching was a natural direction in which to turn. Accordingly Howell wrote a letter to Lord Clarendon, urging a request that he would move his Majesty (Charles II) to let him attend the Lady Infanta (Queen Catharine of Braganza) as her " tutor for languages." As qualifications, Howell mentions his knowledge of Spanish ("with the Portuguese dialect "), Italian and French both for practice and theory. He has, he states, a " compendious choice method of instruction." This request was hardly likely to be granted, but it seems that Charles II had promised to set a mark of his favour on Howell, in recognition of his Dictionary, and this came, after another petition from Howell, in the bestowal of the post of historiographer royal. There is an account [2] of a request in 1633 from Sir Robert Le Grys to the King to act as tutor to the Prince (afterwards Charles II). He undertakes " to render Latin his *linguam vernaculam*, not clogging his memory with tedious rules, after the common pedantic fashion but by a way much

---

[1] *See* p. 520 *infra*.

[2] Cal. State Papers. Domestic Series, 1633. Portuguese is suggested as a subject of instruction for the School of Navigation and Languages, projected by Mr. Maidwell (1705).

more easy ; so that if Sir Robert lived till the Prince were seven years old, the nimblest Latinist should find him his match. Proposes to make the French, for Her Majesty's respect, his first learned tongue and the Italian and Spanish also, so as he shall be able to read, write or discourse therein." [1]

There was, however, one other profession of some importance at the time, besides that of teaching, for which a knowledge of foreign languages was a necessary qualification, viz. that of private secretary to royalty, lords and gentlemen. Angel Day in 1586 describes the education which fits a man for such a profession and desiderates that he be a man " more than ordinarily learned " and that he have " a laudable knowledge of foreign languages." Richard Brathwait (?1588–1673) wrote some Rules and Orders for the Government of the House of an Earl. Of this there was a reprint in 1821. In it

---

[1] With courtier-like consideration, Le Grys continues : " On finding the least discernible weariness in him, Sir Robert would wait upon him to some exercise or recreation, so framed as to be instructive to him. In his recreations Sir Robert would feed his mind with variety of narratives, not such as foolish women use to trouble the peace of tender minds withal, but such as the history of the Bible from Genesis to Acts and what is worth observation in historians of whom Sir Robert has not yet met with anyone that has read more than himself, nor whose memory has more faithfully kept what has been committed to it. At other times he would entertain his fancy with the fables of the poets and the philosophy which is included in those fictions ; finally he would make him familiar with arithmetic, geography, and the art of war."

there is a section on : The Secretary, his Place. Brathwait says :

> He should be a man brought up in the universities, having studied both Logic and Rhetoric ; he is to understand the Latin and Greek Tongues ; also the Italian, French, and Spanish, with other Languages, but also to speak and write well in them, thereby he shall be the better able to discourse with other Noblemen's men and Strangers.

But outside of any systematised instruction, it must be admitted in the case of Spanish, as well as of French and of Italian, many of the active spirits of the age picked up scraps of these languages, knew of the character of books in the subjects in which they were interested, and easily entered into ideas, habits, and peculiarities of these countries. The suggestions which have been made that Shakespere and the better-equipped of his playwright colleagues knew in a thorough and systematised fashion French, Italian, and Spanish, cannot be regarded as sustained by the facts. There certainly was affectation of linguistic knowledge amongst " gentlemen and the followers of fashion."

" It is my custome in my common talke to make use of my readinge in the Greeke, Latin, French, Italian, Spanish poets and to adorn my oratory with some pretty choice extraordinary sayings." So says one of the characters in *The Return from Parnassus*, [1] 1601.

---

[1] Act 4, Sc. 1. *See* also Part III, Act 3, Sc. 3, where ridicule is cast on the book-buying propensities of one of the characters ready to buy books in Spanish and Italian to impress onlookers that he can read languages of which he is ignorant.

But, on the other hand, this apparent depreciation carries with it the rider that their sense of interest and wonder in the newness not only of the New but also of the Old World made their little knowledge go a long way in building up a mental picture of their foreign contemporaries.

The cultivation of Spanish for Commercial purposes came later. The following text-books represent the early stages of this development. In 1704, the large folio *New Spanish and English Dictionary : Collected from the best Spanish Authors both Ancient and Modern.* [Also English-Spanish.] *Likewise a Spanish Grammar more Complete and Easy than any hitherto extant.* By Captain John Stevens. London, 1706.

In 1719, however, was published a text-book for learning Spanish, which ran to the length of 615 pages. Its title is : *Spanish and English Dialogues. Containing an Easy Method of Learning either of those Languages. With many Proverbs, and the Explications of several Manners of speaking, proper to the Spanish Tongue.* . . . By Felix Anthony de Alvarado, a Native of the City of Seville in Spain ; but long since naturalised in this Kingdom ; a Minister of the Church of England as by Law established ; Chaplain to the Honourable English Gentlemen who have Commerce in Spain ; and Translator of the English Liturgy into the Spanish Tongue. London, 1719. At the end of his book de Alvarado writes : " The author of this book teaches in Gentlemen's houses and at home. He liveth in James Street, over against the Rainbow Coffee-house, in Covent Garden."

It is interesting to note that this most comprehensive text-book was issued at the time of the enthusiasm with regard to the South Sea scheme, when, as de Alvarado states, " our trade to Spain is recovered, and the South Sea so far extended and secured ; that this fine [Spanish] language is become much more useful and necessary than formerly." De Alvarado, indeed, seems to take the position in England relatively to Spanish that Holyband occupies with regard to French, and Florio in regard to Italian, though more than a century later. They were all Protestant pastors in London, language schoolmasters, and writers of language text-books.

CHAPTER XIV

TEACHING OF MODERN LANGUAGES

IV. The Teaching of German and Dutch

SEEING that English and German are cognate languages, and trace their linguistic ancestry back to a common speech, called by philologists the Primitive Germanic or Primitive Teutonic (prehistoric) Language, there are good educational reasons, for the comparative study of English and German. Starting from the Low German of northern Germany, the Anglo-Saxon language has had a much more varied history than the High German, for it has taken into its composite development elements from the Celtic, Scandinavian, Norman-French, and Latin at several periods. It is a mixed language, whilst the High German of modern Germany is relatively unmixed. The difference of kind of development in the two nations, typified in their respective languages, in some ways, kept the two nations apart, notwithstanding their far-off common stock, whilst the circumstances of the history of the English nation superinduced forms of culture, thought and language from sources at first as foreign to their original starting-point as to Germany, whilst Germany kept the even tenour of her way, and preserved her national characteristics and language, relatively intact, consolidated, unmixed. As to the comparative merits and demerits of each type of development, nationally and linguistically, there is great debate. But the point which concerns us is that the two nations became foreign to each other in a marked degree, in consequence of this difference of experience. When England came to take an interest in learning foreign languages, the chronological order of study, after the Renascence, was first Italian, soon after, French and Spanish; and of the greater modern languages, German came chronologically last.

There were of course in mediaeval times important points of contact with Germany. As early as the reign of King Ethelred Germans were established in London with privileges confirmed by law. In 1234 the Steelyard or house of the German merchants was a considerable centre.[1] Hanse houses were eventually built at Boston and King's Lynn. Similarly English merchants traded with the Hanse towns, and in 1404, Henry IV constituted the Prussian Company, to which powers were given to deal with the English merchants assembled or resident in the Hanse towns and Prussia. These powers were similarly given to English merchants in Holland, Zealand, Brabant and Flanders 1407, and to those of Norway, Sweden, and Denmark in 1408.[2] Sometimes this trade grew to considerable proportions, and led to struggles only settled by international treaty.[3]

Similarly to the Steelyard in England for the

---

[1] Cunningham : *Growth of English Industry and Commerce*, vol. i, p. 183.

[2] *Ibid.*, p. 371.   [3] *Ibid.*, p. 374.

Hansards there were staple towns or fairs established for the English trade in the Low Countries. There was in London in the fourteenth century an alien Weavers' Gild of Flemings and Brabanters.[1]

But besides commercial and industrial relations there was distinct influence from Germany (a particularly wide term, it must be remembered) on religious affairs, as, for instance, through the marriage of King Richard II with Anne of Bohemia. For the latter brought into England followers who introduced religious relations between England and Bohemia, between the followers of Jerome of Prague and the English Wycliffe. There were visits to England of distinguished Germans in the Norman and in the Plantagenet period. We have seen that English and German students belonged to the same " Nation " in the great University of Paris. A satire of Nigellus Wirecker, himself a student at Paris in the twelfth century, describes the gay and excessive habits of English students, saying of them " sine lege bibunt *Wesheil* et *Drincheil*," showing that English students learned somewhat from their association with Germans in a common " Nation " in the University.[2]

It has been said that four men, Gutenberg, Columbus, Luther and Copernicus mark the transition from the mediaeval to the modern conditions of thought and life. Whether we accept them as

---

[1] Cunningham : *Growth of English Industry and Commerce*, vol. i, p. 313.

[2] K. H. Schaible : *Geschichte der Deutschen in England*, 1885, p. 56.

the four greatest representative names or not, they each offered epoch-making gifts to modern Europe. It is to be noted that Gutenberg, Luther and Copernicus, in as far as they do not belong to the world, are to be identified, chiefly, if not entirely, with Germany. Undoubtedly, from the point of view of teaching, no man has done more for modern education, however indirect his service be considered, than Gutenberg in rendering practicable the multiplication of copies from printing-type, and thus achieving the circulation of books, and creating the possibility of the universal cultivation of reading. It has often been pointed out that the invention of printing was the condition precedent for an effective Luther. The utilisation of the printing-press by the early Protestants multiplied indefinitely the ubiquity of reformers, whose sole resource had been, in former ages, the personal appeal of preaching, a limitation which confined all but the most determined men and those of strong physique to a local vogue and reputation. Lutheranism spread a hundredfold more rapidly, for instance, than Wycliffism could do. Added to this, Luther's translation of the Bible into the vernacular, and his Catechisms, concentrated the new reading public on the sources of their faith, whilst he and his learned followers produced their own credentials and undermined the foundation of their opponents with a publicity unknown before. Yet we must be on our guard against exaggerating the Lutheran influence on England. When Leo X, in 1516, proclaimed his Indulgences, with a tariff of the fees for expiation of each kind of crime, a copy was published in Cambridge by the Chancellor, and over the copy a student, Peter de Valence, challenged the Indulgences as *insanias falsas istas*.[1] This was the English analogue of the stronger defiance of Luther in his posting of his ninety-five theses against Indulgences on the door of Wittenberg Castle Church. Nor must it be forgotten that the English leaders of " advanced " thought were receiving the stimulus of Erasmus, which was working towards a spirit of enlightenment in the realms of the intellect on lines removed, *toto coelo*, from Luther, but which made for a transformation and reformation of the Church from within. Colet and Erasmus were moving the leaders in England " by sweetness and light " when the arch-heretic Luther drew attention and criticism even in distant England by his all-compelling thunderbolts of denunciation against the old Church, and men and nations had to say yea or nay to his doctrines, negative and positive. England, at least, authoritative England, said nay—for many eventful years. From 1517 till 1534 England repulsed the German Protestantism. Henry VIII entered the lists, personally, against Luther, and was dubbed by the Pope himself *Defensor Fidei*. Luther's books were burnt. Heresy of all kinds, chiefly that of the Wycliffian tradition, was fiercely put down, and Englishmen groaned with the foretaste of the Marian persecution in that of King Henry VIII. No doubt the fierce determination and wild-fire success of Luther

---

[1] Mullinger, *History of the University of Cambridge*, i, 557.

struck awe into Henry VIII, lest a similar fever should be aroused in England, which he could not control. But Wycliffe, not Luther, is the Morning Star of the English Reformation. As Dr. Rashdall says: " It is certain that the Reformation had virtually broken out in the secret Bible-readings of the Cambridge reformers before either the trumpet-call of Luther or the exigencies of Henry VIII's personal and political position set men free once more to talk openly against the Pope and the monks and to teach a simpler and more spiritual gospel than the system against which Wycliffe had striven."

Wycliffe had revolted against the authority of the Pope, had denied the doctrine of transubstantiation, had resisted the doctrine of the mass, and especially, along with a continuity of English reformers, had denounced the degenerate friars and monks.

The two men who especially brought about the critical act which definitises the English break with Rome, (viz., the Act of Supremacy of 1536, whereby the King became the Head of the English Church), were Henry VIII and Archbishop Cranmer. The series of acts and events which led to this change were mainly political, and into these it is not necessary here to go. Henry VIII had no kind of sympathy with, or even tolerance for, Lutheranism, and the actions of Cranmer were not due to any share in Lutheran views as such.

The English nationalism was prepared to accept the rejection of the Papal jurisdiction. The nation, too, though not without misgiving and some degree of ineffective resistance, permitted the dissolution of the lesser and greater monasteries and the two Chantries Acts. These were practical measures, on the whole seeming to meet the demands of the reformers wishing for a purer fashioning of the Church within, and at the same time, serving the sinister and selfish designs of the King.

After the Act of Supremacy in 1534, and the Dissolution of the Monasteries in 1536, the King issued the Law of Six Articles in 1539 for the very purpose of suppressing advance towards Lutheranism, after the Commission of 1538, consisting of eminent foreign supporters of Luther, had been in England endeavouring to bring about a *rapprochement* and had proved a failure. With these facts before us, it would seem that Luther's influence in the English Reformation, though real, was indirect.

It is difficult to estimate the German influence on England. Two considerations must be borne in mind. First, that in the fourteenth century Chaucer and others had criticised the wallet of " pardons hot from Rome," whilst Wycliffe had attacked the dogmas of the Papacy and raised a party of opposition, whose combative attitude reached Huss, in Bohemia, and through Huss, and his followers, formed a basis of suggestion to Luther himself in his revolt against Rome. Wycliffe's influence in England survived, if somewhat spasmodically, from his writing of *De Dominio Divino*, to date from the literary side of his activity, in 1376, to 1517, the date of the nailing of the propositions by Luther against the abuse of Indulgences on the Church doors at Wittenberg. It is not always realised that a century and a half of permeating criticism of the Papacy had a specifically English origin, and prepared the ground for Protestantism in England and elsewhere. The German Protestantism, in fact, was aggressively doctrinal. The English Reformation was essentially practical in aim; whilst the English was more conservative than the foreign forms of Protestantism.[1] In 1543 Convocation recommended the general adoption of the old Sarum use for the sake of uniformity, and the Book of Common Prayer was largely a selective adaptation of the old service books, and in 1548, through the energy of Cranmer, and chiefly by his personal direction, the first Book of Common Prayer was compiled. In as far as the second Book of Common Prayer (1552) is concerned, the changes, broadly speaking, are from the insularity of the first book to an " accommodation " to the Reformed Churches abroad, yet rather to the views of Bullinger and Zwingli than to those of Luther. It thus seems that the English Church in King Edward VI's reign had formed views in continuous development with those of Wycliffe, and that, in as far as it had definitised its theology, it was rather inclined towards the views of Bullinger, the successor of Zwingli, than towards those of Luther.[2] The

---

[1] A. F. Pollard: *Cranmer*, p. 221. Mr. Pollard points out that the theology of the first Prayer Book is vague, and that its intention is devotional, not theological.

[2] *Ibid.*, p. 274. The late Prof. S. R. Gardiner held that the English Reformers derived their faith from Zwingli rather than Luther. *Introd. to Eng. Hist.*, p. 108.

main significance of the Protestant movement in England was the creation of the National Church, with the King as head, and a service in the English language, and the preservation, as far as compromise could go, of the old traditions severed from corrupt practices, such as the idolatry of saints, and superstitions such as Churchmen like Erasmus attacked, whilst the Scriptures were introduced in the vernacular as the bulwark of an authority which superseded that of Rome and undermined it. The Church of England, in other words, was absorbed in the nation, and was the expression of the religious side of its life, simplified in doctrine, unified in service, and cleared from old abuses. The aim seems to have been present in the minds of the English leaders to avoid the narrow dogmatism of the foreign Reformers, while being broad enough to imbibe their spirit, as an asset in the new nationalism which the Church as reconstituted typified.

It has been necessary to develop these considerations to explain the fact that German influence on the linguistic side was not so powerful in England as might naturally have been expected. If we do not take into account the foregoing conditions, it is surprising to find for instance that the educational developments of Lutherans present little counterpart in England. Schools were founded and organised in Germany with remarkable rapidity and success. Melanchthon was the preceptor of Germany, the learned classicist to whom Luther and his followers looked up with the utmost respect.

But Melanchthon exercised no influence on English educational development, and his text-books, which played an important part on the Continent in Protestant and even in Catholic schools, are practically unknown in the English schools of the sixteenth and seventeenth centuries. It is the same with Trotzendorf, Neander, Wolf and Bugenhagen. It may safely be said that English educators and schoolmasters later on knew more about the Jesuits and their methods of instruction, than those of the Lutheran schoolmasters. The English schools adopted the text-books of Erasmus and of Vives, not those of Melanchthon, for the first half of the sixteenth century, and in the second half perhaps the text-book chiefly used in teaching Latin speaking was that of Corderius, the schoolmaster appointed by Calvin to conduct his school at Geneva.

Luther, it is true, translated the Scriptures into the vernacular, the New Testament as early as 1517; and from Luther's translation, the first English translators, particularly Tindale, made good use. But the translation of the Testament had been made previously by Wycliffe, and the translation of the Lutherans, though it quickened English interest in the vernacular Scriptures, did not originate the interest. So it was with Luther's Catechisms.

The correspondence by writing between English and German Protestants might lead to the inference that there was involved a stimulus to the learning of German by Englishmen. But such communications as took place either in speech or by writing were for the most part in Latin. Even in the case of Cranmer, there is no definite evidence of his ability to speak German, though the fact that he married a German lady is presumptive evidence in favour of the affirmative.

The Parker Society published over 650 letters of English and foreign writers from Henry VIII's reign to the end of that of Queen Elizabeth. On the English side were Cranmer, Hooper, Partridge, Traheron, Barnes the Martyr, etc. On the German and Swiss side were, in Henry VIII's time, Bullinger (by far the chief), Decolampadius, Grynaeus, Melanchthon, Bucer, Aepinus, Gualter, etc. The correspondence, however, is in Latin, as is shown by the publication of the letters in the original as *Epistolae Tigurinae* in 1848. These letters confirm the view that England owed its Protestantism, in so far as it was influenced at all from the outside, to Zurich and Zwingli, up to the time of Edward VI, and after the time of Mary, to Geneva and Calvin, rather than to Luther and Germany at any time. At any rate, the relations between England and Germany brought about no keenness on the part of Englishmen to learn the German language. For notwithstanding all this correspondence (in Latin) not a single grammar for the purpose of learning German was published in England till 1680.[1] This is a striking indication that

---

[1] 1680. Martin Aedler.

The High Dutch Minerva à la Mode, or a perfect Grammar, never extant before, whereby the English may both easily and exactly learne the Neatest Dialect of the German Mother-Language, used throughout all Europe. Most Humbly dedicated to Prince Rupert. 1680.

the actual teaching of German was a later subject of instruction in England, and less cultivated in the sixteenth and seventeenth centuries than the other languages we have considered, French, Italian and Spanish.

It would, however, convey a wrong impression to suggest that there was no knowledge of German in England. It is true, Lutheranism suffered in reputation amongst the learned, not so much from its appeal to the poor and ignorant, for Erasmus himself had not been lacking in his sympathies for them,[1] but from the supposed discouragement to humanism and the developments of the revival of learning. As Erasmus said : *Ubi regnat Lutheranismus ibi interitus litterarum.* And so we find the teaching of German is not mentioned, nor any great interest shown in the language, even by educationists like Sir Thomas Elyot and Roger Ascham, both of whom were sent on political missions to Germany.

There were bonds of union, however, which involved intercourse and some degree of knowledge of the German language on the part of traders and travellers to the fairs, such as that of Strassburg, but more especially of Frankfort. Merchants came there from all parts of Germany, Switzerland, England, and indeed from Europe generally, with letters, books, and they were the carriers of money and presents. Schaible[2] says in 1538 Partridge sent to

---

[1] *See The English Grammar Schools*, p. 51.
[2] *Geschichte der Deutschen in England*, p. 94.

Bullinger by way of Frankfort Fair, stuff for two pairs of stockings, one white, the other black, six pairs of Oxford gloves " für Frau, Mutter, Bruder und Brudersfrau." The quoted words in German point to Frankfort Fair as stimulating a writing of German, slight as it is, more significant of a knowledge of that language than all the correspondence of the 650 " Zurich letters " of theology. Of English reformers, Miles Coverdale lived eight years in exile in Germany, and translated an English work into Latin and German. Tindale, also, was in exile in Germany, and knew the language. Hooper and Barnes had visited Germany in Henry VIII's reign.

In 1550 the famous John à Lasco came to London, and was entrusted with the founding of a Foreigners' Protestant Church. There was a Dutch (which included Germans and natives of the Low Countries) and a French section, and à Lasco was placed as superintendent of both. Two addresses a week, however, were given in Latin. In 1552, a special French Reformed Church was established in London with Richard Vauville as pastor. The Netherlanders seceded from the original Church and established themselves in the Dutch Reformed Church in Austin Friars. The members of the original Church were absorbed in the population. For the most part they came from the Netherlands and Westphalia, whose vernacular of the Low German type most easily coalesced with English in their language. It is partly for this reason that these refugees undertook to so small an extent the teaching of their own language to English people.

In all English books of the sixteenth and seventeenth centuries *Dutch* means German, and denotes both *Hoch* and *Nieder Deutsche*. In Sir James Melville's Memoirs, 1562, Germany is called *Dutchland* and the language *Dutche*. He says of Queen Elizabeth, " She spoke to me in Dutch (meaning German) bot it was not gud." Many writers of history, Germans amongst others, have made the mistake of saying of Elizabeth that she had spoken *holländisch*, using the word *Dutch* in to-day's sense. Germany was called sometimes Allemaigne, sometimes Germany : and again Dutchland, or High Germany, a fact which had led to numerous mistakes. The English traveller, Moryson, says in his *Itinerary*, 1617, when speaking of the Netherlands : " The country is called the Netherlands because it lies low, but the people in speech and custom are nearly allied to the *Deutschen*. Both are called by a common name, Dutchmen." So, too, there was confusion in America between Hollander and German. Both were called " Dutch," though the former were distinguished as " Amsterdam-Dutchmen." [1]

We thus see that before the Reformation period it was Low German, or as our ancestors called it " Dutch," which was spoken, for instance, by traders from the Hanse towns, and this accounts for the readiness of communication without

---

[1] Schaible, *Geschichte der Deutschen in England*, p. 294.

organised teaching. It was only in the seventeenth century that the High German achieved ascendancy in Northern Germany. High German, therefore, received its sanction with the Lutheran movement itself. Schaible,[1] in his valuable book, makes clear that, in his opinion, it was the English exiles, on their return (when Queen Elizabeth came to the throne) from Frankfort, Strassburg, Basel, Zurich and other places, who chiefly contributed to the advancement of the study of High German in England. They increased the number of Lutheran works known in the country, but chiefly through translation. Professor H. E. Jacobs[2] gives a list of sixty-five Lutheran works translated into English by the end of the sixteenth century. Of course a considerable number of these are from Latin. Schaible also notes that Archbishop Grindal summoned to his aid a German secretary, that Thomas Carius translated German into English, that Bishops Hooper and Parkhurst spoke German thoroughly, and that many English Protestants corresponded with Germans in very good German (but he does not give their names). Amongst diplomats he names Robert Sidney, later Earl of Leicester, as knowing German well, though his distinguished brother, Sir Philip Sidney, was not so successful in learning the language. Hubert Languet, the French refugee at Frankfort, one of the chief of the political agents of the Protestant powers in Germany, suggested as teacher of German for the young Robert Sidney

---

[1] *i.e. Geschichte der Deutschen in England.*
Lutheran Movement in England. pp. 350–358.

a certain Peter Hubner, and gave him the following instructions :

> He was to goad on the young man to industry and not only explain to him such passages in the German language as he would afterwards have to translate into Latin, but also practise him in German conversation. *His practice in German conversation was much more important* than reading German authors, *for German works which aim at the cultivation of the intellect are almost all translated into the language which he knows* (1579).

Another famous Englishman learned his German ; not in Germany, but in Paris. This was John Evelyn in 1646. And James Howell, amongst his many languages did not neglect German, of which language he says : [1] " There is no language so full of more syllables and knotted so with consonants as the German, howsoever she is a full-mouthed masculine speech."

As to the books of instruction for the learning of German by Englishmen, seeing there was no German grammar issued in England till 1680, Mr. Schaible [2] made the shrewd suggestion (though unfortunately he offers no evidence in support of the view) that, earlier on, in England, learners used such grammars as were published in Germany, for Germans, e.g. that of Ickelsamer in 1522, of Oelinger in 1573, Clajus (1578), and the excellent grammar of Schottel in 1641.

There were, however, the polyglot *Colloquies*, [3]

---

[1] *Instruction for forreine Travell*, 1642.
[2] *Geschichte der Deutschen in England*, p. 338.
[3] *See* p. 498 *supra*.

which were originally published in Flanders in 1589, and which included English and *Belgica* and *Teutonica* (Low and High German). The 1639 edition included a short introduction of Grammar.

The *Nomenclator* [1] of Adrian Junius was a comprehensive dictionary for Dutch (Low German) and English and other languages.

In 1627 John Minsheu includes in his dictionary English, Low German (*Belgica*), and High German (*Germanica*).

In 1630 was issued the Jesuits' *Janua Linguarum Silinguis*. This edition was published at Strassburg by Isaac Habrecht. This book was originally published, in 1611, at Salamanca in Latin and Spanish for the purpose of teaching Latin to Spanish youth. Isaac Habrecht's edition includes Latin, German, French, Italian, Spanish, and English renderings of the text.

In 1631, John Amos Comenius published at Leszna his *Janua Linguarum* (called by the same name as the Jesuits' book though quite different in its subject-matter) in Latin and German, and this quickly found its way in various editions and various languages throughout Europe.

In 1654 was published the *Polyglot Dictionary* of Ambrosius Calepinus, edited by Abraham Commelinus in nine languages : Latin Greek, Hebrew, French, Italian, High German, Spanish, English Low German (or *Belgica*.)

In 1660 appeared Henry Hexham's *English and*

---

[1] *See* pp. 516–17 *infra.*

Netherdutch Dictionarie and Grammar, published at Rotterdam.

For Sir Francis Kynaston's proposed studies in the *Musaeum Minervae* (1635) was included one teacher of the High Dutch tongue at £26 a year. In 1648 Sir Balthazar Gerbier sent out the prospectus for his Academy at Bethnal Green, where he proposed to require amongst the foreign languages the teaching of " German and Low Dutch." Later, in 1665, Gerbier went further in the matter by publishing a book entitled :

> *Subsidium Peregrinantibus, as an Assistance to a traveller in his Convers with Hollanders, Germans, Venetians, Italians, Spaniards and French. By Balthazar Gerbier, Knight Master of the Ceremonies to King Charles* I (?). 1665.

Gerbier was a native of Middleburg and came to England in 1616. In 1631 he was a political agent to King Charles I at Brussels. He was a man of projects, and the interest of his proposed Bethnal Green Academy lies in the fact, that to him as a financial speculator, an educational institution on a large scale for the sons of nobles and gentlemen seemed a promising commercial undertaking. It is a good indication of the strong desire for the courtly subjects of education and the difficulty of adequate supply for the demand, and also shows that by the middle of the seventeenth century German had taken its place among the foreign languages desirable to be known by nobles and gentlemen.

CHAPTER XV

TEACHING OF MODERN LANGUAGES

POLYGLOTTISM

THE general opinions of the seventeenth century with regard to modern languages from the point of view of scholarship are brought together by Edward Leigh [1] in 1663. He mentions with approval the *Analogo-Diaphora* (1637) of Peter Bense, professor of languages in Oxford, who in his treatise deals with the " disagreeing concord and the agreeing discord of those three languages, French, Italian and Spanish." Bense himself claimed to show clearly and succinctly the nature and method of each of these languages. His book was therefore a comparison of the resemblances and differences of the grammar and syntax of these three languages.

Leigh characterises the language of the Spaniards as manly, the Italian as courtly, and the French as amorous. The French language is *linguam Romanam rusticam*, whence the term " romances." The silent consonants in French render the genuine pronunciation and reading particularly difficult. Crinesius in his *Discourse on the Confusion of Tongues* (cap. 10) gives " seven general rules of the French

---

[1] In his *Foelix Consortium, or a Fit Conjuncture of Religion and Learning.*

506

pronunciation and many special ones." Isaac
Casaubon is next quoted (*Comment. in lib.* 4,
Strabonis): " For certainly in our France there
are almost as many languages, or certainly as many
dialects and diverse modes of pronunciation as
there are I will not say provinces, but cities in
France."

Juan Huarte, the Spaniard, in his *Examen de
Ingenios para las Ciencias* (1557) (" The Examination of Men's Wits "), discussed the question earlier,
and in one aspect went further even, than Casaubon.
He perceived that there was a psychological as well
as a linguistic problem : " How much," he says,
" the Greeks differ from the Scythians, the French
from the Spaniards, the Indians from the Germans,
and the Ethiopians from the English." Distance
will not account for national differences. " If
we consider even the provinces which surround all
Spain, we may distribute the virtues and vices
. . . allotting to each his virtue and vice respectively. For if we reflect on the wit and manners
of the Catalans, Valentians, Murcians, Granadins,
Andalusians, Estremadurians, Portuguese, Galli-
cians, Asturians, Miquelets, Biscainers, Navarrers,
Aragonians, and Castilians, who sees and knows
not that they differ one from the other, not only
in the lineaments of their faces and make of their
bodies, but also in the virtues and vices of the soul,
and that all this is the consequence of each province
possessing a different temperament ? Nor is this
diversity of manners only to be observed in countries so disjoined, but even in places seated not

more than a little league distant the *variety of wit amongst the inhabitants is hardly to be believed.*"[1]

The Spanish language attracted or rather distracted the attention of the more learned linguists on account of its " corruption," i.e. its divergences from Latin. Scaliger says " a quarter of the Spanish language is sheer Moorish (mere Arabica)." Brerewood in his *Enquiries touching the diversity of languages* (1614) wishes to establish the opposite aspect, viz. the nearness of Spanish to Latin, and says he has seen an epistle written by a Spaniard, " whereof every word was both good Latin and good Spanish." Edward Leigh, in quoting Brerewood, adds : " An example of the like is to be seen in Merula ": *Cosmographia*, part ii, lib. 2, ch. 8. The sum of the whole matter is given by Gesner : " The Spanish language is in affinity to Italian, and is nearer to the Latin language than French, yet approaches it less nearly than Italian." [2]

Leigh evidently gives his preference to French.

---

[1] John Barclay published his *Icon Animarum*, which contains similar national or racial psychology, in 1614.

[2] Conrad Gesner (1516–1565). *Mithridates. De Differentiis Linguarum tum veterum tum quae hodie apud diversas nationes in toto orbe terrarum in usu sunt, observationes.* 8vo. Zurich, 1555. *See* Graesse, iii, 68. Also Allg. deut. Biogr., ix, 112 : " 1555 appeared the remarkable book, ' Mithridates,' an attempt in comparative philology, giving a short delineation of the character of all ancient and modern languages, from the Ethiopic down to Gipsy language, in alphabetical order." On a folding plate the *Pater Noster* is printed in twenty-three languages : Hebrew, Syriac, Arabic, Greek, Romantsch, Sard, Armenian, Bohemian, Groatian, Polish, Hungarian, Welsh, Islandic, English, etc.

If the dropping of consonants makes it difficult to learn, it is on that account " the sweeter." Moreover Scaliger commends the French " as an elegant and sweet language " and prefers it before the Spanish and Italian, and Peter Bense pointed out that " in the Courts of almost all, especially the Western Nations, that language is strong and flourishing." This undoubtedly was so in England at the time Leigh was speaking, for in spite of the fact that Charles II had married a Portuguese wife, his Court brought in the French language so effectually that it is from this time that Latin was dislodged from its position as the secretarial language and French became the English diplomatic language.

One other point in Leigh should be added. " The people," he says, " speak the best French in Blois or Orleans, the best Italian in Etruria, and the best Spanish in Castile." These details show that standards of correctness of speech were at least entering into competition with rudimentary, formal grammar learning, and that living languages had an advantage in the possibility of a test of accuracy such as Latin speaking in the Middle Ages and the sixteenth and seventeenth centuries never had and never could have. But let it be remembered that the impetus which came to the vernaculars, and especially to the comparative study of the foreign languages, came with most authority from such writers as those quoted by Leigh, viz. Scaliger, Casaubon, Gesner, etc., and the vitality of the humanist study of the classics is seen by the annexation of other linguistic territory. As in so many cases the conquered territory received great benefit from the invasion of those superior in intelligence, experience and culture. The great classicists of the seventeenth century were unaware that in the modern languages which served them as showing the corruption of Latin, they were paving the way for studies which would, in the advocacy of some, dislodge the Latin language, the very original itself of their high ancestry. It would perplex the minds of the Scaligers and Casaubons to see the principle of evolution accepted in the scientific teaching of to-day, and then to find in the spirit of the age a tendency to exclude Latin from the schools in which modern languages are to be the main aim; since the evolutionary movement in language as developed by those great classicists and philologists is, probably, the very source from which the scientific tendency of thought had received its main impetus towards evolutionary views in other subjects, unacknowledged as the debt may be.

Method in Linguistic Teaching.

The principle of the comparison of languages which necessarily implies some degree of polyglottism, at least, in the teacher on the basis of the views of a Scaliger or a Casaubon, finds its reflexion in the educational reformers, though with little illustration, as we have seen in the practice of teachers. This aspect of the right method of teaching languages occupied the minds of a number of educational writers, but the outstanding example of the period we are considering is that of John Amos Comenius (1592–1670).

The principles laid down by Comenius are interesting historically as showing the views of " the Father of paedagogical method " in the seventeenth century, shared by a large company of disciples in England and other countries. They are also of merit for consideration even to-day, although as in mathematics and in science, great progress has been made in stating the underlying principles of methods of teaching. It is unnecessary, in view of the numerous treatises [1] on the subject, to enter into a detailed criticism of Comenius' methods, for Comenius' principles were far in advance of the practice of his age or even his own practical application of these to his series of text-books, but a statement of his principles, taken from the *Great Didactic* (1632), is essential for recognising the highest development of the idea of language teaching in the school reached in the period under consideration. Comenius proposes eight rules [2] with regard to the teaching of a " plurality of languages."

i. Each language must be learned separately. First the mother-tongue and then the language of a neighbouring nation. *" For I am of opinion that modern languages should be commenced before the*

---

[1] For instance, S. S. Laurie : *John Amos Comenius.* Monroe : *Comenius* (in Great Educator Series). J. Kvacsala: *J. A. Comenius sein Leben und seine Schriften.* Leipzig, 1892.

[2] These are here taken from Mr. M. W. Keatinge's translation (1896), pp. 357–362, of the *Great Didactic,* the first complete translation into English of the *Didactica magna.*

learned ones." After a neighbouring language, Latin is to be learned. Then Greek and Hebrew.

ii. Each language must have a definite period in which it is the chief subject of study. The mother-tongue, since it is intimately connected with the unfolding of the objective world to the senses, necessarily requires several years (I should say eight or ten, or the whole of childhood, with a part of boyhood). Each foreign language can be sufficiently mastered in one year ; Latin in two ; Greek in one year and Hebrew in six months.

iii. All languages are *easier to learn by practice than from rules. That is to say by hearing, reading, re-reading, copying, imitating with hand and tongue, and doing all these as frequently as possible.*

iv. But rules confirm the knowledge derived from practice in learning ancient and modern languages.

v. Rules should simply state what is correct accidence and construction, not attempt to explain causes, or to philosophise over the grammar.

vi. In the rules for a new language, reference should always be made to what is already known in the learning of a previous language, and stress laid on that which is different from any other language known to the learner. For example, if only what is different from Latin in the usage of Greek be included, Greek grammar may be brought into a few pages and thus be made clear and easy.

vii. The first exercises in a new language must deal with subject-matter that is already familiar. Comenius was surely wiser on this point than much of present-day teaching. He makes the wise suggestion, which was indeed in his day the usual practice, that the first lessons in reading a new language might well be the Catechism or Biblical history, because these were already familiar as subject-matter in the vernacular.

viii. All languages, therefore, can be learned by practice, with rules of a very simple nature, embodying points of difference with languages already known and by exercises which refer to familiar subject-matter.

In learning any language there are these four stages of text-books necessary :

1. The *Vestibulum* for the age of infancy to contain a child's conversation, a few hundred words arranged in sentences to which are added the declensions of nouns and the conjugation of verbs. There will be a vocabulary, Vernacular—Latin and Latin—Vernacular.

2. The *Janua* for the period of ripening boyhood should contain all the common words in the language, about 8,000 in number. These should be arranged in short sentences describing natural objects. There should be short and clear grammatical rules as an aid to writing, and for pronunciation, and for forming and using the words of the language. Also, an etymological Latin—Vernacular dictionary of simple words, their derivatives and compounds ; supplying reasons for the meanings attached.

3. The *Palatium* for the period of maturer youth should contain diverse discourses in all matters, expressed in a varied and elegant style, with marginal references to the authors from which

phrases are borrowed. At the end should be given rules for altering and paraphrasing sentences in a thousand different ways. This will involve a Phraseological Dictionary in the Vernacular, in Latin (and if necessary in Greek).

4. The *Thesaurus* for the period of manhood to contain selections from the classical authors who have written on any matter with serious intent and in a good style, and rules relating to the observation and accurate translation of idioms. Some of these authors should be read in the school ; of others a thorough subject-catalogue should be formed for looking up any subject wanted, giving exact place in the authors. For this stage a comprehensive lexicon is necessary (Vernacular, Latin, and Latin—Greek), which shall include, without exception, every point in each language. " For it is not probable that there exists any language so poor in words, idioms, and proverbs that it could not furnish an equivalent for any Latin expression if judgment were used."

Besides the books specifically written for modern language text-books, we have already seen that, incidentally, books on special subjects included subject-matter in several languages. Thus : Abraham Fraunce's *Lawyers' Rhetoric* took examples from Greek, Latin, English, Italian, and Spanish ; and Drax's *Bibliotheca Scholastica* contained phrases from the same languages ; and Fenton's *Epistles* included examples from French and Italian.

The idea of Polyglottism in the school in the period up to the end of the seventeenth century was chiefly associated with such books as those just mentioned and with dictionaries and similar works. For instance, the great Dictionary of Calepin was issued with words from eleven languages. Basle, 1581. Then there was the following book :

> *Colloquia et Dictionariolum octo Linguarum :* [1] *Latinae, Gallicae, Belgicae, Teutonicae, Hispanicae, Italicae, Anglicae, et Portugallicae,* etc. (By N. Barlement, 1639 (oblong 8vo.).)

This is an English edition of a polyglot manual that had a great vogue. There are Dutch editions (the book seems to have originated in Flanders) in the British Museum in 1589, 1593, 1600, 1630, 1631, and one at Venice in 1656. The earlier editions contained seven languages, the Portuguese language being a later addition.

This international handbook was intended to serve a double purpose, viz. the wants of commercial men and of courtiers. The object is stated by the compiler, to quote from the English portion :
" Beloued Reader, this booke is so new full and profitable, and the usance of the same so necessarie, that his (i.e. its) goodness euen of learned men is not fullie to be praised, for ther is noman in France, nor in this Netherland, nor in Spayne, or in Italie, handling (traffiquant, Fr.) in these Netherlandes, which hath not neede of these seuen speaches that

---

[1] Also known as *The Schoolmaster.* Hoole, 1660, says : " Now I commend to his (the pupil's) own private reading *Dialogi Gallico Anglo-Latin,* by Dugres ; *Dictionarium octo linguarum or the Schoolmaster,* printed formerly by Michael Sparke and *Janua Latinae Linguae,*" etc.

The reference to these books is, of course, for the purpose of practice in Latin phrases, but it is interesting to find such polyglot books brought to the notice of boys.

herein are Writen and declared : for Whether that anyman doo merchandise, or that hee do handle in the Court (*ou qu'il hante la Court*) or that hee followe the Warres, or that he be a travelling man, hee should neede to haue an Interpretour for som of theese seuen speaches." [1]

A much more important series of polyglot text-books were the *Nomenclators* which were the outcome of the research of scholars into the names of things mentioned not only in the classical works of antiquity, but also of mediaeval and Latin writers in history, law, medicine, grammar, etc. Of these the chief is that of Adrian Junius, entitled :

1585.
> The Nomenclator, or Remembrancer of Adrianus Junius, Physician, divided in two Tomes, conteining proper names and apt termes for all thinges under their convenient Titles, which within a few leaves doe follow : Written by the said Ad. Ju. in Latine, Greeke, French and other foreign tongues : and now in English by John Higins : With a full supplie of all such words as the last inlarged edition affoorded : and a dictional Index, conteining above fourteene hundred principall words with their numbers directly leading to their interpretations : Of special use for all scholars and learners of the same languages . . . Imprinted at London for Ralph Newberie and Henrie Denham. 1585. 8vo.

Adrian Junius was born in 1511 or 1512 at Hoorn, in Holland. He studied at Haarlem and Louvain. He also studied physic in Paris and Bologna, where he took his doctor's degree. He became physician to the Duke of Norfolk in England in 1543. He lived

---

[1] Quoted by W. B. Rye : *England as seen by Foreigners.* Introd., p. xxxiv.

in England some years. He compiled a Greek and Latin lexicon, to which he added above 6,500 words. By dedicating this work in 1548 to Edward VI he fell under the displeasure of Rome, and his works were placed on the Index Expurgatorius. He left England, but returned on the accession of Mary, and in 1554, on her marriage to Philip, wrote an epithalamium. He returned later to Haarlem, where he lived until 1573. In the siege of that year he lost his library and the MSS. of a great number of works. He died 1575.

One of his well-known works is :

Adagiorum ab Erasmo Omissorum, Centuriae octo et dimidia. 1558.

His other works are principally commentaries on classical authors. The first edition of the *Nomenclator* was published in Latin in 1567.

The idea of the *Nomenclator* is clearly that of an encyclopedic vocabulary. Its difference, therefore, from Bathe's *Janua Linguarum*[1] (1611) is that the

---

[1] Bathe's *Janua Linguarum*, in Latin and Spanish, had the Spanish translated into English in 1615 by William Welde. In an issue of 1626 John Harmar, Master of St. Albans Grammar School, wrote a Proem, in which he stated the cases of a Portuguese and an Italian who learned English from the book. In 1617, John Barbier, of Paris, produced a quadrilingual edition in London, viz., in Latin, English, French, and Spanish. Barbier added the French, and in addressing the English reader, speaks of the English "Noble Nation, so worthily addicted to the learning of foreign languages." Comenius' *Janua Linguarum* was said to be translated into Latin, Greek, Bohemian, Polish, German, Swedish, Belgian, English, French, Spanish, Italian, and Hungarian—and in the Eastern languages, Arabic, Turkish, Persian, and Mongolian.—(Keatinge : *Great Didactic*, p. 23.)

words are not arranged into sentences, and from its number of words it is much more comprehensive. It was a book of wide circulation and influence, and though not mentioned by Mr. R. H. Quick and Professor Laurie there can be no doubt that it or others of its kind had a considerable direct influence on Comenius. It is the outcome of amazing erudition and research, the enormous labour involved putting the ingenious and painstaking *Janua* (of Bathe) itself into the shade. The writings of sixty-two Latin and Greek poets, fifty-eight doctors, philosophers and rustic writers, sixty-two historians and orators, twenty theologians, thirteen jurists, and fifty-two grammarians, together with forty-four others of the later Latin and Greek authors, have been ransacked to supply material for the names of *things* mentioned in this extraordinary book. In fact, the *Nomenclator* professes to supply the proper names and apt terms for *all things*, under their convenient titles in Latin, Greek, French, and English. It out-Comeniuses Comenius in its encyclopedic detail. There are eighty-nine different subjects for chapters. In Comenius' *Janua* there are 100, so that Comenius gets a better arrangement. There are many subjects in common, such as living creatures, animals, fishes, all kinds of food, trees, vegetables, apparel, buildings, parts of ships, tools, terms in war, games, money, the elements, God and spirits, handicrafts, trades, affinities, etc. Nothing which suggests itself to the mind of the compiler of this book presents any insuperable difficulty in making a Latin name or description available for it, whether the thing were of recent invention or, as one would suppose, so little important as never to have been named in Latin authors. The Latin name for *all* things is always forthcoming.

Living Creatures, as we have mentioned before, ought to be painted, and none but those at the first which are known to children that begin to learn the Latin tongue. Moreover, all those terms or words, whose things thereby signified can be seen and painted, may be taken out of the *Nomenclator* of that most excellent man, Hadrianus Junius, or others ; provided that the exordium or beginning be made from those which are more known. (Eilhardus Lubinus, in Samuel Hartlib's translation in the *True and Ready Way to Learn the Latin Tongue.*)

After the compilation of Adrian Junius's laborious work, such a work as that of John Minsheu [1] became comparatively easy. Minsheu's book includes the languages of the *Colloquia* (in the English edition of 1639 ; the inclusion of Portuguese in the *Colloquia* may have been suggested from its inclusion by Minsheu) with Latin, Greek, Hebrew, and Welsh. Minsheu's book is a considerable advance on the *Colloquia*, though not of the originality of research of Junius. The title is :

Ἡγεμών εἶς τας Γλωσσας. *Id est Ductor in Linguas the Guide into Tongues. Cum illarum harmonia, e, Etymologiis originationibus, Rationibus, et Derivationibus, in omnibus his undecum linguis, viz.* 1. *Anglica.* 2. *Cambro-Britanica.* 3. *Belgica.* 4. *Germanica.* 5. *Gallica.* 6. *Italica.* 7. *Hispanica.* 8. *Lusitanica seu Portugellica.* 9. *Latina.* 10. *Graeca.* 11. *Hebraica.* (With list of subscribers.) Londini, 1617. Also 1626, 1627.

---

[1] See p. 477 *supra.*

In 1660 James Howell, by publishing his Polyglot Dictionary, though limiting it to the four chief modern languages, reaches the highest development of English Polyglot Dictionaries of the period from the point of view of English. It will be remembered he had already produced the definitive edition of Cotgrave's French Dictionary. In his *Lexicon Tetraglotton* he extended the scope to meet not only the needs of the traveller and courtier but also, in his own opinion, the chief needs of the scholar. The title describes the contents :

> *Lexicon Tetraglotton, An English-French-Italian-Spanish Dictionary : Whereunto is adjoined a large Nomenclature of the proper Terms (in all the four belonging to several Arts and Sciences, to Recreations, to Professions, both Literal and Mechanick, etc. With another volume of the choicest Proverbs In all the said Toungs (consisting of divers compleat Tomes) and the English translated into the other Three, to take off the reproach which useth to be cast upon Her, That she is but barren in this point and those Proverbs She hath are but flat and empty. Moreover there are sundry familiar Letters and Verses running all in Proverbs with a particular Tome of the British or old Cambrian Sayed Sawes and Adages which the Author thought fit to annex thereunto, and make Intelligible for their great Antiquity and Weight : Lastly there are five centuries of new sayings which in tract of time may serve for proverbs to Posterity, By the Labours and Lucubrations of James Howell, Esq. : Senesco non Segnesco.* London, 1660. Folio.

Perhaps the most conspicuous work of English Scholarship in the seventeenth century was the Polyglot Bible, edited by Brian Walton, published in 1657. Charles Hoole says of it in 1660 : " This that I have said may seem enough to be learnt at school, but if one desire to learn those oriental tongues in which the great Bible is now happily printed by the great vigilance and industry of Dr. Brian Walton who hath carried on the work to the honour of this nation, the comfort of the poor Church of England, and the encouragement of good literature, in the use of *Introductio ad lectionem Linguarum Orientalium,* and of the Lexicon [1] (which I conceive ere this time is well-nigh finished) made on purpose to explicate the words of the Bible according to their several languages, viz. Hebrew, Chaldee, Samaritan, Syriac, Arabic, Persian, Ethiopic, Armenian, and Coptic, which is a kind of Egyptian tongue." Hoole goes on to explain that he is serious in his suggestion. " Though it be found a thing very rare, and is by some adjudged to be of little use for schoolboys to make exercises in Hebrew, yet it is no small ornament and commendation to a school (as Westminster School at present can evidence) that scholars are able to make orations and verses in Hebrew, Arabic, or other oriental tongues." Hoole's statement is confirmed by a reference to John Evelyn's Diary, under the date 13th May, 1661 : " I heard and saw such exercises at the election of scholars, at Westminster School, to be sent to the University, in Latin, Greek, Hebrew, and Arabic,

---

[1] The *Lexicon Heptaglotton of Oriental Languages* by Edmund Castell to accompany Walton's Polyglot Bible was not published till 1669. But earlier, in 1635, a London publisher, William Jones, had issued the work of Valentine Schindler : *Schindleri Lexicon Pentaglotton, Hebraicum, Chaldaicum, Syriacum, et Arabicum ; . . . in epitomen redactum a G. A.*

in themes, and extemporary verses as wonderfully astonished me in such youths, with such readiness and wit, some of them not above 12 or 13 years of age." Dr. Busby himself wrote a Hebrew Grammar, and though it was not printed the MS. was transcribed for use in the school.[1] He is said to have known enough Arabic to write a grammar. The boys said " he wished it to be thought that all learned tongues were to be got at Westminster."[2]

In each of the chapters on the teaching of languages in England, stress has been laid on the prominent part played by Protestant refugees. The welcome extended to them was denied to Roman Catholic teachers, for whom settlement in England was forbidden. The period succeeding the Gunpowder Plot of 1605 brought with it still deeper distrust of Roman Catholics in England. The effect of these religious and political conditions can be

---

[1] As to the teaching of Hebrew in Grammar Schools *see English Grammar Schools*, Chap. xxxii.

[2] *See* John Sargeaunt : *Annals of Westminster School*, p. 115. The following notice of public teaching of oriental languages in London is in the Thomason Collection of the British Museum Library, dated August 14, 1647. " Sir, you are intreated to give notice in public this next Lord's Day, the 15th of August, that Master Christianus Ravius, heretofore public Professor of the Orientall Tongues in some Universities beyond the Seas, will begin a lecture of these Tongues in London House, God willing, upon Thursday come seven night, the 26th of the instant August." For an account of Ravius, *see* D.N.B., vol. xlvii, p. 319. For the development of Oriental studies in the Universities, though mainly in the eighteenth century, *see* C. Wordsworth : *Scholae Academicae*, pp. 162–170, and pp. 266–268.

traced in connexion with foreign language teaching, as the following decision of a Town Council will show. The licensing of teachers, of course, was ordinarily in the hands of the Bishops, but on this occasion it seems to have been taken over by the Town Authority, by what legal right, if any, does not appear.

> *Constitutions, Laws, Statutes, Decrees and Ordinances of the Bury St. Edmund's Town Council*, 18 July, 1607. *To prevent the infectinge of youth in Poperie by Schoolmasters.* [1]
>
> Item, that the Constables of every ward within this Burgh shall once every quarter of a year certify the Alderman, Recorder and Justices of the Peace, of this Burgh the names of all and every person or persons that do keep any school for the teaching of youth *to write, read, or understand the English, Latin, French, Italian or Spanish tongues*, upon pain to forfeit for every default 6s. 8d., and withal it is ordered that none shall be permitted to keep a school or to teach any children to write, read or understand any of the said tongues other than the Master and Usher of the Free Grammar School, without licence under the hands and seals of the Alderman and chief burgesses or four of them at the least whereof the Alderman to be one, upon pain that every one putting any child to such a schoolmaster to forfeit for every week 6s. 8d.

But as we have seen, the teaching of languages other than Latin and Greek was chiefly carried on outside of the grammar schools, either from private teachers, or by travel. The following instances taken from Aubrey's *Brief Lives* (edited by A. Clark) are representative of the best polyglot Englishmen. John Selden understood Latin, Greek, Hebrew,

---

[1] *Victoria County Hist. Suffolk,* vol. ii, p. 317.

Arabic, " besides the learned modern." [1] James Bovey, (b. 1622), spoke Low Dutch, High Dutch, French, Italian, Spanish, and Lingua Franca and Latin, besides his own. [2] Thomas Hobbes (1588–1679) learned Italian and French, " so as to understand them *mediocriter*." [3] Sir William Plater, Member of the Long Parliament, understood Italian and French well. [4] Sir Thomas Morgan (d. 1679) spoke Welsh, English, French, High Dutch and Low Dutch, " but never a one well." [5] John Pell (1610–1685) understood besides English, Latin, Greek, Hebrew, Arabic, Italian, French, Spanish, High Dutch and Low Dutch. [6] Isaac Barrow (1630–1677) spoke " eight severall languages." [7] Sir Kenelm Digby (1603–1665) "understood ten or 12 languages." [8] To these names may be added William Penn who learned his French, staying at Saumur, and besides French is said to have acquired a " thorough knowledge " of German, Dutch, and Italian, and later on, to have learned " two or three dialects of the Red Men." In a letter to Bradshaw in 1652, Milton described Andrew Marvell as "having gained " Dutch, French, Italian and Spanish as well as being " well read in the Latin and Greek authors." And John Vicars writes at the beginning of the *Works* of Joshua Sylvester (in the edition of 1641):

" Adorned with the Gift of God's good Spirit ;
I mean the Gift of Tongues ; French, Spanish, Dutch, Italian, Latin."

---

[1] Aubrey, ii, 224.   [2] *Ibid.*, i, 112.   [3] *Ibid.*, i, 396.
[4] *Ibid.*, ii, 156.   [5] *Ibid.*, ii, 87.   [6] *Ibid.*, ii, 122.
[7] *Ibid.*, i, 88.   [8] *Ibid.*, i, 225.

But however marked the progress of the cultivation in England of modern languages, European and Oriental, may have been, and there can be no doubt that the French influence on England in the time of Charles II marks a period in the aspirations of the best-educated Englishmen and Englishwomen to have a speaking knowledge of modern languages—yet probably the most substantial result of the new impulses towards language-learning, was the intensified interest in the vernacular. This might be illustrated by the beginnings of systematic study of Anglo-Saxon, by the amazing wealth of literature by which the English language had been endowed in the Tudor and Stuart reigns, but above all, from the pedagogical point of view, by the slow but sure change which had been taking place in the substitution of English for Latin, as the spoken language for oral instruction and as the written language of *all the text-books*. It was only by this revolution that the modern type of school became possible.

CHAPTER XVI

CONCLUSION

THE TRIUMPH OF ENGLISH

As the mountaineer, who is fascinated by a particular peak, cannot satisfy himself until he has scaled the height from every available starting point, and by every practicable route, so the pioneers of learning, once roused to a national consciousness of the glory of our heroes, of the wealth of our national elements, and of the resources of our composite language, became enthusiastic in tracking the paths of the mountain-like material which had to be penetrated before general intelligibility could bring it into the province of instruction. It was fortunate that scholars had been well-trained in the classics, since the mental discipline which had become ingrained in finding paths and gaining heights by patient winning of new ground, inch by inch, made the investigation of the details of modern subjects so much the surer, and so much the swifter. The methods of search and research had been tried on the vast experimenting ground of antiquity. By the concentration of intellectual energy on Greece and Rome, far away from the conflicting self-interests of passion and party in the stormy times of Tudors and Stuarts, the power of contemplation and reflexion over details had made clear the life and conditions of antiquity, and at the same time had revealed to the self-consciousness of the modern students the possibility of the direction of their energies and self-determination to the ever-widening *orbis intellectualis*, in which the thought and knowledge of Greece and Rome found their place, but no longer could remain the infallible standards for hypotheses and conclusions. Not only did the later Renascence scholars long for new fields to conquer, but they had also developed within themselves the necessity for seeking the intelligibility of the new and modern, in the light of the ancient splendour. They wished to interpret whatever they studied closely, exactly, and—magnanimously. In the attempt to bring antiquity to life again, these intrepid discoverers found their own souls re-fashioned with the discipline of truth-seeking, and re-furbished with methods of inquiry which had become almost intuitive. The Renascence spirit within called with irresistible force for application in every department of knowledge and thought, both of the Humanities and of Nature.

Particularly was this spirit active in promoting the sense of glory in our native country. Our dramatists, true sons of the Renascence, even if they knew " little Latin and less Greek," registered with full glow, the state of the consciousness of nationality. The defeat of the Spanish Armada had proved that no flights of imaginative exaggeration were necessary to sustain the credit of English patriotism. Shakespere voiced the swelling joy :

> " This other Eden, demi-paradise,
> This fortress built by Nature for herself
> Against infection and the hand of war,
> This happy breed of men, this little world,
> This precious stone set in the silver sea."

MODERN SUBJECTS IN ENGLISH SCHOOLS

The dramatists' expression of patriotic warmth intensified the scholars' appeal to antiquity. Not without clear conviction, the claim was at last made that England could stand without fear and trembling in comparison with nations of antiquity. Mulcaster[1] gloried in our language because of its antiquity, and Robert Recorde[2] based an argument for learning arithmetic on its 2,000 years' standing in Britain. In connexion with British history, Leland and Camden travelled the whole kingdom with keen delight and determination, to note inscriptions, to seek for records, and to collect traditions as to all the antiquities of the land. The map-makers and geographers joined hands with the historians and correlated their miscellaneous ingatherings of past Britain. Camden coined the name Anglo-Saxons. The historians and chroniclers inspired the lawyers (e.g. Coke, Lambard, Selden, Whitelocke, Hales, Fortescue) to the pleasant task of tracing English law to Anglo-Saxon times, and Milton naturally wished the well-educated youth to acquaint himself with the " Saxon laws " thus collected. The Church-leaders, e.g. Archbishops Parker,[3] Laud, Usher, and Bishop Stillingfleet, rejoiced in Anglo-Saxon lore and were proud to trace the continuity of the English Church to its due antiquity, far prior to the change of the Reformation.

---

[1] p. 9.

[2] pp. 296–7.

[3] Archbishop Parker commissioned John Day, the printer, to cut the first Anglo-Saxon type in brass, in 1566.

The logical step was taken of the study of the Anglo-Saxon language. Materials were collected which eventually made it possible for Dr. George Hickes to publish in 1703–5 the *Linguarum veterum septrionalium Thesaurus grammatico-criticus et archaeologicus*. Then followed *The Rudiments of Grammar for the English Saxon Tongue, First given in English : with an Apology for the study of Northern Antiquities. Being very useful towards the understanding of our ancient English Poets and other Writers*. By Elizabeth Elstob. Lond. 1715.

Miss Elstob on the title-page to her book quotes from a letter, which she had received from one of the bishops : " Our earthly possessions are truly enough called a patrimony, as derived to us by the industry of our fathers ; but the language that we speak is our *mother-tongue ;* and who so proper to play the critics in this as the females ? "

The seventeenth century English grammars had already begun to take a historical attitude in dealing with the subject. Early in the eighteenth century scepticism set in vigorously as to the necessity of the knowledge of Latin and Greek for understanding English grammar. This position is well represented by John Brightland in his *Grammar of the English Tongue . . . making a complete system of English education for the Use of the Schools of Gt. Britain and Ireland*. Lond. 1712.

Brightland points out that if the knowledge of Greek and Latin is assumed as necessary for English Grammar, the greater part of mankind " must spare ten or eleven years in learning dead languages " so as to know their own ! He urges that quite as good a case can be made out for the necessity of " the knowledge of Spanish, Italian, High Dutch, Low Dutch, French, Old Saxon, Welsh, Runic, Gothic, and Icelandic," since our language is more indebted to these than to Greek and Latin. Thus in Brightland we see the direct effect of polyglottism, even on the school text-book. In other words, English was recognised as the central language of study, and classical and all other languages were regarded as subsidiary, though auxiliary.

This great change of attitude, however, is only part of the triumph of English in the period following the Restoration. Latin-speaking in the schools gradually sank from the position of an avowed aim [1] to that of a tradition. The attempt to make the ancient languages live again in schools was quietly given up. Yet the multitudinous new modern subjects, often rising into prominence in private and non-classical schools, were rarely incorporated into the public Grammar School curriculum. In the following century—the eighteenth century—the real educational life and activity was outside of the Grammar Schools, and even outside of the Universities, and is noticeably to be found better established in the Dissenting Academies. In all the newer institutions of learning, English had entirely triumphed as the language in which instruction was to be carried on.

In the sixteenth and seventeenth centuries, the

---

[1] See *English Grammar Schools*, chap. xix.

text-books had been slowly and surely changing from Latin to English. Latin text-books had been adopted necessarily because all the subject-matter of the several departments of knowledge was either to be found in the classical authors, or if in modern foreign authors, all educated people accepted Latin as the international language of communication. But when a foreign country, e.g. France, produced writers in the vernacular of acknowledged authority, French became a necessity for students, entrenching on the ancient sole prerogative of Latin. Moreover, losing ground as the language of intercommunication, the old position of Latin was still more endangered by the growing recognition of the claims of the newly acquired literary possessions bequeathed the country by Spenser, Shakespere, Milton, and the whole galaxy of English writers of the Elizabethan and Stuart periods. Lastly, in all the departments of the school curriculum, the best text-books were, by 1700, to be found in English. Sir Isaac Newton, curiously enough, whilst the greatest of the moderns in his mathematical investigations, may be regarded as the last of the giants in communicating his *opus magnum* in the Latin language instead of in the vernacular.

Now must be recalled some of the land-marks of the conquest of English over Latin, as the language in which text-books were written. It will be remembered that even on the subject of the English language itself, Greenwood (1594), Gill (1621), and Wallis in 1653 had written in Latin. As late as 1703 Dr. Hickes felt surer of attention from educated people for his great work on the Anglo-Saxon language by presenting it in Latin.

Of books used in school, the Authorised English Bible was prepared 1607–1611, though of course the Latin and Greek texts were commonly read in schools. Dean Nowell's *Catechisms* appeared, the larger form in 1570, the middle size in 1572, whilst the *Short Catechism* had appeared in English in the Book of Common Prayer[1] in 1549. Here again, the self-respecting Grammar School preferred to use the Latin and Greek versions (and sometimes even the Hebrew). In 1545 the *Primer* was authorised in English " to be used by every schoolmaster." Other works in religious instruction in the Grammar Schools were some of them in Latin, some in English.[2] In the elementary subjects of reading and writing the tendency set in, earliest of all, towards the vernacular. The Latin and Greek grammar text-books, in the early Renascence times, were all in Latin, and it was only by a fierce struggle that the concession was won of the translation of the Latin grammar, into English, and the early use of Latin authors for reading was won.[3] The first *Rhetoric* in English was that of Leonard Cox in 1524, but it yields in importance to that of Thomas Wilson in 1553. Wilson had previously written the

---

[1] The change of the language in which the Service-Books of the Church were written from Latin to English is a critical event in the progress of the history of the English language as well as of ecclesiastical history.

[2] *See* Excursus on Religious Instruction, 1600–1660, in the *English Grammar Schools*, p. 63 *et seqq.*

[3] *Ibid.*, Chapter on *The Grammar War*, pp. 276–287.

first text-book of *Logic* in English in 1552. William Bullokar produced the leading *English Orthography and Grammar* in English in 1580, though he confesses the subject had been dealt with earlier by Sir Thomas Smith and John Hart. The first Latin-English Dictionary for schools was that of John Withals c. 1554. Thomas Blundeville wrote in English the first *Method of Reading Histories* in 1570. *The Short Introduction to Music* (in English) was issued with Sternhold and Hopkins's *Book of Psalms* in 1549. The first modern treatment of Geography in English was the finely produced book of Dr. William Cuningham, of Norwich, called the *Cosmographical Glas* in 1559. There is the notice of an English book on Drawing in 1573. The first general elementary school book containing English spelling, a short Catechism, historical dates, and numeration, was Edward Coote's *English Schoolemaster* in 1596, though Thomas Johnson's *Pathway to Reading* was published in 1590, and the Horn-book at least dates back, in England, to 1450.[1] As far back as 1526, there was published in English, the anonymous *Grete Herbal*, and the development of Herbals and Animal books marked the advance of the art of engraving (by which they were illustrated) as well as that of Natural History. The typical natural history text-book of the Puritan period was John Swan's *Speculum Mundi* (1635), a book with a Latin title, but with a text in English. The works of English experimental scientists, e.g. those of William

---

[1] *See English Grammar Schools,* p. 171.

Gilbert (1600) and William Harvey (1628) were issued in Latin. The *Mathematical Magic* of John Wilkins (1648) is announced by himself as a subject " not before treated of in this language." Robert Recorde deserves the highest recognition as a pioneer in using English in text-books. He was the first to write in English on the following subjects : arithmetic, in the *Ground of Artes* (? 1540) ; on geometry in the *Pathway to Knowledge ;* on astronomy in the *Castle of Knowledge* (1556) ; and on algebra in the *Whetstone of Wit* in 1557. In 1569 James Peele, schoolmaster, clerk of Christ's Hospital, was the first to write in English on Book-keeping, and John Mellis, schoolmaster, in 1588, expounded in English the art of book-keeping by double entry. In 1570 appeared the first translation into English of Euclid's *Elements* by Henry Billingsley and Dr. John Dee. In 1571 Leonard Digges in the *Pantrometria* wrote in English on mensuration, and in 1579 his son Thomas Digges in English, applied arithmetic to the military art. As to astronomy, though Dr. Robert Recorde's *Castle of Knowledge* (1556) was the first treatise in English on astronomy, it will be remembered that Geoffrey Chaucer wrote in English a *Treatise on the Astrolabe* to " little Lewis, my son," in 1391. The first Tudor book in English for the teaching of French was by Giles Dewes in 1528, though the wider heralding of French teaching was marked by the appearance, in English, of Holyband's *French Schoolemaister* c. 1565. Florio's *First Fruites* was the first text-book in English, for teaching Italian, in 1578. In Spanish, the grammar of de Corro, was translated into English by John Thorius, and published in 1590. Henry Hexham's *Dutch Grammar* appeared in 1660, and the German Grammar by Martin Aedler in 1680, both in English.

Thus by the second half of the seventeenth century every important department of knowledge had been expounded in an English text-book, and in almost all cases text-books had been simplified and adopted for school use in English. There was no reaction from any point once won by the English language. All the chief subjects, ancient as well as modern, were gathered together in English. Even the chief Latin and Greek classical authors were available for the monoglot Englishman in translation.

Institutionally, this movement was represented by the growth of the provision in schools of two divisions, often in two different buildings, in the same town, called respectively, the Latin and the English school. Thus at Exeter, the old Grammar School was re-founded in 1627 with a Latin School and an English School. In 1629 Archbishop Harsnet established a double Latin and English School at Chigwell in Essex, and in 1718 two separate schools, Latin and English, were re-established at Risley, in Derbyshire. The intention was apparently similar to that of the later idea of the modern side in the Public Schools. Unfortunately, the *status* attached to the old Grammar School caused a depreciation of the English School in the two-fold foundations, and the latter often degenerated into an ordinary Charity School. The revolution that had taken place in the sixteenth and seventeenth centuries in the substitution of English for the old ideal of Latin-speaking and Latin-writing, can be explained in a sentence. It was caused by the felt need to enter into the realisation as directly as possible of the vast material of knowledge which had accumulated in every direction of mathematics, the natural and experimental sciences, modern languages, and the technical and practical arts. All this mass of knowledge had become more easily and more comprehensively available in English than in Latin.[1] Whilst, therefore, the ancient classical languages continued to hold the highest *status* in the Grammar Schools, as distinctive of the well-trained scholar, they ceased to be regarded as necessary languages for studies in the subject-matter of concrete knowledge. For the justification of their educational standing, the argument changed from the older utilitarian ground of the subject-matter, the " solid knowledge " contained in the classical languages, to the claim for them of the unique nature of their "formal" discipline, linguistically, and the intrinsically predominant value of the literary and humanistic training to be derived from reading the great writers of antiquity in their own languages.

---

[1] *See* the remarkable prophecy of Mulcaster (1581) on this very point, p. 259 *supra*.

INDEX

38a—(2407)

INDEX

THE END

Printed by Sir Isaac Pitman & Sons, Ltd., Bath.
K—(2407)

THE END